The Crossroads of American History and Literature

Philip F. Gura

The Crossroads of American History and Literature

The Pennsylvania State University Press
University Park, Pennsylvania

Library of Congress Cataloging-in-Publication Data

Gura, Philip F., 1950–
　The crossroads of American history and literature /
Philip F. Gura.
　　　p.　　cm.
　Includes bibliographical references and index.
　ISBN 0-271-01521-7 (cloth)
　ISBN 0-271-01522-5 (paper)
　1. American literature—19th century—History and criticism.
2. Literature and history—United States—History.　3. American literature—Colonial period, ca. 1600–1775—History and criticism.
4. National characteristics, American, in literature.　5. United States—Intellectual life—Historiography.　6. United States—Civilization—Historiography.　7. Historicism.　I. Title.
PS217.H57G87　　1995
810.9′003—dc20　　　　　　　　　　　　　　　　　　95-20048
　　　　　　　　　　　　　　　　　　　　　　　　　　　　CIP

Copyright © 1996 The Pennsylvania State University
All rights reserved
Printed in the United States of America
Published by The Pennsylvania State University Press,
University Park, PA 16802-1003

It is the policy of The Pennsylvania State University Press to use acid-free paper for the first printing of all clothbound books. Publications on uncoated stock satisfy the minimum requirements of American National Standard for Information Sciences–Permanence of Paper for Printed Library Materials, ANSI Z39.48-1992.

For
David, Katherine, and Daniel,
before, through, and beyond whom
these essays were written,

thanks to the example of
Richard Rabinowitz and Paul Levitt,
truth-tellers and true believers both

Contents

	Acknowledgments	ix
	Introduction: Tangents to a Sphere	1
1	The Study of Colonial American Literature, 1966–1987: A *Vade Mecum*	12
2	Preparing the Way for Stoddard: Eleazer Mather's *Serious Exhortation* to Northampton	55
3	Cotton Mather's *Life of Phips*: "A Vice with the Vizard of Vertue Upon It"	64
4	Solomon Stoddard's Irreverent Way	79
5	Sowing for the Harvest: The Reverend William Williams and the Great Awakening	95
6	Early Nineteenth-Century Printing in Rural Massachusetts: John Howe of Greenwich and Enfield, c. 1803–1845	114
7	The Reverend Parsons Cooke and Ware Factory Village: A New Missionary Field	140
8	The Transcendentalists and Language: The Unitarian Exegetical Background	157
9	Elizabeth Palmer Peabody and the Philosophy of Language	174
10	Manufacturing Guitars for the American Parlor: James Ashborn's Wolcottville, Connecticut, Factory, 1851–1856	190

11	Thoreau and John Josselyn	221
12	Thoreau's Maine Woods Indians: More Representative Men	234
13	Language and Meaning: An American Tradition	252
	Index	273

Acknowledgments

These essays were written at different times over the past two decades as part of my continuing investigations into colonial and antebellum history and literature. In most cases, they are not formally linked. I present them together primarily as evidence of methodology, for what they add up to is a statement concerning ways of asking and answering questions about American culture. Put another way, they represent the kind of empiricism necessary to work profitably in cultural studies. By placing them in such proximity, I hope that readers coming to them, whether for the first or second time, will be able to produce intellectual light and heat by striking them against each other.

Because these essays were composed over such a long period, many people have had a hand in their genesis, growth, and fruition. Foremost among those would be my teachers in college and graduate school, most notably Daniel Aaron, Bernard Bailyn, Warner Berthoff, Alan Heimert, Joel Porte, and (though still "only" graduate students) Barry O'Connell and Richard Rabinowitz. In their different ways they helped me find the intellectual routes in which I would go. After them came departmental administrators, who urged me to continue in what then was viewed as a maverick's path. I think here particularly of Howard Munford at Middlebury College, who continues to represent for me the very highest example of collegiality; Paul Levitt, James Kincaid, and Lesley Brill of the University of Colorado at Boulder, and Joseph Flora and Laurence Avery at the University of North Carolina at Chapel Hill. They never were bothered that they had a historian in their literature departments, and allowed me to cultivate my interests as I saw fit.

Colleagues at the institutions at which I have taught have been a constant resource: I mention in particular the Reverend Arnold McKinney and John Conron, both of whom were at Middlebury when I was there; L. Michael Bell, John Stevenson, and the late Keith Thomas at Colorado; and Everett Emerson, Richard Rust, Erika Lindemann, and Robert Bain at Chapel Hill. In the profession at large I am privileged to have learned from Lawrence Buell, David D. Hall, Joel Myerson, and Robert D. Richardson, Jr. The personal friendship of Donald F. Eaton, Richard J. Morey, Harry Crockett, and Glen Blalock also has been very important to me.

Fellowship support for this work came at different times from the University of Colorado, the Charles Warren Center at Harvard University, the National Endowment for the Humanities (for a fellowship at the Institute of Early American History and Culture), and the American Antiquarian Society. At these last two institutions, Thad Tate, James P. P. Horn, and Michael McGiffert (of the IEAHC) and John Hench (of the AAS) made me at home away from home and contributed immeasurably to an intellectual environment.

In the introduction to each essay I suggest in brief compass what was on my mind as I undertook the research that eventuated in the published piece, and I present the work virtually as it appeared, save for the correction of the inevitable typographical errors or infelicitous phrasing, and the occasional addition of an explanatory note. I have resisted preparing a supplementary bibliography for each subject, but if significant work on it has appeared subsequent to my initial foray, I have so indicated in the prefatory material.

Finally, I thank Philip Winsor of Penn State Press for offering me the opportunity to present what I hope readers will find a fragrant, as well as a restorative, potpourri of work in American history and literature. And Leslie, for holding it all together, as usual.

Credits

Chapter 1, "The Study of Colonial American Literature, 1966–1987: A *Vade Mecum*," first appeared in the *William and Mary Quarterly*, 3d ser., 45, no. 2 (April 1988): 305–41, and appears with permission.

Chapter 2, "Preparing the Way for Stoddard: Eleazer Mather's *Serious Exhortation* to Northampton," first appeared in the *New England Quarterly* 53, no. 2 (June 1984): 240–50, and appears with permission.

Chapter 3, "Cotton Mather's *Life of Phips:* 'A Vice with the Vizard of Vertue Upon It,' " was published in the *New England Quarterly,* 50, no. 3 (September 1977): 440–57, and appears with permission.

Chapter 4, "Solomon Stoddard's Irreverent Way," was first published in *Early American Literature* 21, no. 1 (spring 1986): 29–43. Permission granted by *Early American Literature.*

Chapter 5, "Sowing for the Harvest: The Reverend William Williams and the Great Awakening," first appeared in the *Journal of Presbyterian History* 56, no. 4 (winter 1978): 326–41, and is reprinted with permission of the Department of History, Presbyterian Church (U.S.A.), 425 Lombard Street, Philadelphia, Pennsylvania.

Chapter 6, "Early Nineteenth-Century Printing in Rural Massachusetts: John Howe of Greenwich and Enfield, c. 1803–1845," was published in the *Proceedings of the American Antiquarian Society* 101, part 1 (spring 1991): 25–52, and is reprinted by permission of the American Antiquarian Society.

Chapter 7, "The Reverend Parsons Cooke and Ware Factory Village: A New Missionary Field," appeared in the *New England Historical and Genealogical Register* 135 (1981): 199–212.

Chapter 8, "The Transcendentalists and Language: The Unitarian Exegetical Background," first appeared in *Studies in the American Renaissance 1979,* ed. Joel Myerson (Boston: Twayne, 1979), 1–16.

Chapter 9, "Elizabeth Palmer Peabody and the Philosophy of Language," first appeared in *ESQ: A Journal of the American Renaissance* 23 (1977): 154–63, and is reprinted with permission.

Chapter 10, "Manufacturing Guitars for the American Parlor: James Ashborn's Wolcottville, Connecticut, Factory, 1851–1856," was published in the *Proceedings of the American Antiquarian Society* 104, part 1 (spring 1994): 117–56, and is reprinted by permission of the American Antiquarian Society.

Chapter 11, "Thoreau and John Josselyn," first appeared in the *New England Quarterly* 48, no. 4 (December 1975): 505–18, and is published with permission.

Chapter 12, "Thoreau's Maine Woods Indians: More Representative Men," first appeared in *American Literature* 49, no. 3 (November 1977): 366–84. © Duke University Press. Reprinted with permission.

Chapter 13, "Language and Meaning: An American Tradition," was published in *American Literature* 53, no. 1 (March 1981): 1–21. © Duke University Press. Reprinted with permission.

Introduction
Tangents to a Sphere

Although much of Bronson Alcott's writing seems full of the intellectual mist and moonshine that contemporary critics identified with the Transcendentalist movement, occasionally he matched his thoughts to an appropriate metaphor. In *Concord Days,* for example, he wisely observed that, though we may be tempted to regard "truth" as something precise, the knowledge of which is attainable, in fact it is best thought of as "spherical." Thus, unlike something that is circular, it cannot be circumscribed but only *approached* from different tangents, "Of two or more sides," he concluded, "none can be absolutely right."[1]

This felicitous image has stayed with me for two decades, particularly when I write about American culture. Alcott chastens us to realize that, given our culture's depth and breadth, all that any scholar can hope to do is draw tangents to America's sphericity. To expect otherwise is to grossly underestimate the complexity, the very sphericity, of the subject.

Academics, however, are loath to relinquish the belief that, with the right methodology, they might explain the mysteries of American culture in some broad new way. Driven on the one hand, however, by the *beau monde* of academic fashion and on the other by the sputtering engine of the job market (as I write, multiculturalism is in, new historicism is fading, critical theory is out), attempts at such circumscription seem often to change with each semester. Further, such hubristic ambition to "explain" American culture is encouraged by the very insularity of our academic disciplines; until very recently, to think about America as a member of a literature

---

1. A. Bronson Alcott, *Concord Days* (Boston: Roberts Brothers, 1872), 73.

department meant something very different than to consider the topic as a historian or a sociologist or an anthropologist. There exists a level of comfort that comes with the expectation of an audience that basically shares one's investment in a certain methodology and tradition of scholarship. Thus, many scholars' claims to originality evoke Andy Warhol's notion of fame in the postmodern age: they are brief and fleeting, because their methods are so parochial and exclusive.

More recently, particularly in literature departments under the sway of influential practitioners of new historicism, this insularity has begun to break down, but often with questionable, if predictable, results. Scholars of one department, for example, rather than training themselves to work in other disciplines—as a literature professor who wished to write new historicism should learn to "do" history, for example—simply raid the scholarship of another discipline for what they need, with the result having little or no effect on scholars outside their own disciplines.

To return to Alcott's memorable image, rather than viewing American culture as something spherical, scholars too often view it as a circle whose radius and circumference can be ascertained, if only the right cultural (for which, read "disciplinary") calculus is used. By offering the essays that follow—my own tangents to the sphere of American culture—I do not claim to be unmarked by the ambition to make much of little, or at least to make more of it than in retrospect was warranted: that is what the profession (or, better, the professional system, from departmental colleagues to university administrators to fellowship-granting committees) has wanted.

I do claim, however, that this work always has had (and now has different, and perhaps more) value. For at the crossroads of American history and literature where I frequently find myself, I am forced to rethink what I am saying and why I say it by my desire to be taken seriously by at least two disciplines—in my case, usually literature and history. I consciously sought to win the confidence of at least two audiences, either of which might be skeptical of conclusions the other could readily embrace. The result—and this most often has meant my rethinking a piece as a historian rather than as a literary critic—is to make me less willing to aggrandize an argument or to make it serve an overt ideology (though, *pace* those critics who believe that intellectual historians usually have their heads in the sand, I understand how easy such recasting would be).[2]

2. This was particularly so in my *A Glimpse of Sion's Glory: Puritan Radicalism in New*

It is also worth recalling that when some of these essays were written, it was decidedly unfashionable to work from the perspective of "history and literature," something that smacked too much of work in the "myth and symbol" vein of American Studies. But now that the winds of academic fashion again have shifted and interdisciplinarity is all the rage, the implicit methodologies as well as the content of the essays that follow may well prove instructive, sometimes in different ways than when they initially were conceived, written, and published.

Fortunately, the acolytes of the Yale school of literary theory did not shame all of us in graduate school in the early 1970s into thinking that we had to retool ourselves as theorists. Ironically, to have done so would have gained us quicker obsolescence! We resisted co-optation by things francophile and hunkered down in our carrels to study literature in the "old-fashioned" way, in relation to cultural history, as it was being refigured by a new generation of scholars. We emerge now to find the sun shining and a cool breeze upon us. The work presented here gains renewed life as we discover how complex the production of literary discourse was.

These essays constitute what I have come to call, first and foremost, acts of historical recovery rather than of literary interpretation. In each essay (with the exception of the first, which constitutes a lengthy review of two decades of scholarship and a prospectus for further work) I start from something—a little-known published text, an unstudied manuscript source, a little-remarked historical event—that has not yet been foregrounded in discussion of the relevant authors or periods. In some cases I do not merely recover the cultural artifacts from the graveyard of history; I note the possibilities they offer for the interpretation of literary texts. In other cases I have been content with discovery and have left the implications for others to work through. It has always seemed to me more significant, and in many ways more exciting, to perform such acts of recovery than to offer, for example, yet another reading of the symbolism of *Walden* or *Moby-Dick*.

As much as possible, then, I have resisted the notion that I have a special ability to tease from a text some hitherto-unknown meaning. Rather, I have

---

England, 1620–1660 (Middletown: Wesleyan University Press, 1984), which I might have cast, on the one hand, as a history illustrating the dialogic nature of discourse, à la Bakhtin; or, following the more obvious lead of Christopher Hill in his work on English Puritan radicalism, in a Marxist direction. But I was most interested in the act of recovery and wished to leave to others the use of my discursive excavations.

sought to provide the basis for renewed negotiation of both masterworks and the discourse from which they emerged, discourse that, while significant in its own time, frequently has not found the discussion it deserves today. In so doing, I note the distinction between a literary critic and a cultural historian, between one who expends energy to prove that his reading is at least as important as another's and he who marvels at the complexity of any historical moment, and thus at the presumption of anyone who thinks that she might have enough of a handle on an author to venture her notions of what a text finally "means." To put it another way, I have found it fascinating to consider, at different points in colonial and antebellum history, what it was possible for someone to think at a given time, and thus to contribute to the mapping of the elaborate cultural grammar of moments in the past.

I derive my understanding of this cultural grammar primarily from contemporary historians who have refertilized the once seemingly exhausted field of "intellectual" history. Many historians, for example, now view the project of the "intellectual" historian to be the understanding of discourse as a complex social as well as intellectual activity. Thus, David Hollinger, who has done as much as anybody to reinvigorate the field of American intellectual history, notes that the study of the language of any individual is dependent on the recognition that such study "entails interaction between minds." Further,

> it revolves around something possessed in common. Participants in any given discourse are bound to share certain values, beliefs, perceptions, and concepts—"ideas," as these potentially distinctive mental phenomena are called for short—but the most concrete and functional elements shared, surely, are questions. Even when one grants that the choice of questions on the part of the contributors to a discourse is in itself an act of evaluation, and when one grants further that conflicting "answers" offered to these questions will be structured partly by ethical, aesthetic, and cognitive arguments among the participants, it remains that the questions are at the active heart of discourse.

"Questions," Hollinger concludes, "are the points of contact between minds, where arguments are consolidated and where differences are acknowledged and dealt with." Questions, then, of the kind that I have sought to frame in the essays that follow, about revivalism, or Transcendentalist philosophy, or the output of rural printers, are "the dynamisms whereby membership in a community of discourse is established, renewed, and sometimes terminated."[3]

To me, discourse most vividly manifests itself through the mediation of experience and consciousness, in what people have called "ideas"—the idea of factory production, for example, or of a good governor, or of the meaning of language—but which we must strive to understand as more than just the intellectual constructs usually associated with such terms. Once we acknowledge that ideas are articulated within a broad "communicative context," we also realize that any contribution to a discourse is, in Hollinger's words, "no less an 'event' (and no less trivial or momentous in itself) than a bullet fired in a war or the invention of a machine."[4] This is another way of saying, though many of my contemporaries would dismiss the notion, that ideas do indeed have consequences, whether or not all who use them consciously acknowledge the fact.

Discourse then, properly understood, is nothing less than the product of the history and contemporary circumstances of an entire culture, even of those individuals who oppose its premises and thus enter into dialogue with it, as people did with Thoreau, for example, about the meaning of the Native American, or with Elizabeth Peabody about the authenticity of Scripture. Concomitantly, this also implies that

> communication across intellectual levels can be authentic, and that "ordinary people" as well as intellectuals think, even formally and systematically, with or without the same analytic tools used by contemporary intellectuals. Yet the observation *also* recognizes that relatively distinct discourses can develop among people who precisely formulate questions that may be shared with people who remain oblivious to those more specific and often more precise formulations.[5]

---

3. David A. Hollinger, "Historians and the Discourse of Intellectuals," in *In the American Grain: Studies in the History and Historiography of Ideas* (Bloomington: Indiana University Press, 1985), 132. Further references to this essay are given in the text. Also see the various essays in John Higham and Paul K. Conkin, eds., *New Directions in American Intellectual History* (Baltimore: Johns Hopkins University Press, 1979); and Brook Thomas, *The New Historicism and Other Old-Fashioned Topics* (Princeton: Princeton University Press, 1991), esp. 3–50.
4. Hollinger, "Discourse of Intellectuals, 149.
5. Ibid., 147.

In other words, one need not know all the rules of a specific language to speak in and through it, or to be circumscribed by it, just as the rural Massachusetts printer John Howe might not be considered learned in debates about the difference between republicanism and liberalism, even as his career and satiric versifying exemplify it. Thus, the history of discourse, as opposed to the older "history of ideas," treats how a language impinges on all who use it, whether or not they actively participate in its ongoing formulation.

Viewed in this way, what previously we have been content to call "ideas" now must be treated, in Gordon Wood's words, in "an instrumental and rhetorical way—as mechanisms for perceiving, persuading, manipulating, and ordering the world."[6] "Our older assumptions about ideas operating in some sort of spatial separation from social circumstances" is specious, Wood continues; "ideas and symbols do not exist apart from reality out there." They are no less than the "means by which we perceive, understand, judge, or manipulate that reality: indeed, they create it."[7] William J. Bouwsma heartily agrees: "Through language man orders the chaos of data impinging on his sensorium, organizing them into categories and so making them intelligible for himself, manageable, communicable, and therefore specially useful as well as essential to his private adaptation to the world." The "human and social world" with which historians are concerned, he concludes, "might therefore be described as a vast rhetorical production." And it is parts of this "production" that I isolate and elucidate in this volume.[8]

Thus we cannot rest in a mere description of what ideas were but must investigate what they allowed people to do, what they allowed individuals to think and say. And concomitantly, what they did *not* allow: to know what ideas do also implies an understanding of how in their social context they prescribe and circumscribe behavior, indeed, mark what it is possible to think and believe about one's world. The ideas and thoughts that define discourse, Wood notes, form nothing less than a "collective cultural system" that sets limits on what individuals can say and think (and hence do) at any particular moment.[9] Hollinger concurs, for he believes that

---

6. Gordon S. Wood, "Intellectual History and the Social Sciences," in Higham and Conkin, *New Directions*, 35.

7. Ibid., 32.

8. William J. Bouwsma, "From History of Ideas to History of Meaning," *Journal of Interdisciplinary History* 12, no. 2 (autumn 1982): 289–90.

9. Wood, "Intellectual History," 35.

access to the implied power of discourse is not "axiomatic." "Social and political contexts obviously set limits," he observes, "on who speaks about what, and in whose hearing."[10]

To write such history, be it about exclusively literary texts or about such artifacts as occasional broadsides, temperance sermons, parlor guitars, or the books read by rural people, is different in quality and tone from what has come to be called the "new historicism"; it begins in and remains centered around that "hard but unquestionable history" that Thoreau located in an old "fisherman's account current" and everywhere else in the immense fact of the world, or that I discern in the records of an early nineteenth-century printing office or of an antebellum musical manufacturer, not in some preconceived notions of ideological power and hegemony.[11] In other words, these essays most often commence with small pieces of a cultural puzzle. They end by allowing a reader to fit more and more pieces—and eventually the contours of the large picture—into place because of the new space my pieces create. The joy of such work derives primarily from initial discovery and discernment, and later from the reconfigurations that such painstaking work makes possible.

Thus, as this work was produced at different times in the past two decades, I never had in mind any idea that what I was writing—even if it was about such volatile topics as Puritan radicalism, the Industrial Revolution, or perceptions of Native Americans—should fit some preexistent notion I had of ideology or, to use a less fashionable word, politics. Of course, I had a politics and was enmeshed in various cultural webs that I understood were ideologically spun, but it seemed potentially to blemish the integrity of the historical record, the "hard but unquestionable" artifacts that remain from the past, to bring such matters to an investigation of the cultural grammar of another time and place. I seek to preserve artifacts that I believe significant, in themselves and for what they reveal of the complexity of American culture at any given moment. I let them speak first and most powerfully of what they are.

To explain my obsession with such reading, my devotion to empirical history, I must speak more autobiographically. My introduction to the fields

---

10. Hollinger, "Discourse of Intellectuals," 131. Also see John E. Toews, "Intellectual History after the Linguistic Turn: The Autonomy of Meaning and the Irreducibility of Experience," *American Historical Review* 92, no. 4 (October 1987): 879–907.

11. Henry David Thoreau, *A Week on the Concord and Merrimack Rivers* (1849; Princeton: Princeton University Press, 1980), 35.

of history and literature, and thus to the reading of larger cultural issues through their complementarity, came not only through undergraduate and graduate training in those disciplines but also through an immersion in the nitty-gritty of the past at one of the nation's major outdoor museums. Serving both as an undergraduate intern and later a staff member in the department of interpretation (as it came to be called) at Old Sturbridge Village, I was trained in just the kind of intensive reading of the minutiae of the past that I carry over into these essays. The time was the early 1970s, and at such places as Plimoth Plantation and Old Sturbridge Village a revolution in the way such museums presented the past to their myriad visitors was under way.

I could write a separate essay on the nature of that revolution and its effect on museum interpreters, administrators, and the public themselves, but here I simply emphasize the importance to a budding historian of culture of the kind of immersion into the physical landscape, and peoplescape, represented by the museum.[12] Taken into the restoration of a farmer's home, a general store, or a printing office, we were trained to "read" that environment: to ask questions, that is, of the quotidian objects that surrounded us and the museum visitors who would seek understanding and interpretation from the staff. It was heady and exhilarating, and through our internships and our independent research (encouraged by the administration), we investigated byways that soon led us to the thoroughfares of New England history.

One colleague, for example, researched the spatial development of the village "common." Another became expert in the matter of soap and the kinds of cleanliness it permitted. Another researched the holdings and circulation records of village "social" libraries, the lending libraries of the time. My effort, initiated in 1971, resulted in an essay (included here, Chapter 7) on the transformations wrought in an agricultural community as a factory village arose on one of its rivers. Thus, though not the earliest published piece in this collection, "The Reverend Parsons Cooke and Ware Factory Village" is emblematic of my entire enterprise: to show how negotiation of the byways of the past frequently leads us into the main routes of colonial and antebellum cultural history. Some of those efforts,

---

12. See, for example, Stephen Eddy Snow, *Performing the Pilgrims: A Study of Ethnohistorical Role-Playing at Plimoth Plantation* (Jackson: University Press of Mississippi, 1993), for a sense of the revolution wrought in the outdoor-history museums during this period.

my essay on the study of language by the Transcendentalists (Chapter 8), for example, led into central arteries, as several subsequent studies have shown.[13] Others, like the studies of various figures from the Connecticut Valley of Massachusetts (Chapters 2, 4, and 5) limn as completely as I was able the contours of sections of the enormous jigsaw of history that historians, more than literary critics, try to assemble. Still others, like the very recent case study of rural printing in antebellum Massachusetts (Chapter 6), have not yet had their full impact but will contribute to the assembly of a detailed history of reading and of knowledge in the period and thus move from the local to a larger level.

But all the works derive from what one friend called my "antiquarian" bent, something of which I am unabashedly proud. Indeed, he used that term in 1975, in notes taken of my interview for a position at his institution. He had read some of my work on Thoreau, specifically an essay on Thoreau and the early explorer John Josselyn (included here, Chapter 11), and wondered what might come of someone with a mind that ran to such topics at a time when literary theory was ascendant. Although he died before he could read the full shape of my career, I like to think that he would be pleased with what the antiquarian in me has produced. And, completing a circuit with that magical word, I take great pride in my association with the American Antiquarian Society, devoted to the "purpose of Collecting and Preserving the Materials for the History, and for promoting the Arts and Sciences of this Western Continent." To be enthralled with the antiquities of one's place in the world does not strike me as embarrassing. Rather, it signals a rootedness of the kind more and more rare among scholars who climb on a bandwagon without ever understanding the music they were meant to play.

All of the essays that follow had an occasion, indeed, were for me some sort of intellectual event marking what I understood that I was doing. I am most happy with those for which I had to educate myself anew; in this regard the most recent effort, on the history of American musical technology (Chapter 10), is most apropos. But in different ways the reading for the major assessment of research in, and future directions for the study of, early American literature provided the same sort of excitement, as did the

13. I have in mind here Richard Grusin's *Transcendental Hermeneutics: Institutional Authority and the Higher Criticism of the Bible* (Durham: Duke University Press, 1991) and Michael P. Kramer's *Imagining Language in America: From the Revolution to the Civil War* (Princeton: Princeton University Press, 1992).

piece on rural printing, and on Thoreau's understanding of Native Americans. These were labors of love, the more so because I had confidence that, even if I did find the major thoroughfare to which the paths led, the intellectual landscape through which I had to pass en route would be sufficiently satisfying. Remarkably, my confidence was justified, my discoveries reward enough for all the pettiness that academics must endure.

As I suggested earlier, I have not tried to stitch these pieces into a patchwork quilt. Except in a few cases, when the essays were written they were not conceived as part of a larger whole. I claim no preternatural ability to have seen how all one day would eventuate in whole cloth. Rather, I put them here as examples of what the cultural historian can do when his or her eyes are open to read the small print of America's past. Several of them will, I believe, lead others to find that of which I caught glimpses, and others to views that I never imagined. That is my best hope for them.

And I put them here, finally, to honor those who either have believed in the kind of scholarship they represent or in me as I defined myself in and through this kind of work, a hybrid of the disciplines of history and literature, somehow still literary history. As David Perkins recently has noted, even though in our age it has become increasingly difficult to believe in and write about literary history, we still "must read it." He means that even though we cannot attain the ideal of objective knowledge, we still must pursue it, "for without such pursuit the otherness of the past would entirely deliquesce in endless subjective and ideological reappropriations." "A function of literary history is, then," he concludes, "to set the literature of the past at a distance, to make its otherness felt."[14]

Let me close by invoking the example of Nathaniel Hawthorne, among his generation of writers, one of the most interested in the relation of history to literature. In his charming reminiscence, "The Old Manse," which introduces his collection of stories, *Mosses from an Old Manse*, we find a lesiurely discussion of an attic room in his Concord home where young scholars came to study with Ralph Waldo Emerson's grandfather William Emerson, and, later, the venerable Ezra Ripley, had boarded.[15] Therein Hawthorne found many old volumes, presumably the remains of the clerical library. Good historian that he was, he "burrowed among these venerable books, in search of any living thought, which should burn like a coal of fire, or glow like an

---

14. David Perkins, *Is Literary History Possible?* (Baltimore: Johns Hopkins University Press, 1992), 33, 17, 185.

15. Nathaniel Hawthorne, *Mosses from an Old Manse,* Centenary Edition of the Works of Nathaniel Hawthorne, (Columbus: Ohio State University Press, 1974), 10:18–21.

inextinguishable gem." But to his surprise he found no such treasure among the leather-bound books. "All was dead alike," and he could not but muse deeply and wonderingly upon the humiliating fact, that the works of man's intellect decay like those of his hands." "Thought grows mouldy," he continues. "What was good and nourishing for the spirits of one generation, affords no sustenance for the next."

After examining some works that pertained to the more recent Unitarian controversy and noting that these had an effect even more depressing than the more "venerable" tomes, which at least were "earnestly written" and "might be conceived to have possessed warmth, at some former period," Hawthorne lit upon some old newspapers and almanacs. These genuinely excited him, he wrote, for they "reproduced, to [his] mental eye, the epochs when they had issued from the press, with a distinctness that was altogether unaccountable." "It was as if," he continued, "I had found bits of magic looking-glass among the books, with the images of a vanished century in them." Interrogating a tattered portrait of an eighteenth-century divine who had lived in the Manse, Hawthorne wondered why it was that "he and his brethren, after the most painful rummaging and groping in their minds, had been able to produce nothing half so real, as these newspaper scribblers and almanac-makers had thrown off, in the effervescence of the moment."

Hawthorne, I would say, made the same discovery as Thoreau when he marveled at the way a simple workingman's account book could evoke the past. Both writers understood that to know the past as well as we can, we have to work with such traces, to let the shattered bits of mirror reflect what they can of the surrounding age. As Thoreau rightly said, "Critical acumen is exerted in vain to uncover the past; the *past* cannot be *presented*; we cannot know what we are not." Yet, he goes on to say, "one veil hangs over past, present, and future, and it is the province of the historian to find out, not what was, but what is."[16] As long as we recognize that in writing history we write as much about our difference from the past as about the past itself, the project remains honest and worthwhile. As we write, then, as the literary theorists would want us to and as we must, more self-consciously aware of what premises underlie our attempts to recover and narrate the past, we move toward a deeper understanding of that "otherness" Perkins so eloquently describes. The satisfactions from such work, as I can testify, are great, and worthy of consideration.

16. Thoreau, *A Week*, 153.

1 | The Study of Colonial American Literature, 1966–1987
A *Vade Mecum*

The inspiration for this essay came after I had spent a year as a National Endowment for the Humanities Senior Fellow at the Institute of Early American History and Culture at Williamsburg, Virginia, in 1985–86. Surrounded as I was by historians the like of whose intelligence and camaraderie I have encountered nowhere else, I was frequently asked to explain the kind of work that engages scholars in literature departments. Concomitantly, more and more I came to wonder why there remained such a significant distance between members of the two professions, particularly since, as had become evident to me with regard to the field of early American studies, we had so much to learn from one another.

At the instigation of Michael McGiffert, editor of the *William and Mary Quarterly*, I undertook a reconsideration of the ways in which scholars of early American literature had approached their subject, and as well to sketch how such work might be enriched by more attention to the labors of historians of the same period. After the essay was completed, McGiffert decided to run the piece as part of the *Quarterly*'s new "Forum" series, and invited responses by prominent scholars of early American literature. Thus, when this piece appeared it was accompanied by statements from David Levin, Norman Grabo, and Larzer Ziff, and a final comment by me.

The essay proved useful to me in other ways, too, for I was on the verge of taking up the position of editor of *Early American Literature*, replacing my colleague Everett Emerson, who had held the job for two decades. At the same time, with the cosponsorship of the Institute and the University of North Carolina at Chapel Hill, he and I hosted a research conference called "Prospects," devoted to the consideration of what work needed to be done in early American literature in the next decade. This essay greatly aided me in conceiving the shape and function of that event.

Since this essay has appeared, important new work has reshaped the field of early American literature; in most cases it stems precisely from the fruitful conjunction of history and literature that I believe so necessary. I think particularly of David Hall's *Worlds of Wonder, Days of Judgment: Popular Religious Belief in Early New England* (1989) and David Shields's *Oracles of Empire: Poetry, Politics, and Commerce in British America, 1690–1750* (1990), but as well of work in American Puritan studies— Andrew Delbanco's *The Puritan Ordeal* (1989), and Janice Knight's *Orthodoxies in Massachusetts: Rereading American Puritanism* (1994)—that challenges the centrality of Sacvan Bercovitch's work (see below). I could add to this list but point the reader instead to the able summaries of scholarship in the field published each year by William Scheick in *American Literary Scholarship*. Suffice it to say that, as I continue in my position as editor of *EAL,* I am constantly amazed at the continued vitality of the discipline, one whose practitioners have come to acknowledge more than ever that to work therein they must educate themselves in at least two disciplines.

For many years the marriage of convenience between American history and literature, which by the 1950s had become the core of the American Studies movement, at least had the virtue of its fertility. What some later viewed as an accommodation between ill-suited partners had been sanctified at Harvard in the late 1930s, where from the conjunction of these two disciplines there issued a major reassessment of early American culture (for which read "early New England culture"), an achievement epitomized by the works of Perry Miller and the allied scholarship of such of his colleagues as Kenneth B. Murdock, Samuel Eliot Morison, and, for the nineteenth century, F. O. Matthiessen.[1] As a result, through the mid-1960s, in large part because of

---

1. The major scholarship comprises Miller's *The New England Mind: The Seventeenth Century* (New York: Macmillan, 1939) and *The New England Mind: From Colony to Province* (Cambridge: Harvard University Press, 1953); Murdock's *Literature and Theology in Colonial New England* (Cambridge: Harvard University Press, 1949); Morison's *Builders of the Bay Colony* (1930; repr. Boston: Houghton Mifflin, 1958), *The Founding of Harvard College* (Cambridge: Harvard University Press, 1935), and *Harvard College in the Seventeenth Century,* 2 vols. (Cambridge: Harvard University Press, 1936); and Matthiessen's *American Renaissance: Art and Expression in the Age of Emerson and Whitman* (New York: Oxford

Miller's domination of the field, those who entered upon the study of colonial American literature felt compelled to become versed as much in intellectual history as in belles lettres. And because intellectual as well as literary historians took Miller seriously, to study colonial American literature in these three decades meant that one addressed, at least implicitly, two professions.

All this began to change shortly after Miller's death in 1963, an event that for some already has taken on quasi-mythical dimensions.[2] Bit by bit, commencing with the work of social historians such as Darrett B. Rutman and Robert G. Pope, and reaching something of an apogee in the *annus mirabilis* of 1970, when four significant town studies were published by historians, scholars began to chip away at Miller's methodological assumptions and, in some cases, his conclusions about New England Puritanism in particular and intellectual history in general.[3] By the late 1960s all interested parties knew the terms of the divorce. The study of history, under the influence of the *Annales* school, was thought of more and more as an exact social science dominated by demographers and cliometricians. The study of literature became increasingly the realm of those who, equally enchanted by siren songs from the Continent, studied the ambiguity of elaborately structured verbal artifacts. To be sure, students of American literature were among the last to succumb to a mode of interpretation derived from linguistics, structural anthropology, and allied

---

University Press, 1941). Also see Gene Wise, "Paradigm Dramas in American Studies: A Cultural and Institutional History of the Movement," *American Quarterly* 31 (1979): 293–337.

2. See, for example, Sacvan Bercovitch's admission in *The American Jeremiad* (Madison: University of Wisconsin Press, 1978) that in an earlier version of his study he "muted" his dissent from Miller because he was "unwilling to join in the patricidal totem feast following Miller's death, when a swarm of social and literary historians rushed to pick apart the corpus of his work" (xv). Also see Francis T. Butts, "The Myth of Perry Miller," *American Historical Review* 87 (1982): 665–94; and *American Quarterly* 34 (1982), much of which is devoted to a reconsideration of Miller's work.

3. Darrett Rutman, *Winthrop's Boston: Portrait of a Puritan Town, 1630–1649* (Chapel Hill: University of North Carolina Press, 1965), and *American Puritanism: Faith and Practice* (Philadelphia: Lippincott, 1970); Pope, *The Half-Way Covenant: Church Membership in Puritan New England* (Princeton: Princeton University Press, 1969); John Demos, *A Little Commonwealth: Family Life in Plymouth Colony* (New York: Oxford University Press, 1970); Philip J. Greven, Jr., *Four Generations: Population, Land, and Family in Colonial Andover, Massachusetts* (Ithaca: Cornell University Press, 1970); Kenneth A. Lockridge, *A New England Town, the First Hundred Years: Dedham, Massachusetts, 1636–1736* (New York: Norton, 1970); Michael Zuckerman, *Peaceable Kingdoms: New England Towns in the Eighteenth Century* (New York: Knopf, 1970).

fields that focused on *language*—what writers mean by it and how they use it—and concluded in "deconstruction," but even had they more vigorously sought a rapprochement with their colleagues in the history departments it would not have been forthcoming.[4]

The increasing strains between the two fields also occurred almost simultaneously with the maturation of colonial American literature as an independent discipline, symbolized by the founding in 1966 of the *Early American Literature Newsletter* (soon called simply *Early American Literature*) as the official organ of the Modern Language Association's division on "American Literature to 1800." Contributors to *EAL* and others publishing in the field have added distinctive voices that often rise above the general cacophony now heard in literature departments. With *EAL* now in its twenty-first year of publication and showing signs of increased vigor, this seems an appropriate moment to assess the work over the past two decades of scholars of colonial American literature, paying special attention to the direction of studies of the history of early America.

I do not intend what follows to be an all-inclusive bibliographical essay but rather an attempt to present the important lines of inquiry established by scholars of colonial American literature. Readers who seek more inclusive bibliographical information have several resources available to them, most notably the annual review essay on "Literature to 1800" in *American Literary Scholarship* and the detailed listing of books and essays provided in the annual issues of the *MLA International Bibliography*.[5] I assume that, just as students of early American literature constantly are nourished by the work of scholars in other fields, history not the least of them, so the historical profession should be aware of the ways in which the literary

---

4. For a flavor of the issues that structuralist and poststructuralist literary theory has raised, see Richard Macksey and Eugenio Donato, eds., *The Languages of Criticism and the Sciences of Man: The Structuralist Controversy* (Baltimore: Johns Hopkins University Press, 1970); Harold Bloom et al., *Deconstruction and Criticism* (New York: Seabury, 1979); and two important journals that often contain essays on the subject: *Critical Inquiry* and *Representations*. Michael Clark's " 'The Crucified Phrase': Sign and Desire in Puritan Semiology," *Early American Literature* 13 (1978–79): 278–93, indicates to what uses such theory can be put in the study of early American literature.

5. *American Literary Scholarship: An Annual* (Durham: Duke University Press, 1965–). The "Literature to 1800" essays have been written by such distinguished scholars as Richard Beale Davis, J. A. Leo Lemay, Robert Arner, and William Scheick. The *MLA International Bibliography* is published by the Modern Language Association of America. Another invaluable bibliographical tool is James A. Levernier and Douglas R. Wilmes, eds., *American Writers before 1800: A Biographical and Critical Dictionary*, 3 vols. (Westport, Conn.: Greenwood, 1983).

profession approaches its subject and of the conclusions about early American culture that flow from them. That their respective assumptions and conclusions concerning the development of early American history and culture in many cases are not congruent makes it the more important for professors of history and of literature to understand the premises of each others' work.

With regard to the scope of this essay, I follow the lead of the editors of *Colonial British America* and restrict my comments to the study of the literature of British North America before 1763, for two reasons.[6] First, I think it unfortunate—an indication of how suspicion still fouls the air between historians and literary critics—that no scholar of colonial American literature participated in the transatlantic conference from which the essays in Greene and Pole's book were drawn; I intend this essay as a contribution modeled in form and content, as well as in spirit, after those in that volume.[7] Second, practically speaking, literary historians, like their counterparts in the historical profession, have been slow to expand their studies into regions of North America settled by other Europeans. Thus there has been little significant investigation by students of colonial American literature of, say, the literature of French Canada or Spanish Florida, or even of the British settlements in the Caribbean, and virtually no studies comparing the literature of any of these regions with that of the mainland British colonies.[8]

Twenty years of such scholarship does not lend itself to easy organization; yet it can, I believe, be profitably discussed if we consider the following lines of argument. First, the literature of the colonial period most often has been viewed as a prologue to the literature of the United States in the nineteenth century rather than having been considered in its own right

6. Jack P. Greene and J. R. Pole, eds., *Colonial British America: Essays in the New History of the Early Modern Era* (Baltimore: Johns Hopkins University Press, 1984).
7. For a survey of the range of issues and concerns addressed by the contributors to the volume see Greene and Pole, eds., *Colonial British America*, 1–17.
8. The literature of these areas, however, is extensive. See, for example, Donald E. Herdeck et al., eds., *Caribbean Writers: A Bio-Bibliographical–Critical Encyclopedia* (Washington, D.C.: Three Continents Press, 1979), esp. 1–260; Alma Jordan and Barbara Comissiong, *The English-Speaking Caribbean: A Bibliography of Bibliographies* (Boston: G. K. Hall, 1984), and Gordon K. Lewis, *Main Currents in Caribbean Thought: The Historical Evolution of Caribbean Society in Its Ideological Aspects, 1492–1900* (Baltimore: Johns Hopkins University Press, 1983), 29–239. On French Canada see, for example, Claude Thibault, *Bibliographia Canadiana* (Don Mills, Ont.: Longman, 1973), passim, and for literature in English, Reginald Eyre Watters, *A Checklist of Canadian Literature and Background Materials, 1628–1960*, 2d rev. ed. (Toronto: University of Toronto Press, 1972), esp. 3–423.

and terms. Second, colonial American literature has been understood as somehow exceptional, sui generis, rather than dependent in its style and form on cultural norms set in England. Third, in many studies New England has served as a proxy for the British North American colonies generally, with the result that the literature of the distinct regions within the British American empire has not been properly assessed. Fourth, despite an increasing awareness on the part of some scholars of nonreligious forms of discourse, the study of colonial American literature, especially in its New England phase, has been informed primarily by an interest in religious language and symbol. And last, as yet little attention has been paid to "popular" literature in all its various forms. After examining these observations in some detail, I attempt to synthesize what their adherents offer historians of colonial America and, at the same time, how their views might change if they more deeply considered the scholarship of their colleagues in history departments.

By stopping my essay at 1763 I trim about forty years from the field of early American literature as it is usually defined, but I do so for what I consider sound scholarly reasons. The period of the American Revolution and the early republic inaugurated new forms of discourse that were greatly complicated by the first waves of Romantic ideology that by century's end washed the American strand; these new forms require a very different orientation for their interpretation. An assessment of the study of the literature of this period seems best taken up in a separate essay that addresses the very different issues in history and literature raised by the momentous fact of American independence and the country's subsequent search for political stability and cultural identity.[9]

The most significant, and for historians undoubtedly the most problematic,

9. Good general studies of this later period are Emory Elliott, *Revolutionary Writers: Literature and Authority in the New Republic, 1725–1810* (New York: Oxford University Press, 1982); Joseph J. Ellis, *After the Revolution: Profiles of Early American Culture* (New York: Oxford University Press, 1979); Michael Kammen, *A Season of Youth: The American Revolution and the Historical Imagination* (New York: Knopf, 1978); and Kenneth Silverman, *A Cultural History of the American Revolution: Painting, Music, Literature, and the Theatre in the Colonies and the United States from the Treaty of Paris to the Inauguration of George Washington, 1763–1789* (New York: Crowell, 1976). Also see the bicentennial offering of *EAL*, "The Literature of the American Revolution," (Special issue, 1976), and two other issues: 11, no. 1 (1976), the proceedings of a conference at Fordham University devoted to literature of the period 1765–90, and 11, no. 2 (1976), the proceedings of a similar conference held at Williamsburg, Va. Also relevant is William L. Hedges, "The Old World Yet: Writers and Writing in Post-Revolutionary America," *Early American Literature* 16 (1981): 3–18.

development in the study of colonial American literature in the past twenty years has been the reemergence—some would say the irrational persistence—of the notion of profound continuities between early American literary expression and the classic literature of the United States in the mid-nineteenth century, and of the accompanying belief in American "exceptionalism," both literary and cultural.[10] This is especially surprising because, as Greene and Pole emphasize in their introduction to *Colonial British America,* for many years now in the historical profession assumptions about the uniqueness of American culture in the colonial period have been considered wrongheaded, a hangover from the heyday of the "American Studies" movement of the 1950s whose champions assiduously analyzed "colonial developments largely in terms of the extent to which they exhibited a process of Americanization." But, despite growing evidence to the contrary, many literary historians continue to assume that "America, at least in its continental British-American variant, was and had always been fundamentally different from Europe."[11]

We thus encounter what is perhaps the single most important fact as we consider the study of colonial American literature in light of that of colonial American history generally. While historians more and more agree that the American colonies, "no matter how distant they might be from Britain or how much latitude they may have had in their internal development," were all "cultural provinces of Britain," literary historians, particularly those who reside, intellectually or otherwise, in New England, have stubbornly maintained the primacy of colonial literature and culture in the formation of an "American mind." For Emory Elliott, for example, "the task set before the present generation of students" is to "properly assay the impact of colonial Puritanism upon the development of American literature." Seemingly oblivious to the fact that most historians agree that by the beginning of the eighteenth century all the mainland colonies were transatlantic outposts "whose legal and social systems, perceptual frameworks, and social and cultural imperatives were inevitably in large measure British in origin and whose inhabitants thereby shared a common identity as British peoples living in America," Elliott assumes that "Puritanism contained the seeds of political and social ideals, structures of thought and language, and literary themes which inspired both the content and the forms of much American writing from 1700 to the present."[12]

10. See Greene and Pole, eds., *Colonial British America,* 2–7.
11. Ibid., 3.
12. Ibid., 14; Emory Elliott, ed., *Puritan Influences in American Literature* (Urbana: University of Illinois Press, 1979), xii–xiii. Also see the special issue of *Texas Studies in*

We shall return to the novanglophilia that informs such a view, but at this point it is more important to account for the credibility of this seemingly anachronistic notion of the colonial British American roots of the subsequent literature of the United States. In large measure the current popularity of such views derives from the provocative work of Sacvan Bercovitch, who has taken up where Miller left off—some critics would say, has only rephrased Miller's ideas in a vocabulary more relevant to scholars of the present generation—in his claims for the uniqueness of American literature from 1630 on. Bercovitch's reputation rests primarily on two studies, *The Puritan Origins of the American Self* (1975) and *The American Jeremiad* (1978), but his earlier work, particularly his edition of essays on *Typology and Early American Literature* (1972) and a lengthy essay on Cotton Mather published in the same year, as well as an earlier version of what became *The American Jeremiad*, clearly marked the directions his work would take.[13]

The contributors to *Typology and Early American Literature*, including Bercovitch, who provides both an introductory essay and an invaluable bibliography of typological literature from the church fathers on, demonstrate the significance of a mode of interpretation of early American culture whose worth Miller simply underestimated and thus virtually neglected (except in his study of Roger Williams, whose thought he simply misconstrued). In addition to providing the underpinning for Bercovitch's own work, this method allowed scholars in a variety of fields to stake out new intellectual vantage points from which to survey the culture of the colonial period.[14] To be sure, Bercovitch did not single-handedly resurrect inquiry

---

Literature and Language 25, no. 1 (1983), devoted to the continuities between Puritanism and later American culture.

13. Bercovitch, *The Puritan Origins of the American Self* (New Haven: Yale University Press, 1975); *American Jeremiad: Typology and Early American Literature* (Amherst: University of Massachusetts Press, 1972); "Cotton Mather," in *Major Writers of Early American Literature*, ed. Everett Emerson (Madison: University of Wisconsin Press, 1972), 93–150; and "Horologicals to Chronometricals: The Rhetoric of the Jeremiad," in *Literary Monographs,* ed. Eric Rothstein (Madison: University of Wisconsin Press, 1970), 3:1–124.

14. Perry Miller, *Roger Williams: His Contribution to the American Tradition* (Indianapolis: Bobbs-Merrill, 1953); see also Miller's introduction to Jonathan Edwards's *Images or Shadows of Divine Things* (New Haven: Yale University Press, 1948). In a succinct essay, "Perry Miller and the Puritans: A Literary Scholar's Assessment" (*History Teacher* 14 [1981]: 459–67), Everett Emerson discusses Miller's seeming blindness to the typological framework of most Puritan literature. Readers also should be aware of how completely Miller's notion of a Puritan "plain style," as epitomized in his "An American Language" (*Nature's Nation* [Cambridge: Harvard University Press, 1967], 208–40, but announced by him and Thomas H. Johnson decades earlier in *The Puritans* [New York: American Book, 1938], 64–80), has been discredited. See, for example, Norman S. Grabo, "The Veiled Vision: The Role of

into typology in this period—in 1970, for example, Ursula Brumm published *American Thought and Religious Typology*, a translation of a work issued in Germany seven years earlier—but he must be credited with demonstrating how completely biblical analogy permeates American Puritan literature and thus, through his own work and his sponsorship of others', with reorienting scholars of early American literature to the implications of the complex rhetoric that underlies New England Puritan thought.[15] By addressing anew the question of what was *literary* about American Puritan literature, *Typology and Early American Literature* sent students back to the Geneva and King James Bibles, as well as to Benjamin Keach's *Tropologia* (1681) and Samuel Mather's *Figures or Types of the Old Testament* (1683), to crack the linguistic code of New England Puritanism. When Mason I. Lowance, Jr., published *The Language of Canaan* in 1980, with its claims for the persistence of a typological mode of interpretation through the American Renaissance of the 1840s and 1850s, he merely certified what most had come to believe: scriptural analogy lay at the heart of the New England Puritan enterprise and so, by implication, beneath American literature as a whole.[16]

Bercovitch's essay on Mather alerted scholars to the types of concerns that, when elaborated a few years later in *The Puritan Origins of the American Self*, brought this scholar national prominence.[17] Still the best single essay on its subject, "Cotton Mather" traces this minister's literary career with particular emphasis on how, in the *Magnalia Christi Americana* (1702), he "fuse[d] the morphology of conversion (in the biographies) and the flourishing of the theocracy (in the narrative) into alternate perspectives

---

Aesthetics in Early American Intellectual History," *William and Mary Quarterly*, 3d ser., 19 (1962): 493–510. Paul J. Korshin's *Typologies in England, 1650–1820* (Princeton: Princeton University Press, 1982), provides an idea of the ways in which typology is studied in and used to discuss British literature.

15. Brumm, *American Thought and Religious Typology*, trans. John Hoogland (New Brunswick: Rutgers University Press, 1970). It should be noted that some of the essays and the detailed bibliography in *Typology and Early American Literature* first appeared in *Early American Literature*; see particularly vol. 5, no. 1 (1970).

16. Lowance, *The Language of Canaan: Metaphor and Symbol in New England from the Puritans to the Transcendentalists* (Cambridge: Harvard University Press, 1980), esp. 277–78.

17. In addition, in the late 1960s Bercovitch had published several important essays; see especially "New England Epic: Cotton Mather's *Magnalia Christi Americana*," *English Literary History* 33 (1966): 377–50; "Typology in Puritan New England: The Williams–Cotton Controversy Reassessed," *American Quarterly* 29 (1967): 166–91; and "The Historiography of Johnson's *Wonder-Working Providence*," *Essex Institute Historical Collections* 104 (1968): 138–61.

on the work of redemption."[18] In *The Puritan Origins of the American Self,* a hermeneutical reading of the biography of John Winthrop that Mather had included in the *Magnalia,* Bercovitch goes on to suggest how pervasively and indelibly Mather's formulation of "exemplary" biography (and the cultural fact on which he based it, the Puritans' invention of "a colony in the image of a saint") marked subsequent American literature. He argues that, as "the literary *summa* of the New England Way," the *Magnalia* stands at the head of a line of such American literary masterpieces as Thoreau's *Walden* and Whitman's *Leaves of Grass,* works in whose rhetoric an author's personal and corporate identities are similarly conjoined. As a result of the Puritans' legacy in the realm of the American imagination, Bercovitch concludes, all subsequent American writers must compose (for better or for worse) "auto-American-biographies."[19]

In *The American Jeremiad* he further expanded his investigations of the uniqueness and continuity of certain forms of rhetoric in American culture and more openly discussed their part in the establishment and maintenance of that culture's dominant ideology.[20] Deriving his understanding of this term from the social and literary theory of Raymond Williams and Antonio Gramsci, as well as from the cultural anthropology of Victor Turner and Clifford Geertz, Bercovitch discusses the jeremiad as a powerful communal ritual "designed to join social criticism to spiritual renewal, public to private identity, [and] the shifting 'signs of the times' to certain traditional metaphors, themes, and symbols."[21] He also claims—inaccurately, as we now know from Francis Butts—that Miller underestimated the "pervasive theme of affirmation and exultation" that was one part of the jeremiad's equation (the other being chastisement for the present generation's decline from the piety of its predecessors). As Bercovitch sees it, from the days of John Winthrop and John Cotton to the American Revolution and beyond, America's religious and civil leaders institutionalized a rhetorical mode in which, alongside threats of divine retribution for the Puritans' apostasy

---

18. Bercovitch, "Cotton Mather," in *Major Writers,* ed. Emerson, 142.
19. Bercovitch, *Puritan Origins,* 114, 24, and chap. 4, passim; "Cotton Mather," in *Major Writers,* ed. Emerson, 148, 146–48 passim.
20. Bercovitch, *American Jeremiad,* esp. 132–212.
21. Ibid., xi, xii–xix. Antonio Gramsci, *Selections from the Prison Notebooks,* ed. and trans. Quentin Hoare and Geoffrey N. Smith (New York: International Publishers, 1971); Raymond Williams, *Marxism and Literature* (Oxford: Oxford University Press, 1977); Clifford Geertz, *The Interpretation of Cultures* (New York: Oxford University Press, 1973); Victor Turner, *Dramas, Fields, and Metaphors: Symbolic Action in Human Society* (Ithaca: Cornell University Press, 1974).

from the God of their fathers, they sang an incessant "litany of hope" to the rising glory of America.[22] The jeremiad's function thus was to "create a climate of anxiety that helped release the restless 'progressivist' energies required for the success of the venture," even as it operated in a very conservative way, as a tool of a profoundly "middle-class" culture, for the ideological co-optation of any who seriously challenged its premises.[23] Despite its controversial analysis of the underlying premises of the American Dream, more than any other work in the last two decades of the study of colonial American literature, *The American Jeremiad* has convinced scholars of the importance of searching for continuities between the literature of the colonial period and that of subsequent eras—indeed, as some of Bercovitch's adherents would claim, to that of the present day.

Such generalizations have not gone unchallenged, but as yet no one has seriously shaken Bercovitch's or his followers' belief in the notion of the consensus or—to use (as he does) Raymond Williams's term, via Gramsci—*hegemony* that he sees at the heart of the American way. Daniel Walker Howe, for example, has criticized him for underestimating the role non-Puritan groups played in the establishment of this hegemony, and Alan Heimert and Andrew Delbanco, in their recent critical anthology of American Puritan writing, implicitly attack his notion of how and why *English* Puritans became *American,* positing a society much less self-confident than Bercovitch seems willing to allow, an argument Delbanco has elaborated in two recent essays as well.[24] But most intellectual and literary historians defer to Bercovitch's undeniable stature in the field, recently confirmed by his appointment as general editor of the new *Cambridge History of American Literature.*

---

22. Bercovitch, *American Jeremiad,* 6, 9–18; Butts, "Myth of Miller," *American Historical Review* 87 (1982): 687–88; Theodore Dwight Bozeman, "The Puritans' 'Errand into the Wilderness,' " *New England Quarterly* 59 (1986): 231–51, this last a particularly convincing attack on Bercovitch's reading of early American history.

23. Bercovitch, *American Jeremiad,* 23, 18, and 3–30 passim.

24. Howe, "Descendents of Perry Miller," *American Quarterly* 34 (1982): 91–93; Heimert and Delbanco, *The Puritans in America: A Narrative Anthology* (Cambridge: Harvard University Press, 1985); Delbanco, "The Puritan Errand Re-Viewed," *Journal of American Studies* 18 (1984): 343–60, and "Looking Homeward, Going Home: The Lure of England for the Founders of New England," *New England Quarterly* 59 (1986): 358–86. See also Bozeman, "The Puritans' 'Errand,' " and my *A Glimpse of Sion's Glory: Puritan Radicalism in New England, 1620–1660* (Middletown: Wesleyan University Press, 1984), in which I argue for the great variety of religious beliefs carried to and developed in seventeenth-century New England, and demonstrate as well the importance of such heterogeneous ideas for the area's institutional and cultural evolution.

The study of American continuities has not been restricted to those whose reading of Puritan typology necessarily leads them to Bercovitch's particular conclusions about the ideological bases of American culture. I already have mentioned Lowance, whose *Language of Canaan* traces, more in the aesthetic than in the political realm, the evolution of the uses of typology from sixteenth-century English Puritanism through the American Renaissance. Lowance's treatment through the early eighteenth century is a fine study, but when he makes the obligatory leap of faith from Edwards to Emerson, and tries to show "how Puritan epistemology influenced symbolic modes in American literature during the nineteenth century," he is less convincing, primarily because by that time writers were influenced less by scriptural exegesis of the sort Lowance had discussed than by epistemological and linguistic questions that stemmed from an interest in the history of language.[25]

Richard Slotkin's *Regeneration through Violence*, like Bercovitch's *American Jeremiad*, implicitly criticizes certain underlying premises of the American Dream. His argument about the inherent and persistent violence at the core of the American soul admittedly derives from D. H. Lawrence's and William Carlos Williams's criticisms of the white settlers' insensitivity to the American land and its native inhabitants, but Slotkin adds power to their observations by linking them to the myth criticism of Jung and, more directly, of Joseph Campbell to explore the fact and depiction of violence in two and a half centuries of American writing.[26] Like Lowance, Slotkin is at his best when he treats the seventeenth and early eighteenth centuries, particularly in his discussion of the narratives of Indian captivity and witchcraft. In dealing with the nineteenth century he necessarily becomes more selective and so less able to tie off his threads on the warp of "regeneration through violence." It is difficult, for example, to fit Emerson, a central figure in any discussion of nineteenth-century culture, into Slotkin's dark tapestry.

---

25. Lowance, *Language of Canaan*, 2, and chap. 11 passim. See also my review of Lowance's book in *American Literature* 53 (1981): 508–10, and my *The Wisdom of Words: Language, Theology, and Literature in the New England Renaissance* (Middletown: Wesleyan University Press, 1981), esp. chaps. 1 and 2.

26. Richard Slotkin, *Regeneration through Violence: The Mythology of the American Frontier 1600–1860* (Middletown: Wesleyan University Press, 1973). See also D. H. Lawrence, *Studies in Classic American Literature* (New York: Seltzer, 1923); William Carlos Williams, *In the American Grain* (Norfolk, Conn.: New Directions, 1925); and another recent study with concerns similar to Slotkin's, Richard Drinnon, *Facing West: The Metaphysics of Indian-Hating and Empire-Building* (Minneapolis: University of Minnesota Press, 1980).

Whatever their weaknesses, Lowance's and Slotkin's studies are ambitious and have large followings because of the consuming interest of literary historians in what they continue to believe to be the many significant continuities that underlie American civilization—continuities that emerge primarily from a reading of religious discourse. William C. Spengemann, however, has vigorously condemned the search for such connections as a brand of self-serving academic wish-fulfillment. He views scholars engaged in this enterprise as motivated more by their desire to find ways to refertilize the overworked fields of nineteenth-century American literature than by any genuine interest in the earlier literature, a point supported by their final inability to explain how "pre-Revolutionary American writing can have [anything] to do, immediately, with the shape and meaning of North America in the nineteenth century." In the last decade Spengemann has steadfastly maintained that, as he put it in his severe review of Elliott's *Puritan Influences in American Literature,* "to spend our time and energy trying to hang Puritanism about the neck of later American literature, when we don't even have bibliographical control—let alone a first-hand knowledge—of what was written in British America before the Revolution, seems to me at best an idle occupation and at worst a criminally wasteful one."[27]

Here Spengemann singles out perhaps the most important reason for the persistence of the continuities school: that in large measure colonial American literature has gained its definition as a field from questions posed about nineteenth-century literature. As early as 1953, for example, in *Symbolism and American Literature,* Charles Feidelson's interest in the roots of literary modernism sent him to New England Puritan literature to try to explain the precocious use of symbolism by such writers as Hawthorne and Melville.[28] Similarly, Bercovitch, Lowance, Slotkin, and others attempt to answer the all-important question of what is literary about colonial American literature by privileging, implicitly or explicitly, the texts of later American writers and seeking their origin in an earlier discourse.

Because he strenuously urges us to resist this tendency, Spengemann is one of the few literary historians who might feel comfortable with the

---

27. William Spengemann, "Discovering the Literature of British America," *Early American Literature* 28 (1983): 7, and "Review Essay," ibid., 16 (1981): 184.

28. Charles Feidelson, *Symbolism and American Literature* (Chicago: University of Chicago Press, 1953), esp. 77–118. For a recent assessment of Feidelson's significance see Barbara Foley, "From New Criticism to Deconstruction: The Example of Charles Feidelson's *Symbolism and American Literature,*" *American Quarterly* 36 (1984): 44–64.

conclusions about anglicization presented by Greene and Pole. Spengemann has vociferously urged his colleagues to reject the notion of an "American" literature in the colonial period and to focus instead on "the literature of British America," which he defines as "literature written in English before 1765 by persons who spent some time in the New World." Moreover, in presenting this suggestion he intends to expand considerably the canon of what literary historians consider worthy of study; as he put it in a seminal essay in 1983, "the idea of the seventeenth and eighteenth centuries as a tail wagged by a nineteenth-century dog arises partly from the identification of literature with belles-lettres." When the scholar gets away from the notion, which Spengemann sees as implicit in most studies of colonial American literature, that such writing "owes its significance to what comes later, that Hawthorne alone makes John Winthrop worth the attention of literary scholars," he will begin to understand how the writings of British America arise from and refer to "a situation of their own: the extension of British culture into the New World and the resulting impact of this extension on that culture." Then, if historians are correct, students of colonial American literature may come to very different conclusions about nineteenth-century literature and ideology from those popularized by Bercovitch, Lowance, and others—conclusions to which they have been led, as Spengemann wittily puts it, "by a kind of verbal shell game, in which the prestidigitator places his thematic pea under one shell labeled 'Puritan,' makes a lot of rapid movements on his typewriter, and then produces the pea from under another shell marked 'American literature.' "[29] In other words, Spengemann understands that colonial American literature was not formed exclusively by its relationship to religious discourse but by other modes of speaking and writing—the tradition of travel writing, say, or of promotional tracts or natural history.

Ironically, Spengemann may have been brought to such thoughts by Michael Colacurcio's review of Spengemann's own *The Adventurous Muse* (1977), in which he spoke of broad continuities in American literature centered on the themes of exploration and domesticity, and of John Seelye's *Prophetic Waters,* an idiosyncratic work whose basic premise is that "the

---

29. Spengemann, "Literature of British America," 8, 5–6, and passim, and "Review Essay," ibid., 179. Spengemann's views about the conceptual inconsistencies reflected in the study of colonial American literature have changed over the years. Readers interested in his ideas should begin with "What Is American Literature?" *Centennial Review* 22 (1978): 119–38, and follow the essays mentioned above with "American Things/Literary Things: The Problem of American Literary History," *American Literature* 58 (1985): 456–81.

river is a defining agent in the metamorphosis of colonies to republic."[30] In a probing assessment of these two very different books conjoined by their authors' assertions about how certain metaphors rule American literature from the period of exploration on, Colacurcio puts his finger on what historians would find most suspect about the entire "continuities" school of American literary study. If we believe, Colacurcio writes, that "the Pastoral of the Cavalier Garden [both authors treat some examples of southern literature] plus the Holy War for the Puritan Kingdom equals the tragical epic of American empire," we may have "a poor way to know reality." To argue in this manner "makes 'history' not what we need to know to interpret a text, or what a text might enable us to recognize about a real world now remote from our own, but only the figure created by our own geometric (or other metaphorical) arrangement of all the texts within a given field."[31] If Colacurcio had been reviewing more recent examples of the "continuities" school such as *The American Jeremiad* or *The Language of Canaan,* he might have added that often practitioners of such "history" are not that far removed from Cotton Mather's example in the *Magnalia,* presuming to pass off as facts what in some cases are the figures of their heightened imaginations. They would reply that he missed the main point, for such literary scholars are less interested in "history" as the social historian defines it than in how the human imagination *perceived* reality and shaped that perception, through language, for others to understand.

To date, Spengemann and Colacurcio remain prophets without honor in the field. Because of the intellectual glamor that attaches to studies of the connections between colonial American literature and the American Renaissance (and beyond), and, similarly, to those that continue to insist on the exceptionalism of American culture from the days of settlement on, there is little chance to stem the tide of books and essays that derive from what many historians would consider highly problematic assumptions.[32]

30. Spengemann, *The Adventurous Muse: The Poetics of American Fiction, 1789–1900* (New Haven: Yale University Press, 1977); John Seelye, *Prophetic Waters: The River in Early American Life and Literature* (New York: Oxford University Press, 1977), 7.
31. Michael J. Colacurcio, "Does American Literature Have a History?" *Early American Literature* 13 (1978): 129–30.
32. In fairness to Bercovitch I should note that in his most recent work he has deemphasized "continuities" and "exceptionalism" and has begun to sponsor regionalism, ethnicity, feminism, and popular literature—in his term, "dissensus." It is equally important to note, however, that he is now primarily concerned with nineteenth- and twentieth-century American literature, not that of the colonial period. See, for example, Bercovitch, ed., *Reconstructing American Literary History* (Cambridge: Harvard University Press, 1986); Bercovitch and Myra Jehlen, eds., *Ideology and Classic American Literature* (Cambridge: Cambridge Univer-

Often such studies become more problematic because they persist in treating the literature of colonial America as though it were that of New England writ large, with the result that the literature of other areas does not get its due. But as Greene and Pole point out, historians of British America now have developed a detailed classification of regions "based largely upon differences in methods of land use, settlement patterns, socioeconomic organization, and cultural orientation." Thus, although some historians would quarrel with precise boundaries, most would agree that prior to 1763 British America was defined by five important regions—New England, the Middle Colonies, the Chesapeake, the Lower South, and the Caribbean—and some would even distinguish further the "New West" (that is, the backcountry of Pennsylvania, Maryland, Virginia, and the Carolinas, settled after 1730) and the small island colonies of Bermuda and the Bahamas.[33] Few scholars of colonial American literature have concerned themselves with how the experience of people in each of these areas may have drawn from different traditions of discourse for its explication and so contributed to the development of literature quite different from New England's, so undeniably religion-based. Instead, they have continued to think and write as though colonial America were divided into only two regions, New England and the South, and for decades have assigned primacy to the literature and culture of the former—again, often as part of their attempts to display the supposed continuities between the colonial period and the American Renaissance.

There have been some promising developments in studies of the literature and culture of the colonial South, even though most scholars insist on conflating, to the detriment of their work, the regions of the Chesapeake and the Lower South. The most wide-ranging of this scholarship is in the third volume of Richard Beale Davis's monumental three-volume *Intellectual Life in the Colonial South, 1585–1763* (1978).[34] The summation of a remarkable career devoted to southern life and letters, this study builds upon Davis's *Literature and Society in Early Virginia, 1608–1840* (1973),

---

sity Press, 1986); and Bercovitch, "The Problem of Ideology in American Literary History," *Critical Inquiry* 21, no. 4 (1986): 631–53. For his influence on others see, for example, Sam B. Girgus, ed., *The American Self: Myth, Ideology, and Popular Culture* (Albuquerque: University of New Mexico Press, 1981).

33. Greene and Pole, eds., *Colonial British America*, 12–13.

34. Richard Beale Davis, *Intellectual Life in the Colonial South, 1583–1763*, 3 vols. (Knoxville: University of Tennessee Press, 1978). See also Louis D. Rubin, Jr., and C. Hugh Holman, eds., *Southern Literary Study: Problems and Possibilities* (Chapel Hill: University of North Carolina Press, 1975), 21–35, 70–101.

and *Intellectual Life in Jefferson's Virginia* (1964), but in its treatment of literature in relation to culture goes far beyond them in scope, from Maryland to Georgia, and all-inclusiveness, from the Roanoke settlement to the beginning of intra-imperial difficulties with Great Britain.[35] Further, much of the best work on early southern literature in the last twenty years has been done by scholars who challenge the notion that New England writers were the only attending midwives at the birth of the "American mind." Thus, for example, in *Intellectual Life in the Colonial South* Davis objects to the assumption that the New England mind "is the root, the fertile seed, of the living plant which is American cerebral activity."[36] Similarly, J. A. Leo Lemay, in *Men of Letters in Colonial Maryland* (1972), a work that indicates the riches that await the assiduous student of almost any colony outside of New England, urges students to unearth and evaluate the literary riches of other regions. "Just as each colony had its own political, economic, and institutional characteristics," he reminds the reader, "so each had its distinctive literary history." What is needed for each of the colonies, then—be it Maryland, Pennsylvania, New Jersey, or Georgia—is a study that asks "the basic questions about early American literary activity. What literature existed? Who wrote it? Why was it written? How does it compare with similar works? What are its sources and influences? Is it significant in American literary or cultural history?"[37] It may surprise some readers to learn that, even as I write, such questions have neither been asked nor answered for most of the colonies or, in some cases, even for the larger regions of which they were a part.

What is more surprising, however, given the profession's predilection for such scholarship, is the continued lack of a study that treats in significant detail the role of southern language and rhetoric in the subsequent formation of an "American mind" in the nineteenth century.[38] To be sure, some

---

35. Davis, *Literature and Society in Early Virginia, 1608–1840* (Baton Rouge: Louisiana State University Press, 1973), and *Intellectual Life in Jefferson's Virginia* (Chapel Hill: University of North Carolina Press, 1964). Readers should also consult "A Colloquium on the Present State of the Study of Early American Literature and the Contributions of Richard B. Davis to This Study," held in 1977 at the University of Tennessee and published in *Tennessee Studies in Literature* 26 (Knoxville: University of Tennessee Press, 1981), 1–47.

36. Davis, *Intellectual Life in the Colonial South*, 1:xxiii.

37. Leo Lemay, *Men of Letters in Colonial Maryland* (Knoxville: University of Tennessee Press, 1972), x, xii.

38. The most significant effort in this direction remains that of Vernon Louis Parrington, in *Main Currents in American Thought: An Interpretation of American Literature from the Beginnings to 1920* (New York: Harcourt Brace, 1927, 1930). Parrington devotes much energy to tracing Jeffersonian liberalism back to the seventeenth century.

have seen Davis's magnum opus as providing the staging for the subsequent elevation of southern literature to a position at least as lofty as New England's in the development of the culture of the United States, but by Davis's own admission the grounds on which it would assume such a place are considerably different from those by which scholars have proclaimed New England's preeminence.[39] It would be a very different sort of study, based on texts that emerge from much different discourse.

Thus, in his important essay "The Act of Thought in Virginia" (1980), Lewis P. Simpson champions Davis as the scholar who "challenges us to trace and elaborate a Virginian (and an essentially southern) cast of mind" that through its literature can be seen as "distinctive and coherent" as that of early New England. Following Davis's lead, Simpson suggests that this "cast of mind" and the literature it produced were most marked by their "rationality," the hallmark of an essentially secular society, and by the southerners' continued close relationship to the intellectual and social currents of England and Enlightenment Europe.[40] In other words, the literary culture of the South was diametrically opposed in many ways to that of the overtly pious inhabitants of New England, who from their very different New World experience—and their self-righteousness—predicted a divine destiny for their region and developed an extensive literature profoundly shaped by religious language to promulgate their ideas. Needless to say, if those who urge on their readers a vision of colonial American literature as prologue to a subsequent literary flowering are to gain any credence among historians, it will be through the work of those who follow the lead of Davis, Lemay, Simpson, and others whose understanding of the development of southern letters coincides more closely with the general conclusions about the British American colonies to which historians have come. It should be obvious, for example, that the South's consuming interest in things English, from the days of Virginia's settlement on, makes its various colonies prime laboratories to study, not American exceptionalism during the colonial period, but the varying degrees of anglicization through which, many historians argue, all of the British colonies passed as they matured.[41]

This is clearly indicated in Lemay's study of Maryland literature, a

39. See Davis's introduction to *Intellectual Life in the Colonial South*, 1:xxi–xxxi.
40. Lewis P. Simpson, "The Act of Thought in Virginia, *Early American Literature* 14 (1979–80): 253–54.
41. See, for example, the chapters in Davis's *Intellectual Life* that discuss the influence on the colonial South of British fashions in art, architecture, and music.

splendid introduction to the complexity of the southern colonies' relationship to England, and particularly to the attempt by that colony's literati in the eighteenth century to imitate and acclimate modes of British gentility. One need go no further than to Dr. Alexander Hamilton's *History of the Tuesday Club* (c. 1754) to understand that, though British North America had no metropolis comparable to London, the citizens of such provincial capitals as Annapolis strove mightily to stay abreast of, to imitate, and, if their fancy so moved them, to mock the literature and culture of the home country.[42] That Hamilton should emerge, in Lemay's words, "as a major writer of neoclassic prose" will come as no surprise to those who understand that, for an aspiring and talented writer in that time and place, British literature remained the standard by which he sought to be judged and British audiences those whose approbation he most sought.[43] Two other Marylanders who gained British acceptance were the well-known poet of his day, Richard Lewis, whose "A Journey from *Patapsco* to *Annapolis,* April 4, 1730," a high point in neoclassic poetry written in America, was reprinted in England at least five times; and his younger fellow colonist, James Sterling, whose reputation as poet and playwright spanned the Atlantic.[44] Hitherto virtually unknown or, worse yet, dismissed as derivative, the works of these two men (and of course those of Hamilton) epitomize the need for scholars of colonial American literature to consider in depth the transfer of culture from England to America.

We also can learn much about this transit of civilization and its reconstitution in the New World from the life and work of William Byrd II, long enshrined as the "American Pepys" because of his voluminous and detailed diary, whose literary talents extended as well to sharply satirical public prose and highly competent topical verse.[45] Byrd's trips to England as agent

42. Lemay, *Colonial Maryland,* 213–56, esp. 248–54. Robert Micklus is editing the "Tuesday Club" manuscripts, soon to be published by the Institute of Early American History and Culture. See also Micklus, "Dr. Alexander Hamilton's 'Modest Proposal,' " *Early American Literature* 16 (1981): 107–32; Elaine G. Breslaw, "Wit, Whimsy, and Politics: The Uses of Satire by the Tuesday Club of Annapolis, 1744 to 1756," *William and Mary Quarterly,* 3d ser., 32 (1975): 295–306; and Carl Bridenbaugh, ed., *Gentleman's Progress: The Itinerarium of Dr. Alexander Hamilton, 1744* (Chapel Hill: University of North Carolina Press, 1948).

43. Lemay, *Colonial Maryland,* 213.

44. Ibid., 126–84, 257–312. See also Pierre Marambaud, " 'At Once the Copy,—and the Original': Richard Lewis's 'A Journey from *Patapsco* to *Annapolis,*' " *Early American Literature* 19 (1984): 138–52, and Lawrence C. Wroth, "James Sterling: Poet, Priest, and Prophet of Empire," *American Antiquarian Society, Proceedings,* n.s., 41 (1931): 25–76.

45. Richard B. Davis, "William Byrd: Taste and Tolerance," in *Major Writers,* ed.

for Virginia, coupled with an earlier term in London's Middle Temple, indelibly marked his literary interests, and though his plantation at Westover was not home to a group so extraordinary as Annapolis's Tuesday Club, it welcomed guests whose literary and cultural interests were more English than Virginian.[46] Yet precisely for this reason Byrd, like Hamilton, Lewis, and Sterling, has never drawn the attention of scholars in the way his New England contemporaries have. Focusing almost exclusively on religious rhetoric, which they view as an introduction to the literature of the United States of America in the nineteenth century, such scholars fail to grasp that, through 1760, the British American colonies were precisely *that*, a fact widely reflected in the literature of all regions outside New England as well as in some New England writing itself—the sermons of Benjamin Colman or the poetry of his daughter Jane Turell, for example, or the early newspaper essays and the humorous "bagatelles" of Benjamin Franklin.[47] Thus an emphasis on the literature of other regions, beyond retrieving important but still little-known works that would allow us to limn a more accurate portrait of literary activity within these areas, might have the equally salutary effect of forcing scholars to reconsider the relation of New England writers to their British tradition.

But, recalling Greene and Pole's typology of regions, we have to conclude that beyond the boundaries of New England and the larger region of "the South," to this point literary historians have provided little guidance. Few have tried, for example, to distinguish the literary culture of the Chesapeake

---

Emerson, 151–77. See also Lewis P. Simpson, "William Byrd and the South," *Early American Literature* 7 (1972): 187–95; David Smith, "William Byrd Surveys America," ibid., 11 (1976–77): 296–310; and Willie T. Weathers, "William Byrd: Satirist," *William and Mary Quarterly*, 3d ser., 4 (1947): 27–41.

46. Kenneth Lockridge's *The Diary, and Life, of William Byrd II of Virginia, 1674–1744* (Chapel Hill: University of North Carolina Press, 1987) details Byrd's cultural and political interests.

47. See, for example, Teresa Toulouse, " 'Syllabical Idolatry': Benjamin Colman's Rhetoric of Balance," *Early American Literature* 18 (1983–84): 257–74; Pattie Cowell, "Puritan Women Poets in America," in *Puritan Poets and Poetics: Seventeenth-Century American Poetry in Theory and Practice*, ed. Peter White (University Park: Pennsylvania State University Press, 1985), 21–32; Cowell, *Women Poets in Pre-Revolutionary America, 1650–1775: An Anthology* (Troy, N.Y.: Whitson, 1981), 43–54; J. A. Leo Lemay, "Benjamin Franklin," in *Major Writers*, ed. Emerson, 205–43, esp. 205–11, 232–38; Bruce Ingham Granger, *Benjamin Franklin: An American Man of Letters* (Ithaca: Cornell University Press, 1964), 19–50, 181–208; and Lemay, ed., *The Oldest Revolutionary: Essays on Benjamin Franklin* (Philadelphia: University of Pennsylvania Press, 1976). I do not devote more space to Franklin in this essay because in most accounts of early American literature he figures primarily in the period after 1760.

from that of the Lower South, and once scholars undertake the task of demonstrating continuities between the colonial southern mind and the culture of the United States in the nineteenth century, they may further subordinate any such distinctions among regions to what they consider the more important point of continuities between the earlier period and the later.[48] And there has been very little scholarly inquiry into the literature of the middle colonies. Students of the literary development of colonial Pennsylvania, for example, still have to turn to Carl and Jessica Bridenbaugh's *Rebels and Gentlemen: Philadelphia in the Age of Franklin* (1942) to get a hold on the topic and must start from scratch if they wish to study that of New Jersey, Delaware, or New York.[49] This is a particularly unfortunate state of affairs when one considers the rich cultural heterogeneity of these various colonies, with their conglomerate populations of Swedes, Dutch, Germans, and other nationalities. Finally, the Caribbean is virtually unknown to scholars of early American literature, although the recent activity among social historians in this area may prod other students to explore what Spengemann has suggested is a very important vein of British American writing.[50] Such works as Richard Cumberland's *The West*

48. Lemay's *Colonial Maryland* is virtually the only study that treats in depth the literature and culture of a southern colony other than Virginia. In *Myths and Realities: Societies of the Colonial South* (Baton Rouge: Louisiana State University Press, 1952), Carl Bridenbaugh clearly distinguishes the cultures of the regions within the South and speaks briefly about the literary sources. To be sure, the Carolinas and some of the middle colonies date from a much later period than the settlements in New England and Virginia, and thus by 1760 may not have developed so self-conscious an intellectual culture as the longer-settled areas; but socially and economically they saw themselves as different from their neighbors. See David S. Shields's discussion of such regional self-consciousness in "George Ogilvie's *Carolina; or, The Planter* (1776)," *Southern Literary Journal*, special issue (1986), 5–20. This issue also reprints Ogilvie's poem, which was published in London in 1791.

49. Carl Bridenbaugh and Jessica Bridenbaugh, *Rebels and Gentlemen: Philadelphia in the Age of Franklin* (New York: Oxford University Press, 1942). Ned C. Landsman's *Scotland and Its First American Colony, 1683–1765* (Princeton: Princeton University Press, 1985), and Jon Butler's *The Huguenots in America: A Refugee People in New World Society* (Cambridge: Harvard University Press, 1983) alerts us to the richness of these other cultures. I am aware that more intensive study of the literature of these regions may in fact reinforce the centrality of New England to later American history; the very cultural heterogeneity that marked areas like the middle colonies might have prevented these regions from having a more significant influence over other parts of British North America.

50. See, for example, Richard S. Dunn, *Sugar and Slaves: The Rise of the Planter Class in the English West Indies, 1624–1713* (Chapel Hill: University of North Carolina Press, 1972); Sidney W. Mintz, *Caribbean Transformations* (Baltimore: Johns Hopkins University Press, 1974); Lewis, *Main Currents in Caribbean Thought*, esp. 29–170; Roger D. Abrahams and John F. Szwed, *After Africa: Extracts from British Travel Accounts and Journals of the Seventeenth, Eighteenth, and Nineteenth Centuries Concerning the Slaves, Their Manners, and*

The Study of Colonial American Literature, 1966–1987   33

Indian: A Comedy (London, 1771) and James Grainger's *The Sugar-Cane: A Poem in Four Books* (London, 1764), for example, are part of the literature of British North America as much as of England, but the region to which they refer has remained almost exclusively the province of scholars of African-American history and culture.[51]

In addition to studying the uniqueness of colonial American literature as they argue for broad continuities between the colonial period and the nineteenth century, or assessing, with varying degrees of satisfaction, the literature of other regions of British America, scholars of colonial American literature also devote considerable energy and imagination to monographic studies, either essay- or book-length, that treat one author or group of authors, a significant text, or a genre. Not surprisingly, though, such work often is marked by the author's adherence, implicit or explicit, to the sorts of arguments for American exceptionalism and New England's cultural centrality outlined above. To be sure, such scholarship displays the variety of interests among scholars in the field and makes substantial contributions to the study of British North America, but it is also clear that the strength of some of this work has been diluted by overprovincial views of its subjects' uniqueness or significance.

Here I do not speak merely of descriptive, biographical, or genre studies, or even just of "critical" biographies in which an author's works are related to his external biography, but rather of a range of scholarship whose purpose is to illuminate both the author and his culture through an analysis of his literary production. Such monographs are comparable in intention and method, and, in some cases, in final importance to the work of historians who study the social dynamic of individual communities, families, or other small groups in an attempt to relate their subjects to their historical moment. Such scholars not only illuminate the lives of their subjects in elaborate detail and through a variety of methods—

Customs in the British West Indies (New Haven: Yale University Press, 1983); Spengemann, "Literature of British America," 3–16 passim; Tzvetan Todorov, *The Conquest of America: The Conquest of the Other* (New York: Harper and Row, 1984); and Peter Hulme, *Colonial Encounters: Europe and the Native Caribbean, 1492–1798* (London: Methuen, 1986).

51. Cumberland's and Grainger's works are the sort that would be added to the canon of early American literature if more scholars and teachers undertook the kind of research outlined in Spengemann's "Literature of British America," particularly in the author's bibliographical suggestions, 10–15. See also Samuel Keimer, ed., *Caribbeana*, 2 vols. (London, 1741); Nathaniel Tucker, *The Bermudian: A Poem* (London, 1774); and Lewis Leary, ed., *The Complete Published Poems of Nathaniel Tucker together with Columbinus: A Mask* (Delmar, N.Y.: Scholars Facsimiles and Reprints, 1973).

demographic, anthropological, statistical, to name but a few—but also reflect the light so generated on larger issues (the history of the family, say, or the motivations for migration into unsettled areas). So, too, with scholars of literature who similarly restrict their immediate focus: their intensive studies of individuals, texts, or genres often contribute greatly to our understanding of the varied contours of American culture.

Obviously, in an essay of this length one cannot address the full accomplishment of scholars of colonial American literature in this direction; indeed, every major author and genre has had its explicators.[52] Rather, I intend to highlight their work primarily by discussing the range of scholarship on one figure, the poet Edward Taylor, and then by briefly addressing that on a few other important writers, to indicate further both the strengths and limitations of current scholarship and its ramifications for the study of colonial American culture generally.

The scholarship on Taylor indicates the ways literary scholars in the last few decades have approached writers of stature in the colonial period; it also shows the pervasive influence of those who persist in seeking out continuities between Puritan literature and that of the American Romantic period. For two decades after Thomas H. Johnson serendipitously discovered, in 1937, what proved the major part of Taylor's manuscripts, scholarly discussion focused on how and why his imagination and talent stood out in the barren fields of early New England literature. Scholars who knew only Anne Bradstreet's and Michael Wigglesworth's poetry marveled at Taylor's intricate meter and startling use of language, as well as at the intensity of his emotion, and concluded that they had found a belated metaphysical poet, one who, by a time warp often still used to discuss the relationship of English to "American literature," could stand with Francis Quarles and George Herbert, if not quite with John Donne.[53] During this period new poems continued to surface, the extant ones were explicated in all their verbal and rhetorical intricacy (as the school of "New Critics" would want), and scholars of early American literature congratulated

---

52. A perusal of *American Literary Scholarship* over the past two decades bears out this assessment, but see also the entries on individual authors in *American Writers before 1800*, and Emerson, ed., *Major Writers*, passim.

53. The first collection of Taylor's poetry was Thomas H. Johnson, ed., *The Poetical Works of Edward Taylor* (New York: Rockland, 1939), but Johnson announced his discovery of Taylor's verse in "Edward Taylor: A Puritan 'Sacred Poet,' " *New England Quarterly* 10 (1937): 290–322. For Taylor's connection to the metaphysical poets see especially Wallace Cable Brown, "Edward Taylor: American 'Metaphysical,' " *American Literature* 16 (1944): 186–97.

themselves on finally excavating a literary figure about whose talent they need not be apologetic.[54]

In the early 1960s, primarily through the efforts of Donald E. Stanford and Norman S. Grabo, Taylor studies became more sophisticated, particularly as they sought to place Taylor in his immediate context. Stanford's edition of Taylor's poetry, for example, contained a preface by Louis L. Martz, scholar of seventeenth-century religious poetry in England, in which he linked the poet's accomplishment to such works as Richard Baxter's *The Saint's Everlasting Rest* (1650) and thus indicated Taylor's participation in a tradition of meditative verse to which he easily could have been exposed before his departure for New England. Martz's observation prodded scholars to consider a hitherto little-studied manifestation of Puritan piety— meditation—whose recovery (in large part via Taylor studies) eventually renovated our comprehension of New England Puritanism.[55] And as Martz and others framed the aesthetics of Taylor's poetry in its transatlantic context, so Grabo, with his editions of Taylor's *Treatise Concerning the Lord's Supper* and *Christographia,* as well as his *Edward Taylor* (1961; the first full-length critical study of this figure), opened the door to equally important considerations through his knowledge of intellectual history, particularly of Taylor's role in the ecclesiastical debates that rocked the Connecticut River Valley in the late seventeenth and early eighteenth centuries as his neighbor Solomon Stoddard progressively liberalized the

54. See, for example, Thomas H. Johnson, "The Topical Verses of Edward Taylor," *Colonial Society of Massachusetts, Transactions* 34 (1943): 513–54, and Donald E. Stanford, "Nineteen Unpublished Poems by Edward Taylor," *American Literature* 29 (1957): 18–46, and "The Earliest Poems of Edward Taylor," ibid., 32 (1960): 136–51. See also Austin Warren, "Edward Taylor's Poetry: Colonial Baroque," *Kenyon Review* 3 (1941): 355–71, Willie T. Weathers, "Edward Taylor, Hellenistic Puritan," *American Literature* 18 (1946): 18–26; Sidney E. Lind, "Edward Taylor: A Revaluation," *New England Quarterly* 21 (1948): 518–30; and Roy Harvey Pearce, "Edward Taylor: The Poet as Puritan," ibid., 23 (1950): 31–46. On New Criticism see esp. René Wellek, *A History of Modern Criticism, 1750–1950* (New Haven: Yale University Press, 1986), 6:144–58.

55. Stanford, ed., *The Poems of Edward Taylor* (New Haven: Yale University Press, 1960); Martz's foreword is at xiii–xxxvii. The most important assessment of Taylor's relationship to the tradition of meditative verse is Barbara Kiefer Lewalski's *Protestant Poetics and the Seventeenth-Century Religious Lyric* (Princeton: Princeton University Press, 1979), esp. 111–44, 283–316, 388–426; but also see Ursula Brumm, "Edward Taylor and the Poetic Use of Religious Imagery," in Bercovitch, ed., *Typology and Early American Literature,* 191–206, and William J. Scheick, "Typology or Allegory: A Comparative Study of George Herbert and Edward Taylor," *Essays in Literature* 2 (1975): 76–86. In his important work, *The Practice of Piety: Puritan Devotional Disciplines in Seventeenth-Century New England* (Chapel Hill: University of North Carolina Press, 1982), Charles E. Hambrick-Stowe brilliantly outlines the importance of meditative structures to New England Puritanism generally.

qualifications for church membership.⁵⁶ It became clear that, rather than being an anomalous "sport" who lived in isolation in frontier Westfield, Massachusetts, Taylor was genuinely a man of his age, caught in the same aesthetic and intellectual crosscurrents as his contemporaries and determined to navigate by the compass of Scripture as best he could read it.

By 1966, then, when *EAL* was founded and provided a convenient vehicle for Taylor studies, scholarship was advancing in several important directions. Primary bibliographical and critical work continued as more poems and prose writings were discovered, published, and explicated, often within the frame of Taylor's adversary relationship to Stoddard.⁵⁷ Such work proceeded from a new plateau after 1981 with the publication of Thomas M. and Virginia L. Davis's three volumes of Taylor manuscript material, which included his Westfield church records and several treatises written against Stoddard as well as hitherto unpublished "minor" poetry.⁵⁸ The fact, for example, that so many of his poems were either inspired by or related to the central ecclesiastical debates of the age—over the qualifications for communion and the efficacy of the sacraments, to take the most

---

56. Norman S. Grabo, ed., *"Christographia,"* by Edward Taylor (New Haven: Yale University Press, 1962); Grabo, ed., *"Treatise Concerning the Lord's Supper,"* by Edward Taylor (East Lansing: Michigan State University Press, 1966); and Grabo, *Edward Taylor* (New York: Twayne, 1961). For a sample of the critical appraisals these works engendered, see Michael Colacurcio, "Gods Determinations Touching Half-Way Membership: Occasion and Audience in Edward Taylor," *American Literature* 39 (1967): 298–314; E. F. Carlisle, "The Puritan Structure of Edward Taylor's Poetry," *American Quarterly* 20 (1968): 147–63; and James W. Barbour, "The Prose Context of Edward Taylor's Anti-Stoddard Meditations," *Early American Literature* 10 (1975): 144–57.

57. See Robert M. Benton, "Edward Taylor's Use of His Text," *American Literature* 39 (1967): 31–41; Thomas M. Davis, "Edward Taylor and the Traditions of Puritan Typology," *Early American Literature* 4, no. 3 (1970): 27–47, and "Edward Taylor's 'Occasional Meditations,' " ibid., 5, no. 3 (1970–71): 17–29; Dean Hall and Thomas M. Davis, "The Two Versions of Edward Taylor's Foundation Day Sermon," *Resources for American Literary Study* 5 (1975): 199–216; and David L. Parker, "Edward Taylor's Preparationism: A New Perspective on the Taylor–Stoddard Controversy," *Early American Literature* 9 (1976–77): 259–78.

58. The Davises' efforts in the transcription and publication of Taylor's manuscripts, which have been nothing short of heroic, culminated in *The Unpublished Writings of Edward Taylor,* 3 vols. (Boston: G. K. Hall, 1981), comprising *Edward Taylor's "Church Records" and Related Sermons, Edward Taylor vs. Solomon Stoddard: The Nature of the Lord's Supper,* and *Edward Taylor's Minor Poetry*. Particularly valuable is Thomas M. Davis's introduction to *Edward Taylor vs. Solomon Stoddard,* which offers the most complete and accurate account of the relationship between these two ministers. See also Philip F. Gura, "More Treasure from the Taylor Lode," *Early American Literature* 16 (1981): 187–90.

striking examples—reveals much about the centrality of doctrine to the New England Puritan imagination.[59]

As their colleagues prepared important bibliographical and contextual studies, other literary critics explored the range and depth of Taylor's aesthetic achievement, again with important ramifications for our understanding of seventeenth-century Anglo-American culture in general. In 1966, for example, Clark Griffith published the trenchant essay "Edward Taylor and the Momentum of Metaphor," in which he investigated in Taylor's verse the constant juxtaposition of the predictable with the startling, of allegory with conceit, a rhetorical strategy that allowed the poet, Griffith claimed, to probe the problematic Puritan notion of an inscrutable yet somehow—through the covenant, for example—approachable deity.[60] Shortly thereafter, Alan B. Howard, Michael Schuldiner, and William J. Scheick, among others, furthered the discussion of the nature of Taylor's literary imagination as they debated the more specific question concerning the degree to which he bequeathed an original and integrated body of work.[61] Crowning all this scholarship is the chapter on Taylor in Robert Daly's *God's Altar* (1978), a brilliant discussion of the poet's use of metaphor in relation to his primary concerns as a Puritan and a fine example of what a good close reading of poetry can contribute to the study of cultural history.[62]

59. Charles W. Mignon, "Edward Taylor's *Preparatory Meditations:* A Decorum of Imperfection," *PMLA* 83 (1968): 1423–28; Michael D. Reed, "Edward Taylor's Poetry: Puritan Structure and Form," *American Literature* 46 (1974): 304–12; Parker H. Johnson, "Poetry and Praise in Edward Taylor's *Preparatory Meditations,*" ibid., 52 (1980): 84–96; Kathleen Blake, "Edward Taylor's Protestant Poetic: Nontransubstantiating Metaphor," ibid., 43 (1971): 1–24.

60. Clark Griffith, "Edward Taylor and the Momentum of Metaphor," *English Literary History* 33 (1966): 448–60.

61. Howard, "The World as Emblem: Language and Vision in the Poetry of Edward Taylor," *American Literature* 44 (1972): 359–84; Schuldiner, "Edward Taylor's 'Problematic' Imagery," *Early American Literature* 13 (1978): 92–101; Scheick, " 'The Inward Tacles and the Outward Traces': Edward Taylor's Elusive Transitions," ibid., 12 (1977): 163–76. Also see two recent essays on Taylor's interest in medieval numerology: Karen Gordon Grube, "The 'Secret Sweet Mysterie' of Numbers in Edward Taylor's Meditation 80, Second Series," *Early American Literature* 13 (1978–79): 231–37, and Ursula Brumm, " 'Tuning' the Song of Praise: Observations on the Use of Numbers in Edward Taylor's *Preparatory Meditations,*" ibid., 17 (1982): 103–18. Jeffrey A. Hammond, "Reading Edward Taylor Exegetically: The *Preparatory Meditations* and the Commentary Tradition," *Texas Studies in Literature and Language* 24 (1982): 347–71, offers another important reading.

62. Robert Daly, *God's Altar: The World and the Flesh in Puritan Poetry* (Berkeley and Los Angeles: University of California Press, 1978), 162–200.

But once the breadth and significance of Taylor's work were established beyond any reasonable doubt, some scholars began to explore what they took to be his connections to that nebulous entity known as "American literature" and to modern literature and philosophy generally. Karl Keller, for example, sees Taylor as Emily Dickinson's Connecticut Valley second cousin and thus weakens the value of his ambitious study, *The Example of Edward Taylor* (1975).[63] Indeed, Keller views Taylor as an intellectual and spiritual ancestor not only to Dickinson but to any individuals in American culture—the architects of skyscrapers, jazz musicians, the framers of the Constitution, Walt Whitman, and Mark Twain, to cite a few of his examples—whose "art" evidences what John A. Kouwenhoven calls "the national preoccupation with process."[64] "Ultimately Taylor's poems do not *mean* very much," Keller writes, but instead record the process of "a man watching himself in his worthlessness desiring worth." Thus the meaning of his life and art, Keller argues, "lies not in his self nor in his desires . . . but in *the act of desiring*."[65] No one who knows Taylor's poetry will dismiss this last point out of hand, but when Keller tries to make this Puritan poet emblematic of deeper continuities in American culture, and so a godfather to the Manhattan skyline as well as to Whitman's "barbaric yawp," he asks the reader to accept the impressionistic fruits of his lively imagination as hearty scholarly fare. Fortunately, in those parts of the study in which he sticks to the facts—as in his biographical assessment of Taylor or in his relation of Taylor's poetry and prose to his and his contemporaries' concerns—Keller is much more reliable, though admittedly he does not go much beyond what we already knew from the scholarship of Grabo, Davis, and others who have mined the primary sources.

Building on the firm foundation laid by other scholars, literary critics sometimes produce indispensable works. On Taylor such a book is Karen E. Rowe's *Saint and Singer* (1986), which goes far toward providing the synthetic assessment of this figure that both literary scholars and historians

---

63. Keller, *The Example of Edward Taylor* (Amherst: University of Massachusetts Press, 1975). See also Keller's " 'The World Slickt Up in Types': Edward Taylor as a Version of Emerson," in *Typology and Early American Literature*, ed. Bercovitch, 175–90.

64. Keller, *Example of Edward Taylor*, 94–95, and Kouwenhoven, "What is American about America," in *American Literary Essays*, ed. Lewis Leary (New York: Crowell 1960). Another significant book-length study is William J. Scheick, *The Will and the Word: The Poetry of Edward Taylor* (Athens: University of Georgia Press, 1974), which relates Taylor's poetry to his understanding (primarily through Saint Augustine), of the soul's faculties, particularly the will.

65. Keller, *Example of Edward Taylor*, 94.

need. Drawing on four decades of scholarship and commentary, Rowe offers the most comprehensive study we are likely to have of "Edward Taylor's typology and the poetics of meditation."[66] Having as one of her models Barbara Kiefer Lewalski's *Protestant Poetics and the Seventeenth-Century Religious Lyric* (1979), which places Taylor in company with long-canonized seventeenth-century English poets, Rowe goes beyond all previous commentators on Taylor, and on colonial American poetry generally, in the sophistication of her analysis of his verse in light of contemporary theology and aesthetics. This sophistication is engendered by her detailed study and use of yet another recently discovered Taylor manuscript, *Upon the Types of the Old Testament*.[67]

Rowe's strength as a critic resides in her willingness to grapple with Taylor the theologian to better understand his verse. Indeed, her discussion of the prolonged and complex debate among Taylor, Stoddard, and Increase and Cotton Mather over the meaning and purpose of the Lord's Supper is the best we have of the roiled issues, particularly because she carefully integrates material from the newly discovered manuscript and from Taylor's poems to illuminate his passionate interest in covenant theology.[68] *Saint and Singer* places its subject squarely in his complex cultural moment—both British and British American—and thus is particularly satisfying to intellectual historians. At the same time, Rowe uses her knowledge of seventeenth-century intellectual history to elucidate the poetry *as poetry*, even as she accomplishes this through her understanding of Taylor's place in his age.[69] Finally, because she restrains her temptation to draw an imaginary line from Taylor to Dickinson, or to make Taylor speak to the concerns of contemporary critical theorists, her book is a model of informed scholarship, an example of the best work being done by literary scholars.

In the last two decades other major figures have drawn the same sustained attention as Taylor and have become subjects of equally sophisticated studies.[70] To reinforce my point about the tendency of literary historians to

---

66. Rowe, *Saint and Singer: Edward Taylor's Typology and the Poetics of Meditation* (New York: Cambridge University Press, 1986).
67. Charles W. Mignon, "The Nebraska Edward Taylor Manuscript: 'Upon the Types of the Old Testament,' " *Early American Literature* 12 (1977–78): 296–301, and "Christ the Glory of All Types: The Initial Sermon from Edward Taylor's 'Upon the Types of the Old Testament,' " *William and Mary Quarterly*, 3d ser., 37 (1980): 286–301. Mignon has completed his transcription of the entire sermon series, and its publication is imminent.
68. Rowe, *Saint and Singer*, esp. 90–195.
69. Ibid., 229–76.
70. I think particularly of David Levin, *Cotton Mather: The Young Life of the Lord's*

view the literature of seventeenth-century New England as the first act in a drama called "The Development of American Literature," we need only look at recent assessments of Cotton Mather, who is tossed about by the critics the same way Taylor is. We already have reviewed Bercovitch's influential notion of this figure, but the literary scholar who knows his history is hard-pressed to reconcile Bercovitch's Mather with Robert Middlekauff's. I think in particular of the latter's point in *The Mathers* (1971) that, toward the end of his life, Mather was much more interested in transatlantic Pietism and ecumenicalism than in the idea of "America."[71] Again, the problem lies in the fact that one of these scholars is more interested in Mather's legacy in the realm of the American imagination, the other in understanding him historically. One explains his language, the other his actions.

Kenneth Silverman has recently provided what is, for the work of a "literary" scholar, a splendidly balanced portrait of Mather in his age, an achievement the more remarkable considering Bercovitch's current influence on Mather studies.[72] Another significant study that builds on history in a very different way is Mitchell Breitwieser's *Cotton Mather and Benjamin Franklin: The Price of Representative Personality* (1984), in which the author examines the way each of his subjects consciously fashioned a "self" in both his life and, more important, his writings, and in so doing offered "diligent reflections on, rather than reflections of, human life in [his] period." Influenced by Stephen Jay Greenblatt's seminal *Renaissance Self-Fashioning* (1980), Breitwieser similarly advances our understanding of autobiographical statement, in this case in eighteenth-century British American culture.[73] Well versed in intellectual as well as literary history, Breit-

---

Remembrancer, 1663–1703 (Cambridge: Harvard University Press, 1978); Kenneth Silverman, *The Life and Times of Cotton Mather* (New York: Harper and Row, 1984); and Sargent Bush, Jr., *The Writings of Thomas Hooker: Spiritual Adventure in Two Worlds* (Madison: University of Wisconsin Press, 1980).

71. Robert Middlekauff, *The Mathers: Three Generations of Puritan Intellectuals, 1596–1728* (New York: Oxford University Press, 1971), esp. chap. 17.

72. Silverman, *Cotton Mather*, passim.

73. Mitchell Robert Breitwieser, *Cotton Mather and Benjamin Franklin: The Price of Representative Personality* (New York: Cambridge University Press, 1984), 4. A preview of Breitwieser's concerns in this book appeared as "Cotton Mather's Crazed Wife" (*Glyph*, 5 [1978]: 88–113). It should be noted that this now-defunct journal, along with *New Literary History*, served as an important vehicle for studies that draw on contemporary critical theory. See also Greenblatt, *Renaissance Self-Fashioning: From More to Shakespeare* (Chicago: University of Chicago Press, 1980). An earlier study of Puritan autobiography still held in high regard is Daniel B. Shea, Jr., *Spiritual Autobiography in Early America* (Princeton: Princeton University Press, 1968).

wieser convinces us of the complexity of Mather's response to his age, something that, despite his compelling rhetoric, Bercovitch finally does not. In the work of Middlekauff and Silverman, and in a different way in that of Breitwieser, we see an Anglo-American Mather, one who would be much more familiar—and believable—to historians.[74]

One could multiply the examples of how such studies are informed by, and occasionally transcend, the work of scholars who posit what we might term the exponential growth of a genuinely "American" literature through time. Recent scholarship on Anne Bradstreet, to take another example, fits the mold equally well. As early as 1951 in a tercentenary appraisal of this poet, Elizabeth Wade White stressed Bradstreet's importance as "the first Englishwoman who seriously and successfully chose for her occupation the writing of poetry" and in the process noted Bradstreet's indebtedness to her English and Continental predecessors.[75] But in 1966, in a seminal essay by Ann Stanford, the terms by which Bradstreet was judged had shifted. Rather than being a remarkable Englishwoman poet, she assumed a place at the head of "a long line of American writers"—Cooper, Hawthorne, and Melville, among others—"who would express what D. H. Lawrence had called the 'duplicity' of the American literary mind" and who owed, again in Lawrence's words, "a tight mental allegiance to a morality which all their passion goes to destroy."[76] Bradstreet, in other words, for all her uncomfortableness in the New World, was very quickly Americanized. And although Robert D. Richardson, Jr., and others tried to reestablish her importance as a Puritan poet, more and more her poetry was treated as an anticipation of that of subsequent writers—even of Wordsworth and Keats, and, of course, of Emily Dickinson.[77] Despite the numerous important

---

74. An interesting way to sample recent work on Mather is to read the articles devoted to his "Life of Phips" in the *Magnalia,* a text that has come to be regarded as one of the more interesting biographies in Mather's immense history. See especially Jane Donahue Eberwein, " 'In a book, as in a glass': Literary Sorcery in Mather's Life of Phips," *Early American Literature* 10 (1975–76): 282–300; Philip F. Gura, "Cotton Mather's *Life of Phips:* 'A Vice With the Vizard of Vertue Upon It,' " *New England Quarterly* 50 (1977): 440–57; and David H. Watters, "The Spectral Identity of Sir William Phips," *Early American Literature* 18 (1983–84): 219–32.

75. Peter White, "The Tenth Muse—A Tercentenary Appraisal of Anne Bradstreet," in *Critical Essays on Anne Bradstreet,* ed. Pattie Cowell and Ann Stanford (Boston: G. K. Hall, 1983), 56–75, quotation on 70.

76. Stanford, "Anne Bradstreet: Dogmatist and Rebel," ibid., 76–88, quotations on 87. Also see Stanford's *Anne Bradstreet, The Worldly Puritan: An Introduction to Her Poetry* (New York: Burt Franklin, 1974).

77. Robert D. Richardson, Jr., "The Puritan Poetry of Anne Bradstreet," in *Critical*

source studies of her poems that were published throughout the 1970s, she became praised most commonly as the progenitor of American women's poetry, as in Wendy Martin's recent *An American Triptych: Anne Bradstreet, Emily Dickinson, Adrienne Rich*. Martin is not embarrassed to declare that there are "striking parallels" between "the feminist vision and the Puritan vision," the former creating "an alternative response to the patriarchal tradition in art and politics" represented in the latter.[78] As Martin's study indicates, once placed in the context of her time, Bradstreet is used to explain the subsequent development of American literature—in this case, along feminist lines.

Or, to take a final example, consider the treatment over the past decades of William Bradford's *Of Plymouth Plantation*, long accorded a privileged status as a premier work of art in seventeenth-century New England. Thus, while Alan B. Howard has provided our finest analysis of Bradford's history as self-conscious artifact, John Griffith reads the book as one whose "fundamental pattern . . . is that of the American success story," the forerunner, by implication, of Franklin's *Autobiography*, Crèvecoeur's *Letters from an American Farmer*, and a host of other works that treat America as a land of commercial opportunity.[79] Astute critics like Jesper Rosenmeier and Robert Daly have attempted to reestablish Bradford's epic within its proper context, as the history of a tiny colony rapidly overshadowed in significance by its much larger neighbor to the north; for many others, however, Bradford is most important for his report of a series of events that would be replicated countless times in later American history.[80] In David Levin's words, *Of Plymouth Plantation* initiates "a pattern [of mobility

---

Essays, ed. Cowell and Stanford, 101–15; Anne Hildebrand, "Anne Bradstreet's Quaternions and 'Contemplations,'" ibid., 137–44; Daly, *God's Altar*, 82–127.

78. Wendy Martin, *An American Triptych: Anne Bradstreet, Emily Dickinson, Adrienne Rich* (Chapel Hill: University of North Carolina Press, 1984), 6–7, and "Anne Bradstreet's Poetry: A Study of Subversive Piety," in *Shakespeare's Sisters: Feminist Essays on Women Poets*, ed. Sandra M. Gilbert and Susan Gubar (Bloomington: Indiana University Press, 1979), 19–31; Ellen B. Brandt, "Anne Bradstreet: The Erotic Component in Puritan Poetry," *Women's Studies* 7 (1980): 39–53.

79. Alan B. Howard, "Art and History in Bradford's *Of Plymouth Plantation*," *William and Mary Quarterly*, 3d ser., 28 (1971): 237–66; John Griffith, "*Of Plymouth Plantation* as a Mercantile Epic," *Arizona Quarterly* 28 (1972): 231, 233.

80. Jesper Rosenmeier, "'With my owne eyes': William Bradford's *Of Plymouth Plantation*," in *The American Puritan Imagination: Essays in Revaluation*, ed. Sacvan Bercovitch (Cambridge: Cambridge University Press, 1974), 77–104; Robert Daly, "William Bradford's Vision of History," *American Literature* 44 (1973): 557–69.

and prosperity] that has become common in our secular history."⁸¹ In Walter P. Wenska's view, in the book's "disillusionment, lament, and bewilderment, as well as in its assertion of a dream of communal order, it stands as the first of many such examinations and critiques of the American dream."⁸² The issue always returns to representativeness, but representativeness in relation to later American literature and culture rather than to the work's historical moment.

I trust I have made my point about the tendency of scholars to force the connections between major figures of colonial American literature and later writers and themes. But before moving to another avenue of inquiry, let me mention several important studies, frankly revisionist, that take as their subject a genre, or even a ubiquitous metaphor, rather than a single literary figure, for in a few cases these genuinely enlarge our understanding of colonial American literature and culture, in some cases by challenging the religiocentric assumptions of the majority of critics who treat the period. Thus, for example, Wayne Franklin's *Discoverers, Explorers, Settlers* (1979), the best study we have of the literature of exploration and early settlement, focuses on the "enormous Old World energies which went into the attempt at controlling the West by means of the symbol system of language" and thus unpolemically brings to bear on these often-neglected sources the poststructuralist critics' obsession with the linguistic sign.⁸³ In *The Lay of the Land* (1975) Annette Kolodny treats much the same material from a feminist point of view, discerning in the white male's descriptions of the American land in both the New England and southern colonies a metaphorical strategy that readied it for the rapine they soon enough would perpetrate on it.⁸⁴ Seelye's *Prophetic Waters*, though more

---

81. David Levin, "William Bradford: The Value of Puritan Historiography," in *Major Writers*, ed. Emerson, 11–32, quotation on 28.

82. Walter P. Wenska, "Bradford's Two Histories: Pattern and Paradigm in *Of Plymouth Plantation*," *Early American Literature* 13 (1978): 163.

83. Wayne Franklin, *Discoverers, Explorers, Settlers: The Diligent Writers of Early America* (Chicago: University of Chicago Press, 1979), 6.

84. Annette Kolodny, *The Lay of the Land: Metaphor as Experience and History in American Life and Letters* (Chapel Hill: University of North Carolina Press, 1975); also see her *The Land before Her: Fantasy and Experience of the American Frontiers, 1630–1860* (Chapel Hill: University of North Carolina Press, 1984). Other such important studies are Larzer Ziff, *Puritanism in America: New Culture in a New World* (New York: Viking, 1973), and John Owen King III, *The Iron of Melancholy: Structures of Spiritual Conversion in America from the Puritan Conscience to Victorian Neurosis* (Middletown: Wesleyan University Press, 1983).

idiosyncratic, is in this same category, as are the sections of Slotkin's *Regeneration through Violence* that treat the Indian captivity narratives. In such studies the topic at hand becomes the occasion for investigation of wide-ranging cultural concerns of interest to the historian as well as to the literary critic.

The most significant of such studies—in all their variety of subjects and critical modes—can easily be located in the pages of *American Literary Scholarship,* where readers will find the summary of a substantial and ripe harvest. Not so, unfortunately, for my final category of studies of early American literature, those that deal with what for convenience we can call "popular" literature, as distinct from works that have been canonized as the central texts in the field. Historians and literary critics alike are only beginning to explore matters that have concerned British and other European researchers of *livre et société* or *l'histoire du livre* for the past two decades. To be sure, the American Antiquarian Society has begun a program in the History of the Book in American Culture (the first fruit of which is *Printing and Society in Early America* [1983]) and is actively sponsoring literary scholars as well as those in other fields, but America still has no works like Margaret Spufford's *Small Books and Pleasant Histories* (1982), Peter Burke's *Popular Culture in Early Modern Europe* (1978), David Cressy's *Literacy and the Social Order* (1980), or François Furet's *Livre et Société dans la France du XVIII siècle* (1965, 1970).[85]

To date, there are no book-length studies of popular literature, or even of folk culture generally, for British North America, although David D. Hall's recent important essays on Samuel Sewall and other topics suggest that we will soon have an assessment of allied subjects for the New England colonies.[86] We do have a dozen or so essays, of varying quality and import,

85. William L. Joyce et al., eds., *Printing and Society in Early America* (Worcester, Mass.: American Antiquarian Society, 1983). Margaret Spufford, *Small Books and Pleasant Histories: Popular Fiction and Its Readership in Seventeenth-Century England* (Athens: University of Georgia Press, 1982); Peter Burke, *Popular Culture in Early Modern Europe* (New York: New York University Press, 1978); David Cressy, *Literacy and the Social Order: Reading and Writing in Tudor and Stuart England* (Cambridge: Cambridge University Press, 1980); and François Furet et al., *Livre et société dans la France du XVIIIe siècle,* 2 vols. (Paris: Mouton, 1965, 1970).

86. Hall, "The Mental World of Samuel Sewall," *Saints and Revolutionaries: Essays on Early American History,* ed. Hall et al. (New York: Norton, 1984), 75–98; "A World of Wonders: The Mentality of the Supernatural in Seventeenth-Century New England," in *Seventeenth Century New England* [ed. David D. Hall and David Grayson Allen], *Colonial Society of Massachusetts, Publications* 62 (Boston: The Society, 1984), 239–74; and "The

in which scholars of colonial American literature have begun to explore texts whose origins lay in discourse different from the religion-centered one that has most often occupied their field and that thus offer a prime opportunity to link British American to British popular culture. Some of these texts are in fact part of religious discourse but lend themselves to other concerns as well, as in Emory Elliott's essay on the development of the Puritan funeral elegy and Ronald A. Bosco's studies of New England execution sermons.[87] The recent work of Daniel E. Williams on criminal conversion and "rogue" narratives, as well as his explorations of New England pirate literature (particularly Cotton Mather's narrative of William Fly), is more promising because of his willingness to examine the verbal and cultural complexity of texts that hitherto have been read straightforwardly as a form of advice literature.[88] Laurel Thatcher Ulrich's "Vertuous Women Found: New England Ministerial Literature, 1668–1735," is a similar effort, as is Margaret W. Masson's "The Typology of the Female as a Model for the Regenerate: Puritan Preaching, 1690–1730," even if the authors are more concerned with feminist discourse than with the issue of popular culture.[89] Unfortunately, however, none of these scholars investigates his or her topic in a genuinely transatlantic context.

Uses of Literacy in New England, 1600–1850," in *Printing and Society,* ed. Joyce et al., 1–47. For an interesting attempt to read first-generation Puritan literature (particularly John Cotton's works) in light of cultural and material anthropology, see Ann Kibbey, *The Interpretation of Material Shapes in Puritan Culture: A Study of Rhetoric, Prejudice, and Violence* (New York: Cambridge University Press, 1986).

87. Elliott, "The Development of the Puritan Funeral Sermon and Elegy, 1600–1750," *Early American Literature* 15 (1980), 151–64; Bosco, "Lectures at the Pillory: The Early American Execution Sermon," *American Quarterly* 30 (1978): 156–76, and "Early American Gallows Literature: An Annotated Checklist," *Resources for American Literary Study* 8 (1978): 81–107. In *The Puritan Conversion Narrative: The Beginnings of American Expression* (New York: Cambridge University Press, 1983), Patricia Caldwell analyzes the personal narrations of saving grace offered for church membership privileges in Thomas Shepard's Cambridge church, a body of materials one might consider "popular" literary expression. See also George Selement, "The Meeting of Elite and Popular Minds at Cambridge, New England, 1638–1645," *William and Mary Quarterly,* 3d ser., 41 (1984): 32–48.

88. Daniel Williams, "Doctor, Preacher, Soldier, Thief: A New World of Possibilities in the Rogue Narrative of Henry Tufts," *Early American Literature* 29 (1984): 3–20; "Rogues, Rascals, and Scoundrels: The Underworld Literature of Early America," *American Studies* 24 (1983): 5–19; " 'Behold a Tragic Scene Strangely Changed into a Theatre of Mercy': The Structure and Significance of Criminal Conversion Narratives in Early New England," *American Quarterly* 38 (1986): 827–47; and "Puritans and Pirates: A Confrontation between Cotton Mather and William Fly in 1726," *Early American Literature* 22 (1987): 232–51.

89. Laurel Thatcher Ulrich, "Vertuous Women Found: New England Ministerial Literature, 1668–1735," *American Quarterly* 28 (1976): 20–40; Margaret W. Masson, "The

Another major grouping of studies centers on Indian captivity narratives, an indigenously American genre that originated in lay as well as clerical responses to the ordeal of the hostage in the hands of Native Americans (and, occasionally, their French allies), and, as such, one that is not easily compared to British texts. I already have mentioned Slotkin's important work on the psychological and mythic dimensions of captivity narratives in *Regeneration through Violence;* also valuable is his and James K. Folsom's *So Dreadfull a Judgment: Puritan Responses to King Philip's War, 1676–1677* (1978).[90] Their introduction to the reprinted texts offers in abbreviated form some of the most insightful commentary from Slotkin's earlier work. Equally important is the introduction to Alden T. Vaughan and Edward W. Clark's *Puritans among the Indians* (1981), which provides a good starting point for understanding how the conflict of cultures that forms the basis of the captivity narratives became the stuff of literature.[91] The best single essay on the Indian captivity as a literary form is Richard VanDerBeets's "The Indian Captivity Narrative as Ritual."[92] It can be supplemented by David L. Minter's "By Dens of Lions: Notes on Stylization in Early Puritan Captivity Narratives," but, as in many of these studies, Minter has done little with the *audience* for such literature.[93] It is some consolation that all these scholars at least recognize that this genre's relation to popular culture has to be addressed, even if only in passing.

Indian captivity narratives have always received significant attention from literary historians, but the discourse of witchcraft and other supernatural events, a topic open to analysis in a wider Anglo-American context, has hardly been touched. Such writings as Increase Mather's *Essay for the Recording of Illustrious Providences* (1684), for example, and the sixth

---

Typology of the Female as a Model for the Regenerate: Puritan Preaching, 1690–1730," *Signs* 2 (1976): 304–15.

90. Richard Slotkin and James K. Folsom, eds., *So Dreadfull a Judgment: Puritan Responses to King Philip's War, 1676–1677* (Middletown: Wesleyan University Press, 1978), esp. 3–54.

91. Alden T. Vaughan and Edward W. Clark, eds., *Puritans among the Indians: Accounts of Captivity and Redemption, 1676–1724* (Cambridge: Harvard University Press, 1981), 1–28.

92. Richard VanDerBeets, "The Indian Captivity Narrative as Ritual," *American Literature* 43 (1972): 548–62. Also see his *Held Captive by Indians: Selected Narratives, 1642–1836* (Knoxville: University of Tennessee Press, 1973), and " 'A Thirst for Empire': The Indian Captivity Narrative as Propaganda," *Research Studies* 40 (1972): 207–15.

93. Minter, "By Dens of Lions: Notes on Stylization in Early Puritan Captivity Narratives," *American Literature* 45 (1973): 335–47. For another interesting treatment see Roy Harvey Pearce, "The Significance of the Captivity Narrative," ibid., 19 (1947): 1–20.

section of his son's *Magnalia* are unexplored as examples of folk culture.[94] So, too, the realm of devotional literature. It has taken Charles E. Hambrick-Stowe, a historian, to awaken us to the large number of devotional tracts written or reprinted in colonial New England, and no literary historian has yet explored their importance except as they have shed light on Taylor, now canonized as a high-culture figure.[95] The most significant work in this general direction has been David H. Watters's " 'I spake as a child': Authority, Metaphor, and *The New-England Primer*," which discusses how the language of this often-reprinted work helped to maintain certain "authority structures" in Puritan culture. "By learning a set of religious metaphors" through the *Primer,* Watters writes, "the child learns about his or her place in the world" and that religious language holds a "status beyond that of other forms of discourse."[96] A model of careful yet imaginative scholarship, this essay should stimulate others to explore similarly central yet virtually ignored texts in British North American culture that tell us about the Puritans' understanding of the power of language to shape culture.

Other items of interest include Marion Barber Stowell's account of how Nathaniel Ames, the almanac writer, formed his readers' literary taste, and Vern L. Bullough's brief discussion of the sex manuals of "Aristotle" that were popular in the colonies and the early republic. But virtually none of this work addresses colonies outside New England, and none of it is as sophisticated as, say, B. S. Capp's for England in his *Astrology and the Popular Press.*[97] So, too, little has been done on the textual history of

---

94. Increase Mather, *Essay for the Recording of Illustrious Providences* . . . (Boston, 1684); Cotton Mather, "Thaumaturgus," book 6 of *Magnalia Christi Americana* (London, 1702). This section contains "many Illustrious Discoveries and Demonstrations of the *Divine Providence,* in Remarkable *Mercies, and Judgments* on many particular Persons among the People of *New-England.*" The only scholar who is systematically investigating such texts is the historian David D. Hall; see note 80.

95. See note 55. This neglect is all the more surprising when one considers that scholarship on British literary figures—U. Milo Kaufmann's, say, on John Bunyan—has been available for decades. See Kaufmann, *"The Pilgrim's Progress" and Traditions in Puritan Meditation* (New Haven: Yale University Press, 1966).

96. David S. Watters, " 'I spake as a child': Authority, Metaphor, and *The New-England Primer,*" *Early American Literature* 20 (1985–86): 193–213, quotations on 193–95.

97. Marion Barber Stowell, "The Influence of Nathaniel Ames on the Literary Taste of His Time," *Early American Literature* 18 (1983): 127–45; Vern L. Bullough, "An Early American Sex Manual or, Aristotle Who?" ibid., 7 (1973): 236–46. Also see Otho T. Beall, Jr., "*Aristotle's Master Piece* in America: A Landmark in the Folklore of Medicine," *William and Mary Quarterly,* 3d ser., 20 (1963): 207–22. B. S. Capp, *Astrology and the Popular Press: English Almanacs, 1500–1800* (London: Faber and Faber, 1979).

the Great Awakening and the immense literature the revivals engendered throughout the colonies, a topic designed for the literary historian whose work is informed by notions of the literary text as an agent of social control.[98] Nor has there been an adequate study of the literature of the Enlightenment as it affected literary taste or the culture at large.[99] Instead, what frequently pass for "cultural" studies among literary historians are such works as Emory Elliott's *Power and the Pulpit in Puritan New England* (1975), which studies shifts in the archetypal imagery of New England sermon literature in the first few generations of colonists and links such changes to the changing psychology of the populace at large (with no evidence of how the latter group reacted to such shifting metaphors); or, more quirky still, David Leverenz's ambitious *The Language of Puritan Feeling* (1980), the most sustained, if not fully successful, Freudian reading of how the Puritans' literary enterprise influenced personality formation.[100]

Clearly, in the past two decades the promotion of literature and popular culture has had few serious takers among scholars of early American literature, although, as in the case of Cathy N. Davidson's recent work on late eighteenth-century American fiction, they have begun to explore the issue in the post-Revolutionary period.[101] But the field holds great promise for those willing to examine literary forms in their Anglo-American context because such investigations are bound to contribute to the discussion of what has emerged as a major concern among the literary theorists: alterna-

---

98. See Philip F. Gura, "The Discourse of Religious Revival in Eighteenth-Century New England," paper presented at the Institute of Early American History and Culture, March 1986; and "The Great Awakening as a Textual Event," paper presented at the Modern Language Association convention, December 1986. See also David Harlan, "A World of Double Visions and Second Thoughts: Jonathan Dickinson's *Display of God's Special Grace*," *Early American Literature* 21 (1986): 118–30.

99. See, for example, Robert Darnton, "The High Enlightenment and the Low-Life Literature in Pre-Revolutionary France," *Past and Present*, no. 51 (1971): 81–115, and "Reading, Writing, and Publishing in Eighteenth-Century France: A Case Study in the Sociology of Literature," *Daedalus* 100 (1971): 214–56; and Paul J. Korshin, ed., *The Widening Circle: Essays on the Circulation of Literature in Eighteenth-Century Europe* (Philadelphia: University of Pennsylvania Press, 1976). See also, for a slightly later period, Robert B. Winans, "The Growth of a Novel-Reading Public in Late Eighteenth-Century America," *Early American Literature* 9 (1975): 267–75.

100. Emory Elliott, *Power and the Pulpit in Puritan New England* (Princeton: Princeton University Press, 1975), passim; David Leverenz, *The Language of Puritan Feeling: An Exploration in Literature, Psychology, and Social History* (New Brunswick: Rutgers University Press, 1980).

101. Cathy S. Davidson, "Female Authorship and Authority: The Case of Sukey Vickery," *Early American Literature* 21 (1986): 4–28, and *Revolution and the Word: The Rise of the Novel in America* (New York: Oxford University Press, 1986).

tive ways of answering the vexing question of what makes a text necessarily "literary." Further, such interest in other textual paradigms cannot but make scholars rethink the assumptions they have brought to colonial American literature through their concern with the literature of the United States in the nineteenth century. To be sure, the whole question of what "popular" literature is, as distinct from the literature that has conventionally occupied scholars, is far from settled. But, at the very least, the study of other kinds of discourse hitherto neglected or prejudged will expand appreciation of why the literary canon has been established as it now stands. Such study also may aid in that canon's redefinition.

As the above summary indicates, the present center of studies of colonial American literature resides in the supposed continuities between the literature of the colonial era and that of the early national and Romantic periods, or, more specifically, between the language and rhetoric—primarily religious discourse—of Puritan New England and those of the late eighteenth and early nineteenth centuries in the United States as a whole. Although the precise nature of these continuities still rouses vigorous debate, an interest in the persistence for at least two centuries of a special language and set of symbols—the most vivid of which is "America" itself—derived from the New England settlers has superseded questions of region, canonicity, and even critical methodology. In other words, a majority of scholars of colonial American literature continues to seek the roots of American exceptionalism in a historical period in which the colonies were cultural and linguistic appendages of European countries. Even the best studies of individual writers or genres, in which the author has ample time and space to explore the literature contextually, frequently manifest a compulsion to put scholarship to the use of the larger project: the description of a unique national literature whose foundation lies solidly in the seventeenth century.

There is no doubt that this development in studies of colonial American literature has done some good; as in the case of the Puritans' use of typology as an organizing principle in their literature, both literary scholars and historians have become sensitized to rhetorical modes that had been undervalued. Bercovitch's analysis of Puritan literature through lenses ground by cultural anthropologists like Geertz and Turner is a prime example of this kind of scholarship. For many years students of colonial American literature frequently became mired in discussions of ecclesiology or abstract theology; now their eyes are open to the contours of Puritanism as an elaborate belief-system, with its own rituals and taboos, its own internal cultural logic. That such studies, again, often are based on the notion that the United States of America is New England writ large is the price we have paid for these new tools and the skills to use them.

To be sure, not all scholars adhere to the continuities thesis or believe that New England is the omphalos of later American literature, but it is fair to say that dissenters have not yet produced work that is as convincing or compelling as some of that of the continuities school. To put it another way, the field of early American literature has become increasingly divided—as has the profession of literature generally—between cultural historians and critical theorists, the latter reexamining the primary issue of what constitutes "literary" language itself. Until more scholars are willing to take the risk—and an intellectual risk it surely is—of offering an interpretive reading of early American literature that is not New England–based, does not commence from the premise of American exceptionalism from 1620 on, and directly addresses the complexity of linguistic discourse at any moment in history, the continuities school will continue to have its day.[102]

I make so much of this issue because if the study of colonial American literature is to be respectable in the eyes of historians who take colonial British America for their bailiwick, scholars have to be more willing to grapple with the consensus about British North America that emerges from Greene and Pole's book. To take only the most striking example: if, as the British colonies matured into their second century, their inhabitants more and more sought to replicate British culture and society—a desire particularly apparent in the social elites who, as Greene and Pole put it, "by the late colonial period almost everywhere dominated and gave tone and definition to their societies"—how could such societies (specifically those in New England) forge an ideological consensus based on their *difference* from all other nations?[103] This is not to say that such an incongruity is impossible—indeed, one of Bercovitch's points about the rhetoric of the jeremiad is that it can absorb contradictions!—but only that most adherents of the continuities school have not yet seen fit to consider as "literature" any discourse that is not primarily religion-based. Clearly, if their understanding of the development of early American culture is to have more

---

102. See, for example, the provocative essays by Gordon S. Wood, David A. Hollinger, and David D. Hall, in *New Directions in American Intellectual History*, ed. John Higham and Paul K. Conkin (Baltimore: Johns Hopkins University Press, 1979).

103. Greene and Pole, eds., *Colonial British America*, p. 15.

credibility among historians whose conclusions about early American culture differ from theirs, they must address this issue more directly.

The best way to test the interpretation of colonial American literature now so ubiquitously offered is in fact to follow the lead of the critical theorists and thus to reexamine our assumptions about the relationship of language to what we consider "literary," a project that should involve us in rethinking as well both the New England– and religion-centered literature that has constituted the field. We need, for example, to consider figures who work primarily in other discursive fields as touchstones to early American culture. Bercovitch has gotten much grist for his ideological mill by treating Cotton Mather as a representative man, but what if we were to replace him with William Byrd or John Lawson or William Penn, or even Captain John Smith?[104] What would their exemplary lives and writings tell us about British North America? Indeed, the case of Smith is most instructive; as T. H. Breen has recently argued, Smith's astonishing literary career has been virtually ignored by historians and literary critics from the nineteenth century on because his writings tell Americans things they have not wanted to hear—about their pettiness and greed and self-righteousness, for example—rather than about men and women whose selfless behavior could be reported in stories, à la William Bradford and John Winthrop, which in turn could (and did) spawn reverential myths about American origin.[105] Surely, though, Smith's *True Travels* (1630) is at least as important a British North American text as Mather's *Magnalia*. The fact that the book is not set exclusively in America only makes it the more representative of the literature of British America generally, and Smith's relation to his subject bespeaks a very different linguistic paradigm from those we most often have been willing to consider. We could offer other such substitutions. Robert Beverley's *History and Present State of Virginia* (1705) cannot be dismissed from the ranks of histories of colonial America solely on the

---

104. It is important to note that the recently published *Complete Works of Captain John Smith (1580–1631)*, ed. Philip L. Barbour, 3 vols. (Chapel Hill: University of North Carolina Press, 1986) and the ongoing publication of *The Papers of William Penn*, ed. Mary Maples Dunn, Richard S. Dunn, et al. (Philadelphia: University of Pennsylvania Press, 1981–), are providing literary scholars with the reliable texts necessary to carry on the kinds of studies I am suggesting.

105. T. H. Breen, "Right Man, Wrong Place," *New York Review of Books* 33, no. 18 (20 November 1986): 50. This is an essay review of Barbour, ed., *Complete Works of Smith*. Also see Philip F. Gura, "John *Who?*: Captain John Smith and Early American Literature," *Early American Literature* 21 (1986–87): 260–67. On Penn see Richard S. Dunn and Mary Maples Dunn, eds., *The World of William Penn* (Philadelphia: University of Pennsylvania Press, 1986), esp. 3–86, 281–362.

ground that, unlike Mather's *Magnalia,* it contains no transcendent prophecy of Virginia's relationship to the New Jerusalem. Yet it has garnered nowhere near the attention given to a single sermon such as Samuel Danforth's *New-Englands Errand into the Wilderness.*[106]

To place the entrepreneur or the rationalist or the Quaker in a privileged position as an archetypal British North American has a certain dramatic flair, but the real labor must follow: to understand the language of different types of colonists in different regions with the same sophistication displayed by the New England scholars for their subjects' religious discourse. The territory here is virgin; it involves both the proper framing of early American literary expression in its British context and, concomitantly, an understanding of the great variety of expression such a literary and linguistic heritage made possible. This of course would be a mode of analysis acceptable to historians like John Murrin who vigorously propound the "anglicization" thesis concerning the development of colonial American culture.[107] Of equal significance, it would provide scholars of literature with new ways of understanding problematic periods or developments—a way of moving through the eighteenth century without being embarrassed by the amount of energy the colonists expended on religious or political issues to the supposed detriment of belles lettres. From 1730 to 1760, for example, a great amount of topical verse was written by poets throughout the colonies and published in newspapers or on broadsides. This body of material has not been studied in its British American context yet presents abundant evidence of the importance of such discourse to the general reader.[108]

This suggests a final desideratum for the continuing study of colonial American literature. If the new literary history of British North America

---

106. Robert Beverly, *The History and Present State of Virginia* (1705), ed. Louis B. Wright (Chapel Hill: University of North Carolina Press, 1947).

107. Greene and Pole, eds., *Colonial British America,* esp. 13–16, and the essays by T. H. Breen, Gary Nash, and Richard L. Bushman. It was, of course, John M. Murrin who initiated the thesis of "anglicization"; see his "Anglicizing an American Colony: The Transformation of Provincial Massachusetts" (Ph.D. diss., Yale University, 1966). Although nowhere in this essay do I adhere to this thesis as strictly as he does, I must acknowledge that, for my purposes, much of what he says suggests even more strongly that literary scholars have been remiss in not focusing on the broad connections between British and British American culture.

108. For an indication of the wealth of material in such publications see J. A. Leo Lemay, *A Calendar of American Poetry in the Colonial Newspapers and Magazines and in the Major English Magazines through 1765* (Worcester, Mass.: American Antiquarian Society, 1972), and Hennig Cohen, *The "South Carolina Gazette," 1732–1775* (Columbia: University of South Carolina Press, 1953), 181–230.

should reflect a variety of distinctive voices within an Anglo-American culture, it also must focus on the reader's as well as the writer's concerns. The study of newspaper verse is only one of several obvious keys to the mind of the general populace. The literary content of almanacs is another and many chapbooks and frequently reprinted British devotional tracts, as well as those items (tales of pirates, say) obviously produced primarily for entertainment, are of equal significance.[109] We still know too little about what people read and why, be it in Pennsylvania, Maryland, or Connecticut; to help answer these important questions literary historians must pay more heed to the emerging field of *l'histoire du livre* in America. The economics (indeed, the very mechanics) of book publication, the network of local and regional book distribution as well as the international book trade and the profession of authorship—all these topics are intimately linked to the history of colonial American literature as it now must be considered.[110] The diligent labors of many scholars have provided a set of canonical works and writers, but the elaborate and finally all-important background against which these texts and authors are highlighted remains an intellectual blur.

It is unlikely that scholars of colonial American literature and their counterparts in the historical profession will reestablish the relationship that they had four decades ago, but it is not healthy for either group to work as though the other did not exist in the same intellectual universe.[111] Moreover, more than at any other time in the past twenty years, there now is a genuine opportunity for these groups to work together to establish a truly broad-based foundation for understanding literary texts of all kinds in all parts of seventeenth- and eighteenth-century British North America, a project that demands the support of historians of *mentalité* and scholars of *l'histoire du livre* as well as of literary critics conversant with the theoretical premises of the "new historicism." Granted, this essay is devoted to many other scholars besides those who work these particular veins, but

109. See Spufford, *Small Books,* passim; and Daniel Williams, "Puritans and Pirates," 232–51.

110. The essays in Joyce et al., eds., *Printing and Society,* indicate the varied directions such studies can take.

111. One pioneering development for the mid- and late eighteenth century, however, is Jay Fliegelman's *Prodigals and Pilgrims: The American Revolution against Patriarchal Authority, 1750–1800* (New York: Cambridge University Press, 1982). Using literature as an indication of certain important and subtle cultural trends, Fliegelman goes far toward closing the distance between such scholars of the origins of the American Revolution as Bernard Bailyn and Alan Heimert.

it is offered in a genuinely ecumenical spirit to all laborers in the vineyard of early American culture. With regard to what members of the "other" professions can teach historians or literary critics, we should keep in mind a central character of early nineteenth-century American fiction, Harvey Birch, whose "tale," as James Fenimore Cooper put it in his subtitle to *The Spy*, was one of "the neutral ground." There is indeed such a place on the frontiers between both camps, and we should make every effort to meet and trade there.

2
Preparing the Way for Stoddard
Eleazer Mather's *Serious Exhortation* to Northampton

I conceived of this essay, as well as a few others in this book, as part of a large-scale study of the intellectual life of the Connecticut River Valley during the colonial period. Reading Perry Miller's various works on the period made me aware that, from the migration of Thomas Hooker to Hartford, the area always had been a place apart, and as the seventeenth century wore on, it seemed clear that, under the leadership of Solomon Stoddard and others, a variant of New England Puritanism was developed. People like the Westfield poet and minister Edward Taylor, Stoddard's own grandson, Hatfield's William Williams, and Stoddard himself debated issues central to the development of the Puritan theology and society, but on their own terms and with their own emphases. I only completed this history in bits and pieces but was delighted when other scholars, particularly the indefatigable Thomas M. Davis in his work with the Taylor manuscripts, continued to contribute to our understanding of the significance of this variant of New England orthodoxy. I still believe there is a book to be written about this region, a different one than Paul Lucas's *Valley of Discord* (see below), but it will have to be one suffused by economic as well as social history.

Eleazer Mather interested me because he was a member of the clerical family that most dominated affairs in Boston and yet had taken upon himself a mission to the wilds of the Connecticut Valley. Although he did not live long enough to exercise the same kind of influence as his brother Increase or his nephew Cotton, from what I learned of him I understood that the kinds of innovations that Stoddard and others initiated owed something to Eleazer's own tenure in the Valley. In this essay I sketch the nature of that influence.

Despite the extensive scholarship devoted to the Mather family in recent years, one member of its second generation in America, Eleazer, brother of Increase and the first minister of Northampton, Massachusetts, has received little serious attention from students of early American history and culture.[1] To be sure, Eleazer's influence on the development of New England theology never approached that of several of his distinguished relatives, nor did he make any significant mark on Anglo-American politics, as did his illustrious brother and that brother's son Cotton. Eleazer's ministry was hardly a success by any standard; instead of the attention and respect that quickly had accrued to his brother and Harvard classmate Increase in Boston's Second Church, upon his death in 1669 at the age of thirty-two, Eleazer left behind a community badly splintered by ecclesiastical disputes, one whose full support he never had gained.[2]

Yet Eleazer demands attention by his very position in the Connecticut River Valley town that later became the birthplace of revivalism in colonial New England, particularly because Eleazer's difficulties with his congregation set the terms of ecclesiastical debate for his renowned successor, Solomon Stoddard. Though historians usually point to the Synod of 1679 as the beginning of Stoddard's long and often bitter rivalry with the Mathers for the clerical leadership of New England, the antagonism actually began a decade earlier, when Stoddard encountered in Northampton a deep distrust of clerical prerogative, the direct legacy of Eleazer's pastorate.[3]

---

1. For biographical information about Eleazer Mather, see his entry in John Langdon Sibley's *Biographical Sketches of Graduates of Harvard College* (Cambridge: Massachusetts Historical Society, 1873), and James Trumbull, *The History of Northampton,* 2 vols. (Northampton, Mass.: [Press of Gazette Printing Co.], 1898), 199–209. The only historian who has noted the importance of Eleazer and his sermons is Emory Elliott, in *Power and the Pulpit in Puritan New England* (Princeton: Princeton University Press, 1975), 46–47, 103–5, 138–40, but Elliott deals with the sermons more in terms of the psychological condition of the Bay Colony as a whole rather than of Northampton.

2. The best biography of Increase Mather is still Kenneth Murdock's *Increase Mather: Foremost American Puritan* (Cambridge: Harvard University Press, 1925); see also, Robert Middlekauff, *The Mathers: Three Generations of Puritan Intellectuals, 1596–1728* (New York: Oxford University Press, 1971), and Mason I. Lowance, Jr., *Increase Mather* (New York: Twayne, 1974).

3. For the standard view, see, for example, Perry Miller, "Solomon Stoddard, 1643–1729," *Harvard Theological Review* 34 (1941): 277–320.

The chief evidence of the implicit relationship between Eleazer and Stoddard lies in the one work we have from Eleazer's hand, a set of sermons posthumously published as *A Serious Exhortation to the Present and Rising Generation*. Eleazer's injunctions to his parishioners offer an important index to the religious turmoil Stoddard encountered in his first years in Northampton. If we examine these sermons with an eye not only to the colonywide crisis over church membership that followed the endorsement of the Half-Way Covenant by the Synod of 1662 but also to what they reveal of Northampton's peculiar social and ecclesiastical constitution, they indicate how the town's first minister had prepared it spiritually for the later evangelical efforts of Stoddard and his successor, Jonathan Edwards.

Eleazer never explained his decision to put a hundred miles of wilderness between himself and the family home in Dorchester, but Northampton's brief history should have given him pause before he accepted the town's call. Although the area in which the community was located had been purchased from the natives in 1653 and was settled about the same time, its inhabitants waited until 1658 to hire a minister and three more years before gathering a church, an unusually long period at a time when new communities often were settled by groups of emigrants who arrived with ministers in tow. Furthermore, while its settlement was not so overtly the result of ecclesiastical disruption as, say, the neighboring town of Hadley, various groups who had moved to Northampton had left their communities for reasons of religion.[4]

A large number of Northampton's first inhabitants had come from Dorchester, the town from which Eleazer's future father-in-law, John Warham, had led a large emigration in 1635 to the Connecticut Valley at Windsor, a move prompted by his disapproval of the Bay Colony's stringent church membership requirements.[5] These migrants were joined in turn by people from Hartford, where the church had become badly splintered when members were unable to agree on a successor to Thomas Hooker, and from Springfield, which had just experienced an outbreak of witchcraft and

---

4. On Northampton's settlement, see Trumbull, *Northampton*, 1–94.
5. On John Warham's move to Windsor, see Paul Lucas, *Valley of Discord: Church and Society along the Connecticut River, 1636–1725* (Hanover, N.H.: University Press of New England, 1976), 38–40, and B. R. Burg, *Richard Mather of Dorchester* (Lexington: University of Kentucky Press, 1976), 28–32. In 1636 Eleazer's father, Richard, had been prevented from founding a church in Dorchester because other ministers in the colony considered the potential members to have unsound religious principles (see Burg, *Richard Mather*, 32–37).

where the Valley's first citizen, William Pynchon, had lived prior to his censure for publishing a purportedly heretical treatise on the atonement.[6]

We also should not overlook the fact that Eleazer himself greatly contributed to his later difficulties in Northampton: he consented to settle only if he were allowed to bring six or seven prominent Dorchester families with him to serve as "pillars" of the new church and to whom the townspeople had to promise parcels of rich farmland. It had proved difficult to lure a ministerial candidate so far from the preferments he might receive in a more settled area, and the town finally acceded to Eleazer's wishes, but there was a good deal of grumbling about the minister's high-handed demands. Though the Dorchester men soon enough became integrated into the political life of the young community, Eleazer ran into more serious difficulties when the town learned of his adamant opposition to the Half-Way Covenant, the principles of which most of them espoused. He and his brother Increase did little to mask their disagreement with the majority of the delegates at the meetings of the Synod of 1662, and though Eleazer's strong stand against the Half-Way Covenant never resulted in a call for his dismissal, throughout his tenure a majority of the parishioners continually pressured him to accept the Synod's recommendations.[7]

Ecclesiastical matters remained at a virtual stalemate until 1668, when Northampton's settlers, knowing that their minister's ill health prevented any strong resistance to their efforts, initiated a series of town meetings that concluded early the next year with the drafting of a new church covenant to replace the one Eleazer had composed in 1661. Under this new covenant Northampton's citizens extended some of the privileges of membership not only to "the Adult Children hitherto unbaptized of Confederate Beleevers" (that is, to the group for whom the Half-Way Covenant had been designed) but also to any inhabitants who understood and believed "the Doctrine of faith" (even though "but in the lowest

---

6. For a discussion of the trouble in the Hartford Church, see Lucas, *Valley of Discord*, 43–50; on witchcraft in Springfield, see Trumbull, *Northampton*, 1:42–53, and Henry M. Burt, *The First Century of Springfield*, 2 vols. (Springfield, Mass.: Henry M. Burt, 1898), 1:73–89; on Pynchon, see my " 'The Contagion of Corrupt Opinions' in Puritan Massachusetts: The Case of William Pynchon," *William and Mary Quarterly*, 3d ser., 39 (1982): 469–91, and A *Glimpse of Sion's Glory: Puritan Radicalism in New England, 1620–1660* (Middletown: Wesleyan University Press, 1984), 304–22.

7. Trumbull, *Northampton*, 1:79–80, 108–20, 202–3; Robert G. Pope, *The Half-Way Covenant: Church Membership in Puritan New England* (Princeton: Princeton University Press, 1969), 45–46, 51–52, 147–50, and *Massachusetts Historical Society, Collections*, 4th ser., 8 (Boston: Wiggin and Lunt, 1868), 192–94.

degree"), who "Publickly seriously, and freely" professed "their assent thereunto," and who were not visibly "Scandelous in life." By declaring that such people, as long as they did not "essay the breaking in upon the privileges of Lords Supper and votting," were free to present their children for baptism, the congregation urged a step that even the chief proponents of the Half-Way Covenant had not sanctioned.[8]

No doubt drawing on the example of some of the Connecticut churches, which already had experimented with such enlarged membership privileges (and from which some of the Northampton settlers had come), Northampton greatly narrowed the distinction between the church and the world with its new covenant. Membership in the church was to be determined not so much by the minister's private and professional examination of the state of an individual's soul (though the minister technically still held the power over admission to full membership) as by the community's judgment of an individual's adherence to communitywide moral standards. By their new covenant, Northampton's citizens announced that the language of obligation and promise, and a concomitant emphasis on spiritual nurture, hitherto would demarcate the boundaries of their lives as Christians and so would replace Eleazer's insistence that church membership was indissolubly linked to a vivid experience of grace.[9]

Faced with such boldness on the part of his church, in the last month of his life Eleazer again assumed his pulpit, this time to defend his beliefs and actions in the sermons that became *A Serious Exhortation,* the central document for understanding the world that Stoddard inherited. The sermons clearly indicate Eleazer's anger at his people's presumption in blaming the splintered condition of the church on his unwillingness to allow more people into it as probationary members; on the contrary, he saw his people's quarrel with him over church membership as the outward manifestation of a much more fundamental problem—their own moral and spiritual failure as Christians. Thus, as he viewed it, the cause of contention in Northampton lay not with the children of baptized but unconverted parents but with the parents *themselves,* particularly with their refusal to respond positively

---

8. Northampton, First Church Records, 1661–1924, Forbes Library, Northampton, microfilm reel 22, p. 6; quoted in Pope, *Half-Way Covenant,* 147–48.

9. On the importance of church covenants in the late seventeenth century, see Lucas, *Valley of Discord,* 15–16, 107–10, 135–36, and David D. Hall, *The Faithful Shepherd: A History of the New England Ministry during the Seventeenth Century* (Chapel Hill: University of North Carolina Press, 1972), 243–44.

to the evangelical truths that two decades earlier had defined the faith of most New Englanders. The townspeople's creation of a new category of membership that glossed over the spiritual bankruptcy of the older generation allowed them to avoid the real problem, their obvious inability to take godly principles to heart.

In place of their fathers' God, Northampton's citizens had substituted Mammon and paid open tribute to "prosperity" and "outward riches," two of his subordinates who flourished among farmers and traders in the rich bottomlands of the valley; Eleazer implored his people to consider the extent of their devotion to such golden calves. As long as people in the valley continued to "stop the crannies, and fill the empty places of the Heart, with Creature-comforts," there was little likelihood that God would continue to inhabit Northampton.[10]

Eleazer also was troubled by his people's unwillingness to respond to the ordinances of the Gospel he so lovingly offered, a problem that had arisen because of the confusion surrounding the scriptural warrant for the Half-Way Covenant. "When men's hearts are not stirred, and quickened, and warmed" by ordinances, he complained, and when "the Word is lodged only in the Porch, and never comes into the House," people are left only with "something to talk of" and thus neglect the substance of religion. Parishioners came to meetings and heard Eleazer's sermons, promised themselves to Christ, and outwardly paid attention to the minister's sermons; yet it was all too evident that not in the least were they affected by the gravity or joy of the Gospel promises he dispensed. Because of Northampton's lengthy and divisive debates over the Half-Way Covenant, the Gospel ordinances had become "occasions and means of disquiet," which caused the congregation to leave the house of God "with galled and condemned Consciences."[11]

Throughout *A Serious Exhortation* Eleazer attacked the shortcomings of the adult population who first had settled the town. Northampton's citizenry wanted to believe that the Half-Way Covenant would resolve the community's moral and spiritual crisis, yet in their hearts they knew that a

---

10. Eleazer Mather, *A Serious Exhortation to the Present and Rising Generations* (Cambridge: S. G[reen] and M. J[ohnson], 1671; repr. Boston: John Foster, 1678), 8–9. Hereafter cited as *SE*.

11. *SE*, 10–11. On the question of excessive scrupulosity among the laity following the results of the Synod, see Pope, *Half-Way Covenant,* passim, but esp. 132–51, and "New England versus the New England Mind: The Myth of Declension," *Journal of Social History* 3 (Winter 1969–70): 95–108. Also relevant is Edmund S. Morgan's "New England Puritanism: Another Approach," *William and Mary Quarterly,* 3d ser., 18 (1961): 236–42.

man who "hath only a visible interest, an interest in the visible Covenant," could do "no more for his child but leave that unto him." Such individuals, he added, "cannot believe for any more, nor act faith for any more."[12] Worse still were religious hypocrites, who sought to creep under the fold of the Half-Way Covenant, for such had no reason whatsoever to believe that God would be the God of their children "by special grace." Only a true conversion guaranteed sainthood to one's offspring; thus in their hasty desire to adopt the Half-Way Covenant, Northampton's people were creating a church composed primarily of deficient, if well-intentioned, Christians. "*If in your time Profession and Lukewarmness* go hand in hand together," Eleazer predicted, "then in those that come after you, *Profession and Prophaneness* shall go hand in hand together." "If you keep your Religion and Forms with all their buts," he added, "they that succeed will be Professors with their buts."[13]

Thus, the older generation willfully had foregone its responsibility to come to Christ with speed and sincerity, and this moral failure severely threatened the spiritual welfare of the rising generation. *"Why came you into this land?"* Eleazer sharply asked Northampton's elders. *"Was it not mainly with respect to the Rising Generation?"* "Was it to leave them a rich and wealthy people? Was it to leave them Houses, Lands, Livings?" So it appeared, for rather than striving to keep God in the midst of their children, the townspeople, as revealed in the terms of the new covenant, only set themselves more firmly in their profligate ways. People were too apt "to complain against the Rising Generation," Eleazer noted, as though their children's sins surprised them. But the "second Generation seldome or never prove totall Apostates" unless "the first are deep, secret Heart-revolters." "Heart-sins" in the first generation, he warned, "grow into Life-sins in the second." Do not your children, he asked, "see *your* Pride, your Worldliness, your Passion, your Vanity?"[14]

With *A Serious Exhortation* providing our clues, we do well to consider how boldly the lines of contention had been drawn in Northampton in the year before Eleazer's death, and how they remained so defined through the first decades of Stoddard's pastorate. If, for example, Eleazer's troubling analysis of Northampton's moral failure was correct, the adoption of the Half-Way Covenant would only hide, and perhaps aggravate, the wide-

12. *SE*, 18. Elliott, *Power and the Pulpit*, 138–40, remarks on how severely Eleazer chastised the "present" generation, a stance unusual in the late 1660s and early 1670s.
13. *SE*, 18, 22.
14. *SE*, 16, 17, 21.

spread spiritual anxiety in the population. Predictably, given how frustrated the town had been with Eleazer's refusal to accede to their wishes regarding church membership, upon his arrival Stoddard quickly was asked to institute the recommendations of the Synod, a request with which he complied.[15] He also agreed with the town's desire to include more people under a "state of education" by allowing any adult willing to subject himself "to the government of Christ in this church" to become a church member.[16] Thus, as the town had wished, an individual's assent to the doctrine of faith coupled with his good moral behavior was all that was required of him to "own" the covenant like any "half-way" member and so to enter the church's special watch and care.

During the early years of Stoddard's ministry, such reforms failed to eliminate the townspeople's unchristian behavior—behavior to which Stoddard linked the wrathful judgment of King Philip's War—and fewer and fewer people were admitted to full church membership. Stoddard was forced to implement different ecclesiastical measures, ones that themselves exacerbated the particular insecurities that had become so obvious in the town's difficulties with his predecessor. In 1690, for example, when Stoddard openly announced his intention to treat the Lord's Supper as a converting ordinance rather than as a "seal" of the covenant of grace solely, he met such resistance from his congregation that he was forced to hold special meetings of the church to answer their criticism.[17] In the late 1670s, his people had accepted his enlarged definition of church membership, through which any distinction between "full" and "half-way" members essentially was dissolved and which he formally brought to the attention of other ministers at the so-called Reforming Synod of 1679, but when Stoddard attempted to go beyond community-based reform to gather more power to himself by emphasizing the efficacy of the sacraments and, hence, the minister's authority in administering them, his church reacted with the same suspicion and jealousy they had displayed in their battles with Eleazer.[18]

Similarly, in 1700, when Stoddard laid the foundation for a church

---

15. See Patricia J. Tracy, *Jonathan Edwards, Pastor: Religion and Society in Eighteenth-Century Northampton* (New York: Hill and Wang, 1980), 22–23, and Ralph Coffman, *Solomon Stoddard* (New York: Twayne, 1978), 60–62.

16. See Pope, *Half-Way Covenant*, 252–53, and Lucas, *Valley of Discord*, 136.

17. See Lucas, *Valley of Discord*, 157–58, and Thomas M. Davis and Virginia Davis, eds., *Edward Taylor vs. Solomon Stoddard: The Nature of the Lord's Supper* (Boston: G. K. Hall, 1981), 1–49, esp. 18–19.

18. Davis and Davis, *Taylor vs. Stoddard*, 17–19.

defined by geographic area rather than covenantal obligation in his *Doctrine of Instituted Churches,* he again met with resistance from his town and others in the valley because the laity thought increased authority would accrue to the clergy under such a system.[19] Not until 1714 was the Hampshire Association of ministers formed, along the lines of Connecticut's Saybrook Platform, and even then many of the valley's residents continued to doubt the wisdom of allowing ministers so great a degree of independence. The community's fears of ministerial prerogative lay at the root of Stoddard's difficulties in implementing such ecclesiastical reform; as "liberal" a church as Northampton was, the people still wished to claim the primary role in any ecclesiastical decisions that affected the church's identity and moral character. Not forgetting Eleazer's haughty resistance to their suggestions for the spiritual renovation of the community, Northampton's churchgoers remained suspicious of Stoddard's true intentions.

Had Eleazer acquiesced to the town's initial demands for a more liberal admissions policy, Northampton's history might have been more like that of some of the Connecticut churches downriver, in which peaceful accommodation had been reached within a presbyterial polity. In that case Stoddard's attempts to modify the community's understanding of sacramental efficacy and ministerial authority would not have been necessary.[20] By 1669, however, Northampton's situation resembled none more than Windsor's, where Eleazer's father-in-law, John Warham, had plunged the community into years of acrimonious bickering by reversing his initial support for the Half-Way Covenant.[21] Northampton, like Windsor, had studied the wager proposed by the Synod of 1662 and gambled on its promise of moral peace and harmony. Later Northampton church members discovered, to their discomfort, that Stoddard had changed the stakes, and finally even the rules, of the game so that their wager could be maintained with what *he* considered some degree of integrity.

---

19. On the failure of Stoddard's instituted church, see Lucas, *Valley of Discord,* 152–58, and "'An Appeal to the Learned': The Mind of Solomon Stoddard," *William and Mary Quarterly,* 3d ser., 30 (1973): 278–83. The Saybrook Platform of 1708, a revision of the colony of Connecticut's ecclesiastical polity, endorsed the use of ministerial consociations to aid in the regulation of church doctrine and the resolution of clerical disputes. By 1714 the churches of the upper Connecticut River valley in Massachusetts had voluntarily adopted a similar plan of church government, one that emphasized ministerial prerogative at the expense of the laity's, which under more strictly congregational polity had been much stronger.

20. See, for example, the towns discussed in Lucas, *Valley of Discord,* 23–40, 59–71, and Pope, *Half-Way Covenant,* 96–131.

21. Lucas, *Valley of Discord,* 78–82.

3 | Cotton Mather's *Life of Phips*
"A Vice with the Vizard of Vertue Upon It"

This essay originated in my consuming interest in Cotton Mather's *Magnalia Christi Americana,* and more specifically, after having read Sacvan Bercovitch's *The Puritan Origins of the American Self* (1975), in my desire to test that critic's understanding of Mather's use of biography. If any leader of New England Puritanism was different from John Winthrop, on whom Bercovitch focuses much of his book, it was Phips, and in this essay I contextualize these differences.

After many readings of Bercovitch's work, I realized that what I missed in his pyrotechnic readings of Puritan literature was a sense of the thickness of the historical moment. As scholars like Andrew Delbanco and David Harlan have pointed out, when one reads Puritanism through Bercovitch's lenses, one leaves with a sense of having been immersed in an old black-and-white movie that has gone to shades of gray. There is too little contrast, too little sense that within any given situation there were many voices striving against one another, rather than the one dominant discourse that Bercovitch explicates over and over again. There is, in other words, a lot of history that is left out of his accounts, one reason, perhaps, why his stature among historians has never been so assured as it is with literary critics.

Mather's *Life of Phips* makes this readily apparent; his stylization in the *Magnalia* of this man's rise to prominence can only be comprehended when we regard the minutiae of politics in provincial Massachusetts. Of course, as Bercovitch suggests about Mather, in the *Puritan Origins* and elsewhere, always he is writing autobiographically. But in his *Life of Phips* he also feels his way to a new understanding of how citizenship could be defined in the eighteenth-century colonies. The character of the good ruler, as Samuel

Willard termed it, need not be what it hitherto had been, and in Mather's frantic attempt to make sense of his father's appointment of Phips to the governor's chair, we can observe this Puritan patriarch move crablike into the Age of Reason, when politics rather than religion defined good citizenship. The change was momentous and it is nowhere more strikingly described than in Mather's apologia for this bumbling adventurer.

Robert Calef, the improper Bostonian who braved the wrath of New England's orthodox clergy by publishing a severe indictment of the Salem witchcraft episode in *More Wonders of the Invisible World* (London, 1700), also offered (in a postscript) an astute observation on a book recently published in London. He noted that *Pietas in Patriam: The Life of His Excellency Sir William Phips, Knt.* (1697) "pretends to raise a statue in honor of sir William," yet "it appears it was the least part of the design of the author to honor him." "It was rather to honor himself, and the other ministers" that Cotton Mather had composed the work.[1] Not particularly interested in the psychological import of his criticism, Calef spent the remainder of the postscript lambasting Mather (as he had done in the body of his work) for obscuring the Mather family's real part in the witchcraft debacle.

Recent criticism supports Calef's observation and has stressed the degree to which many of Mather's public pronouncements were scarcely veiled psychological projections that resolved tensions arising from his imaginative identification with New England and his almost hysterical awareness that upon him had developed the unenviable task of maintaining the purity of the New England churches.[2] In this regard the *Life of Phips* is a particularly significant document. The seeming incongruity between Mather's

---

1. Robert Calef, *More Wonders of the Invisible World* (1700; repr. Salem, Mass.: J. D. and T. C. Cushing, Jr., 1823), 302. Although the *Life of Phips* was published anonymously "by one intimately acquainted with Him," Calef had little difficulty ascertaining the author. The prefatory leaf, signed by Nathaniel Mather, identified the writer as one so well known for "Integrity, Prudence, and Veracity that there is not any cause to question the truth of what he here relates."

2. See Sacvan Bercovitch, "Cotton Mather," *Major Writers of Early American Literature*, ed. Everett Emerson (Madison: University of Wisconsin Press, 1973), passim. Also Bercovitch's "Delightful Examples of Surprising Prosperity: Cotton Mather and the American Success Story," *English Studies* 51 (1970): 40–43, and Robert Middlekauff, *The Mathers: Three Generations of Puritan Intellectuals* (New York: Oxford University Press, 1972), passim.

flattering portrait and the harsher evidence of contemporary sources suggests Mather's awareness that in New England's history Phips was a crucial figure, one whose behavior had to be explained and justified before the Church's march to the New Jerusalem could continue unimpeded. The subsequent inclusion of this book in the *Magnalia Christi Americana* (London, 1702) further implies its importance and suggests that in the late seventeenth century (whether or not he was aware of it), Mather's understanding of the character and purpose of New England was being transformed, and that in writing his *Life of Phips* he gave to the world what might be termed the first *American* life. Phips had become an emblem through which Mather struggled to understand the contradictions of his own place in the American experience: with the publication of this book Mather could feel more comfortable with his own part in New England's history. He seemed unaware, however, that in the course of his narrative he also had done nothing less than to redefine radically the terms by which future magistrates would be judged.

A glance at the political situation in Boston in 1694 sets the tone for a realistic evaluation of Phips. Called on to give the annual election sermon, the Reverend Samuel Willard adhered to the standards expected for that traditional performance and addressed the General Court on the topic "The Character of the Good Ruler." But the political turmoil initiated by the recent behavior of Governor Phips filled him with trepidation. He knew his words would carry profound contemporary significance and began his sermon by admitting that he was "not ignorant that we are fallen into a critical time," and that he was "far from being ambitious of appearing on the State in this Juncture."[3] It was common knowledge that political factionalism was spreading and that the colony had recently been torn by the refusal of Governor Phips to allow Elisha Cooke his seat on the governor's council.[4] By disallowing the election of this powerful figure, Phips bred more dissension by seeking to implement a law requiring members of the court to reside in the towns they represented, a move

---

3. Samuel Willard, *The Character of the Good Ruler* (Boston, 1694).
4. An opponent both of clericalism and royal prerogative, Elisha Cooke (1637–1715) was the most "loyal" colonist during the negotiations for the return of the charter. In London with Increase Mather as a colonial agent, Cooke had been displeased with Mather's acceptance of the new charter restricting colonial powers. In Boston he was one of the Mathers' most vociferous opponents.

prompted by his painful realization that in the recent election no fewer than ten of his party's men had been dropped from office.

Little wonder that Willard stressed "the proper use of authority" as one of the main attributes of a good ruler: Phips's recent machinations were only the most noticeable in a long list of abuses. On one occasion, falling into a rage, he publicly assaulted with fist and cane Jahleel Brenton, the royal customs officer, after Brenton refused to comply with Phips's request that a certain ship be allowed into Boston harbor duty-free.[5] Later he had beaten Captain Short of the Royal Navy (a partially disabled man) when he refused Phips's demand to allow him to impress Short's crew for one of his own privateering expeditions. Because of such outrageous behavior the governor would soon find himself before King William III answering charges of bribery, piracy, and misconduct in high office; but (perhaps fortunately) Phips died in London (1695) before his guilt could be ascertained. How did this man, so far from representing the character of the good ruler, attain such prominence? Quickly sketching the meteoric rise of William Phips, we equip ourselves, not only to understand the developing political world of late seventeenth-century Boston, but also to comprehend the transformation through which Phips's character would have to pass before it emerged from the complex mind of Cotton Mather.

Phips's life was a testament to social mobility in seventeenth-century New England. Born in 1651, the son of a poor gunsmith in the remote Kennebec region of Maine (then part of the Bay Colony), he early decided that his ambition would take him elsewhere. After a brief period of sheepherding in his native town, he was apprenticed as a ship's carpenter and soon found himself in Boston, where after a few industrious years he had so risen in station that he commanded a coastal vessel and had married the widow of a prosperous merchant. To this point the story was ordinary enough, but it now acquired the tone of romance. Hearing of Spanish galleons that had sunk in the Caribbean, Phips outfitted a frigate and made a trip to the Bahamas in search of this treasure. The voyage failed, but in 1683 (with Yankee presumptuousness), he took himself to London, achieved an audience before Charles II, and charmed the monarch into underwriting another expedition. This second voyage also failed; but in 1686 the persistent Phips imposed himself on the new monarch, James II,

---

5. For the facts presented in this section I am greatly indebted to two essays by Viola Barnes, "The Rise of William Phips" and "Phippius Maximus," *New England Quarterly* 1, (1928): nos. 3 and 4, 271–94 and 532–53.

obtained another vow of support, and shortly thereafter returned to the islands. This time he sailed back to London with more than £50,000 in his hold. This addition to the royal coffers so pleased the king that in 1687, besides granting Phips £16,000 of the treasure, he conferred upon him the honor of knighthood.

Before the outset of the first voyage, Phips and his crew had talked themselves into a brawl in the streets of Boston. When the case came before Governor Bradstreet, this magistrate reminded Phips that he should tame his haughtiness since everybody knew "what he was and from whence he came."[6] As if in answer to Bradstreet's taunt, the adventurer returned to that city in 1688, as Sir William and carried with him a commission as high sheriff of the colony. Moreover, during the course of his treasure hunt, the colony's charter had been revoked and Massachusetts had been joined to the other New England colonies and New York in the Dominion of New England; with his new royal commission Phips was now one of the most powerful officials in Boston. Some prominent men, however, resented this new arrival. As head of the newly created administrative unit, Sir Edmund Andros treated Phips poorly and refused to allow the upstart to appoint his own deputies, claiming that worthy men already held the positions. Never one to take affronts calmly, after vigorous but futile disputation, Phips returned to London to complain of this high-handed behavior. The Reverend Increase Mather, one of the colonial agents negotiating for the return of the charter, was in England at the same time. At this juncture Phips furthered his acquaintance with the minister who (by Phips's admission to Cotton Mather) in 1674 had "first made him sensible of his sins." One wonders if Phips, with his later gift for turning situations to his benefit, realized the significance of this encounter. His association with Increase Mather proved to be one of the most fortuitous events in a remarkable career.

In March 1689, Increase Mather sent Phips hustling back to New England with news of the Glorious Revolution. Disappointingly for Phips, Boston (hearing of William's planned invasion) had already taken the initiative and overthrown the regime six weeks before his arrival. Phips soothed his ego (he would have been pleased to commence a popular rebellion against the despised Andros) and displayed his support for the provisional government by guarding some of the prisoners. He then made a hasty trip to England to ascertain the progress of the charter negotiations, and in 1690 on his return to Boston (perhaps anticipating through an

---

6. Barnes, "Phips," 284.

intimation from Mather that he might soon have the opportunity to serve the colony in some elected capacity) proceeded to justify himself in the eyes of the populace by becoming a church member. Although the colony's charter was not in effect, most people assumed that church membership was the prerequisite for political rights. With this in mind, Phips reported his conversion to Cotton Mather, entered into his church, and within a few weeks was made a freeman of the colony.[7] On the same day these political rights were bestowed, he was named commander in chief of the colonial forces sent to attack the strategic French fort at Port Royal, Nova Scotia. The unqualified success of that campaign brightened his image even more, and with a monopoly of the fur trade the obvious prize, he next broached the idea (equally attractive to the colonial leaders) of an attack on Quebec, capital of French Canada.

This undertaking was rashly conceived and the colonial forces were soundly defeated. The failure to take Quebec proved embarrassing to Phips's ambitions as well as to New England's, and this peripatetic soldier, seeking to redeem himself from what he saw as a personal humiliation, recrossed the Atlantic to petition the king for more troops to renew the assault on the fortress.[8] In London the charter negotiations were nearing an end. Phips's gift of serendipity again became evident as Increase Mather, realizing that the old charter would not be restored and that the new one, with its provisions for a royally appointed governor and for the creation of a franchise based on property rather than piety, would be unpopular with many colonists, tried to save his reputation by requesting the indulgence of naming the first governor and council under the new arrangement. His friend Phips, the native American adventurer, was at hand. Mather knew of his popularity in the Bay Colony and could count on the fact that this new member of his and his son's church would support his political and ecclesiastical views. He was known by and entirely acceptable to King William who, desiring a military man in the office, quickly assented to Mather's proposition.

On 14 May 1692, at the height of the witchcraft panic, Governor William Phips arrived in Boston. At his command, and under the direction

---

7. For an account, see Barnes, "Phips," 288. The confession of faith is printed in Mather's *Life of Phips* and is most readily available in his *Magnalia Christi Americana* (1702; repr. Hartford, 1820, 1853).

8. The Quebec attack failed not through his error but because of a combination of bad weather, sickness, and the ineptitude of the leaders of the flanking force. See George Allan Cook, *John Wise: Early American Democrat* (1952; repr. New York: Octagon Books, 1966), 61–69, for the account of John Wise, chaplain to the expedition.

of Lieutenant Governor Stoughton, a court of oyer and terminer was called, during which session Phips conveniently absented himself by making a trip to the frontier to investigate new Indian difficulties. The witchcraft hysteria got out of control, with accusations being hurled at people as prominent as Cotton Mather and finally even Lady Phips. Phips's political acumen, never great, gave him the good sense to return and to ask the ministers for advice, and shortly thereafter (on their recommendation) he stopped the trials and released the remaining suspects. The spiritual turmoil began to subside, but Phips, trying to govern a colony splintered by political factionalism, blundered into the political errors mentioned at the outset.[9]

He was liked by the populace, but his enemies had continued to sting his pride with allusions to his humble origins.[10] They accused him of choosing his company "out of the mob for the most part, amongst whom noise and strut pass for wit and prowess."[11] Others pointed to his lack of education, claiming that he had just "learned to read since he was Married, and cannot yet read a letter, much less write one, and there being no Carpenter's work in the Government they expect he will not serve long."[12] With such facts before us, it is easy to understand why in his election sermon Willard uttered both a shrill warning and an embarrassed lament. No doubt thinking of his own close association with the Mathers, he declared that it would be "no small Aggravation to our Trouble, to be Wounded with a Shaft of our own Making." Cotton Mather soon took upon himself the extraordinary task of showing that if Phips's career were properly understood, no wound had ever been inflicted. It would prove an intriguing sleight of hand.

In his *Diary* for 1696 Mather reflected on his recently completed *Life of*

   9. Other biographies of Phips draw heavily on Mather's facts and thus run the risk of overlooking many of Phips's difficulties. Alice Lounsberry, *Sir William Phips: Treasure Fisherman and Governor of Massachusetts Bay Colony* (New York: Scribner, 1941) is readable but romanticized. See Francis Bowen, *Life of Sir William Phips* in *Library of American Biography*, by Jared Sparks (Boston: Hillard, Gray, 1837); and Cyrus H. Karraker, *The Hispaniola Treasure* (Philadelphia: University of Pennsylvania Press, 1934).
   10. It is significant that after the Brenton episode witnesses maintained that Phips had just given him a little cuff on the chin! See Barnes, "Phippius," 536.
   11. Barnes, "Phippius," 537.
   12. T. H. Breen, *The Character of the Good Ruler: Puritan Political Ideas in New England, 1630–1730* (New Haven: Yale University Press, 1970), 187. Also, passim, a good account of shifting conceptions of leadership in New England. Breen does not, however, deal with Mather's imaginative use of Phips.

Phips and noted that after he had "considered . . . the memorable Changes undergone, and actions performed" by the late governor, and how these events "had very many things in them" to display the power and wisdom of God, he had then decided to write this man's life "with much Elaboration."[13] With the historical background of Phips's career established, a close reading of Mather's *Life of Phips* displays how much the narrative is (in Mather's understatement) "Elaboration" rather than patent deception: he had not presented falsehoods but instead had displayed a novel biographical emphasis. Rather than composing his *Life of Phips* in the manner of his other "lives" in which "the subject . . . was never glorified in and for himself but for the ulterior purpose of glorifying New England's primitive past," Mather was forced to create a new set of "virtues" to identify his subject, thus making the biography so much more engaging than the conventional, highly idealized lives of Bradford and Winthrop (later to appear in the *Magnalia* with the *Life of Phips*).[14] Besides breaking through the constrictions of his form, Mather, in struggling to defend a man so different from other magistrates he revered, also transformed the vocabulary of political parlance. Discovering Phips's virtues and publishing them with his imprimatur, he lent official sanction to a new era of colonial politics, one in which public patriotism superseded personal piety as the most laudable quality of a good ruler.

Many reasons compelled Mather's imaginative reordering of Phips's career. In purely political terms foremost was Phips's association with the Mather family. As noted, he was Increase Mather's handpicked candidate for the office of governor and as a member of the Mathers' North Church was known to Cotton as well. Discussing the new charter in his *Diary* for "29d, 2m, 1692," Cotton Mather declared that "the Governour of the Province, is not my Enemy, but one whom I baptised . . . and one of my own Flock, and one of my dearest Friends." While we cannot go so far as to claim that he was totally the creation of the Mathers (Fortune claims that honor), Phips owed them so much that, as Barrett Wendell suggested,

---

13. Cotton Mather, *Diary*, in *Massachusetts Historical Society, Collections*, 7th ser., 7–8 (Boston: The Society, 1911–12).

14. William Manniere II, "Mather and the Biographical Parallel," *American Quarterly* 13 (1961): 160. Without doubt the *Life of Phips* is one of the most readable and entertaining pieces in the *Magnalia*, largely because Mather was on this new ground in discussing him and thus did not instantly categorize his experiences. Ironically, then, one has a tendency to believe Mather's account without qualification!

"such a man as this [Phips] might be trusted, if anybody might, to do the will of God as the Mathers expounded it."[15] As it became more apparent to these clergymen that to salvage their conception of New England's part in the history of the work of redemption they had to descend to battle in Boston's politics, it was only natural that they would ally with a man having the charisma of Phips. What they neglected to realize was that while as a military hero of unpretentious origin he captured the popular imagination, Phips had little respect (or the means to procure it) from the Mathers' powerful opponents in the Bay Province.

More interesting were the psychological compulsions forcing Mather's imaginative transformation of Phips. If one takes into account the *Life of Phips*'s subsequent incorporation at the end of book 2 of the *Magnalia* (that portraying "the Lives of the Governours . . . that have been Shields unto the Churches"), it is apparent that Mather's rendering of Phips is linked to Mather's paranoiac attempts to ward off the pressing reality of his personal situation. If Mather were able to order the knowledge of his society's past and present (as he would attempt to do on a vast scale in the *Magnalia*) he might retain what he sensed was a constantly diminishing control over that society. Haunted by the thought that he was to be both prophet and martyr to his people, Mather believed that New England and the Mather heritage had become synonymous. By justifying all that Phips had done for the country and then subtly reminding people that Mather was to be identified with this hero, his legitimacy as the community's leader would be maintained.[16] He faced a crisis in both national and personal terms. Giving shape to a mythology of community leadership he believed consistent with the traditional one, he sought to ensure the supremacy of his political and ecclesiastical views. Both a stimulant to, and a balm for, his ego, the *Life of Phips* was also evidence of Mather's blindness to the fact that the days of John Winthrop could not be restored. Fusing objective reality with his own subjective vision (thus fabricating neither history nor myth but a combination of both), he came to believe that Phips's virtues were as important as Winthrop's. The revealing point is that when he came to write the *Magnalia* he could sing Winthrop's praise in one-fourth as many pages as it took to declare Phips his equal. Even to a declining third generation, Phips's actions needed that much rationalization.

15. Barrett Wendell, *Cotton Mather: The Puritan Priest* (1926; repr. New York: Harcourt, Brace, and World, 1963), 67.
16. Bercovitch, "Mather," passim.

The title page of Mather's *Life of Phips* innocently announced one of the major themes in his evaluation of the magistrate. The book contained (among other things) an account of "the memorable Changes undergone" by New England's most recent leader. But instead of concentrating his attention on the standard "changes" to be recorded in Puritan biography (the establishment of the subject's Christian calling and a description of his final coming to Christ), in the course of this narrative, Mather presented without any inhibition an account of the successes of Phips's secular career, understood throughout as the result, not of exemplary piety but of the intersection of Phips's personal ambition with the blessings of God's providence (that is, luck). Earlier New England Puritans had maintained a belief in society as a hierarchy in which each man would hold his place, but Mather's account of Phips, stressing strongly his constant secular advancement, made the Elizabethans' Great Chain of Being into a multi-runged ladder. Mather treated Phips's ambition (a trait so often cried against in the jeremiads) without any embarrassment. Referring to his simple beginnings, he did not hide the fact that from an early date Phips had "an unaccountable impulse on his mind . . . that he was born to great matters," and suggested that if we were to search history for a parallel life, we might settle on the great Pisarro[!], an implicit recognition that no biblical type had foreshadowed the arrival of William Phips.[17] Even after his rise to prominence, Phips "would speak of his own low beginnings with as much freedom and frequency as if he had been afraid of having it forgotten" (1:199). Cited as evidence of pride in his humble origins, this might more easily be understood as the words of someone boasting (a bit self-consciously) of his remarkable luck, the same ambitious but insecure man who, even after his favorable marriage, yearned for more recognition. He would "frequently tell the gentlewoman his Wife that he should yet be a Captain of a King's ship . . . and that he should be owner of a fair brick-house in the Green-Lane of North Boston" (1:153). A Silas Lapham of the seventeenth century, he is in several places described by Mather as "of an enterprising genius" and of "the Dutch spirit." "He was of an inclination, cutting rather like a hatchet, than a razor."[18]

Some ambition might be excused in one who was conscientiously seeking his Christian calling, but how could Mather sanction the manner in which

---

17. Mather, *Magnalia* (1820 ed.), 1:153. All further citations in text are to this edition.
18. *Magnalia*, 1:154. These character traits might partially explain his inability to manipulate the Boston political factions.

Phips's financial security had been established? In a world marked by the rapid gains and losses indicative of a developing economy, Mather had come to the point where he understood treasure-hunting to be a commendable enterprise for the aspiring Christian.[19] He did not inveigh against the sinful folly of a man's seeking filthy Spanish lucre off the West Indian islands but rather stressed Phips's *diligence* in the enterprise and God's bountiful goodness in granting him success. He pointed to the man's long *patience* in attempting three voyages before having any success and then, reflecting on Phips's offering the king his rightful share of the booty, grandly proclaimed that we might call Phips, "if we please, the knight of honesty, for it was honesty with industry that raised him" (1:158). The ghosts of John Cotton and Richard Mather must have paled when their grandson allowed such a man into his church as a full member, but Cotton Mather knew that in the overturned world of his Boston, Phips emerged as one of the more respectable individuals. Others might have pirated *all* the treasure. Phips, diligent in his peculiar calling (and perhaps anticipating some reward for his "honest labors") at least had shared the profits.

In Mather's narrative Phips emerges as a man of action and decision, one who allowed nothing to sway him from his established plan. Dwelling at length on Phips's military exploits, Mather continued a theme he had initiated in his account of Phips's suppression of an attempted mutiny on one of his Caribbean voyages. His subject had an almost monomaniacal dedication of purpose which in this last case manifested itself by his rushing upon the mutineers and "with the blows of his bare hands" felling "many of them" and thus quelling "all the rest" so that the voyage could continue (1:154). It is indisputable that in military affairs he similarly applied his energies. Witness his remarkable success at Port Royal and the fact that once the dream of defeating the rest of the French Canadian forces came to his mind "it lay down with him, it rose up with him, it engrossed almost all his thoughts" (1:178). The same dedication urged his decision to press the attack on Quebec after the encouraging victory in Nova Scotia. What becomes apparent in these extended military narratives is that Phips was a new type of military leader. The wars fought against the French and Indians were not at all the battles of the Lord chronicled in the accounts of William

---

19. For discussions of the changing social order in late seventeenth-century New England, see Bernard Bailyn, *The New England Merchants in the Seventeenth Century* (Cambridge: Harvard University Press, 1955); and James Henretta, "Economic Development and Social Structure in Colonial Boston," *William and Mary Quarterly*, 3d ser., 22 (1965): 75–92.

Hubbard and Increase Mather.[20] Phips's motivations were based on his ambition to control the *economy* of the northern frontier. When we learn that after the defeat by Frontenac, Phips "underwent a very mortifying disappointment of design, which his mind was, as much as ever, set upon," we should realize that more than a fear of Papist emissaries disturbed his rest: the blow to his expansive ego (as well as to his vision of the fortune to be made from the fur trade and naval stores) prompted his repeated assaults on the French empire (1:172).

Personal motivations aside, Phips undoubtedly was a brave and dedicated soldier who secured the colonists' position in present-day New Hampshire and Maine. His military achievements accounted for a large part of his initial popularity, especially with those who had become more attuned to the things of this world and had recognized the value of the extended northern border he had established. Mather grasped the true import of Phips's hold over popular opinion when he suggested that Phips's military prowess stemmed from "a vast courage, which was always in him to a degree heroical," and to which his professed Christianity added the supposed attribute of virtue (1:198). It is not too much to suggest that Phips was one of the first men in New England's history to emerge in this new heroic capacity. As a man who understood their frontier mentality he maintained an affectionate kinship with the common people and was in turn held in highest regard by those who appreciated his remarkable success.[21] It was more than political manipulation that made him "after his return to his country in his greatness one day make a splendid feast for the ship-carpenters of Boston (1:199). Part of Phips's heroic style was "to study to have his meannesses remembered" even as he assumed the highest position in the province, and it was only the proto-Brahmin stock who refused to acknowledge the symbolic importance he had attained. Unfortunately for Phips, they had enough power to get him recalled to London where for once Dame Fortune failed him.

---

20. See William Hubbard, *A Narrative of the Troubles with the Indians in New England* (Boston, 1677) and Increase Mather, *A Brief History of the War with the Indians in New England* (Boston, 1676).

21. Richard Slotkin, *Regeneration Through Violence: The Mythology of the American Frontier, 1600–1860* (Middletown: Wesleyan University Press, 1973) is the best text with which to investigate the conception of the hero in early American literature. Slotkin has much to say about the emergence of a frontier character who embodies many of the attributes of the wilderness and the Indians and who returns to civilization to use his newly acquired experiences within the context of society.

Ambition, diligence in worldly affairs, military courage and an endearing manner with the lower classes—these were the qualities that contributed to what Mather saw as Phips's most commendable virtue: his patriotism. If any one idea informs the structure of this narrative it is what Mather calls Phips's "love for his country"; in Mather's eyes this patriotism legitimized all the shortcomings that might have condemned other individuals. He admitted that Phips had his detractors "as every raised and useful person must have," but finally each of them would have to confess "that according to the best of his apprehension [Phips] ever sought the good of his country" (1:184). Mindful of his dual audience of Englishmen as well as Americans, Mather took care to add that Phips always "minded the preservation of the King's rights with as careful and faithful a zeal as became a good Steward of the Crown," but from the contemporary evidence (especially his laxity in enforcing the Navigation Acts if a bribe fell his way) this addendum was mere lip service paid to royal prerogative (1:184). Phips was a respectable Englishman when his personal goals coincided with benefit for the Crown, but his main allegiance remained to the benefit he could derive from and for America. Mather was more accurate when he boasted that Phips was a "governour who might call New England his own country, and who was above most men in it, full of affection to the interests of it" (1:183).

Mather referred to Phips's dedication to New England whenever he had to explain the man's embarrassing excesses. He could claim, for example, that Phips's overruling ambition was perfectly justifiable because it channeled his massive energies into the service of his native land. As long as his yearnings for fame and success were linked to military expeditions for the good of the colony, or to actions that strengthened the colonists' position vis-à-vis London, they could hardly be considered sinful. Therefore Mather could harshly remind some ungrateful New Englanders that it was their great fault "no more to value a person, whose opportunities to serve all their interests, though very eminent, yet were not so eminent as his inclinations" (1:205). He made no attempt to conceal the fact that "in his own country of New England" Phips "met with provocations that were enough to have alienated any men living . . . from the service of it," but then admiringly added that rather than striking viciously against his native land, Phips "studied another way to revenge himself upon his country, and that was to serve it in all its interests, with all of his, even with his estate, his time, his care, his friends, and his very life" (1:159). The implication was clear; by refusing to acknowledge the blessing that he was to the interests of their country, Phips's detractors laid themselves open to the charge that their loyalty simply was not so strong as his. The standard for the measurement of this new quality would henceforth be the late governor, and it became another sign of the degeneracy of the times that "the blessing which the country had in his indefatigable zeal, to serve the publick in all its interests, was not so valued as it should have been" (1:201). The New Englanders' failure to appreciate the man who (by any standards but Mather's) exemplified the sins named in the jeremiads became a further sign of their continuing apostasy.

Phips may have been underappreciated because some colonists doubted the questionable standards by which he was to be judged. Or perhaps his enemies knew him too well and realized that Phips's affection for the interests of his country were motivated mainly by self-interest, and that he appreciated America only insofar as it was profitable either to his ego or his purse. The point remained that Mather could praise this incipient American in such a way that the attention he bestowed on New England superseded the level of his religious dedication in marking him as a good ruler. It was not so much that the magistrate had to be ruled by moderation but that his ambitions should coincide with the good of the country. The crisis over the loss of their charter and the experience with the arbitrary Dominion of New England had refocused some of the colonists' attention so that the good magistrate would thenceforth be evaluated not so much with regard to his position as a God-fearing Puritan as by his sense of being an American Englishman. The ship of state began to claim some of the attention hitherto reserved for the rock of the church, enabling Mather to sing Phips's praise in such doggerel lines: "Write now his epitaph, 'twill be thine own, / Let it be *this*, A PUBLICK SPIRIT'S GONE."

Perry Miller noted that after Phips "the governorship was forseeably bound to degenerate from the pinnacle of ultimate adjudication into merely administrative office, and so to lie at the mercy of conflicting interests."[22] The harsh assessment is true, but it is to be recalled that judged through Mather's eyes Phips, for all his ineptitude and corruption, had served his purpose. Compelled to defend Phips's career because of his father's choice of the man as governor, Mather, searching deeply to locate Phips's particular virtues, had to settle for patriotism rather than piety when he came to tell his romantic story. Of the same generation as Mather, Phips stood for a

---

22. Perry Miller, *The New England Mind: From Colony to Province* (Cambridge: Harvard University Press, 1953), 209.

new order in New England. To ensure that his own base of power remained sufficiently attractive, Mather had to join forces with the likes of Phips. His long struggle to convince his readers (and himself) of Phips's grandeur is more than an attempt, imputed to him by Robert Calef, to screen his part in the witchcraft episode. It was no less than a struggle to legitimize a new standard of virtuous leadership and thus to convince people that New England's clergy were still taking their communities to the New Jerusalem. In the Connecticut River Valley another man of heroic stature was establishing in his own way another such territorial commitment. Solomon Stoddard's open communions, and later his revivalistic preaching, were other signs that the old standards of exclusiveness were being replaced by a new community involvement. Lacking the ecclesiastical power of Stoddard, Cotton Mather had to unite his people around a different standard, that of patriotism, of which the late Governor Phips became the exemplar.[23]

If we accept Mather's characterization of Phips as a new American model, we must also realize that the New England magistrate had been defined anew. Ambition could now be sanctioned as long as the subject still pursued the public interest. This was a new kind of stewardship, one that allowed a man to be concerned with the things of this world as long as some of his profits were returned to American soil. It was the beginning of an interesting experiment, one that would bear violently beautiful fruit in later years. With these thoughts before us it should be found perfectly fitting that Phips the American should die with one vision in mind. Even as he awaited prosecution in England, his thoughts returned to the sunken wrecks where he had first made his fortune. He believed that "the Spanish wreck where he had made his first good voyage, was not the only, nor the richest wreck, that he knew to be lying under water" (1:203). This was the man whom Mather had praised so elegantly. The true New England saints had died with different visions before them, but that was, indeed, in another country.

---

23. Robert Pope, *The Half-Way Covenant* (Princeton: Princeton University Press, 1969) is the best study of the background leading to the adoption of less rigorous church admission procedures in the late seventeenth century. On the idea of the "territorial" church, see Perry Miller, "The Half-Way Covenant," *New England Quarterly* 6 (1933): 676–715, and "Solomon Stoddard," *Harvard Theological Review* 34 (1941): 277–320. Both Mather and Stoddard were grappling with the fact that they had to rally people around new standards if they themselves were to remain in power. By allowing all visibly holy members to take communion, Stoddard began to build the idea that the church was a national body to which all people belonged by right. I find it suggestive that at the same time Mather was stressing service to a similar ideal, albeit a more blatantly political one.

4 | Solomon Stoddard's Irreverent Way

This essay constitutes another part of my reconstruction of the intellectual life of the Connecticut River Valley in the seventeenth and early eighteenth centuries. Ever since reading Perry Miller's engaging assessments of Stoddard, in *From Colony to Province* (1953) and elsewhere, I had toyed with the idea of working extensively on this man alone. Indeed, Stoddard still lacks a biographer who has done justice to the complexity of his engagement not only with New England Puritanism as expressed by the Boston-area clergy but with Reformed Protestantism in general. To appreciate Stoddard's mind, one has only to read Jonathan Edwards's appreciation of the intellectual and spiritual achievements of his grandfather, and then to realize that his mental toughness was matched by a willingness constantly to test his ideas against the hard facts of experience. For this reason, as much as for his connection to the "River Gods," Stoddard's was a hard act to follow.

I found most striking in Stoddard his broadside attacks on the filiopietism of so many of his contemporaries and thus focus on that subject. Like Cotton Mather in his *Life of Phips,* Stoddard, too, frequently announced his entry into the Enlightenment, in his case through a willingness to test ideas against the demands of the present moment, not simply to impose its ideas on them. His was, in other words, an interesting and early example of what came to be called "pragmatism" in American thought, although in no sense do I claim that such an attitude toward the world originated either with him or in America. But Stoddard's courage in calling things the way he saw them, especially when the Mathers seemed bent on dressing Puritanism in the emperor's new clothes, was admirable, and worth considering when we note the shape of his grandson's career. Edwards, too, was smart enough to know that occasionally one erred and had to change his mind, a humility not running in the Mathers' genes. Edwards learned that lesson, like so many others, from his predecessor in the Northampton pulpit.

This essay, too, should be considered in light of my engagement with the ideological critics' characterization of the hegemony of New England Puritanism, for to bring Stoddard into the picture is to complicate our notions of New England's third generation. As much as these people were obsessed with a tribal past, they also were beginning to understand that each day brought to them the necessity of careful and honest reevaluation of what they hitherto had taken for granted, a lesson that would hold them in good stead as they moved closer to the pivotal decade of the 1760s. Thus, though usually remembered for his contribution to American evangelicalism, Stoddard, like his contemporary John Wise, also has something to teach us about the sacred cause of liberty, particularly how to judge its demands on one's soul.

In the last decade scholars of American Puritanism have made a concerted effort to place Solomon Stoddard in New England's religious history, but by focusing so intently on the details of his ecclesiology they have lost the proverbial forest in the trees. There is no denying that Stoddard's various ecclesiastical innovations—his sponsorship of "open" communion and an "Instituted Church" the best known—are important to New England religious development.[1] But an equally significant, and enduring, achievement lay in his challenge to the rhetorical strategy through which many of his contemporaries, most notably Increase and Cotton Mather, sought to

---

1. The first important essay on Stoddard was Perry Miller's "Solomon Stoddard, 1643–1679," *Harvard Theological Review* 34 (1941): 277–320, which he later incorporated into *The New England Mind: From Colony to Province* (Cambridge: Harvard University Press, 1953). Among the most important recent assessments are Paul R. Lucas's " 'An Appeal to the Learned': The Mind of Solomon Stoddard," *William and Mary Quarterly*, 3d ser., 30 (1973): 257–97, and his *Valley of Discord: Church and Society Along the Connecticut River, 1636–1725* (Hanover, N.H.: University Press of New England, 1976), chaps. 9 and 10; Thomas Schafer's "Solomon Stoddard and the Theology of the Revival," in *A Miscellany of American Christianity: Essays in Honor of H. Shelton Smith*, ed. Stuart C. Henry (Durham: Duke University Press, 1963); and E. Brooks Holifield's "The Intellectual Sources of Stoddardeanism," *New England Quarterly* 45 (1977): 373–92.

mask their own appropriation and redirection of New England history. While such individuals trumpeted praise for the ecclesiastical order established by their predecessors (even as they irrevocably changed it), Stoddard forced his generation to acknowledge openly that New England's first settlers, for all their wisdom, were not infallible and that neither they, their ecclesiology, nor its contemporary defenders should be treated as such.[2]

As the celebration of New England's past reached a crescendo in Cotton Mather's *Magnalia Christi Americana* (1702), Stoddard openly and consistently attacked such hagiography as a smokescreen behind which many of his countrymen, the rank and file as well as the colony's leaders, played an elaborate sleight of hand with true Protestant principles. This is not to say that Stoddard was a stubborn and virulent antitraditionalist; as much as the next man he respected the piety of New England's spiritual forebears. But like his older contemporary William Hubbard, who in the 1680s had noted that with regard to their church way the early Massachusetts settlers had "walked something of an untrodden path" and were joined together in worship more by "some general profession of the doctrine of the Gospel" than by any wide-ranging consent to a preestablished set of principles, Stoddard understood that there was nothing inherently sacrosanct in the New England Way.[3]

"Experience best fits men to teach others," he counseled young ministers in 1723.[4] Fifty years of experience in the Connecticut River Valley had taught him that ecclesiastical reform, when necessary, would only come about through open recognition that New England Puritanism, be it in 1630 or 1680, never had coincided with God's true intentions for His church. And his various attempts to act on this knowledge both display his central role as a critic of his contemporaries' misguided respect for their history and provide more evidence that, as Stephen Foster recently has written, Puritanism never remained a "fixed state of affairs" but rather was "a volatile synthesis of potentially contradictory impulses kept in equilibrium only by regular shifts in the balance between them."[5]

---

2. Recently Karl Keller has discussed what he terms Stoddard's systematic "co-optation" of earlier ecclesiastical and doctrinal principles for his own purposes; Keller's stimulating essay directly complements what I say in the following pages. See his "The Large, Loose Principles of Solomon Stoddard," *Early American Literature* 16 (1981): 27–41.

3. William Hubbard, *A General History of New England, from the Discovery to MDCLXXX* (Cambridge, Mass.: Hilliard and Metcalf, 1815), 181–82.

4. Stoddard, *The Defects of Preachers Reproved* (Boston, 1724), 9.

5. Stephen Foster, "New England and the Challenge of Heresy, 1630–1660: The Puritan Crisis in Transatlantic Perspective," *William and Mary Quarterly*, 3d ser., 38 (1981): 660.

Historians long have recognized that from the Massachusetts Bay Puritans' arrival in the New World they continually modified their errand into the wilderness, all the while believing that they were preserving its basic integrity. In reality, however, they extended it in ways which, with the blessing of hindsight, we can see as inconsistent with, if not directly contradictory to, their original design for a Bible commonwealth. Their battles with Anne Hutchinson and her supporters during the Antinomian Controversy, their continuing difficulties with the various Rhode Island radicals, their virtual acquiescence to presbyterian innovations in the colony of Connecticut—these factors and others inexorably moved the Bay Puritans to the Synods of 1637, 1648, 1657, and 1662, the most obvious times at which they reaffirmed what they regarded as the basic principles of their church way. After the Synod of 1662 failed to gain the wholehearted endorsement of the laity, the intellectual scrambling of the clergy—particularly of Richard Mather and Jonathan Mitchel—displayed the innovators' growing struggle to keep themselves aligned with the beliefs of their wise and holy ancestors.[6]

Apologists for the Half-Way Covenant gained an important convert in 1671, when Increase Mather, initially an opponent of the results of the Synod, brought his intellectual weight to their side. In that year he dated his preface to *The First Principles of New England,* a collection of writings from the founding fathers which proved that the "new" terms of baptism were *"no Apostasy from the First Principles of* New England, *nor yet any declension from the* Congregational way."[7] This work, and his own able apology for the Synod, *A Discourse concerning the Subject of Baptisme* (1675), joined such works as Mitchel's preface to the Synod's results, John Allin's *Animadversions upon the Antisynodalia Americana* (1664), Richard Mather's *A Defence of the Answer and Arguments of the Synod* (1664), and Mather's and Mitchel's edition of Thomas Shepard's manuscript, *The Church-Membership of Children* (1663), in sealing the testament of the Synod's purported orthodoxy. Increase Mather's belated embrace of the Half-Way Covenant provided its supporters with even more reason to believe that the mantle of the founding fathers still rested on their shoulders.

6. See, for example, my *A Glimpse of Sion's Glory: Puritan Radicalism in New England, 1620–1660* (Middletown: Wesleyan University Press, 1984), chaps. 9 and 10, and Lucas, *Valley of Discord,* passim; also relevant are Robert G. Pope, *The Half-Way Covenant: Church Membership in Puritan New England* (Princeton: Princeton University Press, 1969), 132–84, and Emory Elliott, *Power and the Pulpit in Puritan New England* (Princeton: Princeton University Press, 1975), 43–52.

7. Increase Mather, *The First Principles of New England* (Cambridge, Mass., 1671), a4v.

After the 1670s most ministers fell in line behind the Mathers, stifling lay objections to the Half-Way Covenant and presenting themselves to their congregations as defenders of the faith delivered to the first generation of New England saints. But at this same time from his isolation in western Massachusetts Stoddard began to question the wisdom not only of the precepts affirmed in 1662, but also of those that initially had defined New England's errand into the wilderness. Called to Northampton in 1672 upon the death of the Reverend Eleazer Mather, whose widow he promptly married, Stoddard discovered a congregation eager to practice the principles of the Half-Way Covenant, a desire hitherto stymied by the recalcitrance of Mather, who, unlike his brother, had never accepted the results of the Synod.[8] Stoddard immediately instituted broadened criteria for admission to baptismal privileges. But, not satisfied that complicated distinctions among church members were at all scriptural or, for that matter, expedient, in 1677 he abruptly stopped entering into the church record book an individual's particular membership status. More surprisingly, he soon allowed any church member to approach the Lord's Table, regardless of whether or not he had offered an account of the nature of saving grace on his soul, a requirement reaffirmed at the Synod of 1662. By 1690 he had openly declared the Lord's Supper a converting ordinance and claimed that as such it should be administered to any people who sought it, as long as they were blameless in their outward behavior.[9]

Such innovations certainly were not part of the bargain struck in 1662, and Increase Mather, after Mitchel's death in 1668 the unchallenged intellectual leader of the colony, quickly administered a sanctimonious rebuke. In 1677, when he preached his *Discourse Concerning the Danger of Apostasy* to the Massachusetts General Court, he pointedly expressed his wish that "there be not Teachers in our Israel, that have espoused loose, Large Principles here, Designing to bring all Persons to the Lord's Supper, who have an Historical Faith, and are not Scandalous in Life, altho' they never had Experience of a work of Regeneration on their Souls." He also stepped off the intellectual territory on which he and Stoddard later would battle by reminding the general court that whoever betrayed what "our

---

8. Philip F. Gura, "Preparing the Way for Stoddard: Eleazer Mather's *Serious Exhortation* to Northampton," *New England Quarterly* 57 (1984): passim.

9. The best biographical account of Stoddard's career is Miller's "Stoddard." The shifts of emphasis in Stoddard's ecclesiastical positions are best studied in Lucas, "Mind" and Thomas M. Davis and Virginia L. Davis, eds. *Edward Taylor vs. Solomon Stoddard: The Nature of the Lord's Supper* (Boston: G. K. Hall, 1981), 1–58.

Fathers have taught concerning this matter" and neglected that "which they did with much cost and pains, dig out of the Rich veins of the Scripture," necessarily should be excoriated.[10]

Where Mather got his information about Stoddard is still open to conjecture, though it most likely was from John Russell of Hadley, a longtime opponent of the Half-Way Covenant who in 1681 complained to Increase that "our good Brother Stoddard hath bin strenuously promoting his position concerning that right which persons sound in the doctrine of faith, & of (as he calls it) a Holy Conversation, have to full Com[m]union." To Russell and other conservative clergy in the valley (particularly Westfield's Edward Taylor), the evil tendency of Stoddard's innovations was evident, for "upon the admission of those to full Com[m]union what discipline shall we have or can we expect[?]" Taunting Mather to recall his turnaround on the Synod's results, Russell added that he took "the great care of that matter (if any things be doable in it, which I utterly despaire of) to be upon your selfe."[11] By the time of Russell's letter Increase already had tangled with Stoddard concerning the terms of communion, at the so-called Reforming Synod of 1679, but Stoddard's public victory there had hardly satisfied him.[12] His experience in the Connecticut Valley had taught him that there was much more to be done to aid Christ's cause, but in ways men like the Mathers never could accept.

For nearly a decade following the Reforming Synod Stoddard remained silent about the rationale for his various ecclesiastical innovations. But in 1687, with the weight of two spiritual harvests behind him, he published *The Safety of Appearing at the Day of Judgment in the Righteousness of Christ* and therein seized the opportunity to explain his evangelical suc-

---

10. Increase Mather, *Discourse Concerning the Danger of Apostasy* (Boston, 1679), 14–16.

11. John Russell, "Letter to Increase Mather, 28 March 1681," in *Massachusetts Historical Society, Collections*, 4th ser., 8 (1868): 82–84. For many years Russell was a staunch opponent of the Half-Way Covenant and probably never forgave Increase for his defection to the other side. In this same letter Russell announced to him that "it now stands them in hand, who were of the Synod of 62, to looke to the maintaining of that defense which they p[re]pared in their 4th Proposition for the securing of the Ch[urche]s: from pollutions by unp[re]pared ones incroching upon full Communion in the Lord's Supper & voting." In the fourth proposition the Synod prohibited half-way members from further privileges until they had given a narration of the effects of saving grace upon their souls.

12. Solomon Stoddard, *An Appeal to the Learned* (Boston, 1709), 93–94; Williston Walker, *The Creeds and Platforms of Congregationalism* (1893; repr. Boston: Pilgrim Press, 1960), 419.

cesses. "I have made it my business to gain souls to Christ," he explained in his preface, and his labors toward that end had been rewarded because he had "principally insist[ed] upon such things as have reached the heart of Religion," that is, upon doctrine solidly based in Scripture. In this book Stoddard primarily intended "to clear up the way of Salvation by Christ" and also served notice to the Mathers, who since John Russell's reports had eyed the valley with growing apprehension, that he would "meddle not with those false Doctrines that have been invented by men, in opposition to the truth." A true worker in Christ's vineyard did not wish to gather more power and authority to himself at the expense of true Christian principles, particularly when the former came through a specious reading of the past; as evidence of the efficacy of Stoddard's way, the Lord had kept the church of Northampton sound in faith. In the valley, Stoddard pointed out, ministers did not have to "spend their time in the confutation of such erroneous Opinions" as occupied clergymen in the eastern part of the colony.[13]

As long as Stoddard's ideas were restricted to the valley the Mathers could treat them as aberrations, but with the publication of *The Safety of Appearing*, in which Stoddard urged men to become church members even if they had not yet felt a convincing work of the spirit upon their souls, he marched on the Mathers' home territory, an advance that by the early 1700s became a full-scale attack. Already deeply suspicious of his new relative, Increase had haughtily refused to supply a preface to Stoddard's book, and in the place of Mather's words Stoddard penned his own, explaining to his Northampton church why the example of their piety should be made more visible. Good son of New England that he was, Stoddard noted that his "care" was not "confined" to them alone, for he owed "a regard to the prosperity of other places" as well. If this "small Treatise" is blessed with any success, he continued, it "will be [for] the great security of the Colony against the degeneracy that is begun, and

13. Solomon Stoddard, *The Safety of Appearing at the Day of Judgment in the Righteousness of Christ* (1687; repr. Boston, 1729), ii–iii. All this time, however, Stoddard continued to proselytize for his innovations; see Coffmann, *Stoddard*, chap. 2, and John Russell's letter, above. During these years Stoddard was embroiled in controversy with Edward Taylor, minister to neighboring Westfield. See, for example, Davis and Davis, eds., *Edward Taylor vs. Solomon Stoddard*, introduction; Edward Taylor, *Treatise Concerning the Lord's Supper*, ed. Norman S. Grabo (East Lansing: Michigan State University Press, 1966), iv–xlvii; Taylor, *Christographia*, ed. Norman S. Grabo (New Haven: Yale University Press, 1962), xi–xliv; and David L. Parker, "Edward Taylor's Preparationism: A New Perspective on the Taylor–Stoddard Controversy, *Early American Literature* 9 (1976–77): 259–78.

against those superstitious practices that are entertained in other professing places."[14]

For a decade after the publication of *The Safety of Appearing*, Stoddard again held his tongue, but between 1700 and 1710 he searchingly challenged the image of New England's churches presented in such hagiographic works as Cotton Mather's *Magnalia*. Not satisfied with the evangelical results that followed his allowing all church members to come to the sacrament or, after 1690, his declaration that the Lord's Supper was a converting ordinance, in 1700 Stoddard stirred a viper's nest with the publication of *The Doctrine of Instituted Churches*, a pamphlet so critical of the New England Way that supposedly no Boston printer would publish it. Therein Stoddard rejected the long-standing notion that New England's ecclesiastical system should follow the model of the New Testament churches; instead, he reached back into the Old Testament to reaffirm the efficacy of the Instituted Church, a catholic, sacramental institution that offered man the promises of the Gospel through such ordinances as baptism, preaching, discipline, and the Lord's Supper.[15]

In this doctrinal position-paper Stoddard wryly noted that "in these latter Ages" the nature of church ordinances had been a "matter of great Inquiry," and, as he could testify, all too commonly such inquiries were accompanied by "great Animosities, Discords, and Persecutions." More disturbing, particularly to a man whose life had been devoted to the care and comfort of souls, "Multitudes of People" now were "left at a loss whether there be any certain Rule to Guide" them or even "any certainty to be attained in these Things."[16] Stoddard here recognized what some historians only recently have acknowledged, that the laity themselves, confused by clerical bickering, willfully abstained from the Lord's Supper from fear of profaning that sacrament; to remedy this sad situation he proposed an ecclesiastical reorganization centered on the Instituted Church. Further, ministers like the Mathers only compounded the first generation's errors and engendered more confusion by maintaining that the New Testament offered the only sure guide to church government. Stoddard wanted them to understand that "the Nature of a Church is the same under both Testaments," for "a Church is not one kind of thing in the Old Testament and another in the New." Yet most of these individuals would not acknowl-

14. Stoddard, *Safety of Appearing*, iii–iv.
15. Lucas, "Mind," 261–63.
16. Solomon Stoddard, *The Doctrine of Instituted Churches* (London, 1700), 1.

edge this fact because they had become so "exceeding Tenacious of the Traditions and Ancient Usages of the Church, not considering how dismal a Corruption and Degeneracy did in a little time prevail."[17]

Stoddard told his readers that New England's problems stemmed from an embarrassing misunderstanding by the colony's founders, who in the eyes of their literal and spiritual descendants could have done no wrong. It has come to pass, he continued, that "those things are obtruded upon us as Rules, which were the Blemishes and Errors of the Ancient Church."[18] Moreover, New England's clergy had enshrined some practices that had no relation to the words of Scripture. For example, the notion of individual covenants sworn by members of each congregation, instituted at the time of the Antinomian Controversy, was patently unscriptural. "We read of no such particular Covenant in the New Testament, we have no precept for it, we have no president [sic] for it," Stoddard declared. "There is no Syllable in the Word of God, intimating any such thing, neither is there any need of it." In this matter and others, too many of Stoddard's contemporaries displayed an obsessive "Veneration for antiquity and adopt[ed] the sayings of the Ancient Fathers as Canonical"; but the truth was that the Puritans' slavish allegiance to congregationalism, which they traced back (mistakenly, Stoddard thought) to "the Children of Israels Covenanting with God," was in fact fatuous. "That Covenant of theirs is no other," he maintained, "than what all Christians do make, when they make a profession of Faith and Obedience." Thus, in the place of the congregational system, which was based on "too Lordly a principle," Stoddard encouraged the institution of a "National Church" in which the covenant was a "Publick" one "wherein [God] engages publick Prosperity" to all believers "upon condition of their obedience."[19]

The Doctrine of Instituted Churches proved even more threatening because of Stoddard's elaboration upon the qualifications for communion that followed from his understanding of the Instituted Church. By claiming

---

17. Stoddard, *Instituted Churches*, 3. Pope, *Half-Way Covenant*, 132–51, documents the laity's reluctance to practice the half-way measures. Before his study historians had assumed that the brethren wished to liberalize the membership requirements, but Pope suggests they were more concerned with maintaining the purity of traditional requirements. Also see his "New England versus the New England Mind: The Myth of Declension," *Journal of Social History* 3 (1969–70): 95–108, and Ross W. Beales, Jr., "The Half-Way Covenant and Religious Scrupulosity: The First Church of Dorchester, Massachusetts, as a Test Case," *William and Mary Quarterly*, 3d ser., 31 (1974): 465–79.

18. Stoddard, *Doctrine*, 1.

19. Ibid., 6–8.

that "all such Professors of the Christian Faith as are of blameless Conversation, and have knowledge to examine themselves and discern the Lords Body, are to be admitted to the Lord's Supper," he struck at the root of a distinction the Mathers and other keepers of the New England Puritan tradition had struggled to maintain.[20] Coming so soon after the ordination of the latitudinarian Benjamin Colman to the newly organized Brattle Street Church, *The Doctrine of Instituted Churches* had to be definitively refuted, for in its publication the Mathers discovered what they regarded as yet another part of an extensive plot to sully the purity of the church system they served as high priests.[21]

The Mathers' main rebuttal came swiftly and was continued in a series of publications that mark this decade as one of the stormiest of their careers. In such documents as Increase Mather's *The Order of the Gospel* (1700), the "Defence of Evangelical Churches" Cotton offered as a lengthy preface to his edition of John Quick's *The Young Man's Claim* (1700), and Increase's *A Dissertation, Wherein the Strange Doctrine Lately Published ... Is Examined and Confuted* (1708), they attempted to call back Stoddard and, they believed, the whole Connecticut Valley, from an apostasy that threatened New England's special relationship to Jehovah. But through this decade Stoddard, encouraged by the fact that the Mathers, for all their noise, were progressively losing control over the political and ecclesiastical affairs of Massachusetts, continued to espouse an external covenant that guaranteed all church members access to the church's ordinances.

His responses to the Mathers were hardly moderate. Not surprisingly, he focused on his opponents' excessive and misplaced respect for the colony's first-generation leaders, noting that what had "been counted lawful or duty by our Fore-fathers" too often was accorded sacrosanct authority.[22] "In managing Controversies in Religion," he maintained, "there are two usual Artifices that frequently prove traps to catch the injudicious Multitude." One, which his opponents might be said to have patented, was to "insinuate that the impleaded Opinion is contrary to Purity and Holiness[,] a way to corrupt the Churches and usher in degeneracy." Hereby, he continued, "many men of Tender Consciences are startled, as if there were a Snake in the Grass." The other manner of argument was closely related, "a magnify-

20. Ibid., 18.
21. Perry Miller, *From Colony to Province*, 240–55.
22. Solomon Stoddard, *The Necessity of Acknowledgment of Known Offenses* (Boston, 1710), 17.

ing of such Authors, as do discountenance, or seem to discountenance that Opinion, as if they were but one degree beneath the Apostles." But when Mather argued in this manner, Stoddard told his readers, his "Passionate Lamentations" served only "to swell the Book and make it more in bulk, but not in weight."[23]

Even as Stoddard pilloried the Mathers' and others' excessive veneration of the past, though, he made it clear that he did not reject all the lessons of his predecessors: his quarrel was not so much with New England's errand as with its perversion by those who could read the lessons neither of Scripture nor of history. "It may possibly be a fault and an aggravation of a fault, to depart from the ways of our Fathers," he said in 1708, but "it may also be a vertue, and an eminent act of Obedience to depart from them in some things." Hearing the shrill cries of the Mathers as paranoid attempts to draw attention to their own connections to the New England tradition and so to reestablish some basis for their eroded authority, Stoddard reminded his readers that "we may see cause to alter some practices of our Fathers, without despising of them, without priding ourselves in our own Wisdom, without Apostasy, without abusing the advantages that God has given us, without a spirit of compliance with corrupt men, without inclinations to Superstition, without making disturbance in the Church of God." The key to progress toward God's kingdom was judicious examination of one's religious inheritance and a redirection of faith the better to align the church with the seemingly distant logic of the Gospel plan. Let our ancestors "have as high a character as belongs to them," Stoddard urged, but do not "look upon their principles as Oracles." If the practices of our Fathers in any particular were mistakes," he concluded, "it is fit they should be rejected."[24] The New Jerusalem was not to be realized through the worship of golden calves, even if they were called by such names as Mather, Shepard, and Cotton.

By 1710 Stoddard had stopped sparring with the Mathers. To be sure, even within the valley he had not won many converts to the idea of the Instituted Church; and, true to his own respect for the lessons of experience, in the next decade he acknowledged his failure by switching his support to a presbyterial system similar to that formalized in Connecticut by the

23. Solomon Stoddard, *An Appeal to the Learned* (Boston, 1709), A7r and v.
24. Solomon Stoddard, *The Inexcusableness of Neglecting the Worship of God* (Boston, 1708), ii–iii.

Saybrook Platform of 1708, and by encouraging evangelical preaching among his younger colleagues.[25] But before he settled firmly into his role as patriarch of the Hampshire Association, under whose structure the valley would finally be prepared for the spiritual harvests of the 1730s and 1740s, he allowed himself one more attack on New England congregationalism, particularly on its basis in what he considered the specious authority of New England's Golden Age. The publication in 1718 of his sermon *The Presence of Christ,* preached at Joseph Willard's ordination at a new town in the valley, gave him the opportunity to append *An Examination of the Power of the Fraternity,* a sharp attack on the powers hoarded and abused by the laity themselves through their own stubborn adherence to the principles of the Cambridge Platform.

The occasion for this last venting of Stoddard's spleen was a controversy in the Enfield church, where for at least four years the congregation had been quarreling with their minister, Nathaniel Collins, and finally had tried to prevent his administration of the Lord's Supper. Twice the Hampshire Association, created to arbitrate just such cases, urged an amicable settlement to the difficulties, but the congregation persisted in their animosity toward Collins. In 1724 the association finally concurred in his dismissal; but in 1718 Stoddard, who throughout his career had considered and reconsidered the premises and obligations of the church covenant, found the town's behavior so outrageous that once again he turned his pen to an attack on the traditions through which such behavior was sanctioned.[26] "The mistakes of one Generation," Stoddard proclaimed, "many times become the calamity of succeeding Generations," and his own contemporaries, "unhappy by reason of the darkness of their minds," only increased their confusion by their misguided respect for what they took to be the autonomy of each congregation. "Posterity," he continued, "is very prone to espouse the principles of Ancestors, and form an inordinate Veneration of them, [to] apprehend a sacredness in their Opinions, and don't give themselves the trouble to make an impartial Examination of them, as if it were a transgression to call them into question, and bordered upon Irreligion to be wavering about them." Furthermore, people like those in Enfield who refused the advice of ministerial associations were not only smallminded about the necessity for reformation but also blatantly selfish. Their

---

25. See Lucas, "Mind," 238–42; Schafer, "Stoddard," passim; and Gura, "Sowing for the Harvest: The Reverend William Williams and the Great Awakening," *Journal of Presbyterian History* 56 (1978): 328–35.

26. Coffman, *Stoddard,* 152–53, 160–63; Lucas, "Mind," 285–88.

"carnal interests" have "no small influence upon them," Stoddard noted, "to prevail with them to engage violently in the Vindication" of their ill-formed opinions.[27]

Stoddard's argument reveals much about the widening cleavages within the valley, for as he knew from personal experience, "if any particular Persons have been led by God into the understanding of those mistakes" made by their ancestors and "have made their differing Sentiments Publick, it has proved an occasion of much Sorrow." Anticipating his grandson Jonathan Edwards's later descriptions of the animosity in the valley, Stoddard lamented that "many People have fallen into Parties, whereby a Spirit of Love has been quenched, and great heats have risen."[28] But to his credit, if here he was thinking of the strong reactions to his own arraignment of New England's past (the letters to him from Westfield's Edward Taylor immediately come to mind) he did not become merely self-serving.[29] In his *Examination* he focused on two "eminent instances" of such bitterness in the earlier history of Protestantism.

The first had occurred when Englishmen "cast off the Doctrines of Popery," for this initiated debates over the ceremonies of the church, which even in Stoddard's day were hotly debated in old England. But he was more interested in the second instance, which had occurred in New England itself, when "the first Planters drew up a Platform of Church Discipline, before they had much time to weigh [those] things" that were to determine the colony's subsequent ecclesiastical history. Stoddard knew to what lengths people went to defend the priority of tradition, as long as it served their own interests. Indeed, some colonists had become so "mightily devoted" to the Cambridge Platform that they regarded it as another "Pattern in the Mount." But if the founders of New England had indeed viewed their errand into the wilderness through such a typological comparison, it now was apparent to Stoddard that what they had taken as a type in fact was merely a trope. For his contemporaries to view it any other way stifled the "flourishing of religion."[30]

Throughout this brief essay Stoddard argued vigorously that the brethren themselves, and not the clergy (as the brethren had insisted), had become

27. Solomon Stoddard, *An Examination of the Power of the Fraternity*, in *The Presence of Christ* (Boston, 1718), 1.
28. Stoddard, *An Examination*, 1–2.
29. Norman Grabo, "The Poet to the Pope: Edward Taylor to Solomon Stoddard," *American Literature* 32 (1960): 197–201.
30. Stoddard, *An Examination*, 2–3.

the main stumbling block to the progress of Christ's legions. Jealously guarding the rules of the Cambridge Platform, church members sought to arrogate to themselves yet more power by resisting any attempts (like Stoddard's with the Instituted Church or the Hampshire Association's through its advice in the Enfield disciplinary case) at true Gospel reformation. "The Community," Stoddard declared, "are not men of Understanding," and "a crafty man may lead a Score of them by the Nose." They are "uncapable" of seeing "into an abstruse thing," and if "the government be put into their hands," things "will be carried headlong by a tumultuous cry." In New England, Stoddard reminded his audience, some attempts had been made "to prevent Corruption & promote Edification" by truly following scriptural rule, but the brethren publicly scorned the instigators of such reform. With this in mind he stiffly reminded his readers that it did not become men, no matter who they were, "to reflect upon the Wisdom of God, as if they had understanding to mend His Institutions."[31] By adhering so uncritically to the Cambridge Platform, with its unscriptural stress on the privileges of the fraternity, New England's saints from the first generation on had greatly dimmed the light of their city on a hill. The guidance of the churches had to be returned to men with enough wisdom and learning to discern what Scripture indicated to, and thus what God expected of, a professing people.

From 1718 on, the valley was shaped by just such powerful leaders, among them Stoddard himself, and William and John Williams, the oldest men in the Hampshire Association.[32] And as Thomas Schafer has noted, from this time on the ministers' stress on the word of the Gospel—a renewed emphasis on doctrine—resulted in increasing evangelical successes, beginning with Stoddard's fifth and final "harvest" the same year that he issued *An Examination of the Power of the Fraternity*.[33] Thus by the time John Williams preached Edwards's ordination sermon in 1727, Stoddard's new "way" had been established throughout the valley and down through Connecticut, to such towns as Norwich, which itself experienced a powerful revival in the 1720s. To be sure, it would take until 1735 for Stoddard's successor to establish his reputation as a man whose gifts were comparable to his esteemed grandfather's, but from the moment of Stoddard's death in 1729 Edwards knew how important the lessons of that man's career would

31. Stoddard, *An Examination*, 10–11, 16.
32. See Lucas, "Mind," 283–92, and Gura, "Sowing for the Harvest," passim.
33. Schaefer, "Stoddard," 335–38.

be for his own understanding of how to bring the kingdom of God to America.

Throughout his ministry, then, Solomon Stoddard questioned his contemporaries' excessive veneration of a past that no longer served the complexity of their needs but that was sanctioned for a variety of pragmatic—indeed, often selfish—reasons. To him, his generation's undue respect for ecclesiastical tradition, evidenced most vividly in an uncritical defense of the church covenant, had severely compromised the New Englanders' march toward the New Jerusalem. Based in part on a set of plans hastily drawn by men under particularly stressful conditions, assembled by others who themselves could not objectively read those directions, the spiritual edifice defended by the third generation tottered under the unscriptural weight it had to bear. But with the memory of the founders kept before them in countless sermons and orations by those whose power stemmed from their own relation to the tradition, most New Englanders continued to view the Cambridge Platform and its "elaboration" in 1662 as their guarantee of a special relationship to the God of their fathers.

Too few had the objectivity to see that by 1690 the Mathers were defending a system that John Cotton would hardly have recognized. In the first sixty years of the colony's history the clerical majority had sanctioned many ecclesiastical changes to compensate for their and their parishioners' experiences in the New World. As long as such modifications in the belief-system were slight, and as long as the ministers could persuade others that seemingly novel changes had in fact been anticipated and approved in the writings of the first generation, the weight of the past continued to legitimize present intentions and actions. It was Stoddard who told the truth about the emperor's new clothes.

His unique contribution to New England's development thus consisted of an open declaration that the New England Way should not be considered static; rather, because of unforeseen changes in society, it had to be refined and then measured again against scriptural rule, a fact that accords with our understanding of Puritanism as a dynamic ideological system, one in which change in fact was normative.[34] The Mathers believed that as long as they caught the glorious tide that swelled from the colony's past it would carry them inexorably to the Millennium; openly to challenge tradition was to steer against an almost irresistible current. Experienced spiritual naviga-

---

34. Foster, "New England," passim.

tor that he was, Stoddard understood how frequently a society might have to alter its course to account for the vagaries of time and chance above which no men, no matter in what covenanted society, could rise. He approached teleological questions with a mind bound only to the truth of Scripture, and he insisted that the realization of a Christian commonwealth often demanded a reinterpretation, and perhaps even a serious modification, of ideas and beliefs hitherto thought inviolate.

Practically speaking, this meant that at moments of particular weakness and confusion in New England society Stoddard offered his fellow colonists significant modifications in their ecclesiastical system, what amounted to a major reorientation of their notion of community membership. He firmly grasped that the duplicity or, if you will, the self-deception of men like the Mathers, who sought to maintain their power and authority by claiming that they were the guardians of New England's past and so the guarantors of its glorious future, encouraged spiritual apathy among his contemporaries. While such ideological legerdemain may have fooled some of their supporters some of the time, the low morale within the colony's churches in the early eighteenth century verified the final poverty of their vision.

Thus, while the Mathers may have formulated the most significant imaginative version of American history before Edwards's, the myth's vitality, its appeal to future generations, was assured by men like Stoddard who did not treat the past as a cabinet of sacrosanct relics but rather as a choice storehouse of experiences through which men were obliged to pick and sort to find the truths that best served their spiritual aspirations, an attitude that directly contributed to the development of Stoddard's evangelism in the 1720s, and so to the Great Awakening. The New England of 1720 was not what it had been eighty years earlier, and even then it had not instituted the church as Christ would have had it. Experience had taught Solomon Stoddard that much.

5 Sowing for the Harvest
The Reverend William Williams and the Great Awakening

When I worked on Solomon Stoddard, I always was puzzled by scholars' statements about the power wielded by this "pope" of the Connecticut Valley; they never supplied any evidence that his radical innovations in ecclesiology were welcomed by his neighbors. This essay originated in my desire to find out more about the theological and ecclesiastical positions of some of those other ministers, and I thought it best to start with the individual considered important enough to have preached his father-in-law's funeral sermon on Stoddard's death in 1729.

I discovered that William Williams had been greatly overlooked: with the exception of C. C. Goen, who had noted that the first published account of Edwards's famous "Little Awakening" of 1735–36 appeared as an appendix to a work by Edwards's uncle Williams, no one had examined Williams's role in events leading up to the Great Awakening. In this essay I tried to remedy that situation. Further, though I did not know it at the time, it turned out that as early as the last decade of the seventeenth century Williams, in an important manuscript, had joined Stoddard in defending a more enlarged version of church membership (see my "Going Mr. Stoddard's Way: William Williams on Church Privileges," *William and Mary Quarterly*, 3d ser., 45 [July 1988]: 489–98). Rather than standing in glorious isolation, in his attempts to redefine church membership Stoddard had been joined by the second most influential clergyman in the region.

Although there recently have appeared important studies of the Great Awakening from the standpoint of the new cultural history—I think particularly of Frank Lambert's *Pedlar in Divinity: George Whitefield and the Transatlantic Revivals* (1994) and, though it is not fully satisfactory,

Michael J. Crawford's *Seasons of Grace: Colonial New England's Revival Tradition in Its British Context* (1991)—we still lack a large-scale study of the background and development of the eighteenth-century American revivals as rhetorical, or what one might call textual, events. Such a history, I believe, would be predicated upon treating the work of scores of significant revivalists through the same kind of closely ground lens that I have used here on Williams and elsewhere on Stoddard.

The high opinion Jonathan Edwards had of his uncle, the Reverend William Williams of Hatfield, Massachusetts, offers a seldom-used key to understanding the theological development of the Connecticut Valley just prior to the Great Awakening. At the heart of Edwards's respect for his relative, expressed most vividly in his sermon at Williams's funeral in 1741, was his recognition that from the time of Stoddard's death in 1729 to the arrival of the British itinerant George Whitefield in 1740 the valley was not exclusively under the charismatic influence of Stoddard or his youthful successor. To characterize the 1730s as a time of Edwards's immediate inheritance of power from Stoddard is too simple a description. A thorough history of the valley prior to the Awakening of 1740 can only be assembled if one realizes that what occurred in the three decades before that date was the establishment of a doctrinal and evangelical basis for the eventual outpouring of the Spirit, and that ministers like the Reverend Williams, heretofore neglected, played an important part in that preparatory process.[1]

A major problem confronting students of the period has been one of emphasis: by now Stoddard and Edwards have assumed such stature that the religious history of the Connecticut Valley in the eighteenth century is composed exclusively of them. This has been the assumption of such scholars as Perry Miller and Edwin Gaustad, and the most recent study of the valley essentially reinforces this historical commonplace. The prominence of these two ministers cannot be denied, but to neglect the presence

---

1. Jonathan Edwards, *The Resort and Remedy of those that are Bereaved by the Death of an Eminent Minister. A Sermon on the Death of the Aged Mr. Williams* (Boston, 1741), passim.
   In this sermon Williams is described not only as "a great Divine, of very comprehensive knowledge" but as "emminently an evangelical Preacher." With Williams's death, Edwards believed that "God has now taken our Father and Master from our Head," and "He has removed him that we have been wont to resort to *in difficult* cases for Instruction and Direction."

(and the final significance) of fellow laborers like Williams distorts any representation we give of the period.²

To chasten ourselves for this exclusive concern with Stoddard and Edwards, we need only turn to characterizations of Williams offered by such prominent contemporaries as Charles Chauncy or Benjamin Colman. For example: when late in Chauncy's life Yale President Ezra Stiles asked him for a reflection on the importance of Stoddard, he replied: "I have read all Mr. Stoddard's writings, but have never been able to see in them the strength of genius some have attributed to him." Chauncy then awakened to reminiscence about the valley that had absorbed so much of his youthful vitriol, and he went on: "Mr. Williams, his son-in-law, I believe to have been the greater man, and I am ready to think greater than any of his sons, though they were all men of more than common understanding."³ What will become apparent is that the focal point of this essay is a person historians of the Awakening have too long neglected.

Born in Newton, Massachusetts, 2 February 1665, William Williams was the son of Captain Isaac Williams and Martha, daughter of Deacon William Parker of Roxbury. Few facts are known about Williams's youth, but he was a member of the Harvard College class of 1683 and had as his only classmates Samuel Danforth, later called to the ministry at Taunton, Massachusetts, and his cousin John Williams, who assumed the pulpit in

2. See Perry Miller, "Solomon Stoddard, 1643–1729," *Harvard Theological Review* 34 (1941): 277–320, and *The New England Mind: From Colony to Province* (Cambridge: Harvard University Press, 1953), chaps. 15 and 17; Edwin Gaustad, *The Great Awakening in New England* (1957; Gloucester, Mass.: Peter Smith, 1965); and Edwards, *The Great Awakening*, ed. C. C. Goen, vol. 4 of the *Works of Jonathan Edwards* (New Haven: Yale University Press, 1972). In his biography of Edwards, *Jonathan Edwards* (New York: Sloane, 1949), Miller stresses Stoddard's influence in the valley, but also drops many hints regarding the insidious presence of the Williams clan. For example, he describes William Williams as "the most shadowy figure" in the tangle of church politics in Hampshire County. The most recent study of the valley, Paul Lucas's *Valley of Discord: Church and Society along the Connecticut River, 1636–1725* (Hanover, N.H.: University Press of New England, 1976), while presenting a thorough treatment of the valley's history, continues the imbalance in favor of Stoddard.

3. William Sprague, *Annals of the American Pulpit* (New York: Carter Bros., 1857–59), 1 (Trinitarian Congregational), 207–9, for an account of Williams in which Chauncy's quotation is given. For Colman's praise, see his preface to Williams's *The Great Salvation Revealed and Offered in the Gospel* (Boston, 1717). The only modern historian who gives any space to Williams is Lucas, " 'An Appeal to the Learned': The Mind of Solomon Stoddard," *William and Mary Quarterly*, 3d ser., 30 (April 1973): 257–92, but he still places Williams in the position of being a mere follower of Stoddard; see 289f. Also see Lucas, *Valley of Discord*, 147, 182f., 194f., 257.

the frontier outpost of Deerfield and achieved fame for the relation of his captivity among the Indians, *The Redeemed Captive Returning to Zion* (1707). After the death of his first wife in 1698 William Williams married Christian, daughter of Solomon Stoddard, and through this marriage became part of the politically incestuous tangle of Connecticut Valley families.[4]

On 6 December 1686, Williams was ordained to the ministry at Hatfield, a small farming community across the river from the more substantial town of Northampton where Solomon Stoddard had been minister since the death of Eleazer Mather. The specifics of his external biography are few. After his ordination he remained inconspicuous until 1707, when he ventured into print with *The Danger of Not Reforming Known Evils*, a sermon delivered to his Hatfield congregation on a day of public fast and humiliation. By 1712 he was accompanying Stoddard on one of his annual trips to Boston, the capital of the province, but despite this introduction to Boston's intellectual circle, he waited until 1717 to publish his first substantial work, *The Great Salvation Revealed and Offered in the Gospel*, a treatise important enough to carry a laudatory preface by Benjamin Colman, one of Boston's most respected ministers. In the spring of 1719 the Reverend John Wise saw fit to refuse the honor of delivering the province's annual election sermon; and, significantly ignoring any of the Mathers' candidates, the general court was enough impressed by the Hatfield minister to bestow the privilege upon him. He rode to Boston on the path the colony had once cleared for Stoddard and delivered *A Plea for God*, a classic jeremiad of the period.[5]

In the spring of 1726, with Stoddard already too feeble to make the

---

4. The main biographical sources for Williams's life are *Sibley's Harvard Graduates* (Cambridge: Charles Sever, 1885), 3:263–69; Sprague's *Annals*; *Dictionary of American Biography* (see entries on his sons); and Daniel White Wells and Reuben Field Wells, *A History of Hatfield, Mass.* (Springfield, Mass.: Published under the direction of F. C. H. Gibbons, 1910). For a complete genealogy of the Williams family, see S. W. Williams, *Genealogy and History of the Family of Williams* (Greenfield: Merriam and Merrick, 1847).

5. Wells and Wells, *History of Hatfield*, 107ff. William Williams, *The Danger of Not Reforming Known Evils* (Boston, 1707); also see Samuel Sewall, *The Diary of Samuel Sewall*, ed. M. Halsey Thomas, 2 vols. (New York: Farrar, Straus, and Giroux, 1973), 1:507 and 2:693. It is significant to the history of the valley that *The Great Salvation* appeared just prior to Stoddard's last "harvest" of souls in 1718. Williams's book might have been one of the stimuli contributing to this awakening. See Miller, *Colony to Province*, 299, and Sewall, *Diary*, 2:918, for Wise's refusal to give the election sermon. *A Plea for God, and An Appeal to the Consciences of a People Declining in Religion*, by William Williams (Boston, 1719), is the title of the election sermon.

arduous trip, Williams again was called to Boston, this time to deliver the sermon before the annual convention of ministers. In 1727, the same year his sister-in-law Esther's son, Jonathan Edwards, joined Stoddard at Northampton, eight valley ministers, impressed by his earlier discourses, which gave "abundant proof of his abilities in Practical Divinity," enlisted Williams's support to write a disputative tract against the Antipaedobaptism that showed signs of spreading to their churches. He obliged and did not disappoint them with *An Essay to Prove the Interest of the Children of Believers in the Covenant,* his only venture into theological disputation.[6]

In 1729 the imposing Stoddard fell, and it was no mean indication of his son-in-law's stature that he was called on to deliver the funeral sermon for the Northampton minister. In his moving eulogy he compared Stoddard's death to "the felling of a mighty spreading Tree in a Forest, which greatly thins its Glory" and makes "all the trees about it to shake," leaving a "wide Breech where it stood, which may be long where it is filled again."[7]

But the crowd assembled there was aware that the man delivering these words was himself the most likely to fill that breach: at that moment no one in the valley commanded his prestige. Within a short while he would take over the chair of the Hampshire Association of ministers that Stoddard had organized almost twenty years before as a means of controlling the area politically. Then, once the "freshenings" of grace in the revivals of the 1730s were noticed, Williams capitalized on the increasing fervor among people in the entire Connecticut Valley and published *The Duty and Interest of a People...,* together with *Directions for such as are Concerned to Obtain a True Repentance and Conversion to God,* a book which carried an "appendix" consisting of a letter from the Reverend Jonathan Edwards describing the wonderful work of God in those parts, the first draft of his famous *A Faithful Narrative of the Surprising Work of God* (1737). Williams remained a supporter of the Awakening until his death in September 1741, all the while observing the meteoric rise of his nephew and colleague in the revivals. He fortunately missed the havoc that ensued once

---

6. Williams, *The Great Duty of Ministers to Advance the Kingdom of God, and Their Comfort in Fellow-Helpers in this Work. A Sermon Preached at the Annual Convention of Ministers at Boston, May 26, 1726* (Boston, 1726). Also see Samuel Sewall, "Sewall-Williams Correspondence," in *Massachusetts Historical Society, Collections,* 6th ser., 2:209. See also William Williams, *An Essay to Prove the Interest of the Children of Believers in the Covenant, and the Obligations of Both Parents and Children Arising Thence* (Boston, 1727).

7. William Williams, *The Death of a Prophet Lamented and Improved, In a Sermon Preached at Northampton, Feb. 13, 1729* (Boston, 1729), 23, 28, passim.

the revival fell from the hands of God into those of men with less discrimination than Edwards and he.[8]

The external facts of Williams's biography only take on meaning when the substance of his preaching is imposed upon them; then the particular doctrines he stressed and the manner of his exhortations to congregation and ministers alike assure him a place with Stoddard as one who inaugurated a new era in New England's religious history. Moreover, it is important to recall that Stoddard himself has just recently been comprehended with sufficient subtlety to allow an understanding of his contribution to the American Reformed tradition: Williams's corroboration of the emphases he struck in the later part of his career can be appreciated only when the full contour of Stoddard's mind is visible.[9]

Perry Miller's 1941 essay on Stoddard is the starting point for any discussion of his position in the Connecticut Valley, but the most astute recent judgment of his historical importance comes from a revisionist quarter. Paul Lucas has convincingly delineated the intellectual development of the "pope" of the valley, one that essentially had two major phases. He argues that originally Stoddard's uniqueness resided in his outright rejection of the New Testament conception of a "gathered" church and that as a result of this belief he was "a lonely but vocal exponent of doctrine over discipline." He saw the church as existing through all time on the model of the Instituted Church of the Old Testament, one created or "instituted" by God for the salvation of men through its various ordinances. Stoddard claimed that New England's continual declension (he preached jeremiads as vehemently as any other minister) was caused by the constant

---

8. William Williams, *The Duty and Interest of a People, among whom Religion has been planted, to continue Steadfast and Sincere in the Profession and Practice of It. With Directions for Such As Are Concerned to obtain a true Repentance and Conversion to God . . . To Which is Added, Part of a Large Letter from Rev. Mr. Jonathan Edwards of Northampton. Giving an Account of the Late Wonderful Work of God in those Parts* (Boston, 1736).

9. The major reexaminations of Stoddard are Lucas, "The Mind of Stoddard"; Thomas Schafer, "Solomon Stoddard and the Theology of the Revival," in *A Miscellany of American Christianity: Essays in Honor of H. Shelton Smith*, ed. Stuart C. Henry (Durham: Duke University Press, 1963), 328–61; E. Brooks Holifield, *The Covenant Sealed: The Development of Puritan Sacramental Theology in Old and New England, 1520–1720* (New Haven: Yale University Press, 1974); James Walsh, "Solomon Stoddard's Open Communion: A Reexamination," *New England Quarterly* 42 (1970): 97–114; Edmund S. Morgan, *Visible Saints: The History of a Puritan Idea* (New York: New York University Press, 1963); and Norman Petit, *The Heart Prepared: Grace and Conversion in Puritan Spiritual Life* (New Haven: Yale University Press, 1966).

wrangling over the *disciplinary* forms of the church: as he saw it, men had too long neglected to assume that the essence of the church was *doctrinal* and not disciplinary. Stoddard's early emphasis, then, was not on searching for signs of genuine sainthood but in bringing as many people as possible to the saving ordinances of baptism, prayer, Scripture, preaching, and, most controversially, the Lord's Supper.[10]

But modern scholarship reveals that the Mathers' assumptions of Stoddard's virtual "papacy" over the churches of his area was a myth and that, while his influence was undeniably considerable, "it stemmed from his personality, not from his theology or ecclesiology." The Presbyterianism that arose in Hampshire County after Connecticut opened the way with the Saybrook Platform of 1708 was not based on what Stoddard advocated in *The Doctrine of Instituted Churches* (1700). Instead it was formalized by more traditional men like Hartford's Timothy Woodbridge and Boston's Benjamin Colman. While Increase Mather lost sleep over his mistaken belief that Stoddard spoke for the entire valley, Stoddard's neighbor and friendly disputant Edward Taylor was more abreast of the situation. He reminded Stoddard that he had "so few of the Non-conformists" for him that his doctrine was "a thing well to be suspected"; if the church fathers could not be mustered to his support, few contemporary ministers would risk supporting his assumptions about the true form of the visible church. Formed in 1714 as the northern counterpart of the Saybrook Platform, the Hampshire Association illustrated precisely this point: while Stoddard was its prime mover, William Williams, John Williams, and Hadley's Isaac Chauncy made sure that its structure reflected a more conventional Presbyterianism than that advocated by the Northampton minister.[11]

Lucas's main point is that late in his life Stoddard, realizing the futility of reforming the New England churches on the Instituted model, pragmatically returned to the evangelical principles he had first avowed in 1687 in *The Safety of Appearing at the Day of Judgment in the Righteousness of*

---

10. Lucas, "The Mind of Stoddard," 260ff., and Solomon Stoddard, *The Doctrine of Instituted Churches Explained and Proved from the WORD of God* (London, 1700).

11. Lucas, "The Mind of Stoddard," 261, 267–83. Edward Taylor to Stoddard, 13 February 1667–68, in Edward Taylor's notebook, Massachusetts Historical Society, Boston, and quoted in Lucas, "The Mind of Stoddard," 267. For a discussion of the Hampshire Association, see Lucas, "The Mind of Stoddard," 274–83; and on Presbyterians in the valley, Robert Pope, *Half-Way Covenant: Church Membership in Colonial New England* (Princeton: Princeton University Press, 1969), 75–95. For Saybrook Platform, Richard Bushman, *From Puritan to Yankee: Character and Social Order in Connecticut, 1690–1765* (Cambridge: Harvard University Press, 1967), 150–55.

Christ. He again regarded communion as a preparatory and not a regenerating ordinance and returned to his labors stressing the doctrine of preparation and exhorting ministers to search their own souls for evidence of grace so that they might become more genuinely inspirational in their roles as community leaders. Interestingly, Lucas dates this shift in Stoddard's thought as beginning around 1708 when, in *The Inexcusableness of Neglecting the Worship of God,* he moved back to the more conventional (if still heretical) notion of the Lord's Supper. Here William Williams enters the story, for his first published sermon appeared just prior to that, in 1707. This piece, *The Danger of Not Reforming Known Evils,* the only treatise published from the valley during the Stoddard–Mather controversy over the Lord's Supper, has a literal and symbolic importance to the history of that period.[12]

Delivered on a day of public fast, Williams's sermon follows the standard formula for the jeremiad. His cousin John had just returned from a hellish captivity among the Indians, and Williams was astounded that even with that lesson of chastisement before them his people still had a "readiness" to roll sin "as a sweet morsel under their tongues," suffering their consciences to fall asleep "like a Town unguarded, ready to be a prey to an approaching Enemy." What seemed even worse was that, for an excuse for their behavior, the sinful people explained that they were "not alone in what they do" and that "many Men that know do so, and such as are wise and good Men too." Against this lame excuse Williams sharply reminded them that, if the thing was in its nature evil, "the practice of others will not make it good, how many or whosoever they be." It would be another of the valley's manifold ironies that in thirty years Williams's nephew Jonathan Edwards, would incur the mortal wrath of Williams's own sons for stressing just this point of logic.[13]

The true import of the pamphlet, though, stems from the fact that Williams devoted several pages to the neglect of the Lord's Supper. In doing so he did not at any point come to Stoddard's defense: communion, while necessary as a preparation for grace, was not declared a converting ordinance. Acknowledging that within the valley many such issues were not settled and that there were "some points that are disputable, that persons are not so well satisfied about," he added with an odd twist (which might have been intended for Stoddard) that the "Evils of this Country are for the

---

12. Lucas, "The Mind of Stoddard," 284ff.
13. Williams, *The Danger of Not Reforming Known Evils,* 4f., 7, 13.

most part in such things as are known, yea, such as have been acknowledged" by both civil and ecclesiastical rulers. Ostensibly speaking of his society's sins, could he not have meant errors in doctrine as well? Could Stoddard's unorthodox ideas about the Lord's Supper have been causing undue confusion and keeping people from the communion table? The divine injunction regarding the sacrament was "plain," yet "how many are there who live from year to year in neglect of it" because they pretend "a want of preparation for it and a fear of polluting it," thus implicitly revealing their "slight and low estimate of God's Authority enjoyning it?"[14]

But not one word of the ordinance as a guarantee of conversion, nor any mention of the doctrine of the Instituted churches, both topics over which two of New England's finest minds were arguing bitterly. From this pamphlet could not Stoddard have deeply sensed the fact of his own isolation, that his son-in-law now had published to a wider audience what had been implicitly apparent in Stoddard's prolonged failure to win support for his ecclesiastical position after Colman, Woodbridge, and Simon Bradstreet had published their own Presbyterian manifesto, *The Gospel Order Revived* (1700)?

Whatever its effect on Stoddard, *The Danger of Not Reforming Known Evils* marked the appearance of another important mind in the valley. Despite Williams's silence for the decade, Stoddard knew that if his dominance over the area were to continue he had to adjust his tactics to the demands of his society. With the publication in 1714 of *A Guide to Christ* he had readopted the role of evangelist and had begun to stress the importance of the ministry in the process of conversion, an insidious way to recoup what he saw as the ministers' constantly diminishing prestige. This "small Treatise" in "guiding souls through the work of conversion" was composed "upon the desire of some of the younger ministers" in the area; if William Williams was among them, he made the request in the full knowledge that it was in this same direction of evangelicalism that his own gifts lay. Stoddard was setting the pace, but there were other strong personalities ready to share the work of spreading the Good News. By 1717 Williams had emerged as an undeniable force within the valley.[15]

---

14. Ibid., 17ff. For example, Lucas suggests that other of Stoddard's reforms were not accepted even within his own congregation, and it seems perfectly likely that the Mather–Stoddard debate set off all kinds of questions about the propriety of taking the Lord's Supper. See Lucas, "The Mind of Stoddard," 278.

15. For a discussion of the significance of *The Gospel Order Revived*, see Miller, *Colony to Province*, 244–47; and Lucas, "The Mind of Stoddard," 271f. and *Valley of Discord*,

In his description of character and social order just prior to the Awakening in Connecticut (by extension, an analysis applying to the upper valley as well), Richard Bushman places the conflict between "order and piety" high on the list of strains visible within the social structure and suggests that Stoddard was among the first to recognize the implications of this tension and to act accordingly; that is, to berate the pastors "for the spiritual lassitude of their congregations" and to attempt to give evangelical preaching a firm ground in doctrine.

Beginning around 1717, his neighbor Williams also felt the need to redefine the importance of the ministry within that centrifugal society; if in the discourses which came from his pen over the next twenty years he did not examine the preparation for and signs of conversion so profoundly as did his older friend, he did contribute significantly to the arousal of ministerial interest over the effective preaching of doctrine. His stress on the importance of the Gospel plan of salvation and his belief that the minister's foremost task was to preach the great truths of the Christian religion in as uncompromising and affecting a manner as possible link him not only to Stoddard but to Edwards, who in the 1730s reemphasized (at the expense of the support of some of the Williams clan) that Christians worthy of the name had to accept the Word in all its blinding brilliance. Thomas Schafer has admirably sketched Stoddard's contribution toward the development of a reinvigorated evangelicalism that took into account the ways and means of conversion. Here I outline briefly Williams's efforts to prepare the way for revivalism by his emphasis on what a proper comprehension of doctrine could offer the sinner; it was in plowing this field that Williams made his major contribution to the Awakening of the 1740s.[16]

A thorough reading of Williams's published works reveals that, although it was probably unintentional, he placed more emphasis on the minister and his evangelical role than on the state of the souls he was bringing to Christ: he feared that many ministers were unaware of the true nature of the labors in which they were engaged. He had warned Stephen Williams at his ordination in 1717 that when God sends "any into his Harvest, it is

---

177–82. Schafer, "Solomon Stoddard and the Revival," gives a good assessment of *A Guide to Christ* (Boston, 1714).

16. Bushman, *From Puritan to Yankee*, 178–80. On Edwards's stress on language and doctrine see Perry Miller, "The Rhetoric of Sensation," in *Errand Into the Wilderness* (Cambridge: Belknap Press of Harvard University Press, 1956), 167–83; Schafer, "Solomon Stoddard," passim, talks of the kinds of doctrine Stoddard stressed.

not to Loyter, but to Labour in it." Rather than resting secure without attempting any reform within his congregation, the worthy minister had to realize that his clerical labors never ceased: "the Ignorant must be Informed, the Careless Quickened, the Erroneous Refuted, the Doubting Resolved, the Afflicted Comforted, Self-Deceivers Detected," and Satan's devices "laid open." Such ministers, he told Jonathan Ashley in 1732, "are greatly to blame, who don't maintain a solemn Awe of the Charge that lies upon them."[17]

But more important to ministers than just acquiring a sense of the seriousness of their work was that they had to "grow in Wisdom, Prudence, and Experience" if they wished to be successful in converting souls to Christ. Paralleling the thoughts of Stoddard in *A Guide to Christ* (and anticipating one of the institutional reforms spawned by the Awakening), Williams told new clergymen that they would "have need to Study Men, as well as Books," and above all learn to scrutinize their own hearts so that they would discover "what is necessary to be spoken for Conviction, Direction, and Comfort of others." His plea was for an experiential ministry, not for what Gilbert Tennent later felicitously termed an "unconverted" one: ministers were to preach the Word "not as if a Man were telling a dull Story," but "with Warmth and Earnestness of Spirit." The evangelist's work could not be fruitful unless he had an "Experimental Piety" and the "Presence of the Spirit in its Graces as well as its Gifts." Any "Cowardice in Christ's Cause" was nothing less than "Treachery."[18]

What were the clergy to preach to the people? Addressing the annual convention of ministers in 1726, Williams explained that they "should endeavor the Advancement of the Kingdom" by taking the laws of the Gospel and "pressing them upon the Hearts of Men" until the "Privileges" of Christ's kingdom lay open before them. More explicitly, it involved "clearly" explaining and "solidly" stating "the great Truths relating to Men's Conversion and Reconciliation to God, and [their] Comfort in Christ." In short, the minister had to preach experientially the "Great Salvation Revealed and Offered in the Gospel," the subject of Williams's first major treatise.[19]

The two hundred pages of Williams's book are filled with what he had

---

17. Williams, *A Painful Ministry, The Peculiar Gift of the Lord* (Boston, 1717), 10, 12; *The Work of Ministers, and the Duty of Hearers* (Boston, 1733), 4, 17.

18. Williams, *Painful Ministry*, 21; *The Great Concern of Christians* (Boston, 1723), 20f.

19. Williams, *The Great Duty of Ministers*, 8; *Painful Ministry*, 12; *The Great Concern of Christians*, 27.

learned in his thirty-year ministry in Hatfield. In his preface to it Benjamin Colman did not exaggerate when he reported that "the Reader will find much in a little room" and that the treasure to be mined there was like gold "that may be gathered in Ingots, and does not Lye scatter'd in the dust, nor beaten into Leaves." Williams thought that the most frightening anomaly of the age was that the glory held forth to sinners was in those degenerate times totally neglected: men's memories on this account were "too like Sieves that let out the Flower and retain the Bran." A means to salvation had been provided by Christ and "offered to Men in the *Ministry*," yet the common experience in the province showed that there were "abundance who are nothing the better for it, who obtain no peace nor pardon, no grace or comfort by it":

> They can't tell how to be contented to want Corn and Cattle, and Lands, or such worldly interests, conveniences, and honours that they see others enjoy: but they can bear it well enough to want spiritual and eternal mercies. These things not being obvious to sense, seem like the Poets Elizeum, but as a dream or fancy.

Ministers of the day wrecked their careers against the fact that people had become obsessed with the things of this world. Williams sardonically noted that if "to equal or outshine their Neighbours in Riches and Honours" was more valuable to them "than to have their Souls Adorn'd with Grace," men had every reason to expect upon them such severe judgments as smallpox, earthquakes, and Indian wars.[20]

Against this prevalent apostasy Williams urged men to embrace the Gospel and not to fail "of an Interest in the Grace of God," for the Gospel presented the strongest arguments to further holiness" by giving "the most excellent Pattern for it." But it was "other News that men generally listen after," and undeniable misery could only follow such a tragic neglect of the means of salvation. The only cries one heard were "What shall we eat, What shall we drink?" not "What must we do to be saved?"; and Williams's book reminded ministers to bring people the precise import of this last phase. That Edwards's *A Faithful Narrative of the Surprising Work of God* reported just such a concern suggests the extent of the revolution wrought in so brief a time. *The Great Salvation* warrants and rewards study as a

---

20. Williams, *The Great Salvation*, 13, 115, 118, 122.

succinct exposition of the substance of the evangelist's message. With the lessons of Paul uppermost in his mind Williams was able to compress into its pages the marrow of the Gospel plan and to phrase it in such a way as to move the hearts of his readers.[21]

To what would this concern for the doctrine of the Great Salvation lead? Williams had a ready answer, one epitomized in a letter to Samuel Sewall in 1727 shortly after the aging chief justice sent him a copy of his recently reprinted *Phaenomena quaedam Apocalyptica,* his venture into millennial prophecy first published in 1697. After thanking Sewall for all the "tokens of respect and kindness" he had shown to him and his family, Williams admitted that he concurred with what Sewall had asserted about the "beauty and grandeur of the New Jerusalem," but confessed himself at a loss "why Mexico or indeed any other particular spot on Earth should be pitched upon rather than another" as the site of the great event. If no one place seemed to be described in Revelation, might not the Millennium begin in New England? Though "in many respects" its contemporary situation suggested that God had a controversy with the region, he still thought "it's our duty to plow in hope, as the Apostle's allusion is 1 Cor, 9-10." Williams evidenced a fervor in his evangelicalism because he held to the belief that New England still was the center of the second Protestant Reformation, and the assumptions of his preaching betrayed the fact that he (like Edwards in the 1740s) believed that if the Millennium began in Hampshire County men like him could prepare the way for it.[22]

All Williams's thoughts on revivalism must be viewed within this millennial context, and his last major work, *The Duty and Interest of a People . . . With Directions for Such as are Concerned to obtain a true . . . Conversion,* published after the first major revival in the area in almost twenty years, illuminates his own role in striving to bring the kingdom of God to earth. It also forms one of the strands of that agonizing web spun around Edwards once he took his Uncle William's advice and preached naked doctrine (in this case, concerning justification by faith alone); Edwards's own part in the awakenings of the 1730s and the subsequent

---

21. Ibid., 144, 70, 167. Jonathan Edwards, *Works* (Worcester, Mass.: Thomas, 1808), 3:26.

22. Williams, "Sewall-Williams Correspondence," 250-52. For a discussion of chiliasm during this period (and especially the Mathers' relation to it), see Robert Middlekauff, *The Mathers: Three Generations of Puritan Intellectuals* (New York: Oxford University Press, 1971), chap. 10.

fame he achieved for it deeply aroused the animosity of some within the Williams clan.[23]

The volume that appeared in 1736 is even more interesting when one realizes that Williams's contribution is in two parts. C. C. Goen's opinion that the second piece, *Directions for Such as are Concerned,* is the earlier one—or, if such dating seems arbitrary, is the selection composed more in the heat of the awakenings—appears to be well founded. He notes that "in spite of allusions here and there betraying a confidence in human ability," Williams's doctrine there approaches Edwards's own. In contrast, *The Duty and Interest* "appears to be a post-revival attempt to consolidate gains recently realized" and is on the whole more characteristic of Williams's concern with the reinforcement of doctrine.[24]

The thrust of *The Duty and Interest* suggests that once men realize the great truths of their religion they have an obligation to "teach or propogate" that religion to their children. More important, if the work of God were to continue to grow, it was incumbent upon parents to live "agreeable to the Precepts of Christianity" and to "shew the Amiableness" of it. Reformation began with people, "but thence it is carried on to Families, from thence to Towns, and from them to whole Countries," and Williams offered his timely exhortation in the hope that the awakening the valley was witnessing never would cease and would usher in those glorious days Sewall had described to him. But despite his solid advice, Williams would have to wait another four years before he saw further hope for New England's reformation.[25]

His *Directions* seems a more spontaneous and enthusiastic piece, and for once he ventured onto the ground of Shepard, Hooker, and Stoddard and attempted to understand the psychology of conversion. Williams attempted to impress upon his readers that if they sought conversion they should be careful "to obtain such a one as is sincere and saving," and he resorted to a

---

23. Miller, *Edwards,* passim, is always tantalizingly suggestive about the problems between Edwards and other personalities within the valley. Henry Bamford Parkes, *Jonathan Edwards: The Fiery Puritan* (New York: Minton, Balch, 1930), also makes much of the Williams's animosity.

24. Edwards, *Great Awakening,* ed. Goen, 34ff.

25. Williams, *The Duty and Interest,* 5, 61, 68, 78. Edwards, *Works,* 3:19, for his mention of Hatfield and also Thomas Milner, *The Life, Times and Correspondence of the Rev. Isaac Watts, D. D.* (London, 1834), 546, for a letter of 24 May 1736, from Elisha Williams to Watts describing the revival in his father's parish. Edwards's *A History of the Work of Redemption* (Worcester: Thomas, 1808) in its later pages also stresses the cumulative nature of revivals and displays the same millennial tendencies as Williams's *The Duty and Interest.*

metaphor easily comprehended throughout the valley to make his point. He noted that "the great Worth and Use of Silver and Gold in the management of Business of this World, makes Men very careful that they be not cheated and imposed upon by what is False and Counterfeit; so the many Benefits following upon a true Conversion, should put Persons upon taking all proper Care that they are not deceived about it." Then, like Edwards in *The Distinguishing Marks of the Work of the Spirit* (and more definitively in *A Treatise Concerning Religious Affections*) and like Stoddard in *A Guide to Christ,* Williams discounted mere external reformation as a sign of true grace and emphasized that true converts had to "love and prize Converse and Communion with God" above all the "Increases of Corn and Wine." If persons were deceived in this matter and called that "a Conversion, which is only an illusion of Satan," it was a thing of "Dangerous Consequence."[26]

These treatises take us to the end of Williams's published works, but his intellectual history is not complete without mention of the letter appended to this last publication, a piece subsequently known as the first published version of Edwards's *A Faithful Narrative* (London, 1737), which was added to Williams's work when Colman, so anxious to see the work printed, abridged it and included it in a work by Williams he had just prepared for the presses. He evidently did not clear this liberty with the aged Hatfield minister, an oversight that seems to have deeply offended some of his family. By the spring of 1737 the difficulty this "appendix" had caused became known. Edwards, responding to Colman's apology for making some textual changes without permission, told his Boston editor that someone had "misrepresented the matter" to him: "I always looked upon it as an honour too great for me, for you to be at the trouble to draw an extract of my letter to publish to the world, and that it should be annexed to my honoured Uncle Williams' sermons; and my main objection against it was that my Uncle Williams himself never approved of its being put into the book." If this was the case, one can imagine the Williams's surprise when, on opening the copy of their patriarch's book (on the cultivation of revivals, no less), they found a testament not to his own evangelical labors but to those of his young nephew across the river! C. C. Goen, adhering to a conspiratorial theory, even suggests that no Boston

---

26. Williams, *Directions*, 3, 4, 17f. For a good discussion of Edwards's sense of a genuine conversion, see John E. Smith's introduction to volume 3 of the Yale edition of his *Works*.

edition of a longer version of the narrative appeared that year because the powerful Williams family "might have insinuated to the entrepreneurs of printing that they should ignore" the work.[27]

But more revealing is the fact that despite the explanation Edwards gave Colman in 1737, William Williams himself genuinely abided by that spirit of fellowship he asked of ministers laboring for revivals of religion: if his pique initially had been raised by Colman's innocent presumption, by the next year he had swallowed his pride and added his name to an attestation of the truth of the narrative as it appeared in its first American edition (Boston, 1738). Edwards's trouble would not be with Williams, but with his sons and what they would do after their parents' death.[28]

Led by the domineering and powerful Israel Williams, the family formed an imposing network of commercial and political interests that openly displayed their affection for the things of this world. Once Edwards's attacks on Arminianism had hit close to home (and, more significant, once the awakenings had begun, proving the effectiveness of his doctrinal attack on the heresy, a tactic to which William Williams had urged ministers as early as 1717), they evidenced a "settled personal hostility," one that displayed itself even after Edwards's dismissal. But the aged Williams remained apart from this internecine hatred. Even though there was reputed to be "Bad blood" between his wife Christian and her sister Esther, Edwards's mother, until his death in 1741 Williams continued to labor beside Edwards for the cause of the Awakening.

For example, during the controversy over the ordination of Robert Breck to a church in Springfield in 1735, the first council to examine the issue (and the one that subsequently refused to ordain Breck) later asked Edwards (who had been a member of it) to answer a defense of a second council's approval of the minister. In this task Edwards was urged on "particularly by his uncle, the Reverend William Williams of Hatfield, who was its moderator"; even though his own sons had attacked Edwards for making a noise about the subject Williams had been strong in his own refusal to approve the blatant Arminian. The other members of his family, those who had a vested interest in the kind of duplicity Arminians could countenance and who still smarted from Edwards's refusal to stop preaching against the doctrine in their own area, were less forgiving:

27. Edwards, *Great Awakening*, ed. Goen, 32–41. The letter from Edwards to Colman dated 19 May 1737, is in the Colman Papers at the Massachusetts Historical Society, Boston.
28. See *A Narrative of the Surprising Conversions* (Boston, 1738). The London edition of the year before lacks this attestation.

For fourteen years after that revival, the individual in question [Israel Williams], a near relative of Mr. Edwards, often too visiting Northampton, and always riding by his house, refused except in three instances to enter his door; though Mr. Edwards regularly called on him and his family, and . . . did all in his power to win his kindness.

Against such a display of original sin there was no earthly remedy; justice only would come (as Edwards later was to tell his Northampton congregation when they treated him similarly) when all the participants stood before the throne of God to give an account of their actions.[29]

But in 1741, riding high on the crest of the Awakening, Edwards had no inkling of the lengths to which a family feud could go. It was perfectly fitting that at that moment he was called on to deliver the funeral sermon for his Uncle Williams and perfectly consistent with his view of the basic corruption of all human nature that his own pride allowed him an irony that must have cut some listeners to the quick. After paying his respects to his Aunt Christian, he turned and "in Humility" addressed himself to his "honourable Fathers, the Sons of the Deceased, that are Improved in the same great Work of the Gospel Ministry, or in other Publick Business for the Service of their Generation":

> You will doubtless acknowledge it as an instance of Christ's great Goodness to you, that you have been the Sons of such a Father; being sensible that your Reputation and Serviceableness in your Generation, has been, under Christ, very much owing to the great Advantages you have been under, by his Instructions, Counsels and Education.

Even in their moment of sorrow they must have cringed at the words, for Edwards was telling them that the only influence they had came through their father's reputation, and that, more obviously, not one of them was the man his father was, especially not the arrogant and resentful Israel who,

---

29. Sereno E. Dwight, ed., *The Works of President Edwards, with a Memoir of His Life* (New York: Converse, 1829), 1:122, 126, 433. Also see E. H. Byington, "Rev. Robert Breck Controversy," *Papers and Proceedings of the Connecticut Valley Historical Society, 1882–1903* 2 (1904): 1–19, and Charles E. Jones, "The Impolitic Mr. Edwards: The Personal Dimensions of The Robert Breck Affair," *New England Quarterly* 51, no. 1 (March 1978): 64–79.

while his parent tried to crush evil root and branch, persisted in becoming one of the wealthiest of the River Gods. One hopes that Israel was aware of the most savage irony of all, that his beloved father himself prepared the way for the success of the upstart cousin who now stood over and openly berated him for neglecting his father's counsel. William Williams had never permitted an unchristian bitterness to interfere with his preaching of the Word.[30]

There is no denying that historians of the Great Awakening and of the developing Presbyterianism in the valley, know less about Williams than about Edwards or Stoddard, but enough concerning his career is known to mark him as one of the most interesting and significant ministers in the Connecticut Valley prior to the Great Awakening. The contour of his intellectual life should be studied with Stoddard's, for these two men shared the labor of readying Hampshire County for the outbreak of religious emotion in the 1730s. With the ritual incantation of the jeremiad causing little reform in the lives of their parishioners, both Stoddard and Williams turned their efforts to evangelism. They reexamined the premises of their Christian labors and decided that, to arouse men from their sinful complacency, they had to insist anew on the importance of Reformed doctrine and its presentation in a manner that awakened their congregations to a serious concern with it. Williams's conception of the proper attitude a minister should take if he were to evangelize successfully, and his stress on the doctrine of the Great Salvation revealed and offered in the Gospel, complemented Stoddard's detailed treatises of the nature and necessity of the conversion experience. Together they established the institutional patterns of response for the Awakening; and when any religious emotion became visible, it thus could be channeled in constructive directions: there would be assurance that what one was experiencing was explicable in a religious grammar comprehended by the entire community. To insist that Williams was merely an imitation of Stoddard is to miss the achievement of an influential man.[31]

Williams is also significant as a symbolic participant in the tragic drama that played itself out once Jonathan Edwards began flexing the intellectual muscle he inherited from his grandfather Stoddard. The Williams family, with Williams at their head, formed one of the most important groups in Hampshire County: that Edwards could have remained effective as long as

---

30. Edwards, *The Resort and Remedy*, 19f.
31. Williams, *The Work of Ministers*, 6.

he did in the face of the concerted opposition of Williams's sons and relatives suggests the undeniable strength of the patriarch's influence. The Reverend William Williams, though he knew his young relative already was eclipsing his own greatness, offered a protecting wing to the minister who soon would be regarded as the chief apologist for the Great Awakening. Williams's entire career had been directed toward bringing the kingdom of God to earth through evangelical labor; heeding his own warning about not deprecating another minister engaged in the work with him, he would not stoop to bitterness at the risk of halting an outpouring of God's grace. That was why he sided with Edwards against Arminianism in the Breck case and why, even after the initial shock of seeing his nephew's success touted in his own book, he added his name to those endorsing the account of the wonderful work of God that Edwards provided for the Boston press.

Passing to his heavenly reward at the height of the Great Awakening, a series of revivals that made the excitement of 1735 seem minute by comparison, Williams died believing that the Millennium for which he had worked and prayed finally was coming to pass. "Were there no Plowing or Harrowing," he once wrote, "we could expect no Harvest." It is time that his labors be recognized and that historians realize that the religious soil of Hampshire County was made fertile by his hands, as well as by Stoddard's.[32]

32. Williams, *The Duty and Interest*, 38.

6 | Early Nineteenth-Century Printing in Rural Massachusetts

John Howe of Greenwich and Enfield, c. 1803–1845

This essay returned me to my home turf, in this case to an area a few miles from my home where in the early twentieth century four towns were legislated out of existence by Boston's insatiable need for drinking water. As my interest in the history of the book and of knowledge developed, I stumbled across the fact that in the antebellum period in one of those now-extinct rural communities there had been a printer of some note. Searches in the American Antiquarian Society's holdings and elsewhere convinced me that John Howe's output was worth studying, but, as with so many of my other projects, I had to find a way to make more than a bibliographical footnote of this project.

Serendipitously, I learned that the Howe family had bequeathed a good number of their ancestors' papers to the Society, among them a very detailed "Printer's Book," an account that showed how little we yet knew of what rural entrepreneurs carried out through their printing offices. Concomitantly, I found my way into William Gilmore's marvelous *Reading Becomes a Necessity of Life: Material and Cultural Life in Rural New England, 1780–1835* (1989), to date the most detailed re-creation of the life of the mind in a rural area. In particular, Gilmore's classification of the different reading "habitats" or "communities" to be found even within a small circuit gave me a way to understand Howe's production vis-à-vis that of other, more sophisticated printers.

The result stands as a contribution to the still-emergent field of the history of the book in America, something to which I have given a good deal of my recent energies, particularly through my association with the

American Antiquarian Society's sponsorship of the multivolume *A History of the Book in America,* to be published by Cambridge University Press. In this project my own interests continue to lie, as they did when I began work on my Old Sturbridge Village internship on Ware, Massachusetts, with rural New England in the antebellum period, when forces of change, particularly technological forces, transformed irrevocably what people knew and how they could know it. Writers like Melville in his "Tartarus of Maids" had one way to understand these changes, but the lives of people like John Howe demonstrated other kinds of responses, every bit as worthy of study.

This essay, then, is part of that immense subject that Perry Miller talked about now so long ago, the life of the mind in America. I hope through this offering, and through future work that adds to it, to make a contribution to our understanding of how people—farmers as well as aspiring authors, mechanics as well as publishers—understood what was happening to them. All my work has been devoted to that end, but it cheers me to realize that even in my most recent writing I have continued to be honest to the goal of trying to understand better who we are by contemplating, often through the most quotidian facts, from where we came.

When I first published this essay in the *Proceedings of the American Antiquarian Society,* I included a transcription of Howe's "Printer's Book."

Historians of the book in America who study the profession of authorship in relation to the business of publishing have greatly enriched our understanding of antebellum literature and culture. But to focus, as many do, only on the new nation's urban entrepreneurs—the Mathew Careys and the Isaiah Thomases, among others—is to offer only a partial portrait.[1] We must balance such scholarship against studies of printers and booksellers who performed a critical role in the proliferation and dissemination of the printed word in rural America. Balance is particularly important because,

---

1. On Carey, for example, see James N. Green, *Mathew Carey: Publisher and Patriot* (Philadelphia: Library Company of Philadelphia, 1985), and David Kaser, *Messrs. Carey and Lea of Philadelphia: A Study in the History of the Booktrade* (Philadelphia: University of Pennsylvania Press, 1957). On Thomas, see Clifford K. Shipton, *Isaiah Thomas: Printer, Patriot, and Philanthropist, 1749–1831* (Rochester, N.Y.: Hart, 1948), and Karl Kroeger, "Isaiah Thomas as a Music Publisher," *Proceedings of the American Antiquarian Society* 86 (1976): 321–41.

as William J. Gilmore points out in his painstaking study of material and cultural life in early nineteenth-century Vermont, the apparent uniformity of cultural life in any area often hid enormous diversity. He argues that different living situations shaped distinctive reading communities, which often existed within a few miles of one another.[2] Thus the history of the book, and, by implication, of literary culture, in Concord, Massachusetts, is not that of Concord, New Hampshire, nor even of nearby Sutton, Massachusetts, not to speak of the hamlets to the north and west.[3]

To understand more fully the history of the book in early nineteenth-century America, we must explore the works and days of another category of entrepreneurs: Ebenezer and George Merriam of Brookfield, Massachusetts, say, or Alden Spooner of Windsor, Vermont, or John Howe of Greenwich and Enfield, Massachusetts.[4] Indeed, Howe's career is particularly instructive, because, unlike the Merriams or Spooner, who served what historians call "center villages" at the hub of regional trading networks, Howe lived in a small town in a region of hardscrabble farmsteads, halfway between the commercial centers of Worcester and Northampton, and fifteen difficult-to-travel miles from Brookfield, where the Merriams carried on a very different printing business.[5] Like his neighbors Ezekiel Terry of Palmer or Moses Learned of Wilbraham, Massachusetts, both of whom printed in similar environments and on the same limited scale, Howe never made a living from this work. Yet for thirty years he set type and pulled his press, printing "steady sellers" and original compositions, town-

---

2. William J. Gilmore, *Reading Becomes a Necessity of Life: Material and Cultural Life in Rural New England, 1780–1835* (Knoxville: University of Tennessee Press, 1989), esp. chaps. 4 and 9.

3. See Robert A. Gross, "Much Instruction from 'Little Reading': Books and Libraries in Thoreau's Concord," *Proceedings of the American Antiquarian Society* 97 (1987): 129–88. Recently, David Jaffee has explored the relationships among publishers, purveyors, and consumers of print culture in the new republic; see his "The Village Enlightenment in New England, 1760–1820," *William and Mary Quarterly*, 3d ser., 47 (1990): 327–46.

4. On the Merriams see Jack Larkin, "The Merriams of Brookfield: Printing in the Economy Of Rural Massachusetts in the Early Nineteenth Century," *Proceedings of the American Antiquarian Society* 96 (1986): 39–73 (a model study); and on Spooner, see Gilmore, *Reading Becomes a Necessity of Life*, passim. See also Marcus A. McCorison, comp., *Vermont Imprints, 1778–1820: A Checklist of Books, Pamphlets, and Broadsides* (Worcester, Mass.: American Antiquarian Society, 1963).

5. Jack Larkin, "The Evolution of a Center Village: West Brookfield, Massachusetts, 1760–1850" (Old Sturbridge Village Research Report, 1977), and "The Merriams of Brookfield," passim; see also Joseph Wood, "Elaboration of a Settlement System: The New England Village in the Federal Period," *Journal of Historical Geography* 10 (1984): 311–36.

meeting warrants and almanacs, sermons and bawdy broadside verse.[6] His career documents a neglected facet of the complex history of the book trade in America.

John Howe (1783–1845) was the son of Solomon and Abigail Warren Howe. Solomon Howe was born in Westborough, Massachusetts, in 1750, but early on he moved with his family to Brookfield. After graduating from Dartmouth College in 1777, he returned to Brookfield. In 1791 he moved to Greenwich, Massachusetts, where he served sporadically as a Baptist minister, tended a farm, and, most significant, wrote and sold books, others' as well as his own. One of Dartmouth's early chroniclers observed that Howe's life "was eccentric and desultory," an accurate characterization; but because John acquired his interest in and knowledge of the printer's art from his father, the few facts about Solomon Howe that we can assemble are germane to this study.[7]

From the papers of the Howe family at the American Antiquarian Society, we learn, for example, that within a year of his graduation from Dartmouth, Howe was living in Boston, where he sought information about, among other things, the printer's trade.[8] In one part of his record of this stay, he listed information he wanted to acquire while in the city. He noted that he wanted "to see Mr. Billings" to "get some tunes pick'd out to bring back" to Brookfield. With this individual, presumably William Bill-

---

6. There is no definitive bibliography of Howe imprints, but see Clifford K. Shipton's listing of the Howe publications donated to the Society by Donald Howe, in "Report of the Librarian," *Proceedings of the American Antiquarian Society* 60 (1950): 217–23. This preliminary list is supplemented by Ralph R. Shaw and Richard H. Shoemaker's *American Bibliography, 1801–19*, 22 vols. (New York: Scarecrow, 1958–66), and Shoemaker et al., comps., *A Checklist of American Imprints, 1820–39*, 12 vols. (New York: Scarecrow, 1964–73). Another important resource is the dated broadsides collection at the American Antiquarian Society.

7. For genealogical information see Daniel Wait Howe, *Howe Genealogies* (Boston: New England Historic Genealogical Society, 1929), 304–5 and 325–26. More biographical information on Solomon Howe can be gleaned from Frank J. Metcalf, *American Writers and Compilers of Sacred Music* (New York: Abingdon, 1925), 79–81; George T. Chapman, *Sketches of the Alumni of Dartmouth College* (Cambridge, Mass.: Riverside, 1867), 21–23, quotation from 23, and Donald W. Howe, *Quabbin: The Lost Valley* (Ware, Mass.: Quabbin Book House, 1951), 138.

8. This and the following information about Howe's visit to Boston are found in an unlabeled commonplace and record book among the Howe Family Papers at the American Antiquarian Society that includes some interesting essays and verse written while Howe was at Dartmouth.

ings, the composer and music publisher, he had other business, too, namely, to "get as much intelligence" as possible "concerning his Book [probably the *Singing Master's Assistant,* published that year], & the Aretinian Society," and to inquire how to "get a pencil to draw 5 musical lines at once," to draw musical staffs more quickly.⁹

He also actively pursued other affairs. He wanted to know, for example, "What Mr. Byles will charge for printing eight pages with small types and find ink for its paper—viz., 1,000 half sheets."¹⁰ And, should he decide to do such printing himself, what this same man "or any other Printer" could tell him of "the Cost of Types . . . for enough to set one press with 12 pages on a sheet, in small types, at once." As befitted his vocation as a Baptist minister, Howe also wanted to stop at Jeremy Condy's bookstore to pick up "Locke's Letter on Toleration," "Cato by Young, a Tragedy," and "a calm and candid answer to the question—Why do you dissent from the Chh."¹¹ Finally, he sought to "enquire of Col. Revere or some Engraver, how to make ink for copper-plate, or how to temper Lamp black for that purpose, if it will answer."¹²

Further entries indicate that the young Solomon Howe's stay in Boston was successful. He purchased some sort of press from Billings for 5 £, was quoted a price of "10 £ Lawfull Money in Silver" for "a font for Printing consisting of 300 wt., which will sett 36 Pages," and noted an elaborate recipe for making "Printing Letters," that is, type metal. Further, through the late spring and summer of 1778, he actually worked for Billings in some unspecified capacity, perhaps learning something about composing music

---

9. *The Singing Master's Assistant* (Boston, 1778). On Billings, see David P. McKay and Richard Crawford, *William Billings of Boston: Eighteenth-Century Composer* (Princeton: Princeton University Press, 1975), esp. 41–103. I have been unable to discover the purpose or constitution of the Aretinian Society.

10. This "Byles" does not appear to have had his own press, but perhaps he was a journeyman whom Howe knew well enough to ask for such advice. The aged minister and poet Mather Byles (1707–88) some of whose verse was put to music by Billings, seems an unlikely candidate for this reference; but see Clifford K. Shipton, *Biographical Sketches of Those Who Attended Harvard College,* vols. 4–17 of *Sibley's Harvard Graduates,* 17 vols. (Boston: Massachusetts Historical Society, 1933–75), 7:487–88.

11. On Condy, see Elizabeth Carroll Reilly, "The Wages of Piety: The Boston Book Trade of Jeremy Condy," in *Printing and Society in Early America,* ed. William L. Joyce, David D. Hall, Richard D. Brown, and John B. Hench (Worcester: American Antiquarian Society, 1983), 83–131.

12. On Revere's work as an engraver, see Clarence Brigham, *Paul Revere's Engravings* (Worcester: American Antiquarian Society, 1954).

and publishing it, and was paid in cash for his services.[13] Other entries from 1778 reveal that Howe took in money for schoolteaching and for lending out his horse and purchased a variety of necessities in the city. After the summer of that year, however, the record of his activities in Boston and elsewhere ceases.

We find him again in 1798, when *A Comprehensive Abridgement of Dr. Watts Lyric Poems* was printed in Northampton, Massachusetts, by Andrew Wright "for the Editor" (that is, Howe), to be "Sold by him in Greenwich; by D. Wright in Northampton; by D. Lombard, in Springfield; by J. Chandler, Petersham; by C. Reed, Brookfield; and by Peter Gibbons, Granville."[14] Bound with Watts's *Sublimity and Devotion United*, "Printed for, and sold by S. Howe, Greenwich," this volume marked the beginning of a six-year relationship with Wright, one of the first American printers to use movable type for music publishing. The next year, for example, Wright printed "Typographically" and "For the Author," Howe's own pioneering compilation of tunes, the *Worshipper's Assistant*. Wright also distributed it to such prominent printers and publishers as Benjamin Larkin in Boston, Ebenezer Merriam in Brookfield, Mathew Carey in Philadelphia, and a host of others—all this suitably emblazoned on the title page. With his location in one of the major towns on the upper Connecticut River, an important crossroad of land and water transportation, Wright was obviously well connected to an elaborate network of storekeepers, booksellers, and publishers from New Hampshire to Maryland.[15] Thus, whenever Howe had an item that he thought might be appealing to an audience beyond the local one—his tunebooks, for example—he resorted to Northampton.

Curiously, Solomon Howe did little if any printing himself. There exists

---

13. The records of Howe's business dealings with Billings are tantalizing but inconclusive. McKay and Crawford, in *William Billings*, 107–8, note that Billings indeed printed some of his early works (including *Music in Miniature* [Boston, 1789], a particularly brief and crude production), opening the possibility that Howe might have learned the printing trade from Billings and was paid for work around the shop. Further, the plates of Billings's *The Psalm-Singer's Amusement* (Boston, 1781) were later used by Solomon's son John for a reissue with a new title page, suggesting that they were acquired through Solomon's offices (*William Billings*, 273–74). Also see Richard Crawford, *American Sacred Music Imprints, 1698–1810* (Worcester: American Antiquarian Society, 1990), 493–97.

14. [Isaac Watts], *A Comprehensive Abridgement of Dr. Watts Lyric Poems* (Northampton, 1798).

15. See Paul R. Osterhout, "Andrew Wright: Northampton Music Printer," *American Music* 1 (1983): 5–26, for a useful account of Wright and of music publishing in general in the Connecticut River Valley during this period.

a typographically simple broadside of two religious hymns ("The Divine Law" and "The Beautiful Infant") signed "S. Howe" and dated "March, 1800, Greenwich, (Mass.)"; but that same year "An Elegy on the Departure of General George Washington," dated February 22 and signed the same way in the same typeface, also carried the line, "Sold by E. Larkin, Cornhill, Boston," raising the possibility that both items may have been printed in the metropolis. Further, although in 1807 Howe's *Evangelical Hymns* appeared with the notation that they were "Printed at the Press of S. Howe, Greenwich, Mass.," two years earlier his *Divine Hymns, on the Sufferings of Christ* were printed there by his son John, "For the Author," suggesting that although Solomon owned the press bought from Billings (or another), it was operated by his son. In any event, by 1805, and perhaps as early as 1803, John Howe had assumed the role of printer at the Greenwich press; and after 1807, when Solomon brought out his *Evangelical Hymns*, we find no further notice of his connection to the printing business.

John Howe's career in Greenwich and, after 1814 (when the township was divided), Enfield is more fully documented than his father's activities, particularly in his detailed "Printer's Book" for the 1830s and in his other accounts, as well as through his many imprints. But before we examine his activities in detail, we do well to distinguish Greenwich's material and cultural life from that of nearby communities such as Brookfield or Northampton, both of which also supported printers, albeit on a different scale.

Incorporated in 1749 as the town of Quabbin, "the land of many waters," Greenwich lay in the eastern part of Hampshire County, sixty-five miles west of Boston, hemmed in on three sides by Big and Little Quabbin Mountains and Mount Ram and bisected by the Swift River, which flowed from its source near the New Hampshire border to join the Ware and Quaboag Rivers at nearby Palmer.[16] Bordered on the west by Pelham and Belchertown, on the south by Belchertown and Ware, on the east by Hardwick and Petersham, and on the north by New Salem, Greenwich's terrain was at least as rugged as that of any of its neighbors and was worthy of the same tart remark Timothy Dwight heard uttered about neighboring Ware: "The land was like self-righteousness, for the more one had of it, the

---

16. On Greenwich and its south parish (later the town of Enfield), see Josiah Gilbert Holland, *History of Western Massachusetts*, 2 vols. (Springfield, Mass.: Samuel Bowles, 1855), 2:200–203, 211–14; John Warner Barber, *Massachusetts Historical Collections* (Worcester: Dorr, Howland, 1839), 320–21; and Howe, *Quabbin: The Lost Valley*, passim.

poorer he would be."[17] Through the 1820s most of Greenwich's citizens, never numbering much above one thousand, farmed or tended sheep on the rocky soil; a few of them worked at the mill sites at the town center or at the South Parish, later Enfield, where grist, carding, and sawmills, the staples of any self-sufficient community, were located. In the 1820s and 1830s the Swift River would be harnessed for much larger enterprises, but before that it was known as much for its good sport fishing as for anything else.[18]

Most transportation through the Swift River Valley, as this region came to be called, was over two turnpikes or toll roads. The Sixth Massachusetts Turnpike went from Amherst on the west, through Pelham, Greenwich, Hardwick, New Braintree, Oakham, Rutland, and Holden, and then on to Worcester and Shrewsbury, where it connected to the "great road" from Boston to New York.[19] The other, the Petersham-Monson Turnpike, ran north/south, from Petersham through Greenwich, the western part of Ware, Palmer, and on to Monson, at the Connecticut state line. Access to the lush Connecticut River Valley (and the substantial market-town of Northampton) to the west or to the center village of Brookfield to the east was by the "Hadley Path," which ran from Hadley through Ware to West Brookfield, where it diverged from the "great road." But travel from the valley was a chore, and although Greenwich's storekeepers participated in a trading network that extended beyond the Swift River Valley, in the early nineteenth century most of its citizens' exposure to the larger world came through the merchandise and print culture available therein.

Thus, in the early nineteenth century, the Swift River Valley strongly resembled what Gilmore has described, in central Vermont, as the "self-sufficient hamlet human habitat"—that is, core communities that "mediated between the bustle of village life and the steadier pace of farmstead life"—and a combination of "self-sufficient farmsteads" and "hardscrabble farms" whose families had regular dealings with nearby general stores but had few contacts with print culture beyond what was available through the

17. Timothy Dwight, *Travels through New England and New York*, 4 vols., ed. Barbara Miller Solomon (Cambridge, Mass.: Harvard University Press, 1969), 1:261–62.
18. See Barber, *Massachusetts Historical Collections*, 320–21, and a fascinating imprint, Festus Foster's *Address Delivered at the Ichthyon Feast at Greenwich-Village, Aug. 23, 1826* (Amherst, Mass., 1826) on the occasion of an annual celebration of a Swift River Valley holiday, when all so inclined took the day off to fish the town's rivers and ponds!
19. On turnpikes in the region see Howe, *Quabbin: The Lost Valley*, 155–56, 343. Jaffe, "Village Enlightenment," speaks to the importance of the expanding road networks to the proliferation of print culture; see esp. 334–40.

village storekeeper.[20] Because of Greenwich's distance "from much of the vibrancy of commercial exchange" and the rapid expansion of print culture that by the same period was evident in the "fortunate" or "center" village environment (represented for our purposes by Brookfield, whose population during this period was almost three times that of Greenwich and whose location on the state's major thoroughfares filled its streets with shops and services that catered to large numbers of travelers as well as to a sophisticated market economy), the figurative distance from Greenwich to Boston, or to Brookfield, was much greater than the literal number of miles.[21]

Moreover, a split among the inhabitants of the hamlets proper—Greenwich and, before 1814, its south parish, and the more outlying areas—also is significant to an understanding of the area's cultural development. This is brought out strongly in Francis H. Underwood's *Quabbin* (1893), a rich reminiscence of life in the south parish in the early nineteenth century. In his chapter on the distinctions between inhabitants of the "Village and [the] Country," Underwood noted that the difference between these two groups was "like a gulf between centuries," with "the rooted antipathy on the part of the hill people toward the better-dressed villagers . . . almost past belief." Indeed, Underwood's description of aspects of the hardscrabble farmers' culture is virtually interchangeable with Gilmore's more elaborate analysis: "There were few books (probably not half a dozen to a household), almost no newspapers, no hints of science, and no knowledge of the world, literally or figuratively." In contrast, Underwood notes that, although the villagers were not "greatly distinguished for reading or general intelligence," there was at least "no bigoted preference for ignorance." "If they were not illuminated," he concludes, at least "their faces were turned to the light," primarily because the more well-educated families—of which he notes half a dozen—and the ministers functioned as conduits of information from the world beyond the valley.[22]

The significance of Underwood's pioneering social analysis lies in his description of how Enfield, from 1830 on, entered more fully into "the

---

20. Gilmore, *Reading Becomes a Necessity of Life,* 141–53.
21. Larkin, "The Merriams of Brookfield," 41–44; and Susan Geib, "Changing Works: Agriculture and Society in Brookfield, Massachusetts, 1785–1820" (Ph.D. diss., Boston University, 1981).
22. Francis H. Underwood, *Quabbin: The Story of a Small Town With Outlooks on Puritan Life* (1893; repr. Boston: Northeastern University Press, 1986), 128–30; Gilmore, *Reading Becomes a Necessity of Life,* 146–48.

vast transformation of cultural exchange" that Gilmore delineates for the Windsor District of Vermont, and, by implication, for antebellum rural society generally. But here we jump ahead of our story.[23] For John Howe began his career as a printer precisely at the time Underwood commences his narrative about the "mother town" of Greenwich, "one of the most sluggish of rural communities," "limp and lifeless" if not poverty-stricken.[24] Beginning in 1798, however, it was distinguished from the nearby hill towns—indeed, from most others in New England—by the presence in its south parish of what Solomon Howe himself called "the Chief [good] that's known by mortal men": a printing press, presumably brought there by Howe himself.[25]

Because he himself did not own a font of musical type, Solomon Howe, who by his own admission already had several hundred more tunes that he wished to publish, brought his own compositions to Andrew Wright, as noted above, and for his first five years in Greenwich did little if any printing.[26] But beginning in 1803, with *Howe's Almanac for 1804* and Samuel Dunn's broadside *Elegy, on the Death of Mr. Henery [sic] Cook* (signed and dated "Newsalem, December 1803," with no imprint), his son John's imprints began to appear from Greenwich.[27] In addition to a yearly almanac, issued under one title or another through 1826, each year for the next three decades John Howe printed a few pamphlets or small books, and carried on a good deal of job work, comprising at first, as an advertisement of 1805 put it, "Writ, Summons, Deed, Execution, Certificate, and Note BLANKS," as well as "a Variety of Ballads."[28]

23. Gilmore, *Reading Becomes a Necessity of Life,* passim, but esp. chap. 10.
24. Underwood, *Quabbin: Story of a Small Town,* 39.
25. Howe's encomium to the press is found as an addendum to his broadside of two religious songs, "The Divine Law" and "The Beautiful Infant."
26. In the preface to *The Worshipper's Assistant* (Northampton, 1799), Howe notes that he has "put his own hymns to the following tunes and has in manuscript five hundred more which he intends to publish in the future."
27. See Howe, *Howe Genealogies,* 325–26, for vital information on John Howe.
28. Advertisement appended to Alonso Decalves, *New Travels to the Westward* (Greenwich, 1805). On this same page, Howe noted that he had for sale the following works: "Billings' Psalm Singer's Amusement" at $.61; "Suffolk Harmony" (William Billings, *The Suffolk Harmony* [Boston, 1786]), at $.55; "Howe's Worshipper's Assistant" (Northampton, 1799), at $.25; "Farmer's Evening Entertainment" (Solomon Howe, *The Farmer's Evening Entertainment* [Northampton, 1804]), at $.25; "Young Man's Musical Companion" (Solomon Howe, *The Young Man's Instructive Companion* [Greenwich, 1804]), at $.25; "Hulbert's Marches" (James Hulbert, *Variety of Marches* [Northampton, 1803]), at $.25; and "Complete Fifer's Museum" (James Hulbert, *The Complete Fifer's Museum* [Northampton, c. 1805]), at

We shall return to his lengthy run of almanacs and his job printing, but a brief survey of Howe's other imprints provides an index of his relation to the marketplace in the Swift River Valley. In 1805, for example, in addition to his father's *Divine Hymns,* he issued Alonso Decalves's *New Travels to the Westward,* an account, probably fictionalized, of a trip to "Unknown Parts of Columbia" (that is, the United States) beyond the Mississippi River, through which Howe hoped to capitalize on interest in the Louisiana Purchase.[29]

The next year, in addition to issuing *Visionary Thoughts, or Modern Prophecy,* a strange millennial speculation by Noah White of nearby Barre, he reprinted two "steady sellers," the anti-Catholic pamphlet, *A Narrative of the Life of Mrs. Hamilton,* and William Perry's *Only Sure Guide to the English Tongue,* in its "First Improved Edition" (Howe "omitted the Fables and other matter of small importance" and "substituted matter more useful and Instructive, so that the Scholar may improve in reading and gain useful Knowledge besides.")[30] In the years immediately following, he continued this pattern, publishing popular works (for example, *The Conversion of a Mahometan* [1807], Lemuel Haynes's celebrated diatribe against *Universal Salvation* [1807], and *The Sorrows of Yamba: Illustrating the Cruelty of the Slave-Trade* [1809]) as well as original work by people in the Swift River Valley and the areas immediately adjacent.[31]

These local productions are particularly interesting; in the first two decades of the nineteenth century Howe had a small stable of essayists and poets who took their work to him if they sought wider circulation. Their

---

$.25. Of schoolbooks, he carried "Webster's Third Part" (Noah Webster, *An American Selection of Lessons for Reading and Speaking . . . Being the Third Part of the Grammatical Institute* (one of the many 1804 editions, no doubt), at $.33; "Alexander's Gent's Spelling Books" (Caleb Alexander, *The Young Ladies or Gentlemen's Spelling Book* [Hudson, N.Y., 1802]), at $.25; and "Fisk's Spelling Book" (John Fiske, The *New-England Spelling Book* [Brookfield, 1803]), at $.25. Also, "The Young Gentleman's Pleasant Companion" (Solomon Howe, *The Young Gentleman and Lady's Pleasant Companion* [Greenwich, 1804]), at $.12.

29. Solomon Howe, *Divine Hymns, on the Sufferings of Christ* (Greenwich, 1805). See note 28 for the interesting information about Howe's books in stock that was appended to his edition of Decalves's work.

30. William Perry, *The Only Sure Guide to the English Tongue* (Greenwich, 1806), sig. A1v; (Mrs. Sarah Hamilton), *A Narrative of the Life, of Mrs. Hamilton* (Greenwich, 1806); Noah White, *Visionary Thoughts, or Modern Prophecy* (Greenwich, 1806). See Jaffe, "Village Enlightenment," 329–33, for a discussion of the importance of the concept of reading for self-improvement.

31. Gaifer [pseud.], *The Conversion of a Mahometan,* 10th ed. (Greenwich, 1807); Lemuel Haynes, *Universal Salvation a Very Ancient Doctrine . . . The Second Edition* (Greenwich, 1807); and *The Sorrows of Yamba . . . Third Edition* (Greenwich, 1809).

efforts speak to the question of early nineteenth-century literary culture, particularly in rural environments. One of these writers was Phineas Davison of Pelham. After publishing his *Evangelical Poems* through Ezekiel Terry of nearby Palmer in 1810, he stayed closer to home in publishing its sequels. Howe printed both his *Second Book: Containing Miscellaneous Essays in Verse and Prose; on Divine and Moral Subjects* and a potentially even more marketable one, the *Poor Boy's Pocket Book, or Double Primer*, a spelling book/catechism that included yet another selection of his moral essays.[32] From nearby Oakham came Nathaniel Bolton, whose attack on Thomas Paine's deism, *A Poem: On Infidelity,* Howe printed in 1808; and a Mrs. Mason of Greenwich brought her *Ellegaic* [sic] *Poems* (undated, though typography and paper indicate that it belongs to this period), to which Howe appended a poetic "Address to Christian Parents in Affliction" by Greenwich's minister, Joseph Blodget.[33]

Further, as an 1805 advertisement indicates, Howe published much broadside verse, such as Bolton's "ACROSTIC and Other Poetical Lines on Horace Perkins" ("instantaneously killed by falling from the steeple of the Northborough Meetinghouse on the First Day of July, 1808"); or, more frequently, work by his favorite local poet, Samuel Dunn of neighboring New Salem, who could be counted on to produce verse for any melancholy accident. We already have noted his "Elegy" on Henry Cook; he contributed others on the deaths of young people by drowning, lightning, and disease.[34] Nor did Howe neglect his parent's gift. He issued "The Pass Bell,

32. Phineas Davison, *Evangelical Poems, in Two Books. The First Book: Being the Husbandman's Companion: Showing How Business May Assist Him in His Spiritual Meditation* (Palmer, Mass., 1811); Davison, *The Second Book: Containing Miscellaneous Essays, in Verse and Prose on Divine and Moral Subjects* (Greenwich, 1810); and Davison, *The Poor Boy's Pocket Book, or Double Primer* (Greenwich, 1810). Some copies of the first two titles are bound together (although the pagination is separate), suggesting that Terry and Howe collaborated on this work or, what is more likely, that Davison took the sheets from Terry for Howe to bind with the sheets that Howe had printed.

33. Nathaniel Bolton, *A Poem: On Infidelity* (Greenwich, 1808); Mrs. Mason, *Ellegaic* [sic] *Poems Sacred to Friendship* (Greenwich, c. 1803). On Blodgett, see Holland, *Western Massachusetts,* 2:213.

34. Nathaniel Bolton, "ACROSTIC and Other Poetical Lines on Horace Perkins, who was instantaneously killed by falling from the steeple of the Northborough Meetinghouse on the First day of July, 1808" [Greenwich, 1808]; Samuel Dunn, "Elegy, on the Death Of Mr. Henery [sic] Cook" [Greenwich, 1803]; "An Elegy on the Deaths of William Luce and Warren Molton, who were drowned in a Pond in New Salem, (Mass.) July 23, 1811" [Greenwich, 1811]; "A Poem on the Death Of Miss LUCY CALHOON . . . Of Petersham, who was killed by Lightening June 1, 1806, in the 14th year of her age" [Greenwich, 1806]; "A Poem, on the Death Of Miss HANNAH CUTLER . . . of Greenwich, Massachusetts [Greenwich, 1808]; and "The following LINES were composed on the *Death,* of *Joseph,* and *John Lindsy,* who were

adapted to *Solemnity* by S. Howe," and other anonymous poems that also may have been by his father.[35]

However, when we compare the range of Howe imprints with that of a nearby firm like Ebenezer and George Merriam's, it is evident that he played a limited role in the expansion of print culture in nineteenth-century New England. Moreover, the nature of his business was not determined by ambition or a missionary sense of his role in the information revolution but almost wholly by matters of geography and economics. Because he was not on a major trading route nor in the center of a densely populated region, Howe never negotiated the kinds of extended commercial relationships that printers like the Merriams did with publishers and booksellers up and down the East Coast who printed large numbers of books in sheets in return for other stock or credit.[36] Nor did he have enough customers within a short distance to make him consider printing a weekly newspaper (as both Wright and the Merriams did), whose pages might introduce his customers to the concerns of a larger world. Most of Howe's imprints reveal an opportunistic farmer, storekeeper, and shoemaker who resorted to presswork as a favor to his more literarily inclined neighbors or to turn a quick profit on an item whose appeal, even in the Swift River Valley's limited market, already had been tested.

The exception that proves the rule is Howe's fascinating series of almanacs issued from 1803 to 1826; with them he sought to establish connections to the larger world of printing and publishing, as the Merriams were doing at the same time on an even more ambitious level. For a century the almanac had proved a good seller, but what prompted Howe to move beyond his immediate customers in the Swift River Valley by printing enough to distribute throughout the Northeast remains a mystery. In his address to the reader in his first number, for example, he allowed little more than that he was "a stranger to a great Part of the Public" among whom his "Labours" now were to appear, and on the title page he announced, as he would in almost every subsequent issue, the price per gross ($4.00), as

---

burnt to Death in a Cole-Cabin, in Dana, Worcester County, *Mass.* on the night of the 23d. December, 1809" (Greenwich: John Howe, [1809]).

35. [Thomas Rowe], "The Pass Bell. The Following *Elegant Lines* are supposed to be written by Mr. Thos Rowe, on hearing the Church Bell TOLL" [Greenwich, 1804]. "The Rich Man and the Beggar" [Greenwich, c. 1805]. "Fly Some Angel for the Altar" [Greenwich, 1805]; and "The following LINES were composed on the *Death,* of *Joseph, and John Lindsy,* who were burnt to Death in a Cole-Cabin, in Dana, Worcester County, *Mass.* on the night of the 23d. of December, 1809" (Greenwich: John Howe, [1809]).

36. Larkin, "The Merriams Of Brookfield," esp. 46–48.

well as per dozen ($.50) and individually ($.06), as proof of his ambition to move them beyond the valley, although through what means he intended to do so is not recorded.[37]

The number of each issue that Howe printed is not recorded, although his almanacs for 1822, which exist in three variants, indicate on their various title pages that they are of the "second edition of 5000 copies" and the "third edition of 5000 copies." And as early as 1812, he had boasted to the reader that he had "reason to be satisfied" with his "first number" (under the pseudonym "Philo Astronomiae") because "more than 5000 copies were sold."[38] To be sure, it is unlikely that he had the manpower to produce fifteen thousand almanacs in a few months' time—extant records for 1819 and 1820, for example, show him using only a quire (480 sheets) each year—but such an advertising ploy suggests Howe's attempt to convince the general public of the popularity of his wares.[39]

The almanacs themselves are important cultural documents and were compiled—even the astronomical calculations—by Howe himself, even though, from 1812 onward, he often signed the issues with his pseudonym. The first issues were simply called *Howe's Almanac,* with the addition of the assertive term "Genuine" in 1810. Exceptions were the *Massachusetts Agricultural Almanac for 1821,* which had "a variety of New, Useful, Instructive, and Amusing Matter by a Scientific Gentleman" (probably Howe himself, who in 1811 had signed himself "Professor of Natural Philosophy"), and which was "fitted to the Latitude and Longitude of Boston"; and the *Free-Mason's Almanac for 1826.*[40] In both instances, Howe, no doubt, was trying to widen the almanac's appeal, but his overall economic success in this venture was negligible and is epitomized by one of the humorous "signs" he noted in the almanac for 1813: "When I see men sell property for three-fourths of what it cost, it is a sign they must trade a

37. *Howe's Almanac for 1805* (Greenwich, 1804), [2].
38. *Howe's Genuine Almanac for 1812* (Greenwich, 1811), [2].
39. John Howe account book for 1819–25, in Howe Family Papers, American Antiquarian Society.
40. The almanacs for 1804–11 were signed by Howe; those of 1812–20 were issued under his pseudonym "Philo Astronomiae"; those of 1821–23 appeared with his name, and that of 1824 bore the name "Philo Astronomiae." In 1818, on the title page, he began noting that the almanacs were printed in Enfield rather than in Greenwich. Interestingly, the 1825 almanac carries the name of his brother Silas Warren Howe (1794–1827) in the title (see note 55). Another unusual imprint is Gideon Tenney's *The Pocket Quotidian or Almanac; for the Christian Era, 1810* (Greenwich: for the author, by John Howe, 1809). Why Howe consented to print the almanac of a competitor in the valley (Tenney was from Barre, as stated in the "Editor's Preface Introduction") is a mystery.

good deal to make it profitable. *For those who sell almanacs,*" he then noted.[41] Circumstantial evidence—unfortunately, few of Howe's extant records speak to the years in which he issued his almanacs—indicates no great change in his fortune, either as a printer or a farmer, after he began this series. Whatever else *Howe's Genuine Almanac* was, it was not his ticket to economic independence.[42]

The almanacs are, however, an invaluable articulation of the region's culture. In each issue several pages were devoted to irreverent and bawdy humor, some of it composed by Howe, the rest gathered where he could find it, the targets of which reveal much about the sociology of the valley and rural New England generally.[43] If we keep in mind two points about Underwood's rich reminiscence of nineteenth-century Greenwich—that the community was a battleground for religious ideas and that its inhabitants were enmeshed (as Robert Gross has observed) in a "masculine culture of competitive display" in which "aggressiveness and strength proved the measure of a man"—the almanacs' humor, almost always at the expense of religion, aggressive capitalism, or women (with other jibes at such "strangers" as blacks and the Irish), becomes more comprehensible.[44] We need also bear in mind Underwood's total silence regarding the individual who obviously was one of Enfield's most visible citizens. For Underwood's culture of liberal Christianity and gentility—he left Enfield for a literary life in Boston—was not that to which Howe aspired.[45]

41. *Howe's Genuine Almanac for 1813* (Greenwich, 1812), [25]. *The Free-Mason's Almanac for 1826* (Enfield, 1825) carried this riddle: "Why are almanacs like school-masters? Because people want to get them *cheap*," signed by "*Sad Experience.*"
42. Entries in Howe's account book for 1819–25, in the Howe Family Papers, do not indicate any large purchases of his almanac, nor any sort of trading with other printers and booksellers.
43. Howe rarely offered any attribution for his humorous stories, but the almanac's riddles and puzzles very frequently bore the name of local residents or others who presumably had presented such to him or whose efforts were borrowed by Howe from other publications, a common practice among early nineteenth-century printers. In this regard note a letter from his brother Jedediah (1791–1834), then in New York City, in which Jedediah speaks of providing the almanac-maker with a whole list of "anecdotes." "I give you a collection," Jedediah wrote, "large enough but I fear, not half, perhaps none of them will suit you—I also expect some of them are *old* to you." This same letter reveals that Jedediah was sending along any almanacs he could get his hands on, presumably (again) to provide filler for Howe's issues. Jedediah was in New York around 1822, trying to learn the typefounding trade; see the letter dated May 3 of that year, in the Howe Family Papers.
44. Robert A. Gross, foreword to Underwood, *Quabbin: Story of a Small Town,* xxiv.
45. See Philip F. Gura, "The View from Quabbin Hill," *New England Quarterly* 60 (1987): 92–105, for an assessment of Underwood; and Gross, foreword to Underwood, *Quabbin: Story of a Small Town.*

The manner and substance of Howe's humor can be traced to the counterpoint between hill country and village to which Underwood alerts us. That is to say, Howe's almanacs indicate a rejection of Underwood's and other liberals' support for Enfield's moral reformation at the hands of the clergy and its openness to intercourse with the outside world, when such trade threatened the rural value system that hitherto had defined personal and business relationships in the area. Thus, for example, we find reason for Howe's satiric portraits of the activities of the social reformers who by the early 1820s were on the scene in Enfield and elsewhere in western Massachusetts and his frequent diatribes against what he took to be clerical hypocrisy in general. "When I hear a Minister preach 'peace on earth, good will to men,'" he observed in 1816, "and get wrangled and contend with his parishoners [sic], or suffer the Collector to distrain for his salary, I guess his 'goodwill' is 'towards money' not men." Or, in 1813, "never judge of the preacher's piety by his professional zeal; the semblance of righteousness may be put on as mechanically as a surplice."[46] Howe was not an atheist; he felt no qualms about printing a work like Bolton's against Tom Paine. But he would not tolerate any ministry—Congregational, Baptist, Methodist—who worshiped Mammon, duped their parishioners for private gain, or engaged in moral reform primarily for the sake of their own reputations. Indeed, his most vivid, and lengthy, indictment of the clergy is a broadside that he printed (but probably did not himself compose) in the 1820s called "The True Preacher. A Lecture for the Clergy, of All Denominations," in which the author viciously condemns these "sharpers" who "While we listen,—slip behind us, / Seize our *purses*—cut the strings!" and exclusively claim the role of biblical interpreters. "These *dark sayings* were all handed / Down to us, a holy train: / You and we are both commanded, / You to hear, and we t' explain."[47]

Howe's anticlericalism, a staple of hill-country ideology during this period, was closely linked to equally frequent attacks on the ethic of acquisitive capitalism, particularly when it challenged an economic order still based profoundly on the trust incumbent in "changing works."[48] For

---

46. *Howe's Genuine Almanac for 1816* (Greenwich, 1815), [19]; *Howe's Genuine Almanac for 1813* (Greenwich, 1812), [24].
47. "The True Preacher. A Lecture for the Clergy, of All Denominations" (Enfield, 1834). An account for 1834 with Asa Damon indicates that Howe printed 500 "True Preachers" for him, strongly suggesting that he and not Howe wrote the piece. See John Howe's "Printer's Book," c. 1832, Howe Family Papers.
48. See Geib, "Changing Works," passim; and Bettye Hobbs Pruitt, "Self-Sufficiency

example, in his very first issue of the almanac, in "A New Catechism," Howe defined "the chief end of man":

> To gather up riches, to cheat all he can,
> To flatter the rich—the poor to despise,
> To pamper the fool—to humble the wise,
> The rich to assist—to do all in his pow'r,
> To kick the unfortunate still a peg low'r . . .
> To deal fair with all men, where riches attend.
> To grind down the poor, where there's none to defend them.[49]

Such sentiments, printed in 1804, are the more comprehensible when we remember Enfield's proximity to Pelham, the center of Daniel Shays's populism; but as late as 1821, with the Industrial Revolution about to arrive, Howe reprinted the poem, and sprinkled similar notions throughout other issues. In 1817, for example, in a poem called "The Disenchanted Rich, Are Poor," he sagely observed, "We see, that too much care annoys, / The Pleasures of the great; / But in contentment there are joys, / Beyond the reach of Fate."[50] At the moment when rural New England was about to be irrevocably transformed by the presence of the factory village and the capitalism on which it was based, Howe celebrated the man who was satisfied with his lot and not seduced by the vanities of the world. His almanacs, with the exception of "special" issues like the *Massachusetts Agricultural Almanac for 1821,* in which he tried to cash in on the interest in agricultural reform, sang the virtues of a rural world in which common sense ruled in matters of heaven and earth and the printer himself had more in common with the dispossessed than with the scions of wealth and cultivation. For "the *Printer,* poor Elf, is the servant of all," Howe noted in 1825, "and must *write,* plod and toil, at everyone's call, / Be content with a pittance—he never can attain, / The *road* to preferment, to honor or gain."[51] As we shall see, before long Howe himself had become the servant of those very entrepreneurs who threatened to overturn the value system of the Swift River Valley.

---

and the Agricultural Economy of Eighteenth-Century Massachusetts," *William and Mary Quarterly*, 3d ser., 41 (1984): 33–64.

49. *Howe's Almanac for 1805* (Greenwich, 1804), [28]; *Massachusetts Agricultural Almanac for 1821* (Enfield, 1820), [26].

50. *Howe's Genuine Almanac for 1817* (Greenwich, 1816), [23].

51. *Howe's Genuine Almanac for 1825* (Enfield, 1824), [24].

Howe's ribald humor at the expense of women, which eventuated in some of his most notorious imprints, stems from the same rural ethic, with its regard for a patriarchal moral and domestic order. But it still comes as a bit of a shock to read such stories as that of the "Gentleman who went to his nabor, whose wife had hung herself from an Apple Tree, and begged he would give him a scion" from it, "that he might graft it on his tree." When asked the reason for this request, the man gives a telling response: "Who knows said he, but it may *bear the same fruit*."[52] The women in Howe's almanacs are usually shrews or coquettes, supposedly deserving of such punishment. If they are virtuous, they are praised for the domestic felicity they bring.

Moreover, they are portrayed as profoundly sexual beings who enjoy intercourse and lust after it, as evident in his story about a woman who prosecuted a man for rape. In the trial, the judge asked her if she made any resistance. "I cried out," testified the woman. "Ay, said one of the witnesses, but that was nine months after." This attitude also colors his tale of a "pretty cherry cheeked, fresh colored" girl who went to market to sell her parents' butter and who was seduced by the man who bought the goods. "O you hussy!" cried her mother when her daughter reported what had happened. "You are *ruined!* you are *ruined!*" "Pho, mother," the girl replies, *"I wish I might be ruined so every night of my life, and live to the age of Methusaleh."*[53] These were the jokes of a masculine world in which, as Underwood put it, "modest girls had reason to shrink from young men whose education was acquired at the bar of the tavern" and "uncleanliness in manners and speech, if not universal, caused little remark."[54] Howe knew that he could count on people with such attitudes toward women to savor, and to purchase, whatever he printed that portrayed women in such ways.

How else explain the two remarkable broadsides (probably from the 1830s) as racy as anything printed in that period, "The Fair Maid's Song When All Alone" and "New Catherine Ogee"?[55] Typographically simple

---

52. *Massachusetts Agricultural Almanac for 1821*, [30].
53. Ibid., [30]; *Howe's Genuine Almanac for 1816* (Greenwich, 1815), [21–22].
54. Underwood, *Quabbin*, 46.
55. Although neither broadside has an imprint or any other identifying mark, the cut on "New Catherine Ogee" is the same as that used on "The Gray Mare. Or Johnny, the Miller and Beautiful Kate," which bears the imprint "Printed by S. Howe, Enfield" (c. 1838), presumably referring to his father or perhaps to his brother Silas. (Silas died in 1827, however, which would make the attributed date of about 1838 incorrect.) The other broadside has been long identified by booksellers as a Howe imprint. The author himself, in 1975, purchased a

(although the latter is adorned with a cut that Howe frequently used on other broadsides of the period and which he might have acquired in 1817 in the "New PRINTING APPARATUS" that he announced to his almanac subscribers) and printed on small sheets of paper, both poems center on woman's sexual appetite and her willingness to satisfy it.[56] "New Catherine Ogee," for example, tells the story of a young man who finally succeeds in seducing his female companion in "the *Late Evening Dew*":

> She sat down in silence, I viewed her divine,
> Then hoised her silks, and her linen so fine;
> Her T****s round, and firm, in betwixt them I flew,
> And was lost in delight, in the *Late Evening Dew*.

The point, of course, is his partner's full enjoyment of all unveiled to her:

> She said not a word, about what she did feel,
> But by kisses and squeezes, her love did reveal;
> I tarried there with her, till daylight it grew:
> Then saw her safe home, from the *Late Evening Dew*.

But this description is mild compared to that of "The Fair Maid's Song," sung in the first person (to the tune "White Cockade") and devoted to the narrator's "wonder what the cause can be / The young men do not fancy me," for "I have a thing belongs to me, / Would please a young man handsomely." In five witty stanzas that follow, the fair maid describes her appeal to a miller, a sawyer, a blacksmith, a cobbler, and a teamster, in all cases using the jargon of the man's trade to describe her prized possession. One stanza gives the flavor of the whole:

> If he be a man that makes the shoes,
> His instruments I'll learn to use;
> And when his trade I understand,
> I'll take his shoe-last in my hand:
> His rub-stick, and his welting-bones,
> And hammar [*sic*] well on his lap-stones:

---

copy of both broadsides from a Massachusetts bookdealer as part of a large lot of exclusively Howe family materials.

56. The new printing apparatus was noted in *Howe's Genuine Almanac for 1818* (Greenwich, 1817), final leaf.

And help him work his waxen balls
And quickly drive his pegging awls.

As should be clear from these examples, Howe's attitude toward women reinforces the same ethic he advanced through his treatment of clerics and other "sharpers." And the fantasies on which it was based are clearly those of an eighteenth-century rural world in which women were the property of men, before and after marriage, who took delight in their psychological bondage.[57] When John Howe sought to supplement his income as a farmer or storekeeper, he knew that he could turn to verse like "The Fair Maid's Song" as well as to Phineas Davison's moral essays.

Very little has survived of what Howe printed between 1826, the last year in which he issued an almanac, and 1844, the last year of entries in his printing accounts. Indeed, most extant items are broadsides like the two just discussed, although they cover a wide range of topics, from reissues of popular songs like "The Gray Mare" to a final effort by Samuel Dunn, "An Elegy on the Death of Mr. Harfield Lyndsey," written when the New Salem poet was "91 years 7 months" old. During this period, Howe's sole book was *The Christian's Pocket-Companion, Being a Choice Collection of Devotional Hymns*, edited by Joseph G. Royce and issued in 1826.[58] But here bibliography fails to present the full range of Howe's work, for his

57. The literature on women's position in late eighteenth- and early nineteenth-century New England is large, but see especially Nancy F. Cott, *The Bonds of Womanhood: "Women's Sphere" in New England, 1780–1835* (New Haven: Yale University Press, 1977), Linda F. Kerber, *Women of the Republic: Intellect and Ideology in Revolutionary America* (Chapel Hill: University of North Carolina Press, 1980), and Mary Beth Norton, *Liberty's Daughters: The Revolutionary Experience of American Women, 1750–1800* (Boston: Little, Brown, 1980).

58. On "The Gray Mare," see note 55; Samuel Dunn, "An Elegy on the Death of Mr. Harfield Lyndsey, Aged Twenty-Six Years" (Enfield, 1838). See *Publications of the Colonial Society of Massachusetts* 13 (1910): 140–45, for more information about Dunn. It seems almost certain that Howe also printed Dunn's fascinating *A Word in Season: or, the BURTHEN of SAMUEL, (the son of Richard, the son of Samuel, the son of James the Rhode Islandite,) which he saw while under the mountain, in the land of Prescott, Mass., in the days of James Munroe, president, and David D. Tompkins, vice-president, of the United States of America, concerning the divisions of Christianity. To which is added, some Remarks on those who oppose the Institution of Free-Masonry* (n.p., n.d.), typographically similar to other Howe imprints from the second decade of the century.

The attribution of *The Christian's Pocket-Companion, Being a Choice Collection of Devotional Hymns* (Enfield, 1826) to Joseph G. Royce is found on the title page in manuscript in Howe's account book for 1819–25; for some reason, Royce's name was deleted from the page as printed.

record books indicate a great deal of activity during the 1820s and 1830s, when his imprints are most scarce.

This manuscript record, admittedly fragmentary, exists in various forms. The earliest entries are found in a general account book that covers the period 1819–25 and is devoted primarily to store accounts. In addition to offering a detailed example of the contemporary economic system—based primarily on the barter of goods and services that Susan Geib has described as "changing works"—it records his printing of such items as neighbor Noah White's *An Easy Guide to the Art of Spelling,* various pamphlets for local authors, and frequent job work.[59] But sometime between 1825 and 1832, Howe began to separate his printing accounts from those of his general store; two separate account books, one of which is a detailed "Printer's Book," commence in the latter year.

These two account books are a significant resource for understanding how a rural printer conducted his trade. The earlier record book, for example, is prefaced by an index of twenty-two accounts, primarily from Enfield and Greenwich; approximately fifteen more customers were added to its pages as the years passed. These entries show customers purchasing such goods as cloth (of various kinds), buttons, thread, and other sewing goods; shears and scissors; hair combs and other toiletries; corn, hay, seasonable vegetables such as turnips and onions—all items that indicate a fairly limited supply of merchandise.

In addition, however, Howe's customers often purchased blank paper or printed material—schoolbooks in particular—and used his leatherworking skills. In 1821, for example, Barzillai Newcomb paid for "Scott's Lessons" and "Daboll's Arithmetic," and a year later James Richards's son bought "Comyn's [Cummings's] Geography & Atlas," a fairly expensive item at $1.75.[60] Richards also took two songbooks, "The American Musical Miscellany" and the "Songster's Amusing Companion."[61] Many individu-

---

59. Noah White, *An Easy Guide to the Art of Spelling* (Enfield, 1819), two issues, with variations on 84. Howe charged $56.00 for printing the book, $11.20 for paper, $20.00 for binding four hundred copies, and was paid by note. During this period, he also printed Josiah White's *The Two Witnesses. Rev. XI ... By a Lay Man* (Enfield, 1823), for which he charged a total of $40.00.

60. Jacob Abbot Cummings, *An Introduction to Ancient and Modern Geography ... with an Atlas* (Boston, 1821); William Scott, *Lessons in Elocution* (Greenfield, Mass., 1821, or any number of editions of 1820); and Nathan Daboll, *Daboll's Schoolmaster's Assistant* (New London, 1820).

61. No titles precisely like these are in *American Imprints,* but see *The Musical Miscellany* (New Haven, 1812, or Poughkeepsie, N.Y., 1812), *The Songster's Companion* (Brattleborough, Vt., 1815), and *The Song-Singer's Companion* (Boston, 1818).

als purchased almanacs, usually single copies and presumably Howe's, although in 1820 Chester Hall took six almanacs and a dozen in the following year, perhaps to be resold among farmers in his neighborhood or in adjacent communities; and in 1822 William Joslin came in for a "farmer's Almanac," at $.12.[62] Finally, several individuals enlisted Howe's skills as a bookbinder; in addition to patching shoes for various customers and selling boots and shoes he had made, Howe also rebound books. In 1819, for example, he bound two volumes for Moses Gray, at $.08 each, and a few years later charged Deacon Darius Sabin $.25 for rebinding his copy of the "System of Divinity" (probably Samuel Hopkins's two-volume work by that name).

The extent of Howe's book binding is indicated in the printing records found in this volume. His account with Noah White of Barre, for example, whose spelling book he printed in 1819, indicates a charge of $156.00 for "Printing 7 forms," $11.20 for the paper for the same, and $6.00 for binding 150 copies—$.04 each. Half a year later he bound 350 more at the same price per copy. For Phineas Davison in 1822 he printed a fourteen-page "octidecimo" at $.42 per page and charged $1.32 for binding thirty-three copies, again at $.04 the unit.[63] Smaller items he often sewed in blue paper wrappers, the characteristic covering of many of his extant imprints. In 1824 when local Masons sought to publish the Reverend James Thompson's *Oration* "pronounced before Mount Zion Lodge" in Hardwick, he charged $8.00 for 200 copies of fifteen pages each, $1.30 for paper, and $1.38 for "folding, sewing and blue paper."[64]

Even more revealing of nineteenth-century rural economy, however, was the varied job work he did for individuals and constituencies in the region. Handbills and advertisements were particularly common work. Isaac Magoon of neighboring Ware, for example, paid $1.50 for 200 "Show-bills." For some kind of "sporting Match," Chaney Shaw ordered twenty "Advertisements," evidently large broadsides, for Howe charged him $1.50. Other such work often took the form of labels for goods produced in the general area. In 1824, for example, Warren P. Wing paid $4.00 for

---

62. Perhaps T. Spofford's *The Farmer's Almanac and Register for 1823* (Andover, Mass., 1822), *The Farmer's Almanac for 1823* (Portland, Maine., 1822), or, most likely, Robert B. Thomas's *Farmer's Almanac* (Boston, 1822).
63. There is no record in *American Imprints* of this Davison title.
64. James Thompson, *An Oration. Pronounced before Mount Zion Lodge of Free and Accepted Masons: at Hardwick, Mass., June 24, A.L. 5824. It being the Festival of St. John the Baptist* (Enfield, 1824).

2,300 "Labels for Rifles" and $4.00 more for 400 advertisements "for the same." That same year he ordered thirty-one quires—an immense number—of "Labels for Razors" and four quires of "Certificates of Carding Machines." Earlier, in 1823, when Howe had printed labels for "Blacking" for the partnership of Wing, C. E. Field, and J. Bishop, he charged $.50 per quire and six months later asked $2.00 more for "resetting" the labels and $10.62 for printing 21 quires, 58 sheets of them.

After 1824 Howe also frequently worked for the town of Enfield, printing blank forms for highway, county, and minister's taxes, and town-meeting warrants. And as his publication of Thompson's *Oration* for the Hardwick Masonic lodge indicates, he sometimes worked for local organizations. To the account of James Minds in 1824, for example, he noted 400 "Membership Applications" for their "Chapter," presumably another Masonic group, and also provided "Chapter receipts" and other job work. In 1825 the "Village Encampment," probably a Methodist meeting, was charged $1.25 for 250 "Applications," and the following year "King Hiram's Chapter" was billed for "3 quires blank Requests." School tickets, bills for a "Black-ball," a "family Record" (probably similar to the one extant for Howe's own family) for Asabel Foster—were just part of the varied nature of Howe's job printing before 1830.[65]

His remarkably detailed "Printer's Book, "commencing with accounts for 1832, fills in this picture for the final decade and a half of his life. Organized basically by year, these records show almost exclusively job work, particularly for the growing commercial community in Enfield and its environs. For Harvey Royce, for example, Howe printed three hundred "Watch Tickets," at $.50. In 1833 O. A. Patterson paid him $2.00 for 200 "Tickets or Invitation Cards," and a year later Asa Damon had him work up "170 Laborer's Agreements," presumably for the workforce that began to flock to the nearby Ware Factory Village. The same year, Damon ordered 500 "True Preachers," the anticlerical broadside discussed above, suggesting that he may have written it.[66] Another individual involved in factory village expansion, Col. Alonzo Cutler, ordered "50 Show-bills for sash in Enfield" and the same number for his "Chelmsford factory." During the 1830s, sale notices also were increasingly common, as was Howe's work for the town of Enfield and surrounding parishes and communities.

65. Howe used the same sort of arch, constructed of typographical ornaments, on his own family register that he used on Thompson's oration; these are particularly attractive imprints.
66. See note 47.

The decade ended with orders for a thousand "soap labels" for John Parkman of Ware Factory Village, a twelve-page Sunday School library catalogue, and a broadside "Funeral Hymn," printed for one Cecilia Lammon.[67]

The records for the 1840s show more of the same. In 1841, for example, Amos H. Wyman paid $3.00 for "3700 labels for Garden seeds and paper," and the next year took six thousand more. James Sloan ordered 160 "Show-bills of Pumps." Samuel Tinkham bought "20 Labels for Churns," for $.34; Cyrus Morse and Gilbert Warden of "Newsalem" were charged $6.00 for "One Thousand and 30 Show-bills"; and Joseph Robinson of Hardwick came to town for 1520 labels. In 1843 Anson Newcomb called on Howe to print one of his few pamphlets of the period, 200 copies of "Alonzo and Melissa."[68] The last entry regarding printing occurs on 25 January 1845, noting twenty-eight show-bills for Samuel Tinkham.

By the 1830s and 1840s, then, Howe the entrepreneur had become more and more the servant of the new economic order he had so distrusted; that is, of individuals and companies who needed his skills to label and advertise an ever-increasing number of goods that were turned out in the water-powered factories of New England's countryside. Thus, unwittingly or not, he contributed to the ways in which such hitherto remote areas as the Swift River Valley were pulled into regional and national economies.[69] In the Howe accounts, this change in his role vis-à-vis the commercial economy is most dramatically reflected by the fact that most of the printing debits of the period 1830–45 were not settled through the goods and services that had served as tender in the early decades of the century but rather in cash.[70]

Howe's first account book, for example, shows people paying for store and printed goods through the use of wagons or work animals, assistance in hog butchering, "bleeding Mrs. Howe," "drawing a tooth," "bringing 5

---

67. No copies of the broadside or library catalogue are known.

68. *Alonso and Melissa. Illustrating the Changes of Fortune, and Triumph of Virtue . . . Stereotype Edition.* Entered According to Act of Congress, Jan. 2, 1844 (Enfield, 1844). This bears no relation to the novel by the same name. Where Howe obtained the stereotype plates for this work, if it was so printed, is unknown. He may have gotten the plates through his brother Jedediah, who by this time was a stereotyper in Philadelphia. See the Printer's Files at the American Antiquarian Society.

69. See Gilmore, *Reading Becomes a Necessity of Life,* esp. chap. 10, for more on this transformation.

70. Larkin, in "The Merriams of Brookfield," observes a similar change in the Brookfield firm's settlement of accounts, dating from 1824. He writes, "From then on, paper accounts were settled not by commodity exchange, but almost exclusively in the negotiable instruments of a cash economy" (56).

bundles of paper from Brookfield," making a coffin and a "trundel bed stead," or offering their children for farmwork; others settled their accounts in such goods as pork, onions, dried apples, leather, and hats. Occasionally, an account was settled with a small amount of cash, but most debits were worked or traded off in various ways. Interestingly, the other extant record book for the post-1830 period, that in which Howe kept only his store accounts, reveals local customers (primarily farmers) still paying through goods and services, particularly produce (suggesting Howe's expanding role as a middleman in an increasingly complex trade network), but the business community paid for his labor at the press in legal tender. At his death in 1845, the rural printer had become, among his various accomplishments, another participant in the economic transformation of the rural American countryside, his hitherto unique role as a cultural middleman obscured by his willingness to work, as so many then did, for a price.

The extant records of the Howe family's business offer a rare glimpse into the world of the rural printer in the new nation. Unlike Alden Spooner or Ebenezer and George Merriam, John Howe never reached the point where he served as a middleman to the information revolution that by 1840 transformed rural America. Rather, through most of his career, as evident most vividly in his almanacs but also in many of his imprints of local authors, he represented a conservative rural ethic opposed to the market capitalism on which industrialization was based.

But by the mid-1830s, perhaps from economic necessity, perhaps because he knew that the revolution could not be stemmed, he became a cog in the new social machine that for a few decades promised to turn New England from its slow drift into an economic backwater. Had he lived another ten years, he would have seen, and perhaps greeted, albeit surreptitiously at first, the day when, as Underwood put it, Enfield became "part of the great world, and felt the universal pulsations of humanity," a change effected by "home and foreign news, politics, inventions, and discoveries in arts and sciences," finally a change "brought home to people who never had anything to occupy their minds except neighborhood gossip and sermons."[71]

He lived, however, on the cusp of such changes, his skills put to use as much to resist as to embrace the new order of the ages. Therein lies his interest to us as cultural historians, and to those moralists among us who

---

71. Underwood, *Quabbin: Story of a Small Town*, 271.

might see in the Swift River Valley's transformation, in the 1830s, into the vast wilderness of the Quabbin Reservoir—Enfield, Greenwich, and other surrounding towns simultaneously lost to metropolitan Boston's insatiable need for water and yet their natural setting permanently preserved—a just conclusion to the battle Howe once waged against the forces of change.[72]

72. For the story of the inundation of the valley, see Howe, *Quabbin: The Lost Valley*, passim, and J. R. Greene, *The Creation of Quabbin Reservoir: The Death of the Swift River Valley* (Athol, Mass.: Transcript Press, 1981).

7 | The Reverend Parsons Cooke and Ware Factory Village

A New Missionary Field

As I mentioned in my introduction, this essay stems from the earliest serious "research" that I undertook, as an undergraduate intern at Old Sturbridge Village in Sturbridge, Massachusetts. The attractions of work at this institution were many and deserve an essay to themselves, but surely the chief joy of the internship program, the brainchild of Richard Rabinowitz, was the independent research project each intern undertook. Because OSV (as it is affectionately known) took as its mission to preserve and interpret the everyday life of New Englanders between 1790 and 1840, one's research had to stem from that. One did not propose, for example, to study the career of Andrew Jackson as president but, for example, the support for Jackson and his principles within the political organization of a New England community. Or, to take another example, not the details of the country's trade relations with England following the War of 1812, but rather the way farm goods were marketed in rural "center" villages in Connecticut. The task was to immerse one's self in the particular and therein to find the significant detail, to make a "fact," as Thoreau once put it, "flower into a truth."

Because my hometown of Ware, Massachusetts, was but a stone's throw from OSV, I decided to mine its archives—preserved, as I learned, not in one repository but sometimes in the most unlikely places—for the federal and early national periods. I already had established an interest in religious history, having enjoyed the classes of Alan Heimert at Harvard, and thus was excited when I discovered that a minister from Ware had published a good many books and pamphlets, all part of his crusade against the religious liberalism of the day. The summer's project yielded much from the local church and town records, and when I returned to college in the fall, I asked Heimert to approve my study of Cooke as the subject of my senior thesis. This work, over the period of a year and the distillation of which you read here, proved crucial in determining the topics to which I later would turn my attention.

My immersion in Ware's history also brought me up against a subject I found, and continue to find, of great interest: the development of New England's rural factory villages. Indeed, so taken have I been with the subject that I often think that if I had begun my career in a department of history rather than of literature, my significant work would have been done in that area. Until recently, though, I have not spent much ink in the paths suggested by this first research project but have delighted instead in the increasingly sophisticated literature that has sprung up on the topic—again, not on such enterprises as the Waltham or Lowell mills, but on the transformation of the rural countryside by the arrival of new technology. To interested readers, I strongly recommend the work of Jonathan Prude, particularly his *The Coming of Industrial Order: Town and Factory Life in Rural Massachusetts, 1810–1860* (1983), whom I watched in graduate school as he assembled more and more material for his vast project; Thomas Dublin's recent *Transforming Women's Work: New England Lives in the Industrial Revolution* (1994); and David A. Zonderman's *Aspirations and Anxieties: New England Workers and the Mechanized Factory System, 1815–1850* (1992). I would point out, however, that to date very little work has been done on the topic I take up in this essay.

By the 1830s manufacturing villages like the one in Ware, Massachusetts, were an indelible feature of the New England landscape, providing a much-needed boost to the region's economy. Yet they raised unsettling questions about the moral welfare of communities facing for the first time the social disruption caused by rapid industrialization. As one minister observed, factory villages challenged the "intelligence and virtue" of communities as their inhabitants struggled with the "new direction" given the American genius through its utilization of water power for manufacturing. "Interesting as are the inquiries suggested by this state of things to the statesman and the political economist," Amos Blanchard noted, "questions of vastly greater interest arise in the mind of every Christian" for whom the "moral character" of these institutions remained unproved.[1]

Within these new communities composed of a heterodox and unsettled population some conservative Congregational ministers discovered a new missionary field. Faced with manifold changes in the public's perception of the role and importance of the ministry, men like the Reverend Parsons Cooke of Ware Factory Village regarded the new environment created by the manufacturing villages as a place to redefine their evangelical labors by making a stand against such "heretical" denominations as the Unitarians and Universalists, which flourished there. Rather than journeying to the wilds of Ohio, or, farther yet, to the Sandwich Islands to convert the heathen, Cooke and others chose as their missionary field these communities where the millworking population threatened the older agricultural order with unorthodox opinions and lax moral standards.[2] To follow Cooke's career in Ware Factory Village is to examine at close range not only some of the unsettling social effects of industrialization but also the reaction of one segment of the ministry to the moral and theological complexity engendered by swift technological change.

Incorporated in 1761, the original town of Ware—hereafter referred to as Ware Center—was situated about three miles west of the Ware River, later the source of water power for Ware Factory Village.[3] Until the early nineteenth century Ware's population, numbering about one thousand, was engaged primarily in agriculture. In 1813, however, several grist and

1. Amos Blanchard, introduction to Dorus Clarke, *Lectures to Young People In Manufacturing Villages* (Boston: Perkins and Marvin, 1836), vi.
2. On the changing role of the ministry during the period see, for example, Daniel H. Calhoun, *Professional Lives in America: Structure and Aspiration, 1750–1850* (Cambridge: Harvard University Press, 1965), part iv, and Ann Douglas, *The Feminization of American Culture* (New York: Knopf, 1977), passim. Two other ministers of Cooke's acquaintance and theological persuasion also chose to minister to factory villages. Dorus Clarke was pastor to the church in the town of Chicopee, Massachusetts, from 1835 to 1841 and then joined Cooke on the editorial board of the *New England Puritan*. Jonathan Edwards Woodbridge, Cooke's classmate at Williams, came to the church in Ware Factory Village in 1838. He, too, later joined the staff of the *Puritan*. There is no full-length study of the orthodox ministry's relation to the industrial village of this period.
3. The best general history of Ware is Arthur Chase, *The History of Ware, Massachusetts* (Cambridge, Mass.: University Press, 1911). But also see William Hyde, *An Address, Delivered at the Opening of the New Town Hall, Ware, Massachusetts, March 31, 1847* (Brookfield, Mass.: Merriam and Cooke, 1847), David Coburn, *An Historical Address Delivered at Ware, 1851* (West Brookfield, Mass.: O. S. Cooke, 1851), and Augustus B. Reed, *Historical Sermon, delivered at Ware First Parish, Dec. 2, 1830* (privately printed, 1889).

sawmills along the river were sold to two enterprising merchants from the Worcester area who promptly installed wool-carding machinery in the buildings and built a machine shop adjacent to them. In 1821 the company of Holbrook and Dexter of Boston purchased these mills and 400 acres of adjoining land; and by 1823, through investments from such prominent merchants as the Tappans of Northampton, the Ware Manufacturing Company was incorporated, with a capitalization of $600,000, "for the purpose of manufacturing cotton and woolen yarn and cloth." Vast construction was undertaken on the site, and, as a result, the town's size swelled to 2,045 people, more than half of whom lived in the new manufacturing area.[4]

The most apparent difficulty raised by the factory village was the strain it imposed on the existing civil and religious organization of the town.[5] The millworkers "were a considerable population collected from various parts of the country" and were not closely tied to the agricultural concerns of the old town or to the strongly orthodox community of the First Church.[6] Soon the different interests of Ware Center and Ware Factory Village became visible in local politics; recognizing this, Thomas Dexter, William Bowdoin, and Anthony Olney—all supervisors in the mills and two of whom were Unitarians—petitioned as early as 1825 to change the village's name to "Waterford," presumably to clear the way for its incorporation as a separate town. During the next decade similar actions ensured that religion and politics would become badly mixed as the factory village sought to achieve civil and ecclesiastical independence from the older community near which it had "sprung up as by enchantment."[7]

The movement to acquire town status did not garner enough support, however, and there began a battle to establish what eventually became the East Evangelical Society. But the heterogeneous nature of the factory village

---

4. Margaret R. Pabst, "Agricultural Trends in the Connecticut River Valley of Massachusetts, 1800–1900," *Smith College Studies in History* 26 (1941): 12; Chase, *History of Ware,* 128, 219. For a description of the mills that Holbrook and Dexter purchased, see the contemporary auction notice in the *Manufacturer's and Farmer's Journal* of Providence, Rhode Island, for 15 March 1821; in 1828 a description of the mill village appeared in Jeremiah Spofford, *A Gazetteer of Massachusetts* (Newburyport, Mass.: Whipple, 1828), 317.

5. See, for example, Hyde, *An Address,* 37; and "Town Meeting Records," Ware Town Hall, Ware, Massachusetts, entry for 3 January 1825.

6. John Adams Vinton, "Parsons Cooke," *Congregational Quarterly,* 14 (1872): 220. Moss, Yale class of 1787, repealed the Half-Way Covenant, which had been adopted by his predecessors, and instituted the orthodox Westminister Shorter Catechism, see Coburn, *An Historical Address,* 24–27.

7. Hyde, *An Address,* 37: Reed, *Historical Sermon,* 17.

prevented quick settlement of a minister, and for about a year after its incorporation the "East Parish" was served by clergymen of different denominations chosen by a committee of three men, representing Congregationalists, Unitarians, and Baptists. Importantly, even though the village's inhabitants had been canvassed for their religious preferences, no provision was made for representation of either the Universalists or the Methodists, two groups against whom orthodox Congregationalists in the village would later inveigh so loudly.[8]

At this juncture another group of men concerned with the factory village turned their attention to the area. At their 1826 meeting in Boston, the principal stockholders of the Ware Manufacturing Company addressed the question of who would be sent to Ware to supervise the new establishment. Gardner Green, president of the company, was a Unitarian, as were a majority of those present; but a few in the number, most notably John Tappan and S. V. S. Wilder, were staunch Calvinists. In his capacity as a director of the company Wilder had visited the factory village in 1825, and, particularly because of his business acumen, seemed a likely choice for the job. Moreover, on his visit he had become concerned about the religious tenor of the town. He had ascertained that "the head machinist and agent [of the company] were uncompromising Unitarians," that these men "had placed as overseers in all departments, either Unitarians or Universalists," and that "most of the workmen . . . were of the same persuasion." Disturbed by the heterodox opinions he found in the village, Wilder reported these facts to Tappan and other conservative members of the company.[9]

When at first Wilder declined the appointment as overseer, Tappan hit

---

8. [S. V. S. Wilder], *Records from the Life of S. V. S. Wilder* (New York: American Tract Society, 1865), 202; Milton P. Braman, *A Sermon Occasioned by the Death of Rev. Parsons Cooke, D.D.* (Lynn: Stevenson and Nichols, 1864), 32; Edward Payson Thwing, *A Memorial of Thomas Thwing* (Boston: Lee and Shepard, 1868), 19. Serious organization of the Methodists began in 1826 under the leadership of Joshua Crowell, a tavernkeeper in Ware Center, and Luther Payne of the factory village, but it is difficult to ascertain the strength of their support; see D. Sherman, "Joshua Crowell," in *Sketches of New England Divines* (New York: Carlton and Porter, 1860), 389, 397.

9. This story is told in [Wilder], *Records*, 199, 200. Wilder was a key figure in the early history of the village. Entering the mercantile world as a clerk at the age of seventeen, he was within five years a European agent for the prominent Salem merchant, William Gray; soon after, he accumulated his own fortune. Deeply committed to orthodox Calvinism—he had studied with the Reverend Jedediah Morse of Charlestown, Mass., founder of Andover Theological Seminary—Wilder was an important supporter of many national voluntary societies, most notably a founder and president of the American Tract Society.

upon an ingenious plan to secure the economic and religious well-being of the factory village. As Wilder recalled the moment, Tappan

> whispered in the ear of the President that, in order to induce me to undertake the overseership, he would do well to propose that $3,000 towards building a church be subscribed, on condition that the good people in the neighborhood would raise $3,000 in addition, and then to invest me with full powers to superintend the erection of said meetinghouse and settling a pastor.

The plan was a stroke of genius on the part of the orthodox group, for the majority of the stockholders, realizing how difficult it would be to persuade anyone of merit to venture to Ware, were more than willing to contribute money for the church. Not overly concerned with what kind of minister Wilder would install, they had as their main objective efficient supervision of the mill operation. Wilder realized his opportunity, and when he heard the motion seconded "and saw twenty Unitarian hands erected in behalf of carrying the motion into effect, [he] did not dare disregard the obvious call of Providence." Ironically, the minister whom the company indirectly sanctioned became one of the most vociferous opponents of the Unitarian faith of which the majority of stockholders were members.

When Wilder arrived in Ware he found a young Williams College graduate, Parsons Cooke, preaching to the inhabitants. Thomas Thwing, a cabinetmaker in the factory village, had secured Cooke's services on the recommendation of Edward Dorr Griffin, president of Williams and formerly Thwing's pastor at the Park Street Church in Boston. Initially hired for a one-month period, Cooke fell seriously ill in the autumn of 1825 and remained in the village until the following spring, when he was asked to resume his pastoral labors and was "providentially" discovered by the newly appointed overseer. Wilder lost no time in assuming control of the spiritual welfare of the village. With the "cordial" encouragement of "all the old inhabitants of the neighborhood," he recognized Cooke as an ideal leader of the new church and soon selected him for the position. On 21 June 1826 the young clergyman was ordained and installed as the first pastor of the East Evangelical Church and Society in Ware; the ceremony was held in one of the vacant stories of a new factory building.[10]

10. Thwing, *Memorial of Thomas Thwing*, 20; Vinton, "Parsons Cooke," 222, 223.

Born in Hadley, Massachusetts, in 1800, Cooke attended college at Williams, graduating in 1822. Later he returned to Williamstown to study theology with Griffin, who was, along with Leonard Woods of the Andover Theological Seminary, the intellectual leader of New England's "consistent" Calvinists. They were the conservative opponents of both Charles Grandison Finney's liberal evangelical methods and the theological innovations of Yale's "New Divinity" men, Nathaniel William Taylor and Lyman Beecher.[11] Cooke's alignment with Griffin's party was never in doubt; as early as 24 January 1827, at the dedication of the newly constructed meetinghouse in the village, he boldly declared that *"Christ's dwelling in the flesh"* was the *"principal thing designed to be set forth in the ordinances of God's house."* Echoing the advice John Woodbridge had given him at his ordination, the Ware minister told the congregation that he would stress "the simple fact of Christ's incarnation and crucifixion [which] embraces within its connexions and relations, the whole system of revealed truth. It is the keystone of the arch, remove this and all other doctrines fall."[12]

But holding together the religiously and politically splintered factory village was a difficult task, and it remained to be seen whether Cooke's Gospel could order a community governed as much by the power of water wheels and self-interest as by allegiance to an untried minister and his uncompromising creed.

Cooke was aided in his mission, however, by a strong conception of the role of the ministry, an attitude that greatly influenced his subsequent behavior in Ware Factory Village. Addressing the subject in 1838, a few years after he left Ware, he maintained that his profession's declining prestige was closely linked to its members having become a "hireling ministry" too easily swayed by the temptation of finding favor with

---

11. Biographical data on Cooke can be gleaned from Braman's sermon and, more completely, from Vinton's sketch. The best description of the theological complexities among Calvinists in this period is still Sidney Mead, *Nathaniel William Taylor, 1786–1858: A Connecticut Liberal* (1942; repr. Hamden, Conn.: Archon Books, 1967) but also see Joseph Haroutunian, *From Piety to Moralism: The Passing of the New England Theology* (1932; repr. Hamden, Conn.: Archon Books, 1964), and Frank Hugh Foster, *A Genetic History of the New England Theology* (Chicago: University of Chicago Press, 1907).

12. Parsons Cooke, *A Sermon Preached at the Dedication of the Meetinghouse, belonging to the East Evangelical Church and Society, Ware, Mass.* (Amherst, Mass.: Carter and Adams: 1827), 4, 13. John Woodbridge of Hadley, Cooke's hometown minister and future father-in-law, preached Cooke's ordination sermon, *The Courageous Minister* (Amherst, Mass.: Carter and Adams, 1826); see Sereno D. Clark, *The New England Ministry Sixty Years Ago: The Memoir of John Woodbridge, D.D.* (Boston: Lee and Shepard, 1877), 277, for Cooke's acknowledgment that this sermon was one of the "formative influences" of his ministerial life.

established interests in communities where "erroneous doctrines or laxity of religious character" had prevailed—for example, with Unitarian mill-owners in areas like Ware Factory Village. The ministry, Cooke believed, was appointed "the grand instrument for saving the world" and served as "the central wheel that keeps all the rest in motion"; but by paying more homage to Caesar than to Christ, it had voluntarily relinquished this trust. Communities like the factory village had to be shown that the true dignity of the office lay "not in pompous displays of eloquence nor in prodigious exertions of intellect," but primarily "IN CAUSING ITS INFLUENCE TO BE FELT" by publishing the everlasting Gospel.[13]

Once installed over the village church, Cooke first attempted to reassert the clergy's importance by nurturing religious revivals. Like his mentor, Griffin, he believed that if a minister honestly preached the Gospel message, the groundwork would be laid for an outpouring of the Spirit. Deriding evangelists like Finney who claimed that revivals could be effected anywhere, anytime through proper evangelical coaching, Cooke insisted that such remarkable events came only through the grace of God. Soon Cooke's attitude bore visible fruit: Wilder noted that in 1827 "there was a wonderful display of the power and grace of God" in Ware Factory Village, "in the conviction and conversion of sinners by the faithful, pungent preaching and parochial visits of the reverend pastor."[14] Moreover, this revival was not isolated (it soon extended "into most of the neighboring towns"), and the excitement that accompanied it momentarily quelled the strife between Ware Center and the village. As early as the fall of 1826 the Reverend Augustus Reed of the First Church had noticed that "there was an unusual solemnity in the minds [of his own] people," culminating in a revival the following spring, and both he and Cooke shared another period of conversions in 1831.[15]

But the perennial difficulty with revivals—no matter how extensive—is their short life, and Cooke soon learned that the evangelical sparks struck by his preaching to the millworkers yielded no constant fire: within a few months of his first conversions the inhabitants of the two villages had

13. Parsons Cooke, *The Antidote; or, The Ministry Worth Preserving* (Boston: Whipple and Damrell, 1838), 9, 12, 13.
14. For Cooke's views on revivals see *Causes of the Decline of Doctrinal Preaching* (Boston: Marvin, 1841), 18–20, and *Recollections of Rev. E. D. Griffin* (Boston: Massachusetts Sabbath School Publishing Society, 1855), 126; [Wilder], *Records*, 201, for the description of this revival.
15. The Rev. Augustus Reed in "Records of the First Church, Ware," Young Men's Library Association, Ware, Massachusetts, entry for 2 June 1828.

returned to their bickering over such issues as road building and parish boundary lines.[16] Failing to reunite the community permanently through the instrument of the revival, Cooke began a relentless attack on what he took to be the predominant doctrinal errors of other denominations within the town. During his Ware years he gained statewide notoriety as one of the most tenacious defenders of "consistent" Calvinism. Important, too, in formulating his moral argument against Unitarianism and Universalism, he frequently linked the emergence and popularity of these groups to the growth of the new factory villages themselves. Cooke thought the people of Ware—and of New England as a whole—were becoming blind servants to Mammon; but in driving home this observation he revealed an inadequate knowledge of how deeply in thrall to this god the populace already was as well as his own inexperience in dealing with the decade's social complexity.

Cooke's most vigorous assaults against Unitarianism came in the lull between the revivals of 1827 and 1831 and were instigated in part by "his senior brethren"—perhaps Wilder or Thwing, but more probably by Griffin himself.[17] His attack commenced with the publication of a Fast Day sermon delivered in Ware in 1828—*(Unitarianism, an Exclusive System)* which drew a sharp answer in the *Christian Examiner* from the prominent Unitarian state justice, Isaac Parker. Cooke speedily answered Parker in a thorough rejoinder and in 1831 treated the subject again when he brought out *A Remonstrance Against Established Religion in Massachusetts*.[18] The titles belie the political content of Cooke's first publications; as he himself explained the origin of these polemics, after encountering the Unitarian element in Ware Factory Village and elsewhere he had become convinced that "when the rights of conscience, and the interests of religion are jeopardized by political management, it is needful and proper that a voice

---

16. For Cooke's disappointment in revivals see, for example, *The Antidote*, 42, and *Modern Universalism Exposed, in an Examination of the Writings of Walter Balfour* (Lowell, Mass.: Asa Rand, 1834), 235. For examples of Ware's quarrels, many of which were carried on through the late 1820s, see "Town Meeting Records," 3 January 1825 and December 1825, and "Records of the East Evangelical Church," Ware Trust Company, Ware, Massachusetts, entry for 30 December 1828.

17. Vinton, "Parsons Cooke," 224; and [Wilder], *Records*, 211.

18. Parsons Cooke, *Unitarianism, an Exclusive System; or, The Bondage of the Churches that were Planted by the Puritans* (Belchertown, Mass.: Sentinel and Journal Office, 1828); *A Reply to a Letter to "The Christian Examiner"* (Boston: Peirce and Williams, 1829); and *A Remonstrance Against Established Religion in Massachusetts* (Boston: Pierce, 1831). Isaac Parker, *Letter to the Rev. Parsons Cooke* (Boston, 1828; reprinted from *Christian Examiner*, November 1828).

of rebuke should come out from the sanctuary."[19] By sounding his trumpet against Unitarianism Cooke believed he was aiding the cause of his own beleaguered denomination and that of the fractured village to which he ministered. Overseers like William Bowdoin had to be shown that adherence to the Unitarian creed might make them successful businessmen but would not ease their way to heaven.

Cooke attributed the spread of Unitarianism to the new economic system. "The active and stirring character" of the present age "aggravates the difficulty" of preaching Calvinism, he observed in another of his pamphlets; "the mind and body of the business world is propelled by steam." More important, these novel changes in a people's notions of time and space created "an excess of immediatism" that makes "the public mind tinder to every wandering spark of error." The sublime connection between man and God was not easily recognized in such times, and Cooke pleaded with his people to recognize that "the age of human invention, the age of steamboats and railroads, will not bring any improvement to that Gospel, which was published eighteen hundred years ago."[20]

It was the Unitarian faith that best lent itself to this age of energy; by stressing the moral perfectibility of man the Unitarians encouraged people to believe that works of human invention contributed to their spiritual progress. Even more insidiously, the Unitarians had advanced their cause through control of the state's economic and political system. "It has come to this," Cooke lamented: "a man cannot, and does not expect to obtain any office, without first giving proof of his hostility to the religion of his fathers," a fact that gave the Unitarians "an almost unlimited sway over all young and enquiring minds." Looking east to Boston, he saw all the major political offices held by liberal Christians, a situation that revealed his most base conspiratorial fears. "This [Unitarian] establishment," he noted, "is the work of many years[,] and the chief influence by which it has been brought to its present maturity, has been a secret control over the distribution of public offices and the enactment of laws."[21] Similarly, since the appointment of Henry Ware to the Hollis Chair of Divinity, Harvard College, too, had become "a mere adjective to the Unitarian church"; and Judge Parker's decision in the famed "Dedham Case" (1818) allowing a

19. Cooke, *A Remonstrance*, 21.
20. Cooke, *Causes of the Decline of Doctrinal Preaching*, 7, 15, and passim; *A Sermon, Preached in Ware Village, Mass., April 12, 1835* (hereafter, *Farewell Sermon*) (Boston: Pierce, 1835), 18.
21. *Unitarianism*, 5–10.

parish to control church property formerly held only by church members provided evidence that Unitarian control extended even to the state supreme court.[22] The only solution to such economic and political tyranny, Cooke concluded, was for the citizenry to exercise their power to vote, to cast their ballots "on the side of religious freedom and equal rights" in an attempt to evict the Unitarians from office.[23]

If these early writings display Cooke's preoccupation with the Unitarians' usurpation of wealth and power formerly accorded his own denomination, his later diatribes against Universalism reveal a fear of this particular creed's attraction to the countless millworkers who were far removed from the influential spheres the Unitarians controlled. In *Modern Universalism Exposed* (1834), his book-length reply to the works of Walter Balfour, Cooke argued that Universalism was a faith adopted by someone "determined to indulge in forbidden gratifications," and as such "originates rather in the desire of the mind, than in the face of solid proofs." Like its upper-class counterpart, Unitarianism, this creed appealed to those who believed that "the whole design of religion is not to please God, but men," allowing them to "screen" themselves behind Universalism's "miserable doctrines." "The Unitarians have sown the seed," Cooke proclaimed, "and the Universalists are reaping the harvest."[24]

More than his polemics against the Unitarians, Cooke's anti-Universalist writings display a concern with the implications of doctrinal errors on personal conduct. "If I would attain to the exalted blessedness of Universalism, taste its fruits, and exhibit its practical results," Cooke sarcastically told his readers, "I must believe . . . that the soul's condition in its future state, is not at all affected by conduct and character here." As he interpreted the Universalists' promise, man, not having to worry about the prospect of eternal punishment, would be justified in doing anything he pleased to procure personal pleasure and advancement; there were no overriding moral restraints to prevent his claiming as much privilege as he desired. "If Universalists are not better than their theory," Cooke declared, "if they

---

22. For the controversy over the Hollis Chair, see Conrad Wright, "The Election of Henry Ware: Two Contemporary Accounts," *Harvard Library Bulletin* 17 (1969): 245–78. Parker's ruling in favor of the church "society" (all members of the parish regardless of whether they had given evidence of conversion) over the church "members" (those who were members in full communion) allowed the more numerous, and often less orthodox "society" members to control church affairs. After this decision many churches, acting upon motion from the societies, discharged orthodox ministers to hire liberals, often Unitarians.

23. *A Remonstrance*, 5, 13, 23, 24.

24. *Modern Universalism Exposed*, 232, 227, 192, ix.

have no regard to the consequences of their conduct, they come up to our idea of unprincipled."[25]

Like Unitarianism, Universalism seemed particularly threatening to such places as the factory village. In areas where the population was unsettled and living in an unnatural proximity, and where there was no well-established moral authority, Universalist ideas could easily "abate the force of moral principles, vitiate the moral taste, and throw a man under the dominion of appetite." Moreover, the numerous youths in such communities were particularly susceptible to Universalist errors, for theirs "are minds so loosely balanced, and ill-formed, that one of the most trivial objections to the truth is enough to upset all their belief." To gain youthful support, the Universalists play on "the price of reason ... characteristic of the youthful mind"; there is "no soil more fit for Universalist cultivation, than that composed of [youthful] ignorance and self-deceit." Thus, Cooke feared that the "consistent" Calvinists were losing the support of an entire generation, sealing their isolation from political and ecclesiastical power for decades. He warned his people that "the mischievous consequences of error are cumulative, [and] human minds are so linked together in this world, that we can set no bounds to the transmission of sentiments, characters and dispositions, from one to another."[26] With the Unitarians siphoning off the godly youth with promises of wealth and privilege, and the Universalists subverting them by appeals to their self-indulgence, Cooke felt he had good reason to shout his warnings against such heresies in his community.

The true extent of the doctrinal threat the Unitarians and Universalists posed in the factory village, however, is questionable. Although appearing prominently in the writings of such orthodox inhabitants of the town as Cooke, Wilder, and Thwing, these denominations are not mentioned in the church disciplinary records until 1838, after Cooke had left the area. Rather, these records display a heightened concern with moral transgressions that Cooke *attributed* to laxity of doctrine, suggesting that his real concern—and that of other members of his denomination—was not so

---

25. Ibid., 191, 236.
26. The factory village's population was composed largely of "immigrants" from within a twenty-mile radius of the town, many of whom contributed to the unsettled character of the community by removing to such new manufacturing areas as Warwick, Rhode Island, and Paterson, New Jersey, within a few years of their arrival in Ware. Moreover, the town's population density increased dramatically during this period, from 35 persons per square mile in 1800 to 72 in 1830. See membership lists in "Records of the East Evangelical Church," and Pabst, "Agricultural Trends," 68. Cooke, *Modern Universalism Exposed*, 236, 243, 246.

much with the doctrinal positions of Unitarians or Universalists per se, but rather with the very instability of the social order he encountered in the factory village and in nineteenth-century New England generally.[27] Adherence to one denomination or another may not have been so significant as Cooke's surprise and frustration at the shifting moral sensibility that accompanied rapid industrialization.

If the mind and body of the business world in Ware Factory Village were indeed propelled more by steam than by the Gospel, Cooke's vehement denunciations of Unitarians and Universalists may have been nothing more than a demonstration of his own inability to accept the manifestations of an age that ran so counter to his cherished beliefs and expectations. Further, Cooke's troubled later years in the village display just how badly he misread the needs of this community. In the 1830s Ware did not require the rigors of orthodox doctrine, but a wide humanitarian sympathy for the diversity that now characterized its population.

If attempts to reform the factory village were hindered by the very relationship of the community's vices to the character of the age, Cooke showed no signs of relinquishing the battle against them, a fact apparent in the unsettling controversy over temperance reform that resulted in his eventual ouster from the town. Cooke regarded intemperance as one of the prime consequences of lax doctrine in factory towns; and in Ware, where by one contemporary report "the labourers in the shops, in the buildings, at the dam and canal, had every man his bottle," the problem was particularly acute.[28] On 4 July 1829, at the same time as he was so pointedly challenging the Unitarian establishment, Cooke preached an incendiary sermon before the Ware Village Temperance Society in which he accused intemperance of "palsying the physical, mental, and moral powers of the people." Delivering his chastisement on a national holiday renowned for the tippling it encouraged, Cooke linked overindulgence in drink not only to immorality, but to the very prosperity of America. While "great complaint is now made of the universal stagnation of business, of the failure of credit, and of approaching poverty," yet one cause, he observed, was sufficient to have produced it all—"the taxation brought upon us by the use of ardent spirits."[29]

27. "Records of the First Church, Ware," 2 June 1838; and "Records of the East Evangelical Church," passim.
28. Hyde, *An Address*, 45.
29. Parsons Cooke, *An Address Delivered to the Ware Village Temperance Society . . . July 4, 1829* (Brookfield: Merriam, 1829), 4, 13.

While many of the audience agreed with such sentiments, Cooke's solution to the problem proved disturbing. *"No man or body of men can rationally expect to exert an influence against intemperance,"* he proclaimed, *"without first themselves renouncing entirely the use of spirits."* Trying to accomplish with temperance reform what he failed to do with his revivals—to unite Ware's heterogeneous community—Cooke stressed the catholicity of this cause. "The ground on which we act is broad enough for all," he proclaimed. "Ours is the work of no sect or party," and "it appeals to the heart of every friend of man." But the very nature of his subsequent demands undercut his ecumenical design: How could one pretend to bring peace to a community while promising the curse of Meroz upon those who did not enlist in the temperance ranks? "Ours is the cause of God," he declared; "and if those bought with the blood of Christ will stand aloof, when the world declares neutrality as an enemy, methinks angels will weep over your ingratitude and folly." Allowing no fence-straddling in his audience, he forthrightly told them that "you do stand in the way if you withhold your name and influence." One either supported the cause or not, and "actions speak louder than words."[30]

Cooke's ultimatum, tendered by countless other ministers in the 1820s and 1830s, rankled moderate members of the town, and his subsequent actions did little to curb their anger. Within a few days of his sermon Cooke circulated a petition in which the signer pledged lifetime abstinence from alcohol; while Cooke claimed that the Temperance Society's members used the pledge "more to regulate their own practices, than to influence the practice of others by a show of their opinions," the townspeople quickly recognized the moral suasion involved.[31] Moreover, in 1832, after another such sermon "which offended many in both societies," members of both the First and East parishes, tired of Cooke's claim that without pledging total abstinence "your vote is against us, your example is against us," separated themselves from their societies to form a third church. While a new congregation was not then gathered, these dissidents hired a Unitarian minister from Boston to preach to them "four Sabbaths"; more significant, "the bitter feelings" caused by Cooke's words and the response they brought "lived on till the generation were all gone."[32]

There is no doubt that Cooke's attempt at temperance reform was

---

30. Ibid., 8, 13, 16, 17.
31. Parsons Cooke, *Moral Machinery Simplified* (Andover, Mass.: Pierce, 1839), 29.
32. Chase, *History of Ware,* 183.

partially successful. For example, in an 1833 town meeting Ware's citizens voted to instruct their representatives "to use their influence to obtain a revision of the license laws in such a manner as to promote the great moral reform now going on through the aid of temperance societies."[33] But such decisions were not reached without striking deep wedges into both parishes. When to such difficulties were added other controversies in which Cooke had been embroiled (for example, the anti-Masonic movement of the late 1820s) his effectiveness as a moral leader became severely compromised. Toward the end of 1834 he became aware that he was losing the support of certain influential members of the town who were increasingly troubled by his severe demands. "There are some particular obstructions to my influence and usefulness here," he tersely noted in the church records. "Past experience and present indications are such to convince me that while I remain, the influence of some members of the church will be found in some points conflicting with my own."[34]

By 23 March 1835 the situation between the intractable minister and his parishioners had so worsened that the church voted to release him from "that part of the contract which requires him to give six months notice of his intention to leave." While the names of those who forced his resignation are lost, his pointed comments in the *Farewell Sermon* he delivered nine years to the day after the factory village church was constituted reveal more fully his perception of the opposition he encountered. "I know not that I ever stood in this pulpit," Cooke told the assembly, "under the influence of a fear to utter any rebuke or principle of doctrine which my conscience was convinced ought to be uttered." Moreover, he added, "since I first came upon this ground, I never felt the force of a temptation to keep back what is profitable, through the fear of offending any hearer." Cooke's error—if it may be so called—was in his *not* giving people what they wanted to hear. His forceful personality and unbending will had made him probe the town's wounds with an unflinching hand, and he finally had struck too many nerves in his influential supporters. Warning the people that "the dismission of a pastor may prove a signal for bringing into action elements of strife, that had slumbered before," Cooke took leave of the village, confident that he had been faithful to the sacred trust he had defined nine years before.[35]

33. "Town Meeting Records," 11 November 1833 and 2 March 1835.
34. "Records of the East Evangelical Church," 23 March 1835.
35. Ibid., 23 March 1835; *Farewell Sermon*, 17.

Despite Ware's rejection of his labors, Cooke's star continued to rise. Soon afterward he was called to the First Church of Lynn, Massachusetts, one of the state's largest manufacturing towns, where he remained until his death in 1864. He had always maintained that manufacturing communities constituted the most challenging ministerial field. "I have always felt and still feel that comparatively few congregations require and give scope for more talent, wisdom and energy in their minister," he once said, and his success in building and maintaining a strong parish in Lynn testifies to his own possession of these virtues.[36]

He also continued his statewide work on behalf of what he always called his "Puritan" faith. In 1840 he founded a religious periodical, the *Puritan*, which in 1841 was moved to Boston and became known as *The New England Puritan*; this journal exercised a wide influence in New England's conservative church circles on both theological and practical matters. In 1849 it was merged with one of the country's oldest religious newspapers, the *Recorder*, to become the *Puritan Recorder*, and Cooke's connection with it as an editor and contributor continued until his death. Moreover, in addition to such editorial labors, he continued his writings against Unitarianism and Universalism, as well as against such novel movements as spiritualism, and his reputation as one of the most articulate spokesmen for "consistent" Calvinism continued to bring him fame. He also repaid a long-standing debt to an old teacher by compiling the life of Edward Dorr Griffin.[37]

But Cooke's formative years in Ware Factory Village constitute the most interesting part of his career. At the age of twenty-six he discovered in Ware's "discordant, repellant, excitable" population a major challenge to the Puritan tenets he so firmly avowed. For nine years he met that challenge by holding the attention of the town's diverse religious interests in one large, if heterodox, congregation. Troubled by the moral confusion he saw around him in the young and transient population of the village, Cooke tried to strengthen the orthodoxy of the East Parish and simultaneously to

---

36. Cooke in "Records of the East Evangelical Church," (spring 1835), and Vinton, "Parsons Cooke," passim.

37. Vinton, "Parsons Cooke," 237, 238. Other of Cooke's writings include *A Century of Puritanism and A Century of its Opposites* (Boston: Whipple, 1855), *Female Preaching Unlawful and Inexpedient* (Lynn, Mass.: Newhall, 1837), *Necromancy; or, A Rap for the Rappers* (Boston: Congregational Board of Publication, 1857), and *A History of German Anabaptism* (Boston: Tappan and Perkins, 1845).

unite its interests with those of the older First Parish through such means as revivalism and temperance reform. He also struck forcefully at the doctrinal errors he claimed were responsible for the community's moral laxity; but finally Ware would not tolerate his uncompromising efforts to instill orthodoxy. As Cooke's successor in Ware, the Reverend Cyrus Yale, told the community, in Ware in past years there had been "manifestly too little of self-diffidence and too much self-confidence—quite too much of a fault-finding spirit, . . . a readiness in many to push forward their own darling measures . . . with reckless indifference to the opinions, feelings, and interests of their fellow men." Yale might well have been describing the legacy of his predecessor, but his words applied just as forcefully to the bustling economic community that had been spawned in the Industrial Revolution. In Ware, Yale noted, there was too much "ultraism, at either end of the scale," and such a diversity of interests would not disappear just because one man preached against it.[38]

Here an anecdote is instructive. The East Parish's deacon, Thomas Thwing, once confided to his pastor, the Reverend Griffin, that he wished to become a missionary to some heathen land, but his plans were disrupted by a long illness. Later, when Griffin visited his old parishioner in Ware Factory Village, the illustrious minister recalled the moment. "You wanted to go on a foreign mission," he said, "but the Lord hedged up your way. *This* is missionary ground. Now let us see what you will do *here*."[39] This true story might well have been told of Thwing's minister in Ware, Parsons Cooke, for in his attack on the liberal theology and lax morality of his day, a battle he chose to fight in a mill village, Cooke displayed the missionary zeal Griffin respected.

By 1835 Ware Factory Village had proved itself impervious to such an evangelical message. As he later did in Lynn, Cooke had to learn to live among differing and competing denominations, some of which had members for whom material prosperity and secular advancement outweighed the spiritual treasure he offered. But in the 1820s, not yet having taken the full measure of the factory village's contribution to New England's moral landscape, Cooke sought to preserve the awful mystery of religion in the face of those who were awed by nothing but canals and power looms. In the decade following his departure from Ware Factory Village his rude awakening to this fact would be shared by countless others.

38. Cyrus Yale, *A Sermon Delivered on the Day of Public Thanksgiving, Dec. 3, 1835* (Boston: Perkins and Marvin, 1837), 19, 20.
39. Thwing, *Memorial of Thomas Thwing*, 20; Vinton, "Parsons Cooke," 221.

8 | The Transcendentalists and Language
The Unitarian Exegetical Background

One of the first topics that engaged me for any considerable length of time was my study of the philosophy of language among the Transcendentalists. Although I had gotten into the subject through an interest in Thoreau's philological explorations, I knew full well, particularly after studying Perry Miller's *The Transcendentalists: An Anthology* (1950) inside and out, that to understand people like Ralph Waldo Emerson and Theodore Parker, one had to wrestle as well with those intellectual figures from whom such more radical reformers had emerged. Thus this foray into the subject of language among the Unitarians.

Because I was not writing a full-scale study but only seeking to understand the main positions on the philosophy of language expressed by the Unitarians, this piece stands only as an introduction to the topic. It seems to me that it still awaits its scholar, for I did not spend enough time on the gradual acceptance of German biblical scholarship among the American community. Since my own work on the subject (*The Wisdom of Words: Language, Theology, and Literature in the New England Renaissance* [1981]), others have taken it up; in particular, I would point to Richard Grusin's *Transcendental Hermeneutics: Institutional Authority and the Higher Criticism of the Bible* (1991), even though his study, like mine, is not the all-inclusive one that we yet need, a work on the scale of Hans Frei's *The Eclipse of Biblical Narrative: A Study in Eighteenth- and Nineteenth-Century Hermeneutics* (1979).

But the point remains: for antebellum thinkers the study of language was central, particularly as exponents of the Higher Criticism forced one to acknowledge the relativity of even the most revered literature, Scripture itself. It is testament to the sophistication of scholars like Andrews Norton and Moses Stuart that they did not shy away from engagement with such topics. If their negotiations of theories of language did not yield the same sort of excitement as did those of Emerson or Horace Bushnell, it was through no fault of their intelligence; rather, their imaginations remained constricted by the internecine wars over the denominationalism that so marked the ecclesiastical complexion of their age.

Scholars of Transcendentalism recognize the importance of language in the early nineteenth century, and point to the "Language" section of Emerson's *Nature* and the manifold punning in Thoreau's *Walden* as evidence of a widespread concern with the significance of words.[1] Recent critics have gone further afield and discovered in Thoreau an obsession with the speculative philological theories of Europeans such as Charles Kraitsir and Walter Whiter, and have demonstrated Emerson's indebtedness to Sampson Reed and Guillaume Oegger, who showed how Swedenborgian correspondence was applicable to the study of language.[2] But there has been no explanation *why* this concern with language was so widespread in Transcendentalist circles. One answer lies embedded in the theological controversies in which New England divines were engaged.

Between 1820 and 1850 New England witnessed a lively debate over the

---

1. On Emerson, see for example, Vivian Hopkins, *Spires of Form: A Study of Emerson's Aesthetic Theory* (Cambridge: Harvard University Press, 1951); Sherman Paul, *Emerson's Angle of Vision: Man and Nature in American Experience* (Cambridge: Harvard University Press, 1952); and *Emerson's "Nature"—Origin, Growth, Meaning*, ed. Merton M. Sealts, Jr., and Alfred R. Ferguson (New York: Dodd, Mead, 1969). On Thoreau, see David Skwire, "A Checklist of Wordplays in *Walden*," *American Literature* 31 (November 1959): 282-89; Gordon Boudreau, "Thoreau and Richard C. Trench: Conjectures on the Pickerel Passage in *Walden*," *ESQ: A Journal of the American Renaissance* 20 (2d quarter, 1974): 117-24; and Christopher Collins, *The Uses of Observation: A Study of Correspondential Vision in the Writings of Emerson, Thoreau and Whitman* (The Hague: Mouton, 1971).

2. See Michael West, "Charles Kraitsir's Influence Upon Thoreau's Theory of Language," *ESQ: A Journal of the American Renaissance* 19 (4th quarter, 1973): 262-74; West, "Scatology and Eschatology: The Heroic Dimensions of Thoreau's Wordplay," *PMLA* 79 (October 1974): 1043-64; West, "*Walden's* Dirty Language: Thoreau and Walter Whiter's Geocentric Etymological Theories," *Harvard Library Bulletin*, 22 (April 1974): 117-28; and my "Henry Thoreau and the Wisdom of Words," *New England Quarterly*, 52 (March 1979), 38-54. On Emerson and Reed, see Clarence P. Hotson, "Sampson Reed: A Teacher of Emerson," *New England Quarterly* 2 (June 1929): 249-77 (still the starting point for examining Reed's influence); and on Oegger, see Kenneth Walter Cameron, *Emerson the Essayist* (Raleigh, N.C.: Thistle Press, 1945), 1:295-302.

origin and meaning of language, with roots in the dialogue that began when Immanuel Kant rejected Lockean sensationalism as a satisfactory epistemological model. This debate was most noticeable in the conflict between the Unitarians, who championed an empirical reading of Scripture, and the Trinitarians, who attempted to defend a more orthodox reading of the Bible by adopting a "symbolic" view of its language.[3] The issues of this debate suggest not only why the study of language was taken seriously by contemporary theologians, but also how such people as Emerson, Theodore Parker, Bronson Alcott, and Henry Thoreau were linked through their belief that many of the important philosophical problems of the early nineteenth century stemmed from differing conceptions of language and its uses.

The study of language in that age was part of a rational climate of philosophical and religious thought with humanistic implications difficult for our generation to comprehend. As Hans Aarsleff has noted, in the nineteenth century the budding science of philology attempted to answer such questions as "What was the origin of thought?" "Did the mind have a material basis?" "Did mankind have a single origin?" "Was the first language given by revelation, or had man invented it in the process of time?"[4] But historians seeking an explanation for the Transcendentalists' interest in the philosophy of language do not acknowledge how many of the main figures of the movement were themselves exposed to just such questions, and that the terms of this theological debate, especially with respect to the accuracy and relevance of language to eternal matters, were of considerable importance to many Transcendentalists.[5] As the conversations over exegesis became more strident, and as the participants read more widely in European philology, what had begun as an attempt to discredit the interpretations of scriptural language that gave rise to

---

3. Jerry Wayne Brown, *The Rise of Biblical Criticism in America: The New England Scholars* (Middletown: Wesleyan University Press, 1965), is the best introduction to the topic of scriptural interpretation in the nineteenth century. Also see Daniel Walker Howe, *The Unitarian Conscience: Harvard Moral Philosophy, 1805–61* (Cambridge: Harvard University Press, 1970), for a brilliant analysis of the philosophical position of the Unitarians.

4. Hans Aarsleff, *The Study of Language in England, 1780–1860* (Princeton: Princeton University Press, 1965), 4.

5. Clarence Faust, "The Background of Unitarian Opposition to Transcendentalism," *Modern Philology* 35 (February 1938): 297–324, offers aid in locating the first points of tension between the two groups. Lawrence Buell, *Literary Transcendentalism: Style and Vision in the American Renaissance* (Ithaca: Cornell University Press, 1973), has important sections on the Unitarian background (see especially part 1), but Buell stops short of discussing the connections between scriptural exegesis and language theory.

denominational bitterness opened the doors to a novel theory of literary symbolism that had its counterpart in the thought of the European Romantics.[6] But this transformation had its beginning in the early 1800s, when liberal ministers resorted to the philosophy of John Locke in order to buttress their theology against attacks by Trinitarian opponents.

The belief in religious voluntarism—developed as a corollary to the United States Constitution—provided the starting point of a fifty-year debate over the nature and meaning of language. Attempts to interpret certain biblical texts bred a widespread concern with exegesis; although theologians and philosophers had earlier recognized that many of their disagreements stemmed from questions of interpretation never had there been such a plethora of readings of important biblical passages. What was the proper form that baptism should take? Would there be everlasting damnation for all sinners? How much free will does man possess?[7] Similar questions tormented the consciences of many Americans who had never known so chaotic a religious situation; still, while such controversies excited many denominations, the issue of immediate concern here is the Unitarians' extended defense of their own methods of biblical exegesis. Here we can locate the formulation of the philological premises against which many Transcendentalists later rebelled.

By 1820, "liberal Christianity" had emerged as a separate and powerful denomination with a philosophical framework built on the empiricism of John Locke, but this proto-Unitarian group soon came under increasing attack by those who found its principles fatal to vital religion. The reaction of Sampson Reed, the Swedenborgian druggist whose *Observations on the Growth of the Mind* (1826) was one of the earliest premonitions of dissent within the liberal ranks, serves as an example. In his "Oration on Genius" delivered in 1821 when he received his M.A. from Harvard, he irreverently declared that Locke's mind would not always remain "the standard of

---

6. See, for example, M. H. Abrams, *Natural Supernaturalism: Tradition and Revolution in Romantic Literature* (New York: Norton, 1971), especially 17–71, where he argues that "the characteristic concepts and patterns of Romantic philosophy and literature are a displaced and reconstructed theology." What has not yet been demonstrated is how a similar transformation was occurring among the American Romantics.

7. The bibliography on these topics is lengthy; as good a starting point as any is Sydney Ahlstrom, *A Religious History of the American People* (New Haven: Yale University Press, 1972). William R. Hutchison, *The Transcendentalist Ministers: Church Reform in the New England Renaissance* (New Haven: Yale University Press, 1959), is a good source from which to begin study of the theological divisions between the Unitarians and Transcendentalists, but Hutchison does not stress the difficulties over the differing epistemologies.

metaphysics." Nurtured on "common sense" empiricism when he was at Harvard, Reed (through the aid of Swedenborg's works) already had begun to pierce the shallowness of empirical philosophy.[8] He reminded his listeners that, given the developments in philosophical Idealism, "had we a description of it [the mind] in its present state, it would make a very different book from 'Locke on the Understanding.' " His tone was belligerent, and the next twenty years saw a major assault against the Unitarians stem precisely from his observation. And Reed's judgment was no exception; as a recent critic has noted, as long as the debate over Transcendentalism raged, "the name of John Locke" remained "integral to its philosophical history . . . a symbol of commitments too diverse and too profoundly rooted to permit facile compromise."[9] Among the various constrictions of the Lockean mind, the men who later came to be called "Transcendentalists" discovered a conception of language that did not square with their philosophical Idealism.

In many of the religious controversies of the 1820s, the age-old argument of how the written or spoken word impressed its significance upon men, of how language made its meaning, had resurfaced. Even in America this question was not new: a hundred years earlier Jonathan Edwards had confronted a similar query and, with the aid of the then novel Lockean epistemology, had refashioned Calvinism into a profoundly emotional, yet intellectually respectable, system.[10] But in the next century men began to reexamine the relationship between word and thing, and the theory of language outlined in the "Third Book" of Locke's *Essay Concerning Human Understanding* seemed appropriate only when they professed to live by their rational understanding alone. When some dissidents began to speculate that some of man's thoughts were intuitive, Locke's theory came under increasing criticism, even though, as Perry Miller has pointed out, such attacks did not immediately demolish his well-wrought edifice.[11]

Locke's declaration of how *arbitrary* words were is what appealed to the Unitarians. In the empirical system, words were perceived merely as exter-

---

8. Sampson Reed, "Oration on Genius," in *The Transcendentalists: An Anthology*, ed. Perry Miller (Cambridge: Harvard University Press, 1950), 55.

9. See, for example, Cameron Thompson, "John Locke and New England Transcendentalism," *New England Quarterly* 35 (December 1962): 435–57.

10. For Edwards's use of Lockean epistemology in his reinvigoration of language, see Perry Miller, "The Rhetoric of Sensation," in his *Errand into the Wilderness* (Cambridge: Harvard University Press, 1956), 167–83, and his *Jonathan Edwards* (New York: William Sloan, 1949), 43–70.

11. Miller, "Rhetoric of Sensation," 168.

nal stimuli, and the "truth" of language consisted of its utility. The source of meaning was simply "rational usage derived from sensory perception." Words were a contrivance designed for human convenience and, if they came to be used by men as the "*signs* of their *ideas*," this was not through any "natural connection, that there is between particular articulate sounds and certain ideas," but only through a "voluntary imposition, whereby such a word is made arbitrarily the mark of such an idea." The languages of the world thus had no underlying unity, and words "in their primary or immediate signification" stood for nothing universal, but only for the ideas "in the mind of him that uses them." If men employed terms for which they had not experienced some sensory analogue, they could not know the meaning of what they said. Conversely, words themselves were not universal symbols; the truth of each idea had to be learned empirically by each man to whom the word-idea was expressed.[12]

The implicit analogy between Locke's theories on government and language is evident and has been recognized. Both were artificial constructs resting upon a contract voluntarily entered, or, more precisely, upon a *contextual* arrangement. As with the rules of a political state, "neither vocabulary nor syntax had an inherent or organic rationale" but were created to serve particular needs—in this case, communication. Words were not gifts from God standing as precise ciphers to reality but only "noises, having no transcendental or preternatural correspondence with what they name." The meaning of meaning was a private or, at best, a narrowly cultural experience, and acts of human communication were only approximations of ideas experienced, not magical incantations of the ideas themselves.[13] Language, then, was to be interpreted by the intellectual tools given men as rational creatures. Words were implements forged for a particular situation, and the continuity of meaning from generation to generation came through the agreed-upon usage of articulate men.

In the early nineteenth century, when such theoretical premises were applied to the religious situation in New England, the issues grew thornier. What happened when one tried to explain the words of Scripture? Could the word of God merely be contextual and not possess some further, or absolute, significance? According to Lockean premises, if the Bible was the word of God, it was the word of God understood *as set down by men in a*

---

12. John Locke, *Essay Concerning Human Understanding*, ed. Russell Kirk (Chicago: Gateway, 1956), xlii, 132, 137, 141, 172.
13. Miller, "Rhetoric of Sensation," 169.

particular place at a particular time and so had been affected by the vagaries of historical circumstance. Language was not divine inspiration but inspiration affected by the limitations of time and chance above which no human being could rise. Thus the Unitarians' main interest was in the reliability of the empirical evidence surrounding scriptural testimony. It never occurred to them that words themselves could be viewed as vitally provocative symbols that transported men to an awareness of secrets that had no relation to their sensory experience.

While some New England liberals—most noticeably Joseph Stevens Buckminster—had become interested in the "Higher Criticism" of the Bible developed by such European scholars as Johann Jakob Griesbach and T. G. Eichhorn, what these Americans neglected to realize was that the recent scholarship in the German universities came as a result of the intellectual freedom Kant's distinction between the real and phenomenal worlds had given men who sought an accurate transcription of the Bible.[14] Within a few years the corollaries to Kant's system opened a Pandora's box for American biblical commentators who failed to consider the epistemological consequences of Kantian idealism. Only the more resilient among them could adjust their beliefs to those propositions that suggested that the key to man's spiritual existence was found in his Reason. A look at the controversy over scriptural testimony between the Unitarian Andrews Norton and the Trinitarian Moses Stuart illuminates how such a glaring philosophical oversight contributed to the Unitarians' already crabbed intellectual position.

Norton, who subsequently achieved fame for his attack on Emerson's "Divinity School Address" (1838), was a chief expositor of the Unitarian view of the Bible. He had read theology with Henry Ware, who in 1805 had been appointed to the Hollis Chair of Divinity at Harvard, a gesture

---

14. Brown, *Biblical Criticism,* chaps. 1 and 2, offers a good understanding of the European exegetical background that affected the figures discussed in this essay. The school of "Higher Criticism" treated the Bible like any other ancient text and sought to establish definitely the temporal and grammatical context of Scripture. In the hands of the "higher critics" the Bible became more of a sourcebook for moral illustration than the unadulterated words of God. In this matter, the influence of J. G. Herder was profound; see Robert T. Clark, *Herder: His Life and Thought* (Berkeley and Los Angeles: University of California Press, 1955), esp. 295–97.

Joseph Stevens Buckminster was a brilliant Unitarian clergyman installed at the Brattle Street Church in Boston who had assembled a large collection of European theological works. His early death, at the age of twenty-eight, robbed Unitarianism of one of its most articulate spokesmen.

that assured the Unitarian ascendency at that institution. Earlier, Norton had been under the tutelage of Buckminster himself, whose large library offered a solid introduction to contemporary European theology. Installed as the Dexter Professor of Sacred Literature at the Harvard Divinity School, Norton had by 1819 read enough German criticism to begin his lifelong project of proving the "genuineness" of the Gospels.[15]

His chief gadfly, Moses Stuart, an orthodox Trinitarian, held the Chair of Sacred Literature at Andover Theological Seminary, the institution founded to counter Harvard's liberalism. Stuart was "probably the best read scholar" in biblical criticism in New England, and his saturation in the German scholarship was so profound that at one point the Andover trustees began to fear for his orthodoxy. They investigated his beliefs but, because they realized that if their clergymen were to maintain the orthodox position against the Unitarians they had to adopt similar methods of textual scholarship, Stuart escaped with merely a censure.[16] When in 1819 William Ellery Channing delivered his famous sermon on "Unitarian Christianity" at the ordination of Jared Sparks in Baltimore, Stuart was presented with the opportunity to attack the Unitarians head-on.

The heated exchange, which began when Stuart attempted to refute the arguments Channing had advanced against the "unscriptural doctrine of the Trinity," revolved around the ultimate authority invested in scriptural language. For Stuart the question was, What did the writers mean to convey in the biblical passages? Once the textual scholar had treated the Bible with the same grammatical and literary tools he would bring to any other ancient book, that is, once he had discerned the words' *meaning*, the text, being the word of God, was authoritative. "It is orthodoxy in the highest sense of the word," Stuart declared, and "everything which differs from it, which modifies it, which fritters it away, is *heterodoxy*, is heresy." His only query was what thought the language of this or that passage conveyed. When this was answered "philologically," a Christian "had to believe what is thought, or else to reject the claim of divine authority." Simply stated, scriptural studies were to be conducted by one's philology independent of one's

---

15. See Brown, *Biblical Criticism*, 29–39, for background on Norton.
16. Brown, *Biblical Criticism*, 45–47, 58. For background on Andover's founding, see Daniel Day Williams, *The Andover Liberals* (New York: King's Crown Press, 1941). For the story of the controversy over Stuart's orthodoxy, see Henry A. Pochmann, *German Culture in America: Philosophic and Literary Influences* (Madison: University of Wisconsin Press, 1957), 128–31.

philosophy. But after that investigation, the truth discerned was a binding truth, for the Bible was an inspired text.[17]

Channing contended that, before any text could be considered as authoritative as the Trinitarians suggested, it had to agree with the general spirit of the Bible and be part of the universal truth revealed by Christ and His disciples in the New Testament. The question he posed was not only what the original writer meant to convey but, whether his text had validity for all ages or merely applied to the local, temporal situation. The underlying assumption was that the *interpreter himself* could distinguish between what Theodore Parker later called "the transient and permanent" in Christianity. Channing maintained that in parts the Bible was composed of other than divine utterance, and in many places dealt with subjects on which men received ideas "from other sources besides itself," subjects such as the "nature, passions, relations, and duties of man." Moreover (and this was blasphemy to any Trinitarian), man was expected to "restrain and modify" scriptural language "by the known truths which observation and experience furnish."[18] Trinitarians like Stuart rejected this idea because it gave final authority to man's reason rather than to divine revelation; to Stuart's thinking no one had the authority to modify propositions to make them agree with man's limited experience. God's word had a divine significance that did not change over time. Truth remained constant, and to assert the contrary was only one more display of man's sinful nature.

In opposition to the Unitarian position, Stuart sought to establish the theological authority of the Bible by using exegetical scholarship *within* the tradition of orthodox Calvinism. Just as Edwards had adopted Lockean epistemology for his own purposes, Stuart went to the German scholars to reinforce beliefs he already held. The Unitarians broke new ground with their conception of Christ as human being and not part of the Godhead in the orthodox sense, a suggestion that Stuart regarded as heretical arrogance, the rash judgment of men trying to ascertain too much through their rational faculties. In a crucial admission, Stuart stated that many of his fellow Trinitarians who still believed in the inscrutability of God would never undertake (as the Unitarians did) to "describe affirmatively the distinctions of the Godhead." Such terms as "the proceeding from the

---

17. See Brown, *Biblical Criticism*, 44, and Moses Stuart, *Letter to Channing* (Andover, Mass.: Flagg and Gould, 1819), 11.

18. Brown, *Biblical Criticism*, 65. Channing, quoted in Faust, "Unitarian Opposition," 302–4.

Godhead" and "the Logos made Flesh" were merely "a language of approximation," feeble attempts to describe the indescribable. Men of humility made no claim to know the literal significance of such terminology; and, while language expressed enough of the truth to "excite our highest interest and command our best obedience," its function was only suggestive. Men had to realize that the final truth at which language hinted emitted a constant light only partially disclosed through the symbolism of words.[19]

Channing was not an outstanding textual scholar and did not reply directly to Stuart's attack on his sermon, but the redoubtable Norton needed no prompting to enter the fray. *A Statement of Reasons for Not Believing the Doctrines of the Trinitarians,* the locus classicus of the Unitarians' understanding of language, appeared that same year, 1819, and was reprinted several times, achieving its final form in 1833.

Norton's arguments were patently simple. Supporting his position through the German Higher Criticism, he restated Locke's principles of language and suggested that even biblical words were only "human instruments for the expression of human ideas." It was impossible that words should express anything else but an "idea or aggregate of ideas which men have associated with certain sounds or letters." Thus, the word had no other meaning, was not inherently symbolic. Words always had to represent something that "the human understanding is capable of conceiving." Thus, all that had ever been written down (in Scripture and elsewhere) could be understood rationally by intelligent men: so far as any words have meaning, he declared, "they are intelligible." And while Norton was generous enough to admit that there were some truths that finally were incomprehensible, they were such as could not be expressed through verbal signs. It was not his purpose to speculate on such hypothetical matters: his research led him to grapple only with the "historical circumstances surrounding scriptural language, its peculiarities of idiom, and the prepossessions of writer and audience." *How* divine wisdom was transmitted to earthly creatures, especially when that wisdom contradicted "common sense," was something he did not condescend to consider.[20]

---

19. Stuart, quoted in Williams, *Andover Liberals,* 19.

20. Andrews Norton, *A Statement of Reasons for Not Believing the Doctrines of the Trinitarians* (Boston: Walker, Wise, 1859), 162. Norton first responded to Stuart in two reviews in the *Christian Disciple* for 1819, and later expanded one of these pieces into *A Statement of Reasons.* Also, see Hutchison, *Transcendentalist Ministers,* 14, 54. The Unitarians' main premise here was that man's means of perception were not impaired at the Fall; hence, he was capable of ascertaining truth through his rational faculties.

Norton thought that the art of interpreting the Bible derived its origin mainly from what he termed "the intrinsic ambiguity of language." But rather than maintaining, as Stuart did, that some important concepts were to be approached only through figurative or symbolic forms, Norton resolved questions of ambiguity in a straightforward, unimaginative way. He declared that "when the words which compose a sentence are such that the sentence may be used to express more than one meaning, its meaning is to be determined SOLELY by a reference to EXTRINSIC CONSIDERATIONS." Stated more bluntly, this meant that one's intuitions, the flights of imagination during a state of inspiration, had nothing to do with understanding the truth of a scriptural passage. Cultural differences accounted for most misrepresentations of language because "figures and turns of expression familiar in one language are strange in another"; and proper interpretations of passages that seemed to "bear a Trinitarian sense" could be achieved definitely through a consideration of "the character of the writer, his habits of thinking and feeling, his common state of expression . . . his settled opinions and beliefs . . . the general state of things during the time in which he lived [and] the particular local and temporary circumstances present to his mind while writing."[21] The words chosen by a writer thus were the result of his social and historical context. It never occurred to Norton that in a transcendent moment a man might be aware of things never perceived before, or that such visions might become an unshakable part of his faith, Christian or otherwise. To Norton's mind, intuitive principles, and symbolic representations, had no place in the life of the rational individual.

Norton's intellectual tragedy was his profound inability to fathom how language, if understood in a more figurative sense, extended the boundaries of the religious sensibility. If language were more than just the fabrication of human minds, if it were also an image or shadow of a divine thing, could it not be that through a wise submission to his intuition man could discover new dimensions to his religious experience? Norton and other Unitarians would not accept this. They believed that God's revelation to man did not extend to language. Revelation was conceptual rather than verbal, and the recovery of those concepts that would return men to the purity of the original churches was the exegete's primary goal. That this conceptual truth was available to rational man and that language was of secondary importance and not within its very self the embodiment of truth were cardinal assumptions of the liberal Christians of the day.

21. Norton, *A Statement of Reasons*, 138, 148, 149.

This brief survey of a complex field is meant to suggest that speculative minds in the early nineteenth century found themselves in a crisis of rhetoric similar to that which preceded the Great Awakening a century earlier, and that by the 1830s the debate over language had become centered on the authenticity of words in the Bible. Soon there arose yet another school of thought, the members of which declared that, contrary to what both the Trinitarians and Unitarians held, verbal communication among men was based on more than an arbitrary imposition of meaning upon sound by man himself. As one critic of the symbolic mode in American literature has suggested, this new group, composed mainly of disaffected young Unitarians, was engaged in nothing less than an attempt to rescue the sterile intellect of the day from Lockean sensationalism by showing how "controversy grew out of the nature of logical language," thus implying that "the full substance of theology could never be rendered in creeds at all, but only in complex symbols."[22]

By the 1830s these men had begun to adhere to an idealistic philosophy offering them what seemed a more convincing description of the human mind than that proposed by Locke. They understood that Unitarianism needed a new emotional and spiritual foundation, one offering the recognition that the divine worked in and through the world; and they found that they could provide this basis by incorporating the twin streams of German Idealism and English Romanticism into their faith. Along with Coleridge and Wordsworth, these young men came to believe that nature, more than the Bible, displayed the revealed will of God, and that, as Kant had suggested, one had to respond to nature, as well as to Scripture, with one's intuitive faculty.[23] Once the value of this "Reason," as the intuition came to be known, was recognized, it followed that, if man's verbal signs came from his observation and understanding of the natural world, there might be some reason why a word meant such a thing. From the higher critics they had learned to read Scripture for its conceptual truth, but the emotional response necessary for genuine religious sentiment was to be provided

---

22. Charles Feidelson, *Symbolism in American Literature* (Chicago: University of Chicago Press, 1953), 97; also all of chapter 3, in which he discusses the American symbolist tradition. He does not satisfactorily explain, however, the immediate origin of the nineteenth-century American symbolists' concern with language.

23. Good general studies of the Transcendentalists' philosophical beliefs are Harold Clark Goddard, *Studies in New England Transcendentalism* (New York: Columbia University Press, 1908), and Alexander Kern, "The Rise of Transcendentalism, 1815–1850," in *Transitions in American Literary History,* ed. Harry Hayden Clark (Durham: Duke University Press, 1953).

by their grasp of how Reason assimilated the language of nature, which in turn corroborated the truths of the Christian religion.

The subtlety here is that the controversy over scriptural language was resolved tangentially as younger Unitarians flocked to the New Thought and became aware of a "language of nature." This does not assert that any man read his Coleridge or Swedenborg primarily to discover a new way to structure his understanding and usage of language. But once Americans understood the new philosophical propositions that allowed them emotional faith, they also discovered the implicit connections between the new epistemology and religious language. In the idealistic system, for example, transcendental knowledge was defined as "theoretical knowledge about the necessary principles of all knowledge."[24] The way man encountered the world was necessarily founded upon a priori principles that Kant defined as in advance of any experience understood in the strictly empirical sense. This was a declaration that man saw differently than any Lockean had ever imagined; and, if one *saw* differently, did not this also imply that these sights and insights might be *communicated* differently as well? If a realm of intuitive knowledge did exist, could it not be that, just as nature derived its meaning from its relation to that ineffable Oversoul so too did language have its roots in that universal ether?

Emerson's struggle with the tenets of his Unitarian faith serves as an example of the manner in which many Transcendentalists had to reconsider the premises of language in their attempts to overcome the Lockean epistemology absorbed from their mentors. His sermon on "The Lord's Supper," delivered in 1832 after he had decided that he no longer could administer that sacrament in good faith, is based upon the exegetical principles of the very Unitarians whose judgment in matters of doctrine he was beginning to question. As he explained, his rejection of the ordinance of the Lord's Supper came from a rational examination of the scriptural evidence for administering the sacrament; and, after carefully examining the texts, his heartfelt conclusion was that "Jesus did not intend to establish an institution for perpetual observance when he ate the Passover with his disciples." Emerson decided that the ritual of the Lord's Supper was based on local, Hebraic custom, and that Christ's followers (especially Saint Paul) erred in their assumption that Christ meant the institution to be maintained permanently after His death. The historical evidence from the Evangelists

---

24. See Walter Leighton, *The French Philosophers and New England Transcendentalism* (Charlottesville: University of Virginia, 1908), 1; and Kern, "Transcendentalism," n. 252.

suggested that "we ought to be cautious in taking even the best ascertained opinions and practices of the primitive church for our own." Moreover, ironically displaying true Unitarian colors, Emerson warned his contemporaries that on such doctrinal matters they should "form a judgment more in accordance with the spirit of Christianity than was the practice of the early ages."[25] Sifting through the historical and textual evidence, he had used the Unitarians' exegetical principles against them and decided that the commonly accepted practice of Communion was not in line with the deeper, more intuitive truths of the Christian religion. But by the time he came to address the graduating class of the Divinity School in 1838, his reasoning on matters of scriptural language had evolved in new directions, marking a more decisive break with the faith of his fathers. His exposure to Swedenborgian and Coleridgean thought already had produced new fruit in his first book, *Nature* (1836), in which the section on "Language" spoke his interest in an organic language of natural forms. The new principles he brought to his understanding of the nature of theological language, however, are more evident in his interpretations of the functions of the ministry outlined in the later address.

The key proposition concerning language that Emerson advanced in the "Divinity School Address" was akin to Stuart's sense that the literal, contextual meaning of scriptural language was not so important as its more symbolic function, its ability to suggest truths beyond the ken of man's rational understanding. Speaking of Christ, whom Emerson here began to describe as a divinely inspired poet, he noted that "the idioms of His language and the figures of His rhetoric" had "usurped" the place of His "truth," resulting in churches being built on His "tropes" rather than on His "principles." More important, however, was that men had to derive His principles *intuitively,* and not merely through the study of the historical context of scriptural words. Emerson believed that the revelation to the present age was that the laws of God, best expressed in human terms in the life of Christ, were also reflected through all nature and so were not just the property of men who, once upon a time, had captured Christ's "tropes." The man who attempted to speak the truths of the Christian religion "as books enable, as synods use, as fashion guides, and as interest commands," merely "babbles," for the true seer had to attend to the language of nature as well as to the contextual base of biblical language. Rather than seeking biblical exegetes, in the class of 1838 Emerson sought "the new Teacher

25. "The Lord's Supper," 10–11, 21.

that shall follow so far those shining laws [of nature] that . . . he shall see the world to be the mirror of the soul" and "the identity of the law of gravitation with the purity of the human heart." Truth, then, was not the truth because the Evangelists so recorded it, but because the men "to whom the soul descends, through whom the soul speaks," had witnessed it and spoken it in words that were themselves the expression of the laws of nature and God.[26]

Emerson's later essay "The Poet" developed further this concept of inspired language; rather than just serving as an example of his own conception of language, however, what is most important about the arguments Emerson initially made against "historical Christianity" in this address is their similarity to those advanced by other members of the Transcendentalist circle. For example, Theodore Parker's reaction to the Unitarian creed, best studied in his *A Discourse of Matters Pertaining to Religion* (1842), was based largely on his understanding of the distinctions between those parts of the Bible he termed "transient," that is, the rituals and myths that reflected the time at which the scriptural evidence was compiled; and the "permanent," those sections where the truth and beauty of the passages overrode any temporal references. He sought "to recall men from the transient Form to the permanent Substance"; and, taking the Unitarians' biblical criticism as a starting point, he demonstrated that they simply had not been honest to the principles of their theory. All that mattered was the "Substance" of the language, the higher truths that Scripture suggested. These transcended earthly bounds and were what was *suggested* by the poetry of the Bible. "Man is greater than the Bible," Parker concluded. It was the "inward Christ" (by which Parker meant man's intuition), and not His words, "which alone abideth forever."[27]

Parker's understanding of the transience of men's words was shared by Bronson Alcott, who was so moved by his new understanding of biblical language that in his Temple School he trained his young scholars to be aware of the deeper significance of words; that is, to comprehend the truths that went beyond the mere temporal significance given them. After the children had gone through their elementary philological exercises (a daily event in his school), Alcott never failed to remind them that "the contempla-

26. "Divinity School Address," in *Nature, Addresses, and Lectures*, in *The Collected Works of Ralph Waldo Emerson*, ed. Alfred R. Ferguson, 1 vol. to date (Cambridge: Harvard University Press, 1971–), 1:81, 84, 93.

27. Theodore Parker, *A Discourse of Matters Pertaining to Religion* (New York: Putnam, 1876 [1842]), 7, 354ff. All of book 4 ("A Discourse of the Bible") is pertinent here.

tion of Spirit in God is necessarily wrapt up in a study of language" and leads upward to "the study of the Soul." He was so convinced of the importance of a true understanding of the language of natural forms that his description of Jesus was as a "Teacher" who sought to "renovate" humanity through a "genius" which depended on language that was like "the living Word, rising spontaneously in the soul, and clothing itself" in images taken from "majestic Nature."[28] From people like Sampson Reed and Coleridge, Alcott learned to read the Scriptures through his intuitive faculty and had to leave behind his conservative friends in his search for a true life of the Spirit.

Even Henry David Thoreau, whom we do not usually number as one deeply concerned with scriptural exegesis, did not escape the influence of the debate over biblical language. His *A Week on the Concord and Merrimack Rivers* (1849) contains a long section (in the "Sunday" chapter) in which he expresses his disgust at the current state of Christianity, a disenchantment stemming from his recognition that, because men had become so involved with the logical consistency of their creeds and language, they neglected the essence of Christ's message. He sarcastically asked if contemporary theologians had "learned the alphabet of heaven," so sure were they about the nature of that spiritual realm. He continued: ". . . and can you count to three? Do you know the number of God's family? Can you put mysteries into words? Do you presume to fable the ineffable? Pray, what geographers are you, that speak of heaven's topography? Whose friend are you that speak of God's personality?"[29] His contemporaries labored over such propositions because they assumed that their logical faculties could define the precise meaning of God's wisdom, when, as Thoreau well knew, the substance of it was never to be truly comprehended. "Think of repeating these things [God's truths] to a New England audience!" he exclaimed. Christ's statements "never were read, they never were heard," because men refused to pierce the rotten diction to the truth behind, a truth as often indicated in the language of nature as through the words of men. "I believe in the forest, and in the meadow, and in the night in which

---

28. On Alcott's use of the philosophy of language in his Temple School, see Odell Shepard, *Pedlar's Progress: The Life of Bronson Alcott* (Boston: Little, Brown, 1937), 112–218. Alcott, quoted in Elizabeth Palmer Peabody, *Record of a School, Exemplifying the Principles of Moral Culture* (Boston: James Munroe, 1836), vi; and Alcott, *Conversations with Children on the Gospels* (Boston: James Munroe, 1835–37), 1:xxxiv.

29. *A Week on the Concord and Merrimack Rivers*, vol. 1 of *The Writings of Henry David Thoreau*, 20 vols. (Boston: Houghton Mifflin, 1906), 71, 73.

the corn grows," he later stated. It was only when men used the alphabet of nature for understanding God's wisdom that the spiritual life became readily apparent.[30]

Coming under the influence of novel philological theories, Thoreau went on to use the American language with rare integrity. But, like Emerson, Parker, and Alcott, he was drawn to reconsider the premises of vocabulary because of the culturewide concern with the power of language to convey the truths of the Christian religion. Emerson redefined the meaning of symbolic discourse for later American writers; Parker, in his insistence on the substance rather than the forms of religion, developed a theology beyond dogma; Alcott used the study of language as a startling educational tool; Thoreau energized his prose style until it became memorable in American literature.

There were also many other significant figures, from Elizabeth Palmer Peabody to Horace Bushnell, whose thoughts on language were greatly influenced by the contemporary debates over scriptural exegesis and each of whom needs more scholarly treatment.[31] Anyone seriously undertaking a study of the philosophy of language in nineteenth-century America has to deal with the peculiarly religious basis of that interest. Once men began to leave behind the premises of Lockean sensationalism and posited that the language they used was not totally arbitrary, and, moreover, that the word of God bore some relation to the language of nature from which man's vocabulary came, the enterprise of scriptural exegesis, especially as practiced by the Unitarians, proved woefully inadequate. It is, indeed, a long way from the Divinity School in Cambridge to the shores of Walden Pond, but, at least where language is concerned, the path is not so indirect as one might first think.

30. "Walking," *The Writings of Henry David Thoreau*, vol. 5, *Excursions and Poems*, 225.

31. On Peabody's interest in language, see her "Language" in *Aesthetic Papers* (Boston: E. P. Peabody, 1849); John B. Wilson, "Grimm's Law and the Brahmins," *New England Quarterly* 38 (June 1965): 234–38; and my "Elizabeth Palmer Peabody and the Philosophy of Language," *ESQ: A Journal of the American Renaissance* 23 (3d quarter, 1977): 154–63. On Bushnell, see H. Shelton Smith, *Horace Bushnell* (New York: Oxford University Press, 1967), a fine critical anthology with frequent mention of Bushnell's theory of language; Frederick Kirschenmann, "Horace Bushnell: Cells or Crustacea?" in *Reinterpretation in American Church History*, ed. Jerald Brauer (Chicago: University of Chicago Press, 1968); and Harold Durfee, "Language and Religion: Horace Bushnell and Rowland G. Hazard," *American Quarterly* 5 (spring 1953): 57–70.

9 | Elizabeth Palmer Peabody and the Philosophy of Language

In the recovery of antebellum women's history, Elizabeth Palmer Peabody has never received the kind of sustained attention that her contemporary and acquaintance, Margaret Fuller did, perhaps in part because she was not so flamboyant. But as I studied the problem of language and meaning among the American Romantics, I quickly realized that Peabody was every bit the intellectual that Fuller was, and that she had made significant contributions to the debates over the origin and interpretation of Scripture and thus, by implication, about the philosophy of language itself. Indeed, Peabody served as a kind of spiritual midwife to all manner of intellectual projects, and it does her great disservice to remember her primarily as the model for Miss Birdseye in Henry James's *The Bostonians*.

We remember less about her—she still has not had a modern biographer—in part because she did not make the cause of women's rights central to her reform efforts, although her incredible bustle of activity at every hour testified to what a woman could do when she put her mind to it. Unlike Fuller, who had, and cultivated, an immense ego, Peabody was content to work in the trenches, in Bronson Alcott's Temple School, for example, or as William Ellery Channing's amanuensis, or as an agitator for Native American rights. Further, I think that it is honest to admit that her gifts were neither literary nor organizational. Rather, she exemplified the exhilaration of Transcendentalist philosophy translated to the practical realm.

Anyone who wishes a view of the variety of her intellectual activities should visit Bruce A. Ronda's engaging *The Letters of Elizabeth Palmer Peabody, American Renaissance Woman* (1984), the introduction to which provides as good a sketch as we have of Peabody's busy life. Whoever wishes to locate the range of her writings must search through various periodicals as well as in the few book-length works (primarily compilations of such occasional pieces) that she published. But such a search will be well worth the effort. In many ways, Peabody offers a key to the Transcendentalist movement: to understand her intellectual obsessions as well as her seemingly limitless capacity for service in the cause of reform is to be brought to the heart of antebellum American culture. When the full contours of her remarkable life are sketched, the interest in language that I here document will find its proper space, for Peabody, as much as Emerson, Thoreau, Parker, and others, knew that one of the things that most distinguished their age from others was the necessity for reconceptualizing how one can say what one means.

The original note to the essay read: "I would like to thank Professor Walter Harding for giving me the opportunity to read a draft of this essay at his National Endowment for the Humanities Seminar in Concord, Massachusetts, in the summer of 1976; and Professor Joel Porte for his long encouragement of my study of language among the Transcendentalists. Richard Morey and Donald Eaton graciously criticized an earlier version of the manuscript. This essay is given to Professor John Conron in partial payment for his exuberance and affection."

Octavius Brooks Frothingham's *Transcendentalism in New England* remains, even after one hundred years, one of the most perceptive discussions of the Transcendentalist movement. Writing forty years after Emerson's *Nature* had shattered the still-youthful Unitarian synthesis, Frothingham noted how in New England "the ideas entertained by foreign thinkers blossomed out in every form of social life." New England furnished "the only plot of ground on the planet where Transcendental philosophy had a chance to show what it was and what it proposed," and the distinctive element of American Transcendentalism was just this pragmatism. "The test of a truth," Frothingham concluded, is its "availability," and in the New World "the thinker was called on to justify himself on the spot by building an engine, and setting something in motion."[1]

He was speaking of such famous enterprises as Brook Farm and Henry

---

1. *Transcendentalism in New England* (New York: Putnam, 1876), 105–6.

Thoreau's sojourn at Walden Pond, but his words apply equally well to Elizabeth Palmer Peabody's role in the discussion among Transcendentalists in the 1830s and 1840s of the philosophy of language, a subject with humanistic implications increasingly difficult for our generation to comprehend. The Transcendentalists' concern with this topic had its roots in the controversy over biblical exegesis that surfaced when the Unitarians openly challenged the Trinitarian reading of Scripture, and their interest spread after the dual streams of German Idealism and Swedenborgian correspondence laid the foundation for an understanding of language significantly different from one based on Lockean empiricism. Hans Aarsleff, in *The Study of Language in England, 1780–1860,* touches the heart of the matter when he explains that, in the nineteenth century, language study, even when called philology, was not merely "a matter of knowing the forms, syntax, phonology, historical relationships and other aspects" of particular tongues. The questions were of larger significance. "What, for instance, was the origin of thought? Did the mind have a material basis? Did mankind have a single origin? Was the first language given by revelation or had man invented it in the process of time?"[2] If we understand that the scholars involved in this study considered their work an attempt to answer such questions and to apply the answers *practically* to such spheres as theology, education, and literature, their dedication to what in retrospect seems like inane, or at best, antiquarian wordplay becomes meaningful. Among the American Transcendentalists involved in this reexamination of language, Peabody was the premiere purveyor of language theory, both in its theoretical and practical aspects.[3]

John B. Wilson recently concluded that Peabody learned her methods of "searching history, language, and literature for spiritual truths" from a study of J. G. Herder's *The Spirit of Hebrew Poetry,* which she used as a textbook in her "conversation classes" for ladies of Boston and which she reviewed for the *Christian Examiner* in 1834. This review, which establishes the tone for much of her later theorizing, deserves close scrutiny, especially

2. (Princeton: Princeton University Press, 1967), 4.
3. Biographical information on Peabody is available in Ruth M. Baylor's *Elizabeth Palmer Peabody, Kindergarten Pioneer* (Philadelphia: University of Pennsylvania Press, 1965), which contains an important bibliography of her writings as well as a list of books published under her imprint. Louise Hall Tharp's *The Peabody Sisters of Salem* (Boston: Little, Brown, 1950) lacks scholarly apparatus but draws the parameters of Peabody's life well. The only essay that suggests Peabody's association with language theorists is John B. Wilson's "Grimm's Law and the Brahmins," *New England Quarterly* 38 (1965): 234–38.

because it illustrates that the origin of the concern over the philosophy of language can be traced to the problem of establishing the authenticity of scriptural texts, one aim of Herder's book.[4] Peabody begins in a manner typical of her Unitarian upbringing, stressing that the words of the Old Testament were the product of men who were "limited in their power of taking in what was so freely poured upon them by their partaking in the spirit and character of the age in which they lived." This notion of language was expressed by many Unitarians schooled in Locke's *Essay Concerning Human Understanding,* who saw words as merely the arbitrary creations of men for the purpose of communication among themselves. But Peabody, already showing signs of her reading in Idealistic philosophy, discusses the *poetry* of the Scriptures, what she describes as the "expression of abstract and spiritual truths by sensible objects, by the forms, colors, sounds, changes, [and] combinations of external nature." This poetic language existed because "the human mind in its original principles, and the natural creation, in its simplicity," were but different images "of the same creator, who linked them for the reciprocal development of their mutual treasures."[5]

Primitive languages thus were "naturally poetic," but, as a society "ramified" and people talked by imitation and custom and not from their primitive experiences, a thousand arbitrary and accidental associations "connected themselves with words and deadened the impressions" they would naturally make on people. Suggesting a theory of the development of the forms of language similar to that advanced in 1836 by Rowland Gibson Hazard (whose works Peabody later published), she saw language as moving to a level of "analytical" (today we would call it *technical*) expression where words no longer were pictures of the natural world but were merely social conventions. This language was commonly known as *prose,* and, while it provided a more precise expression of the differences among things, it sacrificed the "force, impressiveness, and exciting power" of poetry. The most poetic expression of all thought, then, existed in the early stages of the human mind, *but* (and this was critical for those engaged in philological study) since poetry had formed the basis for the first language, "it must always exist as a part of all [subsequent] languages." Proceeding from this premise, Herder then explained the primitive poetical radicals of the Hebrew language and pointed out that the true genius of the

---

4. Wilson, "Grimm's Law," 234.
5. Elizabeth Peabody, "Spirit of Hebrew Poetry," *Christian Examiner* 60 (May 1834): 174, 175.

Hebrew tongue was displayed in its "formation and derivation of words from the original roots, and of those original roots from external and internal nature."[6]

Peabody coupled her study of Herder with what she knew of Greek mythology and discovered "the basic allegorical truths between the poetry of both cultures, which allowed her to assign a symbolic character to identical root words" in the languages. This enterprise led to a vision of primitive man as an original poet who named everything around him through the interaction of his speech instinct and the natural environment; that is, it proved that originally there was a reason (explained by the common origin of all things in the Oversoul) why such a word meant such a thing. For Peabody, the chief lesson of Herder's volume was the suggestion that, if we went back far enough in his study of language, we could not only locate the original roots of a tongue but ascertain how these roots *themselves* were derived from "external and internal nature." This theory—and here is the linchpin of the meaning of language for Transcendentalists—implied that there was a universality to the oldest roots of languages that, if properly understood, revealed what Peabody's friend Bronson Alcott called a "Universal Grammar." This grammar, in addition to providing a key to the more economic assimilation of the various modern tongues, also demonstrated the common origin of all men's thoughts in nature's reflection of the Oversoul. And if all language was derived from a common source—the interaction of Reason with Nature—it declared a brotherhood of man far more inclusive than any defined by the arbitrary claimers of American *political* democracy.[7]

What Peabody and others were seeking in the 1830s and 1840s was a theory of language that refuted the empiricists' claims that all words were arbitrary signs with no final relation to the things they named. This search was part of their general revolt against Lockean epistemology, but it soon involved them with reform in other areas. Peabody's early essay on Herder epitomizes this concern with a *natural language,* the parts of which were intimately connected to the objects of the exterior world; for convenience this sense of a transcendent correspondence between words and things can be termed a belief in a "language of nature" that returned men to a more primitive (that is, *vital*) relationship to the world they inhabited.

One result of Peabody's continuing interest in a theory of language

---

6. "Spirit of Hebrew Poetry," 175–76.
7. Wilson, "Grimm's Law," passim.

compatible with Idealistic philosophy was her sponsorship and publication of the works of theorists whose ideas interested her, most prominently the Rhode Island industrialist Rowland Gibson Hazard and the Hungarian philologist and schoolmaster Charles Kraitsir. Both men advanced theories similar to the one Peabody had groped toward in her essay on Herder; and, while ultimately Kraitsir is the more influential, together they suggest how and why a theory of a language of nature could make a difference in spheres of practical activity.

In 1836 Hazard anonymously published *Language: Its Connexion with the Present Condition and Future Prospects of Man*. Peabody, then serving as what might be called private secretary to William Ellery Channing, transcribing his sermons for the press, was so taken by the book that she promptly read it aloud to the Unitarian divine. In a reminiscence, she recalled that Channing immediately "recognized a rare metaphysical genius in its author," and that the following summer he wrote her from Newport that he had discovered the identity of the author, met him, and thought that he would be "a star in the intellectual firmament by-and-by."[8]

The attraction this homespun philosopher had for Peabody and Channing (Hazard admitted to writing his booklet "in fragments on steamboats, at hotels, and during such hours as could be spared" from his business dealings) resided in his articulation of an epistemology remarkably similar to that being introduced into America by such thinkers as Coleridge and Victor Cousin. Hazard's biographer had astutely recognized this as early as the 1880s, when he mentioned that the distinctions in language Hazard described were not wholly unlike "the distinctions made by Kant and afterwards in a modified way by Coleridge" between the functions of the Reason and the Understanding. Hazard had concluded that behind every

---

8. [Rowland Gibson Hazard], *Language: Its Connexion with the Present Condition and Future Prospects of Man by a Heteroscian* (Providence: Marshall and Brown, 1836), reprinted in Rowland G. Hazard, *Essays on Language and Other Papers*, ed. Elizabeth Peabody (Boston: Peabody, 1857), and Rowland G. Hazard, *Essays on Language and Other Essays and Addresses*, ed. Caroline Hazard (Boston: Houghton Mifflin, 1889). The best modern essay on Hazard is Harold A. Durfee's "Language and Religion: Horace Bushnell and Rowland G. Hazard," *American Quarterly* 5 (1953): 57–70. Biographical information is available in William Gammell, *The Life and Services of the Honorable Rowland Gibson Hazard* (Providence: Reid, 1888). The Channing anecdote is found in Elizabeth Peabody, *Reminiscences of Reverend William Ellery Channing* (Boston: Roberts, 1880), 185–86. It is worth noting that Peabody also translated and published a selection from a work of the French Swedenborgian, Guillaume Oegger: *The True Messiah, or the Old and New Testaments examined according to the principles of the language of Nature* (Boston: Peabody, 1842).

word man uttered there was a primitive nonverbal stage when all he had was an "ideal" or "primitive" perception of the thing in his mind. "Primitive perceptions" were the feelings men had *before* they possessed the proper word or sign to fit their ideas expressly, the *cause* of the effect we call language. In Hazard's words, they consisted in one's "impression of things, and all the images, sensations and emotions of the mind which are independent of words, and which having a separate and prior existence, induce us to resort to language when we would impart them."[9]

But just as Herder had revealed that people no longer understood the poetry of Scripture, Hazard, too, saw men as having strayed from this "language of ideality" (as he termed it) that best expressed their primitive perceptions.[10] Men now resorted to a "language of narration" that expressed their basic thoughts without any high degree of connotation or the need for the "imaginative or reasoning power," or to a "language of abstraction" that was used in contemporary logical discourse (for example, in barren theological treatises). These forms did no justice to the innate linguistic capabilities of men, and Hazard called for a return to a language that allowed men to discover "the relations among their perceptions" without being first obliged to express them abstractly and to rediscover the language of poetry where "instead of the immediate connection between words and ideals, the associations between the ideals themselves are made use of" (*Language*, 12–14).

Hazard's implication throughout was that, while the languages of narration and abstraction were needed for *persuasion*, the language of ideality was necessary for *conviction*. Poetic discourse had to be used in religious discussions, especially to show that "the power of perceiving truth in the form of ideals" (as opposed to dry abstractions) was the principle necessary to nurture a faith. He posited a gradual unfolding of human nature until men realized through these primitive perceptions the religious truths by which they had to live. To his mind there was a direct relationship between the language of ideality and man's attempt to comprehend the divinity of divinity: through the language of poetry man came to understand how his "finite spirit" blended with "the infinite" so that men always were holding "communion" with omniscience. The poet, the highest example of man using language, became, like Emerson's model, a "liberating god" (*Language*, 88, 135).

---

9. Gammel, *Life,* 18; Caroline Hazard in Hazard, *Essays,* 11–17.
10. Durfee, "Language and Religion," 63.

Peabody was enough taken by such ideas to publish a large selection of Hazard's essays in 1857, long after she had been introduced to more sophisticated theories of language. What appealed to her was Hazard's sense that there existed a language that addressed itself "to all, and which may be understood by all," one that (like Hebrew poetry) tapped deep roots within racial memories and spoke of the bond of all men. In his intuitive moments, man felt the conviction inherent in a language that demonstrated that "God, through the medium of His works, holds communion with the soul, shadows out the mysterious relations which exist between visible and invisible, the finite and infinite." This sentiment dovetailed perfectly with the New England Idealists' sense of a Reason, the promptings of which could be felt in moments of pure transcendence. And more important, as Harold Durfee has shown, it was a sentiment that linked Hazard, as well as such Transcendentalists as Peabody and Theodore Parker, to such important theologians as Horace Bushnell, who also advanced the premise that the most profound religious truths could be offered symbolically, that is, through the language of ideality.[11]

Another of Peabody's important essays on the subject of language is her review of the "Preliminary Dissertation on Language" prefixed to Bushnell's *God in Christ* (1849), one of his most important theological formulations. This review-essay first appeared in her own magazine, the short-lived but significant single issue of *Aesthetic Papers*, which she published after the demise of *The Dial* (which in its last two years also appeared under her imprint), and she used the appearance of Bushnell's work to attract more notice to her important discovery, the work of the Hungarian émigré Charles Kraitsir.[12]

Trained as a doctor, Kraitsir was swept up in the revolutionary activity in Poland in 1830 and forced to emigrate to France and England. By 1833 he came to America and in Maryland established an academy on the model

---

11. Hazard, *Language*, 131. Durfee's article is provocative throughout, and I am indebted to it for many of my initial formulations about the role of language in religious discourse.

12. Horace Bushnell, *God in Christ. Three Lectures Delivered at New Haven, Cambridge, and Andover, with a Preliminary Dissertation on Language* (Hartford: Brown and Parsons, 1849). For a sense of how important Bushnell thought the "Dissertation," see Mary B. Cheney, *Life and Letters of Horace Bushnell* (New York: Harper's, 1880), 90 and 192. On Bushnell and language, see Frederick Kirschenmann, "Horace Bushnell: Cells or Crustacea," in *Reinterpretation in American Church History*, ed. Jerald Brauer (Chicago: University of Chicago Press, 1968). Elizabeth Peabody, "Language," *Aesthetic Papers* (Boston: Peabody, 1849). Her essay on the "Dorian Measure" in the same issue also is pertinent here.

of the European *Gymnasium*. His pedagogical gifts, especially in language, attracted wide notice, and in 1840 he was named professor of modern languages at the University of Virginia. But the growing furor over slavery rekindled his libertarian feelings; he removed to the Boston area and, in 1844, began a successful series of lectures based on his unusual philological theories. By 1845 Peabody, still living a penurious existence despite the intellectual success of her bookstore and publishing ventures, became a teaching assistant in the academy he started in Boston.[13]

Peabody was interested in Kraitsir's claim for a theory of language that would unlock foreign tongues and make language study easier. From the copious notes she made of his public lectures, she published his *The Significance of the Alphabet* (1846), a pamphlet that—despite Kraitsir's (and several reviewers') claims that it was an aid in the instruction of foreign languages—proved one of the most remarkable philosophical documents of the period. Presented with an opportunity to review Bushnell's book on a similar subject, she took the time to compare it closely to Kraitsir's.[14]

Bushnell, Peabody said, understood that his topic—God in Christ—could not be broached without "falling upon language itself" and considering its nature more profoundly than had yet been done. Moreover, he realized that men were "linguistic, as truly, as naturally, as they are locomotive or intellectual"; therefore he saw the a priori reason to believe that language was *not* arbitrary nor accidental, but sprang *from nature*, to which it had a vital connection. Thus, the Hartford theologian was close to saying that men named things through a preestablished law connecting the mind and the natural world ("Language," 215–16).

But Bushnell did not perceive that "the same laws of imagination determined the elements of single words to their subjects, so that every word which is not an imitation of nature, like *hum, buzz, boom*, is, as it were, a poem, in short, that there is some natural and inevitable reason why every word should be what it is." Viewing the seeming confusion of the various tongues, Bushnell retreated to the empiricists' position that

---

13. Biographical information on Kraitsir is slight. A scarce pamphlet, *Karoly Kraitsir* (n.p., n.d.) was left to the Harvard College Library in 1863 by Charles Sumner. More readily available is the summary of that source in Michael West, "Charles Kraitsir's Influence on Thoreau's Theory of Language," *ESQ: A Journal of the American Renaissance*, 19 (1973): 262–74. West is the most profound student of Thoreau's knowledge of nineteenth-century philology; see his "Scatology and Eschatology: The Heroic Dimensions of Thoreau's Wordplay," *PMLA* 89 (1974): 1043–64.

14. Tharp, *Peabody Sisters*, 213–14. Kraitsir, *The Significance of the Alphabet* (Boston: Peabody, 1846).

language was "the creature of convention" and did not see that "within the multitudes of languages, and beneath the confusion of tongues, there must be something of a universal character, which gives meaning to the articulations of sound." In short, what he missed was the philological speculation of Kraitsir, who had shown (at least to Peabody's satisfaction) that the key to the study of languages lay not in their sounds—which *did* vary greatly for the same object in different tongues—but in the very *articulations* of sound ("Language," 215).

What Kraitsir had discovered after years of study in the modern languages was that a unity derived from certain *organic* principles underpinned speech. "All men," he declared, "however diverse they might become by conflicting passions and interests, have yet *the same reason* and *the same organs of speech*," and the underlying unity of all languages is based on a *physiological* premise: man could produce only a limited number of sounds through his vocal organs. The relationship between a man's consciousness (his Reason) and his organs of speech *was* language. Speech, concluded Kraitsir, was but "the explosion of reason," and it had to explode in one of three ways: from the throat in *gutturality*, from the lips in *labiality*, or from the teeth in *dentality*. Let me quote his explanation at length:

> Languages therefore have a certain unity. Differing superficially more or less, they begin to resemble each other, as soon as the observer goes beneath the surface; and they unite at the centre into three fundamental articulations, symbolizing the three organs of speech by which they are severally made, and correlative to three obvious categories of nature, cause, living and moving effect, dead or dormant effect. . . . There are three classes of sounds, in consequence of the harmony between our organs and the several categories, into which nature is divided in our conception. On examining languages we find the general fact that the causal is not expressed without the guttural, what is living and moving not without labials and linguals; what is dead or dormant not without dentals.

Kraitsir thus posited an amazing correspondence between the worlds of matter and spirit; for articulated sounds, the way air filtered through the throat, lips, and teeth, were a function of how man's Reason comprehended a stimulus in relation to the three great organic categories of existence: birth, life, and death. The voice modification made by men who in speaking brought "the external universe into relation with the spirit within themselves" was *the* constant underlying all languages.[15]

Kraitsir conceived of the purpose of his speculations as chiefly *educational*, revolutionizing the teaching of foreign languages. He was concerned with the perversion of spoken English and the fact that words "as pronounced" no longer "symbolized ideas" as they had when they first exploded from man's Reason. One had to *read* the words to discern any difference between *know* and *no*, or to see any *"angle* in *knee*, any *ken* in *knowledge*, and *keenness* in *knife*, any *getting into things by gnawing."* People tended to drop gutturals from their speech but, luckily for those trying to ascertain the roots of different languages, kept them in their writing. Taking the Latin language for his key, Kraitsir believed that if men, in learning it, took care not to soften their gutturals and to pronounce their diphthongs as diphthongs, all other languages could be more easily assimilated. Men would learn that languages of the same family "told tales on one another" and that "the same raw material lay at the bottom of the great variety of tongues" (*Significance*, 25).

Peabody easily transferred the implications of Kraitsir's "glossology," as he named his science, from the *educational* to the *theological*. She praised Bushnell's suggestions that there was "a *logos* in the forms of things" by which they were prepared to serve as "types or images of what is inmost in our souls" and that "the outer world which envelops our being" was itself a "language" of sorts. But, she noted, he missed the point that language represented not only *external* nature but "the ideas of man and the operations of his mind." In short, Kraitsir provided scientific, philological proof of Emerson's premises in *Nature*, that words were signs of natural facts; natural facts, signs of spiritual facts; and all nature the symbol of spirit. An awareness of the true form of language with its "direct reference to organic sounds" revealed the "original poetry of the unworn human mind" and thus verified Herder's and Hazard's sense of the keen power and truth of the primitive language of ideality ("Language," 215–18).

Peabody closed her assessment by quoting from a letter Kraitsir had received from one who had attended his lectures on the structure of the universal language:

> The identity of roots presented by him affects the imagination with a sense of the closest fraternity, and revealed to my mind with new

---

15. Kraitsir, *Significance*, 3–4; Kraitsir, *Glossology: Being a Treatise on the Nature of Language and the Language of Nature* (1852; repr. New York: Norton, 1854), 114.

force the words of an eloquent advocate for the study of language who, on dwelling upon the sympathies it stirred up, exclaimed with the prophet. "Have we not all one father? Hath not one God created us?" ("Language," 224)

Peabody saw Kraitsir's theories, then, not only as revolutionizing the teaching of foreign languages but as making men aware of their common brotherhood under God. And the men who saw this most clearly had learned the true relation of the articulations of sound to the Reason as man encountered the things of this world through that faculty and attempted to describe his sights to another. Language was perceived not only as a tool of communication, but as itself a veritable revelation.

Mary Lowell Putnam, a proper Bostonian who in 1849 reviewed Kraitsir's work for the *North American Review* under the bland running title of "The Pronunciation of the Latin Language," put the matter even more succinctly. She identified the genius of Kraitsir as residing in his understanding that language offered a profound insight into man's *spiritual* relationship to nature. Kraitsir demonstrated that "in the childhood of man, when nature mirrored herself in his thought, and thought passed unconsciously into instinctive speech, what is now called metaphor was then natural language."[16] This was precisely the understanding to which the artist Henry Thoreau would come when he transformed the philologist's theories for his own literary and teleological purposes. That, however, is another story.

Thus Elizabeth Peabody became particularly enamored of certain philological theories that presented evidence that originally man used what we call a language of nature, a vocabulary that derived its force from a symbiotic relationship between man's highest faculty, his Reason, and the natural world. She initially was attracted to the ideas of men like Hazard and Kraitsir because they provided a theoretical foundation for a renewed understanding of the metaphors in which Christian (and *all*) history was written. Hazard and eventually Bushnell came to believe that religious truths could be expressed only through the rhetorical forms of symbol or paradox—that is, in a *poetic* mode—and Peabody saw in their theories the injection of faith and ideality necessary to keep Unitarianism a viable faith in the nineteenth century. Further, Kraitsir's painstaking etymological

---

16. [Mary Lowell Putnam], "Review of Kraitsir's *Significance*," *North American Review* 67, nos. 142–43 (January and April 1849): 167.

studies (in 1852 he published his massive *Glossology: Being a Treatise on the Nature of Language and the Language of Nature*) provided what many thought a *scientific* proof of the universality of the symbols men made and used. Peabody's wholehearted espousal of his concepts is more evidence of the Transcendentalists' insatiable desire to perceive, or provide, a philosophical unity to a world that by 1840 seemed badly fragmented.

But one other aspect of Peabody's interest in philology remains: the eminently practical activity of the use of language theory in the educational experiments she and Bronson Alcott performed at the latter's Temple School in the 1830s. Noticing Peabody's pedagogical gifts, Alcott had enlisted her to teach Latin for two hours a day to the young Brahmins enrolled in his classroom, but she was so taken by the master and his methods that she began spending all day in the school and took the lengthy notes that she published in 1835 as *The Record of a School, Exemplifying the Principles and Methods of Moral Culture*. According to Odell Shepard, the most important exercise of the day in the Temple School "was the defining of words, in which Alcott lost no opportunity to draw (some would say drag) in a moral, spiritual or philosophical lesson." The "Explanatory Preface" Peabody contributed to the 1836 edition clarified how these lessons were carried out.[17]

The novelty of Alcott's school, she explained, arose from the "psychology" (that is, that Idealistic epistemology) on which he based his philosophy of education. He believed that the contemplation of spirit was "the first principle of Human Culture and the foundation of self-education." Rather than paying undue attention to the outside world, children should examine their spiritual depths and *then* look outwardly at the material presence. Nature was only to be made use of as "imagery to express the inward life we experience." The vocabulary lessons that began each day were designed to teach children to handle words in just this "spiritual" way, to make them speak of "the outward as the sign of the inward" principles that they intuitively understood but were in danger of forgetting as they matured into the materialistic nineteenth-century world (*Record*, iv–v).

Alcott's lessons in language were admitted "to be the most valuable," Peabody reported, and many were struck with the "advantages, necessarily to be derived from the habit of inquiring into the history of words from

17. For Peabody's role in the Temple School, see Tharp, *Peabody Sisters*, passim, and Odell Shepard, *Pedlar's Progress: The Life of Bronson Alcott* (Boston: Little, Brown, 1937), 112–219; quotation here is from Shepard, 168. Elizabeth Peabody, *The Record of a School, Exemplifying the Principles and Methods of Moral Culture* (Boston: Munroe, 1836).

their material origin, and throughout the spiritual application of them, which the imagination makes." She attested to Alcott's ability to make his students aware that words were the keys to understanding the *deeper* language that suffused nature and illuminated man's spirit—a language, in Sampson Reed's phrase, not of words but of things.[18]

Illustrating again how all these applications of language theory were interwoven, she mentioned that Alcott believed that the "contemplation of Spirit in God" was "necessarily wrapt up in a study of language." His description of Jesus (taken from his *Conversations with Children on the Gospels*) virtually portrayed the Christ as a poet whose success in enlisting people for his cause for more than eighteen hundred years was accounted for by his genius for language. Christ influenced people because of his concern with the "living word," which rose spontaneously from His son and clothed itself "in the simplest, yet most commanding forms." As expressed in the Gospel parables, Christ's ideas became "like the beautiful yet majestic nature" whose images He "wove so skillfully into his own diction," and the best way to understand His message was to parse and spell His words with primitive imagination.[19]

Alcott's lessons on the Gospels, then, took the form of reading the biblical lesson for the day and asking the children for their "associations with words, their impressions of events, the action of their Imagination, and the conclusions of their Reason upon them." Here is an example using the word "type."

> One boy said [it was] a metal letter which is used to stamp signs upon paper. What is a word or type the sign of? said Mr. Alcott. They severally said, of a thought, of an idea, of a feeling; of an object; of an action; of a quality. Language, Mr. Alcott said, is typical of whatever goes on within us, or is shaped out of us. What is the body the type of? of a mind. What is the earth a type of? of God; mind; heaven; were the several answers.

---

18. *Record*, vi. The presence of Sampson Reed is implicitly behind much of this essay. His *Observations on the Growth of the Mind* (Boston: Hilliard and Metcalf, 1826) greatly influenced both Alcott and Emerson. See, for example, Clarence P. Hotson, "Sampson Reed, A Teacher of Emerson," *New England Quarterly* 2 (1929): 249–77; and the section on him in Kenneth W. Cameron's *Emerson the Essayist* (Raleigh, N.C.: Thistle Press, 1945).

19. Peabody, *Record*, x; Bronson Alcott, *Conversations with Children on the Gospels*, 2 vols. (Boston: Munroe, 1836–37), 1:xxxiv.

Some people "think and say," he continued, "that the outward and natural things are all because they do not know what they are typical of." But he could show them that *all* outward things "proceeded out of those spiritual realities, of which they are types." This is a far cry from John Locke's position on the nature of the real world and how man came to describe it (Peabody, *Record,* xi, 75).

What Peabody and Alcott together sought in their teaching was to ascertain those primitive forms of words that related men to the natural facts whence they then could mount to the spiritual realm. They desired to assemble (in Alcott's words) "a spelling book containing the roots of language and nothing more," and both lamented that no "Universal Grammar" had yet been discovered so that all languages might be taught with equal facility and with an eye toward the spiritual and moral meanings of their vocabularies. Hints toward this "Universal Grammar," Peabody continued, anticipating Kraitsir, came from the Latin language, in which the articulation of sound was regarded as a "material" and where air was an element that was "hewn and carved into harmonious and beautiful forms *to give outness* to the movements and modifications of their thought" (*Record,* xxix, xxxv). In studying the Latin language, one discovered "an architecture of sound" and "theme syllables" that defined "in forms as with a graver's tool" every shade of meaning. Moreover, both Alcott and Peabody always stressed that the attainment of any practical facility in languages—of understanding their architectural tectonics—was but the preliminary to a moral understanding of the word, especially in its Christian form.

Despite such high-minded principles, the Temple School was soon forced to close because its preceptor sinned against the twin Boston taboos of race and sex. Parents were irate to discover that in his conversations on the Gospels, Alcott was drawing out his students on the intricacies of the Immaculate Conception, and the last children were withdrawn when he admitted two black youngsters to the school. But while it was in operation, the Temple School proved itself an educational enterprise of critical importance to the Transcendentalists' belief that the leading-out of a preexistent spirit was the main occupation of those educating the nation's youth. The practical success of the venture is attested to by an enthusiastic student; the wonderful line is recorded in Peabody's journal: "I never knew I had a mind till I came to this school." The evidence suggests that the reason for such sentiment lay in the imaginative stress placed on language at that

Masonic Temple on Tremont Street while Alcott and Peabody were teaching there (*Record,* 69).

This essay has suggested, first of all, the sheer *complexity* of language study as it was discussed among the Transcendentalists; and, second, that Elizabeth Palmer Peabody was one of those most concerned with the meaning of language for her generation. With her, language theory was more than an obsession: it was a matter of epistemological integrity. She knew that, if we rejected Lockean empiricism for German Idealism, we must rethink our attitudes toward the origin and function of language. The philosophers of language to whom Peabody was drawn were those who explained man's symbols in ways that suggested the inextricable tie between the natural and moral worlds. Language was anything but arbitrary for men like Hazard and Kraitsir, Reed and Oegger. There was a veritable *Reason* to it, and man had best heed it if he wanted to comprehend his transcendent nature. For the Transcendentalists the word was, indeed, with God, but in a way that reflected their readings among nineteenth-century language theories more than a belief in the infallibility of scriptural revelation.

10 Manufacturing Guitars for the American Parlor

James Ashborn's Wolcottville, Connecticut, Factory, 1851–1856

In this essay, my interest in American factory production merged with research I had begun into the history of antebellum music in its vernacular forms. For many years I had been immersed in the study of the production of early American stringed instruments—specifically the banjo, guitar, and violin—and in their repertoire as performed in parlors and on the early stage. When I learned that a friend had acquired a detailed account book of an antebellum stringed instrument maker from Connecticut, I leaped at the idea of working with the item. As far as I knew, with the exception of the records of the C. F. Martin Company of Pennsylvania, no such account books had come to light.

As I have said earlier, writing this essay constituted an entirely new education for me: not only did I have to learn more about the construction of early instruments but also of the history of American manufacturing itself. My conceptual breakthrough came when I realized that I had more to tell than just the details of this one small rural Connecticut factory. I really was on to a case study of how traditional craftsmanship was transformed under the pressures of the market economy. One small artifact, an account book, had opened an entire world of early American factory production.

Of course, behind this history of technology lay my understanding that music, like literature, has a language, and a history, of its own, and that the cultural historian who seeks to examine a period in any depth must familiarize herself with the varied discourses of the age. If any doubt, for example, that the study of vernacular music can help us decipher the cultural grammar of a moment in history, a look at Eric Lott's *Love &*

Theft: Blackface Minstrelsy and the American Working Class (1994) should dispel any doubts. Although I cannot yet pretend to have contributed anything as pathbreaking as Lott has to the field of American cultural history, this essay signals the growth of seeds planted a long while ago, twenty years or more, when I first became engaged, as a hobbyist, with early American music, as well as one of the directions my future work may take. Finally, I note that since this essay was published, I have acquired the Ashborn account book for my own collection.

By the mid-1850s Americans were awash in popular music. With the spread of labor-saving technology and the concomitant extension of leisure, Americans not only flocked to musical theater and the minstrel shows but also purchased hundreds of thousands of pieces of sheet music intended for performance in the parlor, the center of the new domestic sphere. Familiarity with such folios, songs meant to be accompanied by piano or, with increasing frequency, the guitar, as well as purely instrumental music, marked those (particularly women) who aspired to middle-class respectability. The phenomena of such immensely popular performers as the Hutchinson Family singers and Jenny Lind, the "Swedish Nightingale," who toured the United States to packed houses, and of composers such as Stephen Foster, whose song sheets were eagerly purchased by his admirers, signaled the nation's infatuation with popular music.[1]

But while we recently have learned much about the cultural role of music (what we might term its varied "consumption") in antebellum America, we

---

1. See, for example, Russell Sanjek, *American Popular Music and Its Business: The First Four Hundred Years*, 3 vols. (New York: Oxford University Press, 1988), 2:1–125 passim; Gerald Bordman, *The American Musical Theater* (New York: Oxford University Press, 1978); Carl Wittke, *Tambo and Bones: A History of the American Minstrel Stage* (Durham: Duke University Press, 1930); Robert C. Toll, *Blacking Up: The Minstrel Show in Nineteenth-Century America* (New York: Oxford University Press, 1974) and *On With the Show: The First Century of Show Business in America* (New York: Oxford University Press, 1976); Nicholas Tawa, *Sweet Songs for Gentle Americans: The Parlor Song in America, 1790–1860* (Bowling Green, Ohio: Bowling Green State University Press, 1980), and *A Music for the Millions: Antebellum Democratic Attitudes and the Birth of American Popular Music* (New York: Pendragon Press, 1984); E. Douglas Branch, *The Sentimental Years, 1836–1860* ([1934] New York: Hill and Wang, 1965), 175–88; Harry Dichter and Elliott Shapiro, *Handbook of Early American Sheet Music* (New York: Bowker, 1941); and W. Porter Ware and Thaddeus C. Lockard, Jr., *P. T. Barnum Presents Jenny Lind: The American Tour of the Swedish Nightingale* (Baton Rouge: Louisiana State University Press, 1980).

know little about the production and distribution of the instruments used to accompany it, particularly those produced far from urban markets but clearly intended for them.[2] Given the pervasiveness of this interest in music in antebellum culture, it is important to understand who produced such parlor instruments and how.[3] Moreover, because the interest in popular music coincided with the rise of the manufacturing system, and thus with an expanding economy that both required and engendered new distribution and market systems, case studies of those who produced musical instruments allow us to understand better the transition from artisanal to factory production in this crucial period of America's economic history.[4]

In the antebellum period James Ashborn's guitar factory in Wolcottville (now Torrington), Connecticut, which he operated for almost two decades beginning in the late 1840s, became one of the country's chief sources of parlor guitars. Ashborn's career thus provides an important view of the evolution of rural artisanry to factory production through urban retailing in this period, and hitherto undocumented details of stringed instrument-making as well. In particular, his and his financial partner A. N. Hungerford's accounting journal from April 1851 to January 1856 outlines supply, improvement, and building accounts, expenses for labor, numbers and types of instruments manufactured, and Ashborn and Hungerford's financial arrangements with the music trade in New York City, where Ashborn's guitars were sold.[5] These records and his extant instruments themselves

---

2. Gary J. Kornblith, "The Craftsman as Industrialist: Jonas Chickering and the Transformation of American Piano Manufacturing," *Business History Review* 59 (autumn 1985): 349–69, provides one of the few discussions of this subject.

3. Here I distinguish the production of such parlor instruments as the pianoforte and guitar from that of brass or wind instruments intended for bands and orchestras, which have received more attention. See, for example, Robert E. Eliason, "The Meachams, Musical Instrument Makers of Hartford and Albany," *Journal of the American Musical Instrument Society* 5–6 (1980): 54–73, and *Keyed Bugles in the United States* (Washington, D.C.: Smithsonian Institution Press, 1972).

4. See, for example, Susan E. Hirsch, "From Artisan to Manufacturer: Industrialization and the Small Producer in Newark," in *Small Business in American Life,* ed. Stuart W. Bruchey (New York: Columbia University Press, 1980), 80–99; and Kornblith, "The Craftsman as Industrialist," passim.

5. James F. Bollman of Arlington, Massachusetts, the present owner of the Ashborn and Hungerford account book, has generously allowed me to study and quote from it. I cite this book by monthly account rather than by specific page so that the date of a transaction is readily apparent.

Internal evidence indicates that the accounting journal is written in Hungerford's hand. Before each person or company's listing in the monthly accounting, for example, there is a reference number, which never changes throughout the years covered by the book. By Hungerford's name is the number "1." Further, at p. 141 of the book an external auditor has

illuminate ways in which Ashborn, after identifying a large and dependable market, sought local investment from those who already were engaged in—and thus knowledgeable about—the ways in which manufactured goods could be distributed, and then modified a traditional craft to produce guitars in greater numbers and at a good profit. He accomplished this primarily through standardized and simplified construction of his instruments, consolidation of hitherto segregated segments of guitar manufacture in one factory, and the assembly of a workforce whose labor was divided to expedite assembly of the guitars and their accessories. Ashborn's career thus offers a unique starting point to reconstruct a little-studied aspect of American cultural and economic history.

Ashborn's guitar works were located in the town of Torrington in northwestern Connecticut. Thirty miles west-northwest of Hartford and part of the "Windsor Patent" that was incorporated into Litchfield County, Torrington had been settled in the 1730s when Connecticut's expanding population sought new farmland throughout the western regions of the colony. But by the late eighteenth century the town was not known so much for its agricultural improvements as for its extensive hardwood forests, which contributed to the success of Ashborn's guitar works as well as to the burgeoning wagon-making activity so prevalent in the area, and its plentiful mill sites, situated as it was on the Naugatuck River. Like so many New England communities blessed with these resources, by the 1820s Torrington grew in importance as its grist and sawmills, and its artisanal workshops for the production of tool handles, carriages, and other wooden goods, were joined by factories built specifically for the manufacture of woolen and cotton yarn and cloth, and shortly thereafter of other goods.[6]

Thus, from an early date mill sites and craft workshops were strung up and down the Naugatuck River from Torrington proper, giving rise to

---

written at the bottom of the page that he has examined the "accounts of W[illiam] H[all] & Son & A. N. Hungerford April 20 to Feby 1st 1855 & find bal[ance] in favor of Wm H & Son 2113.09." At the least, this indicates that Hungerford took care of the accounting of the business. For a good discussion of the different kinds of accounts kept in rural areas in antebellum America, see Winifred Barr Rothenberg, *From Market Places to a Market Economy: The Transformation of Rural Massachusetts, 1750–1850* (Chicago: University of Chicago Press, 1992), 61–65.

6. My historical information about Torrington comes primarily from Samuel Orcutt, *Torrington, Connecticut, From Its First Settlement in 1737, with Biographies and Genealogies* (Albany, N.Y.: J. Munsell, 1878). I also have used the manuscript "United States Censuses (Population) of 1850 and 1860," primarily to ascertain the ages and occupations of people involved with the guitar works.

numerous factory villages that, though technically part of the incorporated communities, quickly assumed identities of their own. One such was Wolcottville, on a site north of town where the road from Litchfield met that to New Haven. In 1813 Joseph Allyn, who had purchased the waterpower privileges in the area, in turn sold them to members of the prominent Wolcott family. Caught up in the spirit of entrepreneurship that marked the period, they lost no time in erecting a sizable woolen mill. As a gesture of thanks to its chief proprietors the residents named the community after them.[7]

By the mid-1830s Wolcottville had become the "principal village" of Torrington and, by John Warner Barber's account, contained (in addition to the woolen factory) about forty dwelling houses, a Congregational meetinghouse, another meetinghouse used by other denominations and an academy, four stores, and two taverns. Barber also noted that a short distance from the factory "an establishment for the manufacture of brass" was being built. After several reorganizations, this became, in 1841, the Wolcottville Brass Company, owned by Israel Coe and John Hungerford of Wolcottville, and Anson G. Phelps of New York City; it was the largest manufacturing enterprise in the area.[8] It joined the Alvord Carriage Company, begun in 1831, and soon thereafter other establishments for the manufacture of woolen and cotton goods, and of chairs.

Torrington's forests and water power in themselves do not suggest an overriding reason why James Ashborn chose to manufacture guitars there; the town shared these resources with any number of communities throughout western Connecticut. His reason may have been personal: born in England around 1816, in Torrington he could have joined those of his countrymen who had been recruited by Israel Holmes, the principal manager of the projected brass works. In the late 1830s he had crossed the Atlantic to procure machinery and workmen, and after much hindrance from those who sought to prevent export of the requisite technology and labor, he finally succeeded in bringing to Wolcottville thirty-eight English men, women, and children.[9] Given Ashborn's skills as a designer and

---

7. In *The Roots of Rural Capitalism: Western Massachusetts, 1780–1860* (Ithaca: Cornell University Press, 1990), Christopher Clark comments on how frequently such communities were named after "a leading craftsman or entrepreneur" (231). Clark's study, although restricted to western Massachusetts, is germane as well to the economic development of the region around Torrington.

8. John Warner Barber, *Connecticut Historical Collections* (New Haven, Conn.: Durrie and Peck, 1838), 495–97.

9. Orcutt, *Torrington*, 101–2.

draftsman, evident in the two patents he secured for improvements to his musical instruments (see below), he may well have found his way to Wolcottville to join the recruits.

Ashborn evidently arrived in Torrington in the mid-1840s; the Census of 1850 lists him as having four children, aged six to thirteen, all of whom had been born in the State of New York. We know nothing of his first wife, but in December 1847 he married Lucinda Smith of Torrington—he was then residing in neighboring Litchfield—and in 1859 Maria L. Cook, daughter of Luther and Bethiah Cook, also of Torrington, by whom he had one more child. In 1850 when he was thirty-four, he called himself a "Mechanic" (that is, a skilled artisan) and noted $2,000 in real estate, an amount that had grown to $7,000 by the next census, at which time he also noted $2,000 personal estate. We also know that, true to his English upbringing, he was a member of the Trinity Episcopal Church in Torrington, and of the Seneca Lodge of Masons. Coupled with his substantial real estate, his membership in these organizations suggests Ashborn's prominence in the community, a fact to which his townsmen testified in 1864 when they elected him to the state legislature. For whatever reason, his guitar factory closed at about the same time, but the town historian noted that Ashborn continued to live in the community until his death on 7 December 1876.[10]

We also know that, like many other artisans in that entrepreneurial age, Ashborn sought financial backing from local sources to realize his ambitions, in his case, to build a guitar works to capitalize on the nation's growing interest in popular music, particularly among those who found the cost of the piano, the major parlor instrument, prohibitive. Costing a tenth or less of this instrument, the guitar promised to bring music into even more American homes.[11] At a time when most of these instruments were

---

10. This information is gleaned from Orcutt, *Torrington,* passim, and from the manuscript "United States Census (Population) of 1850."

11. The important point here is that, in the early phases of industrialization, artisans themselves took the initiative in moving toward factory production and themselves sought financial backing from local capital. That is, the impetus for industrialization only infrequently came from capital itself. Clark, *Roots of Rural Capitalism,* chap. 7, comments on how frequently skilled craftsmen sought to expand their works by appealing to local sources of credit; see especially 238–39. Also see Hirsch, "From Artisan to Manufacturer," passim; Kornblith, "The Craftsman as Industrialist," 354, who notes that the piano-maker Jonas Chickering also sought such financial backing, and that, as in the case of Ashborn and Hungerford, he and his partner John McKay divided their attention between what each knew best, that is, production or finance; and Judith McGaw, *Most Wonderful Machine: Mechanization and Social Change in Berkshire Paper Making, 1801–1885* (Princeton: Princeton University Press, 1987), parts 1 and 2.

made in Europe, Ashborn believed that he could produce them as well and at a profit, and he convinced the young Austin N. Hungerford of Torrington, whose family already was well established in large-scale manufacturing and thus who knew firsthand what it took to make such a venture successful, to become his business partner.

Born 20 October 1824, Austin Hungerford was the second child of John Hungerford, originally of Southington, Connecticut, and Charlotte Austin of Wolcottville, whom John married in 1820 after the death of his first wife, Elizabeth Webster. John had opened a store in Wolcottville shortly after its first woolen mill was constructed and before long had acquired an interest in the factory enterprise. From that point he turned his attention primarily to manufacturing. In 1844, for example, he and F. N. Holley formed the Union Manufacturing Company, another local woolen concern, and Hungerford also joined two others as an owner of the local brass mill, which he eventually bought outright. On his death in 1856 he was one of the wealthiest men in the community.

His son Austin, one of fourteen siblings, inherited his interest in business. In the Census of 1850, when Ashborn described himself as a "Mechanic," Hungerford prominently listed himself as a "Manufacturer" (presumably of guitars), just as his father had, and for several more years he and Ashborn conducted a successful business. Sometime between 1856, when the extant guitar-factory record book ends, and 1860 Hungerford evidently left both the business and the area. His financial backer departed, Ashborn had no qualms about listing himself in the 1860 census as the sole "Guitar Manufacturer." We know little else of Hungerford, except that he married Sarah Prindle, of Rochester, New York, had one child, Harrie Prindle, and died in November 1873.[12]

We do know, however, that with Hungerford's capital and connections to the larger commercial world Ashborn manufactured thousands of guitars and shipped them to New York City via the newly completed Naugatuck Railroad, which by 1850 had transformed the economic landscape of the

---

Kornblith observes that Chickering's least expensive pianos cost in the neighborhood of $200, while some of Ashborn's guitars wholesaled for one-twentieth that price. In July 1855 Ashborn and Hungerford secured for Clark Downs, a Torrington "Trader," a piano from New York, at the cost of $276.25.

12. Orcutt, *Torrington*, 512–13, and passim. Because the extant account book ends before all its pages were utilized (see note 5 above), and with an accounting of the finances, it seems possible that it was indeed at this point that Hungerford quit the partnership.

Naugatuck River Valley.[13] With a rail head in Wolcottville, Ashborn and Hungerford, like other entrepreneurs in the area, gained direct and quick access to New York City, the nation's metropolitan center, and as well to its burgeoning musical industry. More than anything else, this railroad gave Ashborn the incentive to locate his guitar works in Wolcottville and thus made possible his prominence and financial success.

By 1851, if not a few years earlier, he and Hungerford, following a common pattern in this early period of American manufacturing, made exclusive arrangements with large-scale distributors in one commercial center—in this case, with the New York music retailers William Hall & Son, and Firth, Pond & Company—to distribute Ashborn's guitars; in so doing, they assured themselves of a large share of that city's trade in guitars as parlor instruments.[14] If the numbering system Ashborn used to mark his guitars is accurate, by 1851, when the extant record book commences, he already had built close to 2,000 guitars. His works, employing up to ten

---

13. The Naugatuck Railroad was completed in 1849 and ran from the manufacturing town of Winsted (north of Torrington) down through Waterbury to Bridgeport, where it joined the New York and New Haven Railroad. Obviously, this rail line, its connection to the New York and New Haven making possible rapid and easy transportation to New York City, made possible, and lucrative, Ashborn and Hungerford's guitar manufactory. See Sidney Withington, *The First Twenty Years of Railroads in Connecticut*, Connecticut Tercentenary Pamphlet No. 45 (New Haven, Conn.: Connecticut Tercentenary Commission, 1935); and for a larger view of the impact of railroads on the economy, Thomas C. Cochran, *Frontiers of Change: Early Industrialization in America* (New York: Oxford University Press, 1981), 100–110; and Albert Fishlow, *Railroads and the Transformation of the Antebellum Economy* (Cambridge: Harvard University Press, 1965).

14. Such arrangements were typical of the antebellum music trade. In Boston around the same time, for example, both Elias Howe and Oliver Ditson similarly had established themselves as giants in the retailing world, acting as purveyors of instruments manufactured specifically for them as well as of sheet music and other accessories. See Christine Merrick Ayars, *Contributions to the Art of Music in America by the Musical Industries of Boston, 1640–1936* (New York: H. H. Wilson, 1937), 12–14, 28–34, 265–66, and passim; James F. Bollman, "The Banjomakers of Boston," in *Ring the Banjar: The Banjo in America from Folklore to Factory*, ed. Robert Lloyd Webb (Cambridge: The MIT Museum, 1984), especially 47–48; and Sanjek, *American Popular Music*, 2:107–11, 118–19.

It is interesting to note that though by 1830 New York City had become, as Nancy Groce has observed, the nation's center for instrument manufacture (surpassing Philadelphia), there in fact were few guitar-makers in the city, its reputation for instruments based primarily in piano manufacture. Indeed, once Christian F. Martin left the city in 1839, Louis Schmidt and George Maul, in partnership between 1839 and 1858, were the sole guitar-makers of any size and prominence. See Groce, *Musical Instrument Makers of New York: A Directory of Eighteenth- and Nineteenth-Century Urban Craftsmen*, Annotated Reference Works in Music No. 4 (Stuyvesant, N.Y.: Pendragon, 1991), xii–xiii, 107, and passim.

workers at any one time, had become not only an important part of Torrington's booming economy but the nation's largest supplier of parlor guitars. No other firm, not even that of the renowned Christian F. Martin, who like Ashborn manufactured instruments in a rural area (in Nazareth, Pennsylvania) and marketed them through New York City, rivaled Ashborn's production.[15]

Where and how did Ashborn make his instruments? At first his workshop was modest in scale. Sometime in the late 1840s, perhaps with Hungerford's support, he had bought from Lyman Clark a shop that had previously been used to make hayrakes, and fork and hoe handles. This building probably resembled any small early nineteenth-century woodworking shop—the one, say, in which one of his workers, Benjamin Smith, a cabinetmaker originally from Pennsylvania who had owned a small-scale Wolcottville furniture factory, had labored.[16] The large open work area would have been dominated by a variety of saws and simple lathes run off leather belts and wooden shafts from a water wheel powered by the Naugatuck River, whose course had been dammed to turn it—hence, such entries in the factory's expense account as that for August 1851 in which the owners recorded the payment of $10.00 for "Repairing [the mill] Wheel" and in July 1854, when they noted, $4.37 for "Repairs to Dam, etc."[17]

15. The manufacturing statistics of the United States Census of 1860 indicate that Martin produced only thirty-three guitars per year. See Peter Danna, "Guitar," *New Grove Dictionary of American Music*, 4 vols. (New York, 1986), 2:297. Also see Mike Longworth, *Martin Guitars: A History*, 3d ed. (Nazareth, Pa.: Longworth, 1988), passim.

16. Smith is the only one of Ashborn's employees who in the United States Census of 1850 listed himself as a "Cabinet Maker." On woodworking in general in this period, see the bibliographical guidance of Brooke Hindle, *Technology in Early America: Needs and Opportunities* (Chapel Hill: University of North Carolina Press, 1966), and of Nina E. Lerman, "Books on Early American Technology, 1966–1991," in *Early American Technology: Essays in the History of Making and Doing Things from the Colonial Era to 1850*, ed. Judith McGaw (Chapel Hill: University of North Carolina Press, 1994), 358–429. In particular see Wayne Franklin, *A Rural Carpenter's World: The Craft in a Nineteenth-Century New York Township* (Iowa City: University of Iowa Press, 1990); and Nathan Rosenberg, "America's Rise to Woodworking Leadership," in *America's Wooden Age: Aspects of Its Early Technology*, ed. Brooke Hindle (Tarrytown, N.Y.: Sleepy Hollow Restorations, 1975), 37–62.

17. In May 1852, for example, Charles Bradley paid twenty-five cents for "use of Lathe," indicating that Ashborn indeed used this tool, perhaps to turn his patented wooden tuners (see below). On water power in this period see Charles Howells, "Colonial Watermills in the Wooden Age," in Hindle, ed., *America's Wooden Age*, 120–59; and Gary Kulik, "A Factory System of Wood: Cultural and Technological Change in the Building of the First Cotton Mills," in *Material Culture of the Wooden Age*, ed. Brooke Hindle (Tarrytown, N.Y.: Sleepy Hollow Press, 1984), 300–36.

For several years this old rake factory evidently served Ashborn's purposes, although the owners frequently noted repairs or modest physical improvements to it in a separate "Improvement Account." In May 1851, for example, Ashborn and Hungerford installed blacksmithing equipment to facilitate metal work—$25 for a "Blacksmith Shop and Tools," and a year later paid Ralph Palmer for "Repairing [a] Shed." By the early fall of 1852, increased demand for Ashborn's guitars by the New York music houses and expanded manufacture of guitar strings led to construction of a new and presumably larger factory. In a new "Building Account" Ashborn and Hungerford noted considerable expenditures for the factory's construction: 3000 bricks ($18.00), lumber ($60.10), foundry castings ($323.85), shafting ($72.32), and belting ($5.75), and pay not only for Russell Goodnow and his carpentry crew, but for a "machinist," an "Irishman," and the chief builder, Willys Curtiss, who received $281.53. Within a few months there was a noticeable increase in the size of shipments of both guitars and strings to New York, without, however, a concomitant rise in expenditures for labor, suggesting that the innovations in production that Ashborn initiated in his factory (see below) were carried out even more expeditiously in the new plant.[18]

Within the factory, as one might expect in a business based on woodworking, saws were the most important, and most frequently mentioned, tools, and by far the most expensive. In August 1851, for example, the partners bought from J. Atkins & Company a "22 in[ch] veneer saw" for the considerable sum of $17.00, and two months later from the same source secured a twelve-inch "cir[cular] saw" for $3.00 and six "scrapers" (edge tools used in lieu of sandpaper for smoothing wood before final

18. Although monthly production rates of guitars continued to fluctuate after the building of the new factory, on the average Ashborn and Hungerford were able to ship about two to three dozen more guitars per month immediately after its construction. In 1851, for example, the number he made varied from 36 to 77; but after the completion of the factory, in December 1852, he produced as many as 96, 112, and 119 instruments per month, with aggregates in the seventies quite common. As noted, in the year after the factory completion, the overall labor cost per month did not rise more than about $20 (averaging about $300) and in some months was actually lower than it had been in 1851.

The new factory, however, does not seem to have affected production of the strings as much. The factory shipped this item regularly between April 1852 and June 1853, and then more sporadically, often a few months going by before they sent another shipment. During that period of steady production, they shipped as few as 48 dozen (in September 1852) and as many as 252 dozen (in February 1853, shortly after the factory was completed). It seems more likely that Ashborn used the new space for the more expeditious manufacture of the instruments and perhaps sought the new building because, once he undertook to make strings, his space had become cramped.

finishing) for $1.30. In July 1851 they bought "files" for $3.00, and in March 1852 paid out fifty cents for "filing [a] saw" and at the same time purchased "belting" ($3.12) to turn machinery. In 1854, perhaps to outfit further the new factory building for increased production, they purchased a "saw arbor" for $14.00, a "saw frame" for another $12.00, and subsequently noted the acquisition of a "cross cut saw" ($3.38) and several more circular saws ($15.00).

Such equipment itself brought Ashborn and Hungerford income from both local and distant sources. On several occasions, for example, they allowed the Alvord Carriage Manufactory, by the 1850s one of Wolcottville's largest employers, to use their saws to prepare wood for their own works. More often, however, ever alert to opportunities to enlarge their profit margin, Ashborn and Hungerford performed work for the New York companies with whom they already had established extensive business arrangements for the sale of their instruments and the procurement of raw materials not obtainable locally. In particular, they often sawed lumber for William Hall & Son's urban piano factories where the instruments were assembled, thus contributing in another way, as they did in their own factory, to the increased specialization of labor that had come to mark factory production.[19]

Their accounts with Hall & Son, for example, show them frequently "sawing articles for piano forte work." In February 1852, they charged the company $19.00 for "sawing long blocks" and another $46.00 for "21 days sawing on piano work and lumber," and in December of the same year, $42.50 for "sawing piano work." Some of the lumber from which these pieces were cut had been sent by the company from New York City, some procured locally from the same lumbermen who sold Ashborn and Hungerford wood for their guitar work.[20] Even the by-product of such

---

19. Kornblith, for example, notes that in an attempt to economize by division of labor, the piano manufacturer Jonas Chickering utilized workers in several different locations around Boston to prepare the components of his instruments (360–62). Also see Sean Wilentz, *Chants Democratic: New York City and the Rise of the American Working Class, 1788–1850* (New York: Oxford University Press, 1984), who observes that New York, "with its immense labor pool, its credit facilities, its access to prefinished materials from Britain and New England, and its transportation lines, was a superb site for producing finished consumer goods, for local consumption or shipment elsewhere." The out-of-shop contracting that characterized such work, he concludes, created a kind of "bastard artisan system" in which the old distinctions among craftsmen on the basis of skill was undermined as manufacture was subdivided into various tasks (111–13).

20. The New York State Census (Manufacturing) of 1855 indicates that both William Hall & Son, and Firth, Pond & Company held large stocks of wood. The latter's inventory,

contract work had value. On several occasions Ashborn and Hungerford used hogsheads of sawdust as credit toward purchases at the Wolcottville Brass Company, which presumably used the material in their metal casting process or as packing material.

Aside from the "scrapers" just noted and a reference to a lathe (see note 17), Ashborn and Hungerford never mentioned the various hand tools used by antebellum woodworkers, perhaps because, as was often the case in this period of transition from artisanal to factory production, many employees may have still owned their own.[21] But materials for the assembly and finishing of the guitars—hide glue and varnish—appear frequently in the accounts. Ashborn obtained his glue locally from the merchants Holcomb & Lyon ($16.11 worth in July 1852, for example, and a large purchase, for $47.72, in April 1853); and prepared his varnish, commonly made to an artisan's own specifications, from a variety of ingredients secured from Alvord and various contacts in New York City.

In August 1851, for example, as credit for some brass wire the Wadhams Manufacturing Company, a local cotton factory, had bought from them, Ashborn and Hungerford received amounts of "vitrol" (sulfate, probably for coloring) and "aqua fortis" (nitric acid for solvent), and in September took a gallon and a half of "Japan" (a lacquer) from Alvord's carriage works, along with a gallon of turpentine. The next month Ashborn himself was reimbursed for securing two gallons of alcohol ($1.40) and two gallons of shellac ($.50) for the factory; later he bought three "glue pots," and a "varnish rack" from which to hang the instruments until dry. In October 1851 Ashborn settled on F. W. Parrott as his regular supplier of japan, buying thirty gallons, enough to last a year and a half.

Ashborn and Hungerford also purchased brass from which to manufacture frets and other guitar hardware. For some of this material, particularly the "rolled brass" which might also have been used for the base of the guitar tuning machines, they turned to the nearby Wolcottville Brass Company, owned by Hungerford's father. They also employed others to prepare the metal to Ashborn's specifications. In April 1851, for example, Edward Langdon contracted to make forty-four brass castings for $11.00; in July, fifty-seven for $13.11; and as late as February 1854, another 104, at $31.28. While we cannot be sure just what Langdon was casting, there

---

for example, listed $10,000 in "lumber"; the former held $2,000 in "iron and wood stocks." See Groce, *Musical Instrument Makers of New York*, 52, 70.

21. See, for example, Hirsch, "From Artisan to Manufacturer," 87.

is little doubt about what Emery Morris, a thirty-year-old employee who called himself a "Mechanic," provided. Listed in the "Labor" accounts alongside other workers and paid at the high rate of $1.25 per day, he also machined "set screws and wheels" for the guitar tuning machines, a task for which he was paid separately. In July 1851, for example, the company paid Morris $13.00 for eleven days' labor, and an additional $18.00 for seventy-two "sett screws and wheels," a type of entry repeated every few months until April 1852, when his daily rate rose to $1.50 and the days he worked per month increased significantly, which suggests that from that point on he machined these parts as his regular task.

The heart of the guitar-making enterprise, though, lay in the wood from which Ashborn constructed his instruments, and he used what was customary for nineteenth-century guitar-making: spruce, a softwood, for the top, sides, and back of the instrument; rosewood, mahogany, or (occasionally) maple for veneering the sides, back, and neck; maple, cherry, or some other hardwood for the neck itself; and dense and resilient ebony or rosewood for the fingerboard, and sometimes for peghead veneer. Ashborn obtained his stocks both from local sources and via rail through the New York firms to whom he and Hungerford sold their guitars and who received substantial credit for supplying exotic woods.

Ashborn got spruce, for example, from both local lumbermen and through Hall & Son of New York. In July 1851 he and Hungerford credited that firm's account for $47.85 for 1,595 feet of spruce; and in June 1853, $50.67 for another 1,528 feet. Moreover, in February 1852 they paid $83.36 to Hall & Son for "white wood" (that is, bass), which Ashborn probably used for the blocks and braces inside his instruments; but he was as likely to get this wood locally, from the lumbermen Smith & Hawley, say, who in June 1853 brought in 502 feet of "white wood" ($22.59) as well as 146 feet of "Spruce Plank" ($2.34). Another frequent local supplier was Clark Downs, listed in the Census of 1850 as a "Trader." In March 1853 he and Hungerford bought 2,359 feet of "Whitewood" from him.

Some of the maple that Ashborn occasionally used for the sides and necks of his instruments, as well as for his "piano work," also was obtained locally, as it was one of the most common hardwoods in the region. Winthrop Cook, a "Lumber Man," frequently supplied it, bringing in 862 feet in December 1851, along with 1,295 of bass, netting him a total of $30.13. The next winter he returned with 141 feet, for $17.63; and in April 1854 he received $20.51 for 167 feet. Occasionally, Ashborn got this wood from New York—a fifty-foot plank in June 1851, and 1,410 feet in January

1853; and at other times evidently took in a surplus locally for resale to Hall & Son, perhaps for their piano factory. That was the disposition of a load Cook brought in 1851. Cook also supplied local woods that could be used for instrument necks: 300 feet of cherry ($9.00), 157 feet of apple ($9.42), and 310 feet of maple ($3.87) in March 1853; and more cherry and some butternut in August 1853 for $7.15. On another occasion Ashborn and Hungerford purchased 106 feet of cherry for $3.18 from the latter's father at the Wolcottville Brass Company. One last hardwood that appears in the accounts is holly, which Ashborn obtained through Hall & Son. It was inexpensive—100 feet for $1.50 (June 1852).

Ashborn obtained the tropical woods favored by guitar makers for the body and fingerboard of their instruments through the New York firms, and these goods constituted one of his and Hungerford's major expenses. At the same time that they bought a sizable amount of bass from Hall & Son in July 1851, for example, they also took "2 Rose wood Logs" for $30.00 and "1 13 in[ch] Mahog[any] Plank" for $8.16. A year later they acquired ninety feet of mahogany for $14.40, and in January 1853 an unspecified amount for $14.65. As this indicates, rosewood was very expensive—another log bought in April 1854 cost $40.50—but essential. All of Ashborn's higher-grade guitars had rosewood veneer over their spruce sides and backs, and he utilized it as well for the fingerboards on some instruments. Ebony was equally dear, with $22.19 paid for an unspecified amount in December 1853, and $65.00 for an undecipherable amount in July 1854. More unusual yet was cocus wood, also known as Jamaican ebony, a wood favored by flute manufacturers but that could be used in guitar work as well. In March 1852, J. Firth & Hall was given $12.50 credit by "Scrap Cocus."[22]

Ashborn and Hungerford sometimes acted as brokers and sold smaller pieces of these exotic woods to local craftsmen. On several occasions Arvid Dayton, who since 1840 had manufactured pipe and then reed organs in a factory near Ashborn's, occasionally bought small pieces of ebony; and Downs took a "block" of rosewood the day he brought in 3,600 feet of hemlock (a wood Ashborn may sometimes have substituted for spruce for the guitar tops or backs).[23] More anomalously, in February 1855 Ebenezer

22. Evidently, even after they had formally separated their businesses, John Firth and William Hall continued to do some business under the name of J. Firth & Hall, for this designation occurs on a few occasions in the record book, never, however, concerning the receipt of goods produced by Ashborn and Hungerford.

23. On Dayton see Orcutt, *Torrington*, 84–85, 428–32. He built his first pipe organ in

Welton, a "Button Maker," bought an entire rosewood log for $22.00, a purchase that probably went a long way in his craft.

With these materials Ashborn and his workmen manufactured an astonishing number of instruments. Until July 1854 he and Hungerford meticulously listed by serial number all guitars sent to Firth, Pond & Company, and William Hall & Son: a typical entry reads, "12 No 3 Guitars and Cases / Nos 2938 to 2949." Even though they inexplicably stopped noting the serial numbers after that date, they continued to enumerate the guitars carefully. Between April 1851 and December 1855 the factory produced 3,152 instruments, an average of 54 per month, with as many as 119 shipped in June, as few as 12 in December 1854, none at all in October and November of that year, and in January 1855, a slowdown that may bear some relation to an audit of their accounts with Hall & Son (see below). Finally, Ashborn and Hungerford most often shipped instruments in increments of twelve, and the most common amounts per shipment were four and five dozen.

By the time that Ashborn was building guitars, the few American makers produced what was known as the "Spanish guitar" (as opposed to the "English" guitar or cittern), that is, a six-stringed instrument whose basic design, and popularity, had been established on the Continent in the early nineteenth century.[24] The bodies of such instruments were smaller than those of most twentieth-century guitars and ornamented in a variety of ways, accounting for significant difference in prices. This explains Ashborn's designation of six different grades for his guitars, identified by a numeral from one through six (stamped inside the guitar on its center strip) and increasing in cost upward. During the period covered by the account book, the company shipped 916 No. 1's (priced at $8.50), 1,016 No. 2's

---

1840, and in 1846 his first reed organ, evidently one of the earliest of its kind in America. In 1855 he developed a different sort of board for the organ's reeds that Torrington's historian writes, "proved to be the greatest improvement in reed organs, that has been effected." Orcutt continues, "This invention consisted in arranging the reed board so as to have two and a half sets of reeds [or more] all to operate *with one set of valves*, having dampers placed over each half set to be raised by stops, so that either set or half set, can be played alone or at the same time."

24. See Harvey Turnbull, *The Guitar: From the Renaissance to the Present Day* (New York: Scribner, 1974), chaps. 4 and 5; Tom and Mary Ann Evans, *Guitars from the Renaissance to Rock* (New York: Facts on File, 1977); Tom Wheeler, *American Guitars: An Illustrated History* (New York: HarperCollins, 1990); and George Gruhn and Walter Carter, *Acoustic Guitars and Other Fretted Instruments: A Photographic History* (San Francisco, Calif.: GPI Books, 1993), 9–15.

(at $9.75), 576 No. 3's (at $11.50), and 406 No. 4's (at $14.25). Numbers 5 and 6 were quite expensive—$17.50 and $25.00, respectively—and were built in very small numbers, usually three and never more than six instruments sent to New York at one time, for a total of seventy No. 5's and sixty-six No. 6's.[25]

Ashborn's guitars had a body size about the same as those popularized by Louis Panormo, a leading maker in England in the early nineteenth century. In many particulars, however, they differed, which suggests that the details of Ashborn's construction were his own and were intended to expedite construction of the instruments to meet the increasing demands of the New York market. For example, Ashborn simplified production by making his guitars all the same shape and size, eliminating the need for different-sized molds and jigs for shaping the instruments' ribs or for different scales for marking the frets. Such standardization also suggests that the factory's price scale was set primarily by the degree of ornamentation on each instrument.[26]

25. Although the ornamentation varies somewhat within each grade of Ashborn's guitars, I offer the following general descriptions to indicate variations between the different grades themselves. Ashborn's least expensive guitar, the No. 1, had a minimum of decorative binding around the top perimeter and the sound hole. In addition, unlike on higher-grade models, the fingerboard sometimes was made of rosewood rather than ebony. The No. 2 had its maple sides and spruce back veneered with rosewood, had more decorative binding around the top of the instrument, and three-line purfling around the bottom edge. The fingerboard on this style was ebony, and the peghead veneered on the front with the same wood and with rosewood on the back.

No description of a No. 3 instrument has yet been provided, but the No. 4 also had the rosewood veneer over its sides and back, ebony binding and white side purfling around its body, three-line purfling around its back, neck and peghead veneered with rosewood, an ebony fingerboard, and many-lined rosette rings around the sound hole. The No. 5 was similarly appointed but with a nine-ply binding around the top, five-ply around the back, and five-ply around the edges of the sides as well. No description of a No. 6 has yet been provided.

Ashborn occasionally made even more ornate instruments. Thus in October 1851, Hungerford noted "2 Extra Guitars and Cases" at $25 and that December recorded "4 Extra Guitars & Cases / Ivory Bands" at the extraordinary price of $42.75 apiece. These may well have been bound with the ivory that the company occasionally received from their New York retailers. In September 1855, for example, Hall & Son received $20 credit for fifty pounds of "Scrap Ivory." None of Ashborn's highest grade instruments have come to light, however.

26. On Panormo, see Turnbull, *The Guitar*, 68–70; Alexander Bellow, *The Illustrated History of the Guitar* (Rockville Centre, N.Y.: Franco Colombo, 1970), 173, 177–79; and Stewart Button, *The Guitar in England, 1800–1924* (New York: Garland, 1989), 210–41, 311–15. The only other guitar works for which we have records dating back to the mid-nineteenth century is the C. F. Martin Company of Nazareth, Pennsylvania, arguably the most famous guitar-maker in the world, who from the 1840s on manufactured guitars in a variety of sizes as well as with distinctive ornamentation. See Longworth, *Martin Guitars*, passim; and Gruhn and Walters, *Acoustic Guitars*, 16–28. As noted above (note 15), Martin's

Further, from extant Ashborn guitars it appears that their basic construction, whatever their grade, was remarkably consistent, as befitted factory production. The top was spruce, braced with a three-stave fan set into a peaked crossbrace, a design fairly common to contemporary "Spanish" guitars. The sides were spruce or maple; if the former, usually veneered with rosewood or mahogany. The back also was rosewood or mahogany, from two pieces of closely matched grain, lined with spruce and joined without any center stripe.

Ashborn's guitar necks were assembled from three pieces of hardwood (like maple) and sometimes veneered with mahogany or rosewood, an appointment not common in antebellum guitars. Further, his manner of attaching the neck to the body offers a striking illustration of how he adapted traditional design to more rapid factory production. He performed this important task with the use of a dovetail joint and the addition of a short collar glued to the back, a particularly expeditious manner of assembly. In contrast, the "Spanish" heel more commonly seen on antebellum guitars was attached by slotting the sides of the body into the neck, which then continues a short way into the body, a method that requires more tedious adjustment and thus allows for more variation among instruments.[27] Finally, Ashborn spliced the peghead to the top of the neck with a distinctive "diamond" joint that permitted a large gluing surface and thus a strong bond, a method he used on his banjo work as well.

---

production was much smaller than Ashborn's, no doubt in part because he continued to make his instruments as a craftsman rather than a factory producer.

27. For this insight, and for my general description of the construction of Ashborn guitars I am indebted to Juris Poruks of Montreal, Quebec, a collector and scholar of Ashborn guitars (letter to the author, 23 March 1994).

Ashborn's banjos also display the same sort of technological resourcefulness, particularly with regard to the manner in which the calfskin head is stretched over the banjo's rim. In the 1840s, the first decade in which this instrument was commercially produced, most makers essentially modified a drum assembly for the banjo's rim; that is, they stretched the skin over the head by means of several individual brackets that were tightened with nuts. One extant Ashborn banjo in fact is constructed this way; but several others illustrate a novel modification, a wooden bracket band that is glued to the side of the rim, with the brackets tightened into it by means of a key that turned a small nut assembly inside the band. Thus, no holes had to be drilled through the rim, as in the other assembly, to hold the shoes through which the brackets fit. Ashborn's assembly thus kept down the overall weight by eliminating the shoes and larger nuts, and also preserved the integrity of the rim for acoustic purposes, no shoe holes being necessary. Ashborn's bracket band thus constitutes a notable increase in sophistication in the way the banjo assembly was conceived, and prevented him from having to manufacture or purchase more brass parts. Finally, it is worth noting that, though he did not patent this assembly, it performs the same function and is analogous to the rim of the famous A. C.

No doubt because their new factory helped them increase production without incurring significantly greater labor costs, Ashborn and Hungerford kept the prices of their guitars constant between 1851 and 1856, and sold the instruments to both of their New York buyers for the same price. Finally, it is worth noting that in their June 1855 account with Hall & Son, Ashborn and Hungerford listed two new items: eight dozen "Maple Guitars & Cases" for $720, making these the least expensive of the company's productions; and a dozen "No. 3 Guitars & Cases New Style" for $156, more expensive than the standard No. 3.

Ashborn's guitar construction thus indicates how he modified traditional artisanal production of his instruments to meet the demands of factory production by means of his standardization of the basic construction of all models and a novel assembly of the neck to the body. But his technological and entrepreneurial genius is evident as well in the guitar accessories that he and Hungerford provided the New York market.

The most important example of such innovation pertains to the instruments' tuning mechanisms; Ashborn was so interested in their design that he obtained two United States patents for improvements to such devices. Presumably he installed these on many of his guitars, but he also sold them separately; they appear in the business records as "Pat Heads wood parts" or "pat peg heads & wood parts," shipped in batches of six or a dozen at the price of $2 for each set (presumably to be resold to other guitar manufacturers in the city or elsewhere). These novel tuning mechanisms bespeak Ashborn's interest in mechanical design as well as his desire to simplify the manufacturing of his guitars. Rather than having to purchase or painstakingly machine what then were called "patent heads"—that is, a set of metal (usually brass) geared tuners inserted in the peghead for tightening the strings, the components that Emery Morris machined for him—Ashborn replaced such costly items with modified, more efficient versions of wooden violin-style tuners that could be turned on his own woodworking equipment.

On 16 April 1850, for example, Ashborn obtained United States patent no. 7,279, for a "Guitar-Head and Capo Tasto," that is, a peghead tuning mechanism and a capo for changing the pitch of the strings (see below). This tuner is what one music historian describes as a "windlass," a peg-

---

Fairbanks "Whyte Laydie," c. 1901, an assembly patented by Fairbanks' chief designer, David L. Day.

and-spindle mechanism to enable one to tune more easily and precisely than with the older violin-peg-style tuner or the metal "patent heads," which Ashborn found undesirable not only because of the "great cost of a guitar head thus constructed" but also because "the weight of all these pieces of metal injuriously affects the vibrations of the instrument."[28] His solution was to make a larger-sized spindle to attach to the head of the guitar but not protrude on the back side, connected by catgut to a regular-shafted violin tuner passing all the way through the peghead, slightly behind the spindle for that string. When the violin-type tuner was turned, the resulting action was like that of a windlass: easier, more accurate adjustment without the cost or weight of the brass tuners.

Ashborn's second patent, for a "Tuning-Peg for Guitars," is even more ingenious and, like his first innovation, is made wholly of wood in a shape that he could easily produce on a simple lathe. This patent is for what we might term a multiratio tuning peg. Citing the same defects in tuning mechanisms that he noted in his 1850 patent, in United States patent no. 9,268, issued 21 September 1852, Ashborn described a tuner with "that part of the wooden peg which is fitted to and turns in the handle of the instrument, and which may be called the journal, of much greater diameter than the barrel or part on which the string is coiled or wound up, and thereby giving such leverage to the surface of which makes friction and which resists the tension of the string as effectually to hold the string without the necessity of wedging or driving the peg too hard." The result was a larger hole in the peghead into which the "journal" was fitted, but Ashborn obviously thought that the ease with which such pegs could be made and the efficiency and accuracy gained in tuning were significant.[29]

In addition to producing novel tuners, Ashborn and Hungerford decided to manufacture other key components of the guitar, thus obviating the need

---

28. For information about Ashborn's patents I am indebted to Edmund Britt of Wakefield, Massachusetts, who generously shared his research with me.

29. It is difficult to gauge the success or popularity of Ashborn's patent innovations because most of his extant guitars carry the more traditional brass tuning machines, leading one to speculate that most of his instruments left the factory so equipped. It is interesting to note, however, that the one No. 5 guitar located to date in fact carries his pegs, as well as a stamp on the back of the peghead, "J. Ashborn / Pat. 1852," suggesting that he may have installed such pegs on his high-grade models. We also know that he sold his patented pegs separately, through the New York music dealers, so that other guitar-makers might adopt them on their own instruments. Further, Ashborn also used his patented pegs on his banjos, for Britt owns an Ashborn banjo stamped with the 1852 patent whose head is drilled for the pegs. Other of Ashborn's banjos, however, were fitted with brass tuning machines, and still others with regular violin-style pegs.

to purchase them from other suppliers. As noted above, their decision to construct a larger factory building was based not only on their wish to produce more guitars more economically but also in their decision to expand their manufacture of wound guitar strings. After they discovered that it was more economical to produce these items for Ashborn's own guitars in their own factory rather than secure them through New York, they also realized that string-making per se could be profitable.[30]

Prior to the summer of 1851, for example, they had received strings for Ashborn's guitars from either Firth, Pond & Company, or Hall & Son. After that date these items begin to appear as goods made in the Wolcottville factory to be shipped exclusively to Hall & Son with Ashborn's guitars (presumably Firth, Pond & Company had their own supplier of such strings). Indeed, string-making soon became so important a component of their business that, in April 1852, the partners started a separate "String Account" in their ledger to record the purchase of the materials needed to make them. Their new building, completed that autumn, thus would have housed lathe-like machines, running at low speed, to perform the winding of strings, and Ashborn would have trained some of his employees in this specialized work, a further division of labor necessitated by bringing hitherto different parts of the guitar industry under one roof.[31]

Once Ashborn and Hungerford decided to manufacture strings on a large scale, they also began to take as credit from the New York firms large amounts of different-gauged silver wire, and of the silk thread around which the wire was wrapped to make the three lowest strings of the guitar.[32] In September 1851, for example, they paid $4.50 for "16 [presumably a gauge] Silver wire" and $6.75 for "no. 18," and that same month returned to Hall twelve dozen "No. 6 Strings" for $7.80, and the same quantity of "No. 5" for $6.60. They also purchased "no. 13" gauge wire, presumably for the fourth strings. Interestingly, they never recorded the manufacture of first, second, or third strings, usually made from twisted strands of gut, but

---

30. Little is known about early American string manufacture. The music historian Arthur Schrader has indicated that in the United States in the 1850s the manufacture of wound strings was still very unusual, with most of these products still imported from France or Italy (letter to the author, 8 February 1994). Laurence Libin, however, notes that he has found records in the Moravian Archives in Bethlehem, Pennsylvania, of string-making among the Moravians there in the eighteenth century (letter to the author, 22 February 1994).

31. On such division of labor see, for example, Kornblith, "From Craftsman to Industrialist," passim; and Hirsch, "From Artisan to Manufacturer," 87 and passim.

32. I am indebted to Libin and Schrader for information relating to the nineteenth-century manufacture of guitar strings, and of capos as well.

only the three larger-gauge strings.[33] In May 1852, for example, Ashborn and Hungerford sold Hall forty-two dozen "Super Extra 4th" strings at $31.50, twenty-four dozen "Super Extra 5th Strings" at $13.20, and the same quantity of "Super Extra 6th Strings" at $15.60. After April 1852 they used this designation, "Super," for all their strings and shipped comparable amounts to New York each month, between September 1851 and January 1856—a total of 5,212 *dozen* strings.

Ashborn and Hungerford also manufactured and sent to New York three other items worth mentioning. First, virtually all the guitars Ashborn built were shipped in wooden cases made in the factory, items probably constructed by some of the lower-paid employees. From the few instances when he and Hungerford shipped the instruments without such protection (in November 1852, for example), we know that their wholesale price included $2 for each case (see November 1852). Moreover, Ashborn sometimes had his employees work on special orders; in July 1853 he and Hungerford shipped Hall & Son three dozen violin cases at a dollar each. On occasion, too, the company shipped wooden "Bridges," presumably for violins or violoncellos (which Ashborn occasionally repaired), but perhaps for guitars, to be sold like his patented tuners, to guitar-makers in New York or elsewhere. In March 1852, for example, Hall & Son gave $2 credit for twelve of them. These were not, however, common items in the accounts.

More significant was production of what then was called a "capo de astra," to hold down the guitar strings at a certain fret to change the pitch of all strings played above that point. In the manufacture of this item we again see Ashborn's technological genius. During this period capos usually consisted of a metal or wooden bar faced with buckskin (hence the $4 purchase of this item in February 1854 from a local tanner) and attached around the guitar neck to hold down the strings at a certain fret. Tension was provided by a gut string wrapped once around the neck and tightened with a short fiddle-style peg fitted to a hole in the top of the bar. In his 1850 patent, however, Ashborn noted that hitherto the use of a capo is "attended with great difficulty" because the tension on the strings might easily be lessened or released if the gut slipped. He modified this design so that the capo could be more easily adjusted by "an eccentric roller, the

---

33. Nor do the records show Ashborn and Hungerford purchasing the lighter gauge strings or the material from which to manufacture them. Presumably, they continued to acquire these from other sources, though the items do not appear in the credits of the New York firms' accounts, nor of anyone else's.

periphery of which is turned down in the middle to correspond with the underside of the handle." When the roller was properly positioned, as illustrated in Ashborn's patent drawing, "the capo tasto or pressure plate is drawn down tight on the strings," but when it was turned halfway around, "then the plate is not drawn onto the strings and the whole apparatus can be pushed back onto the head."

Despite the seeming complexity of his description, Ashborn's capo is in fact a simple mechanism, a variation of which still is manufactured; though it did not bring him a great amount of income, he could market this essential item at a good profit.[34] In October 1851 Ashborn and Hungerford sent Hall & Son 400 "Cap de Astra" at twenty-five cents each. This was a sizable markup over the $22.50 that they paid Morris, who also made parts for the firm's metal tuners, to produce them. In February 1852, Firth, Pond & Company got them at the same price—$17.75 for seventy-one "Capo de Astris"—and two years later Hall & Son took 1,000 for $250.00.

Departing from earlier practice in musical instrument–making, a highly specialized craft in which a master worked by hand on instruments from start to finish and trained apprentices in the same steps, Ashborn produced his guitars in what we might term a mechanized workshop. He used some water-powered machinery and a small number of employees—in his case, never more than ten—whom he supervised in tasks subdivided in order to produce the instruments more efficiently. In addition, some employees would have been assigned primarily to other tasks in the manufactory, the construction of wooden cases for the instruments, for example, or the winding of strings.

As we already have noted, from extant records we can discern some of the discrete tasks assigned to workers in the factory: Emery Morris's machining of parts for the brass tuners, for example. More striking is Isaac

---

34. Evidently Ashborn did not think it efficient or profitable to manufacture a few other items necessary to the completion of his guitars if they could be obtained cheaply enough from specialized shops in the city. When the guitars were strung, for example, the strings were held in place at the bridge by bridge pins and at the peghead with either brass tuning machines (it is unclear if the factory produced its own) or Ashborn's patented pegs. If the former, the buttons used to turn these machines, like the bridge pins, were made from rosewood, ivory, or mother-of-pearl, and were acquired through Hall & Son or Firth, Pond & Company. In August 1851, for example, the factory got 1,000 "Ivory Buttons" from the latter company; but Hall & Son was a more frequent supplier: 1,200 "Guitar Pins" for $15 in June 1852; two weeks later another 2,000 "Bridge Pins" for $32; thirty-six "Ivory Buttons" ($1.13) in September; and $7.00 for 500 "pearl pins"—that is, mother-of-pearl, probably for Ashborn's higher-grade instruments—in January 1854.

Thornton's work as a "Polisher," as he termed himself in the Census of 1850. An Englishman about the same age as Ashborn, and like him an immigrant to Torrington from somewhere in New York, Thornton, who remained in the factory throughout the period for which we have records, may well have come to the area with his employer. Ashborn paid him well for "polishing" or "polishing and bridging" the guitars, with his rate set by the style of instrument on which he worked. In June 1851, for example, he received $10.08 for polishing twelve "no. 1 guitars," $10.80 for twelve "no. 2," and $12.00 for a dozen "no. 4," a pay scale that remained standard throughout the period. If Thornton "bridged" the guitars as well (that is, properly set the height of the bridges and glued them in place), he received almost a dollar more per dozen instruments (November 1853).[35]

By 1852, though, Hungerford stopped noting such pay for individual jobs and simply listed the number of days these men worked. In Morris's case this eventuated, in April 1852, in a raise of twenty-five cents per day to $1.50, while as early as October 1851 Hungerford simply listed the hours Thornton worked, at $1.50 per day, the highest rate the factory paid. Such changes in the way Hungerford kept the labor account may have had something to do with the move toward a factory system in which specialized work that hitherto was performed in addition to one's regular duties now became one's main task.

The variation in pay among the employees gives further indication of the different kinds of work performed in the factory. At the top of the scale, at $1.50 per day, were four employees whose names were listed in the labor account as long as Hungerford recorded the pay of individual workers. He unfortunately halted this practice in October 1852, when the new factory was being built, beginning then to record simply a monthly total for labor expense: Thornton, married and with three children (one of whom had been born in New York); Charles Lamb, a forty-two-year-old "Mechanic," married with one child; Cornelius Rinders (whose rate was raised from $1.25 to $1.50 in April 1852); and Burris Manville, who began work in August 1851. In May 1852 thirty-five-year-old John Huke, who recently

---

35. Ages given are those declared by the individuals in the United States Census of 1850 unless otherwise indicated. There is little information on which to compare workers' wages in the music industry, but the New York State Census (Manufacturing) of 1885 indicates that William Hall & Son, who employed about twenty-five men and five boys at their New York piano works, paid an average of $28 per month per worker; and that William Badger, a "manufacturer of musical flutes" who employed only two men and one boy, paid all three a total of about $65 per month. Groce, *Musical Instrument Makers of New York*, 70, 7.

had come from Prussia with his wife and three children, also joined the workforce at the high rate. Interestingly, in the Census of 1860 Lamb, Thornton, and Huke all listed themselves as "Guitar Makers," a description presumably fitting their considerable responsibilities in the factory, while Manville, who left the establishment in the late 1850s, became a wagonmaker. Elisha Loomis, a "Mechanic" who worked for Ashborn only from July 1851 through February 1852 but at the high rate, subsequently became a gunsmith.

Chester Smith, who at the age of thirty also had termed himself a "Mechanic" but a decade later was another of Ashborn's "Guitar Makers," led a second tier of employees whose wages were set between $1.00 and $1.30 per day. A bachelor who boarded, as many lower-paid workers did, with a family in Torrington, Smith's peers were Ernest Young, who made $1.30 a day, and Timothy Hart, who began at $1.10 but soon worked himself to that same rate. Also, by July 1852, George Sherman, another "Mechanic" who was with Ashborn throughout the period for which we have records, moved from $1.05 to $1.33, and thus was clearly a member of this second group of skilled employees, though he evidently left the firm before the Census of 1860, from which he is absent.

Employees whose wages were below $1.00 a day, the rate of unskilled laborers in that period, occupied the final tier in the factory, and among this group there was not so much loyalty to the enterprise. Some like Dennis Kelley and Andrew Booter worked only two months at the rate of $1.00; and Thomas Woodrow or Martin Judd worked fewer than six months at the rate of $.50 per day. Alexander Inwood worked about a year, at $.65 a day, leaving a Mrs. Brown, who worked for $.50 a day, as the only steady employee among this group, who by their transience never moved up the wage scale as, say, Hart or Sherman had.

At its largest, Ashborn's workforce numbered about ten but more regularly consisted of around eight employees. With very few exceptions—Thornton and Huke, and Benjamin F. Smith, the "cabinetmaker" from whom Ashborn had purchased his first factory and who worked for him for seven months (April–October 1851) at the $1.50 per day rate)—the employees (a total of twenty-one over the period from 1851 to 1856) all were from Connecticut, and those for whom we have records were in their twenties or early thirties. Few listed any real or personal estate, with the exception of Loomis, an older man, who in 1860 listed $2,000 in real and $1,000 in personal estate; Manville, by then a wagonmaker, with $1,500 personal estate; Benjamin Smith, who returned to cabinetmaking and noted

$300 personal estate; and, most surprisingly, the immigrant Huke, with $1,000 real and $200 personal estate. Thus, as was the case in many of the region's factory villages, whose populations experienced considerable mobility, few of Ashborn's lower-paid employees had put down roots in the community. Virtually none of the lower-paid workers were present for either the 1850 or the 1860 census, indicating, again, their transience.

As was the case in other such mill villages, some of Ashborn's workers took part of their wages in goods, which he and Hungerford provided either through their local connections or those in the city. Chester Smith and Thornton occasionally took barrels of flour, for example, at $5.75 per barrel; and on one occasion Inwood secured a No. 1 guitar for $8.00 (at the same price at which the factory sold them to New York and the only one of Ashborn's instruments we know of that did not go to New York), and a "book and fork" for $1.00 (March 1852). Other arrangements also were made between employer and employee. Hart, for example, rented a house from Ashborn, paying $5.50 for fifty days (April 1852). And occasionally a worker was remunerated for performing some task for his employers that was unrelated to guitar work. In July 1851, for example, at the height of the haying season, Martin Judd got $2.00 "extra for haying," which suggests that his low wage at the factory was predicated on his being just such an unskilled "laborer," as many in Torrington identified themselves in census records.

It is difficult to be more specific about work inside the factory, but the employees evidently worked twelve-hour days: Manville's account in January 1852 shows him paid for "14 $7/12$" days. Further, the core employees—Chester Smith, Lamb, Rinders, Sherman, Judd, and Manville, for example—worked on the average between twenty to twenty-five days per month, though in some months they dropped from fifteen to seventeen days. Interestingly, such short work months do not seem to bear any relation to seasonal agricultural work, as they might have earlier in the nineteenth century. Often the longest work months at the factory were in the spring and summer and the shortest in the colder seasons, reversing our expectations about laborers who might work for the guitar factory while also managing their own farms, and suggesting that the factory operated less efficiently in colder months when the Naugatuck froze over, thus limiting the supply of water for power.

Finally, it is worth noting that Ashborn and Hungerford's average expenses in their "Labor Account" from April 1851 to April 1854 were about $290.00 per month, with as little as $212.27 paid out in September

1852, when the new factory construction began, and as much as $388.29 in December 1853, the month before the company sent a particularly large order of instruments to New York.[36] As dear as some of their woods were, Ashborn and Hungerford's largest monthly expense went to the skilled labor force without which they could not have produced so many guitars.

Ashborn and Hungerford's financial arrangements with Hall & Son, and Firth, Pond & Company were complicated, but it is clear that the scale of the Wolcottville guitar manufactory was the result of sales to these music retailers. In marketing their guitars through these firms, Ashborn and Hungerford connected themselves to the giants of America's music business. In 1855, for example, one of the years in which they sold guitars and other accessories to Firth, Pond & Company, a New York trade paper reported that firm's annual income at $150,000: $70,000 from sheet music, $50,000 from pianos, and an additional $30,000 from other musical merchandise.[37] Against these numbers the income from Ashborn and Hungerford's guitar factory looks small, but operations like theirs fueled the economic growth of such large music companies by providing merchandise that could not be made, or made so cheaply, in the city. Concomitantly, the New York merchants' willingness to market as many guitars as Ashborn produced (there is no evidence that he held any in inventory nor did he sell to any other company) verified his hunch that Americans would eagerly purchase well-made, indigenous instruments.

The owners of the two music companies with which Ashborn and Hungerford dealt—the only businesses comparable in size in New York were the music houses of Horace Waters, and Berry & Gordon—had a long and tangled history. John Firth and William Hall had met as soldiers in the War of 1812 and subsequently worked in New York City for the flute manufacturer and music publisher Edward Riley; both Firth and Hall married daughters of their employer and so became brothers-in-law.[38] In

---

36. Libin has suggested that this particularly large order may have been related to a surge of sales due to the famous New York Crystal Palace exposition (letter to the author, 16 March 1994).

37. *New York Musical Review,* cited in Sanjek, *American Popular Music,* 2:71–72.

38. This and the following information on John Firth, William Hall, and Sylvanus Pond comes from Groce, *Musical Instrument Makers of New York,* 51–52, 70, 126; Sanjek, *American Popular Music,* 2:59, 65–66, 71–72; and from the notes of Robert E. Eliason of Lyme, New Hampshire, who generously made them available. Evidently the detailed financial records of these firms are not extant, although some of Firth, Pond & Company's contracts with Stephen Foster are held by the Music Division of the Library of Congress.

1821 they opened a music store on Pearl Street in New York and by 1827 had become music publishers, capitalizing in particular, as one music historian has remarked, on the new public enthusiasm for minstrel music.[39] In 1832, they moved to Franklin Square and soon took in as a partner Sylvanus Pond, who had been associated with the Meacham piano factory in Albany and who headed up the firm's new piano-making venture at a branch store and music manufactory at 239 Broadway.

This partnership, known as Firth, Hall, & Pond, lasted until 1847, when Hall withdrew and with his son James took over the Broadway store, selling and repairing musical instruments, publishing sheet music, and continuing to make pianos. Now competitors in their attempts to secure instruments for the trade, both Hall & Son and Firth, Pond & Company, recruited Ashborn to provide guitars for their firms. Indeed, Firth and Hall may well have been introduced to him and his work through their interest, then as the partners Firth & Hall, in Asa Hopkins's flute manufactory in "Fluteville," a part of Litchfield adjacent to Wolcottville, where Ashborn lived after his removal from New York but prior to locating permanently in Wolcottville in the late 1840s.[40] The New York firm in 1845 purchased this factory, which had been operating since 1834, Hopkins and his workers thereafter making wind instruments solely for Firth & Hall, just as Ashborn and his workers later produced guitars solely for Hall & Son, and Firth, Pond & Company, though their factory was not owned by either New York firm. Such specialized manufacture for one large and steady market, a hallmark of the transformation from craft to industrial production, was common in this early period of American industrialization.[41]

Of course, Hall & Son's, and Firth, Pond & Company's interests in Ashborn and Hungerford's guitar works comprised only a small part of their business empires, but because information about their arrangements with various suppliers of musical merchandise is virtually nonexistent, what we learn from the accounts of Ashborn and Hungerford is significant. Each month Hungerford meticulously recorded transactions with these two companies. Typically, he listed as debits the amounts of the different grades of guitars he and Ashborn shipped, noting the instruments' serial numbers, as well as the amount of strings (in dozens) and other items they provided or work their employees performed (numbers of patent tuners, capos, or

39. Sanjek, *American Popular Music*, 2:59.
40. On Asa Hopkins and Fluteville, see Groce, *Musical Instrument Makers*, 52.
41. On such unidirectional manufacture for the new markets see, for example, Clark, *Roots of Rural Capitalism*, 232–36, and McGaw, *Most Wonderful Machine*, 117–27.

bridges, for example, or the sawing for piano work or, occasionally, the repair of some instrument like a violin, accordion, or guitar that one of the companies had sent Ashborn). Hungerford also indicated the days on which the factory shipped the items or performed the work; in any given month he and Ashborn often sent goods to the same firm in several different shipments.

The companies' credits to Ashborn and Hungerford were of two kinds, cash in the form of bank drafts payable in ten, twenty, thirty, sixty, ninety, and occasionally up to 120 days; and goods, usually materials Ashborn needed for his guitar work but had difficulty obtaining locally: exotic woods like mahogany, rosewood, and ebony, for example, or the silver wire and silk (an undecipherable amount, for example, for the considerable sum of $110.00, from Hall & Son in June 1855) needed for string manufacture. Occasionally, the companies supplied Ashborn and Hungerford with other items: reams of paper, for example, or, in July 1852, three "Refrigerators," or most surprising of all, in April 1854, "Oysters," for which Ashborn and Hungerford shared a cost of almost $35.00!

When Hall & Son or Firth, Pond & Company wrote bank drafts to Ashborn and Hungerford, they often issued a series of them on one day, payable at different times over the next few months, a standard practice in the contemporary business world, and they did so usually only once or twice in a given month, even if the guitar works shipped items in several different batches. Most commonly Hungerford seems to have handled such business affairs, for a frequent notation in the records shows him paid $.50 for "Going to Bank." The institution Ashborn and he used was in Winsted, at the northern terminus of the Naugatuck Railroad, and may have been a branch of the sizable Phoenix Bank, mentioned once by name in the records.[42] In addition to depositing drafts from New York, the two business partners also issued their own notes to local people in payment for other purchases for the factory, and frequently drew substantial amounts of cash—sometimes $100.00 or more—for themselves, presumably salary as well as reimbursement for goods procured or work carried out for the factory.

For example, while it is unclear if Ashborn accompanied all the com-

---

42. On Connecticut banking in this period see Francis Parsons, *A History of Banking in Connecticut,* Connecticut Tercentenary Pamphlet No. 42 (New Haven, Conn: Connecticut Tercentenary Commission, 1935), and Joseph G. Woodward, "Commerce and Banking in Connecticut," in *The New England States,* ed. W. T. Davis, 4 vols. (Boston: Hurd, 1897), 2:617–82.

pany's shipments to New York, he was frequently reimbursed for traveling to the city to deal with the music companies; in contrast, Hungerford made the trip only a few times. Indeed, "Ex[penses] to NY" for Ashborn is one of the most common entries in the journal and is to be distinguished from payments for "Cartage" (usually quite small), which probably indicate transport of the guitars to, or of supplies from, the train depot in Wolcottville. Oddly enough, there are no entries specifically for railroad freight charges, which must have been substantial but which, through previous arrangement with Ashborn and Hungerford, may have been absorbed by the New York firms, paid to the train company upon arrival of the goods.

Over the five years covered in this account book, Ashborn and Hungerford did approximately 75 percent of their business, worth $40,000, with Hall & Son, and the remainder, about $7,000, with Firth, Pond & Company. Because these parties presumably had been dealing with each other prior to April 1851, though, and after January 1856 as well (when this particular account book closes), it is difficult to assess the overall profitability of their venture. Further, Hungerford did not calculate elaborate yearly balances in this accounting journal, perhaps completing that work in a separate ledger.

But in February 1855, probably at the request of Hall & Son, the journal's accounts were audited: in another hand someone noted at the bottom of a page that "We ex[amined] accounts of W. H. & Son and A. N. Hungerford April 20 to Feby 1st 1855 & find bal[ance] in favor of Wm H & Son 2113.09." This might help explain why during the same years the two New York companies' payments in cash and goods to Ashborn and Hungerford totaled less than their debits, $39,300 for Hall & Son, and $8,150 for Firth, Pond & Company. Other evidence of such external audit appears on the very last page of the ledger. In yet another hand, in pencil, is written "Cr[edit] by 2,578.26 bal[ance] as ex[penses]."

Finally, in addition to drawing cash from the factory's account, on three occasions Ashborn and Hungerford each took a substantial amount listed as a "Dividend," indicating that they were to share profits in the enterprise. In April 1852, for example, each took $1294.62; the following April $1324.74; and in November 1853, $1869.67, at which time Hungerford also gave his partner a note for $245.69 from the general account. These numbers indicate that, whatever the precise condition of Ashborn and Hungerford's accounts with the New York music retailers, their enterprise provided a substantial return.

Without doubt Hungerford kept other account books for this company. For example, standard numbers that are prefixed to each account throughout the journal indicate that he transferred the information into a more formal ledger in which each party was debited and credited by corresponding number.[43] The information we have on James Ashborn's guitar factory, however, provides much insight into the ways in which a rural artisan, by securing local capital and entrepreneurial expertise, and locating a large and dependable market, adapted his craft from workshop to factory the better to produce goods for urban retailers. And in this regard Ashborn was representative: with increased access to railheads, countless other skilled artisans who previously had plied their trades for a local or, at best, regional, market, now had the incentive to expand their operations as they could move their wares through the nation's largest entrepôts. Such unidimensional production, specialized for one market, provided the spokes that strengthened the nation's emergent commercial hubs.[44]

Moreover, Ashborn is highly significant in the history of the American music trade. In 1854, for example, John Weeks Moore, the compiler of an encyclopedia of music, noted that hitherto most guitars used in America had been imported from France, Germany, and Spain, but that these were "weak in tone" and could not "stand the severe changes of our climate." But because of increased interest in the instrument, he continued, "several American houses" had begun to manufacture guitars "which we think will prove rich in tone, and being made here, will stand the severest tests of this

43. Further, we know that Ashborn made banjos, marked with his name as well as that of one of the New York firms through whom he sold his guitars. Yet in the extent records there is no mention of banjos, which suggests both that their manufacture was not something in which Hungerford had invested and that Ashborn may not have made that many of them. Despite the popularity of these instruments on the minstrel stage, for example, their market was nowhere near that of parlor guitars.

After the Civil War, however, the banjo became a very popular parlor instrument. See Karen Linn, *That Half-Barbaric Twang: The Banjo in American Culture* (Urbana: University of Illinois Press, 1991), chap. 1; and Robert Lloyd Webb, "Confidence and Admiration: The Enduring Ringing of the Banjo," in Webb, ed., *Ring the Banjar*, 1–36.

44. In her study of the industrial transformation of the Berkshire paper industry Judith McGaw observes that "like Berkshire paper mills, most American factories during the Industrial Revolution were relatively small concerns, owned by proprietorships and partnerships, located in small towns and rural areas, and operated by relatively modest work forces and locally resident entrepreneurs." She also notes that, thus considered, "the tale of American mechanization is essentially a story of many small men and women making small decisions; accumulating capital, acquiring machines, and reordering work incrementally." *Most Wonderful Machine*, 8. This of course precisely describes Ashborn's guitar works.

climate."⁴⁵ Whether or not he knew it, he most likely was speaking of Ashborn's instruments, among the earliest American guitars and those which could be found more commonly than any other. Thus, the simple facts of Ashborn and Hungerford's business—where they got their raw materials, how many workers they employed and at what tasks and daily rate, how the company's accounts with the large music retailers were conducted, to offer just a few examples—facts that we simply have not hitherto known or been able to verify for the antebellum stringed instrument trade, assume great importance.

We do not know what happened to Ashborn's guitars once Hall & Son, and Firth, Pond and Company received them, though some obviously were sold through their music emporiums and others shipped to outlets in other cities, along with the thousands of pieces of sheet music these companies distributed. Completing the circle of production, distribution, and consumption, we know that eventually the guitars found their way into the hands of those who used them to accompany popular music and, implicitly, to declare their allegiance to certain class values that parlor music had come to represent. Thus, if, as Moore noted of the guitar, "the demand for this beautiful and graceful instrument" had "of late so increased" because it had come "into very general use," Ashborn's guitar works offer an important benchmark for considering how Americans before the Civil War came to acquire one of the musical instruments, and the genteel status, they so eagerly sought.⁴⁶

---

45. John Weeks Moore, *Complete Encyclopedia of Music* (Boston: O. Ditson, 1854), 353.
46. Moore, *Encyclopedia*, 353.

11 | Thoreau and John Josselyn

I have probably written more about Thoreau than about any other author, and I certainly know that I have been engaged by his writing more than by any other's—indeed, since my early teenage years. My discovery of him, through the guidance of a junior high English teacher, allowed me to merge my interests in natural history and writing, and, eventually, as Thoreau himself might have put it, in natural with supernatural history. Although I am the first to acknowledge how difficult a man he could be, Thoreau remains a permanent part of my consciousness, in ways that Emerson, for example, never can.

This was my first published piece on Thoreau and as well my first academic publication, written when I was about to venture onto the job market that had begun its infamous retraction. And so it was this essay that prompted one interviewer, as I have noted in the Introduction, to wonder if I might be a mere "antiquarian."

I hope that readers of the piece will understand why I believe that I am not. While not making any great claims for the final significance in Thoreau studies of what follows, I argue that this essay gave an early indication of the kinds of topics that attracted me—in this case, Thoreau's interest in an obscure seventeenth-century travel writer and amateur herbalist—and how I could find in them connections to larger discursive worlds. Here I wanted to know why Thoreau, particularly in *A Week on the Concord and Merrimack Rivers* (1849), so frequently invoked New England's early exploration literature. Was *he* a mere antiquarian? If not, what did he take from the past that served his prose, as well as his life? I offer some suggestions herein.

What delighted Thoreau about Josselyn and others who had celebrated the American landscape was their privileged vision: they saw America before white settlers had transformed it into, as Emerson might have said, mere commodity. They wrote of things that already in Thoreau's time were beginning to pass (the bounty of nature, to take one example); and Thoreau strove to find in what remained of that pristine world the same kinds of excitement and enchantment that Josselyn, William Wood, and others reported. As far as these writers were from a "Transcendental" vision, they knew that in America the land mattered in some special way, that it impinged on their consciousness with such a force that they never could be the same. It was Thoreau's gift, first, to be able to engender in himself a similar excitement even through a nature greatly diminished in its luxury, and, second, eventually to propagate his insights in prose that continues to stir his readers. In some small way, in this essay I was beginning to understand the miracle of that achievement.

"[O]n the fifteenth of August [1663] I arrived at Scarborow, the habitation of my beloved Brother, being about a hundred leagues to the Eastward of Boston; here I resided eight years, and made it my business to discover all along the Natural, Physical, and Chyrugical Rarities of this New-Found World."[1] Thus did John Josselyn, "an Englishman of gentlemanly connections," describe the circumstances that eventually led to the publication of his *New Englands Rarities Discovered*, which appeared in London bookstalls in 1672. Evidently this attempt at a natural history of the "New-Found World" proved popular: within two years it was followed by *An Account of Two Voyages to New England* in which Josselyn included a more detailed topographic description, as well as a long section on the native inhabitants whom Josselyn, adding his theory to a plethora of others, "judged to be of the Tartars called Samonids that border on Moscovia."[2]

---

1. John Josselyn, *New Englands Rarities Discovered* (London, 1672). As early as 1634 his brother Henry had been at Piscataqua in the interest of Captain John Mason. But by 1636 he was listed on the Council of Gorges' Province in Maine, where he spent the rest of his life. He later became deputy-governor of the province, living all the while at Black-point near Scarborough. He died c. 1683, leaving no descendants. See also *Transactions and Collections of the American Antiquarian Society* 4 (Worcester, Mass., 1860): 107–8.

2. John Josselyn, *An Account of Two Voyages to New England* (London, 1675). Reprinted in the Massachusetts Historical Society, *Collections*, 3d ser., 3 (Boston, 1833). The references to Indians are in *New Englands Rarities*, 5.

This work, taking its title from the brief though intriguing accounts of two voyages (in 1638 and 1663) to visit his brother in the New World, also met a favorable reception, and "The Second Addition" appeared in 1675.[3]

A reading of Josselyn's two books might suggest that they are early collections of American natural history or but another form of English promotional literature, descendants of such works as Francis Higginson's *New Englands Plantation* (1630) or John Smith's *Advertisements for the Unexperienced Planters of New England* (1631).[4] If we consider them, however, as precursors to those narrations of physical and spiritual adventure undertaken by later American writers (and in at least one case offering direct inspiration to a writer of the American Renaissance), they occupy a more significant place in the development of American literature. In his dedication to *An Account,* Josselyn himself points us toward this appraisal: he thoughtfully presents his latest book "To the Right Honourable, and Most Illustrious the President and Fellows of the Royal Society." While this might have been a reflection of his pleasure in the Society's favorable notice of *New Englands Rarities,* it seems more a challenge to his contemporaries (and to us, now blessed with the vision to place such works in the framework of later literature) to accept his books, not as curiosities, but as candid and artful attempts to capture the essence of his New World experience and to reflect on the lessons learned through it. For a gentleman familiar with Lucian, Pliny, and Du Bartas, to a writer who seasoned his pages with proverbs from the Italian and who had read the divine Perkins, as well as Sandys's *Travels* and the trials of Captain John Smith, the "voyage" did not remain straightforward narration but became instead (as it would for so many later American writers) a literary vehicle for his observations, a convention around which to organize his perception of natural American things.[5]

Josselyn can be read as one of the earliest writers in an American

---

3. *New Englands Rarities* was not reprinted until 1860 (see above), and later was issued separately in 1865 by William Veazie of Boston in a limited edition. In 1972 the Massachusetts Historical Society printed a facsimile on the 300th anniversary of the first issue. *An Account of Two Voyages* first appeared in London in 1674, was reissued in 1675, and then not again until 1865 when Veazie issued it as a companion volume to *New Englands Rarities,* again in a small edition. Josselyn's first trip to America in 1638 lasted but fifteen months. The second, begun in 1663, lasted eight years.

4. Higginson's work praised a land where "a sup of New England's air is better than a whole draught of Old English ale," while John Smith spent most of his time outlining for the many Puritans about to join Winthrop's vanguard "The Pathway to Experience to Erect a Plantation."

5. *New Englands Rarities* (all citations from the 1860 edition), 113–14.

tradition linking such seemingly diverse figures as Samuel Sewall, a conscientious Puritan spellbound in the face of Plum Island's natural beauty, and John James Audubon, whose journals embrace the virgin lands in which he lovingly sought his birds of America. Or John Lawson, whose obsession with the American Indian permeates his pioneering *A New Voyage to Carolina* (1709) and John Fremont who, on his expedition to the Rocky Mountains, finally came to terms with the vast wildness that still defined America. Such men have in common an elation at the continent unfolding before them and a consciousness of America's power over their imaginations. Thus John Josselyn, spiritual antecedent to all these explorers, could in the aftermath of the bloody Pequot War and, later, through the growing anxiety over the Stuart Restoration, record for us not the theological and political wranglings of the Bay Colony, but the constant wonder of seventeenth-century New England.

"Glow-worms here have wings," he once reported from Scarborow (describing what we would call a firefly), "and there are multitudes of them insomuch that in the dark evening when I first went into the Countrey, I thought the whole Heavens had been on fire, seeing so many sparkles flying in the air."[6] To a man as open-eyed as Josselyn such wonders of the visible world never ceased, and one takes special delight in the knowledge that another purveyor of such profoundly simple pleasures acknowledged him a literary ancestor. Thoreau noted approvingly that "the strong new soil" spoke through seventeenth-century writers like Josselyn, and both Thoreau's language and literary strategy reflect the vigor he often glimpsed in early travel narratives.

> What a strong and healthy, but reckless, hit-or-miss style had some of those early writers of New England, like Josselyn and Wood and others elsewhere in those days; as if they spoke with a relish, smacking their lips like a coach-whip, caring more to speak heartily than scientifically true. They are not to be caught napping by the wonders of Nature in a new country.[7]

By the time Thoreau made his first excursion to the Maine woods in 1846 his brother had died; but the two weeks spent with John voyaging on the

---

6. *An Account,* 293 (all references are to the 1833 edition).
7. William Wood, author of *New England's Prospect* (London, 1634), "a true, lively, and experimental description of New England in fine Elizabethan prose." Henry David Thoreau, *Journal* 7:108–9, in *The Writings of Henry David Thoreau* (Boston: Houghton Mifflin, 1906), hereafter cited as *Journal.*

Concord and Merrimack Rivers provided Thoreau with the inspiration for a narrative containing many parallels to the works of his admired Josselyn. His affinity for chroniclers of early American history is evident throughout his writing: Edward Johnson and Daniel Gookin, both mentioned in *A Week on the Concord and Merrimack Rivers,* are but two of the more familiar examples. To these should be added later writers like John Warner Barber, whose state "Historical Collections" Thoreau seemed particularly to admire, and John Hayward, whose various New England state gazetteers offered Thoreau that choice amalgam of historical anecdote and natural history that he could imaginatively synthesize in his own work.[8]

Men like Barber and Hayward, though, were writing *after* the fact, and Thoreau's more enthusiastic respect for the earlier historians stemmed from his awareness that they offered undiluted history, his belief that "certainly [Josselyn's] generation stood nearer to Nature, nearer to the facts, than this, and hence their books have more life in them.[9] Standing nearer to the facts, either *literally,* when Thoreau recognizes (in his long digression on the Poet in *A Week*) that "the scholar may be sure that he writes the tougher truth for the calluses on his palms," creating sentences "tough, like hardened things, the sinews of deer, or the roots of the pine"; or, *figuratively,* when he demands that a line read "as if its author, had he held a plow instead of a pen, could have drawn a furrow deep and straight to the end."[10] What else could explain Thoreau's marvelous decision to include in *A Week* the stark figures presented in "Fisherman's Account Current" of 1805: "one cod line," "one brown mug," and "a line for the seine." "Hard, but unquestionable history," says Thoreau, constantly alive to the evocation in such a firsthand source.[11] While Barber and Hayward were halted at cataloguing facts and could read no farther, Thoreau read both books and nature with such creative imagination. In Josselyn too he discovered the freshness of one to whom facts were at least equally expansive, and to whom (in Henry James's words) history was never in any sense the

---

8. John Warner Barber (1798–1885), a Connecticut engraver who began to write popular historics using personal recollections of the people involved in historical events. His best-known works are *Massachusetts Historical Collections* (1839) and *History and Antiquities of New England, New York, and New Jersey* (1841). John Hayward (1781–1862) is best known for his *New England Gazetteer* (1839) and *Gazeteer of Massachusetts, New Hampshire, and Vermont* (1849).
9. Thoreau, *Journal,* 7:108–9.
10. Thoreau, *A Week on the Concord and Merrimack Rivers* (1849; Princeton: Princeton University Press, 1980), 107.
11. Ibid., 35.

immediate crudity of what "happens," but the much finer complexity of what we think of in connection with it.

References to Josselyn appear twice in the "Saturday" section of *A Week*, both times in regard to Thoreau's descriptive catalogue of fish to be encountered in Concord River (these descriptions themselves being a fair parallel, albeit in much more detail, to Josselyn's insistent listing in both his published works).[12] The allusions are brief but illuminating as to the care with which Thoreau assembled his materials when composing the book: the fragments from Josselyn preview Thoreau's own attempts at writing a vital language. He tells that "Old Josselyn, in his 'New England's Rarities,' published in 1672, mentions the Perch or River Partridge," and later speaks of the "Pickerel, Esox reticulatus, the swiftest, wariest, and most ravenous of fishes, which Josselyn calls the Fresh-Water or River-Wolf." What Thoreau wholeheartedly admires in these excerpts is that "hard, but unquestionable history" he discerned in the "Fisherman's Account Current," the writer's ability to invoke the true *spirit* of the thing through the colloquial *name:* writers like Josselyn (he once had noted) "use a strange, coarse, homely speech which cannot always be found in the dictionary, nor sometimes be heard in polite society, but which brings you very near to the thing itself described."[13] How we marvel, then, when Thoreau a few paragraphs later (answering his own call for "sentences that are verdurous and blooming, as evergreen and flowers, because they are rooted in fact and experience") brings us so near the essence of another fish, "the Horned Pout, Pimelodus nebulosus, sometimes called Minister, from the peculiar squeaking noise it makes when drawn out of the water (and which) is a dull blundering fellow, like the eel vespertinal in his habits and fond of the mud."[14] Delighted with the power of language in Josselyn, whose vocabulary could still be so picturesque, Thoreau was reinforced in his own purpose to compose sentences in so vascular a style that they would bleed if one cut them.

---

12. One should recall that Thoreau's first published effort, "Natural History of Massachusetts" (in the *Dial* for 1842), was a review of the Massachusetts state *Reports* on the "Fish, Reptiles, and Birds; the Herbaceous Plants and Quadrupeds; the Insects Injurious to Vegetation; and the Invertebrate Animals of Massachusetts," and offered Thoreau the opportunity to remark philosophically (so much in the manner of his later style) on individual natural facts that for him were always flowering into truths.

13. Thoreau, *Journal*, 7:109.

14. Thoreau, *A Week*, 31, a comment every bit as sharp as Josselyn's remark that most New Englanders were "of a Linsie-woolsie disposition, of several professions in religion, all alike Aethopians white in the teeth only" (*An Account*, 331).

In *A Week* Thoreau also reflects Josselyn's respect for narrative springing from firsthand knowledge of natural fact, for only then (Thoreau believed) could writing be organic and evocative. Whether it was a book of seventeenth-century exploration or nineteenth-century economy, it "should contain pure discoveries, glimpses of terra firma, though by shipwrecked mariners, and not the art of navigation by those who have never been out of sight of land."[15] Josselyn, anticipating the charge that his books included only travelers' tales, had used the same image when he denounced his hypothetical critics as "a sort of stagnant, stinking spirits, who, like flyes, lye sucking at the botches of carnal pleasures, and never travelled so much Sea, as is between Heth-ferry and Lyon-Key; yet notwithstanding, (sitting in the chair of the Scornful over their whifts and draughts of Intoxication) will desperately censure the relations of the greatest of Travellers."[16] He wanted people to know that he too reported "pure discoveries": indeed, why need Josselyn exaggerate the New World's bounty when he could relate as a matter of calm fact that "in Anno Dom. 1670 [Herring] were driven into Black-point Harbor by other great fish that prey upon them so near the shore, that they threw themselves (it being high water) upon dry land in such infinite numbers that we might have gone up halfway the leg amongst them for near a quarter of a mile."[17]

If one were alive enough to observe them, such wonders never ceased: one hundred and seventy-five years later Thoreau could still (in the same matter-of-fact tone) record a similar incident, relating how he once saw the "fry [of Shiners], when frightened by something thrown into the water, leap out by dozens, together with the dace, and wreck themselves upon a floating plank."[18] The diminution in scale is amusing but does not alter the fact that these are two writers whose fascination resides in their abilities to weave such "fabulous" truths imaginatively into their texts: intellectual speculation was fine, but equally important was a glimpse of terra (or aqua!) firma. "Better that the primrose by the river's brim be a yellow primrose, and nothing more, than that it should be something else" through the flowery misrepresentations a "scholar" might toss around it. Josselyn

15. Thoreau, *A Week*, 98.
16. Josselyn, *An Account*, 234.
17. Ibid., 273 (incorrect pagination, should be 283).
18. Thoreau, *A Week*, 30–31. It might bespeak the havoc wrought on nature by two centuries of exploitation: even Josselyn lamented that he had "seen threescore broods of young Turkeys on the side of a Marsh, sunning of themselves betimes, but this was thirty years since, the English and Indians having now destroyed the breed" (*New Englands Rarities*, 9).

early on realized that it was "a good proviso of a learned man, never to report wonders, for in so doing, of the greatest he will be sure not to be believed, but laughed at."[19] Thoreau, who throughout his writing remained grounded in solid observation, also knew that all observable nature was itself "fabulous" and, for the transcendent observer, all ponds without bottom.

In September 1853 Thoreau journeyed to Maine for the second time, and as he boarded the Boston-to-Bangor steamer (with the Chesuncook Lake region as his destination) the narratives of Josselyn were freshly recalled. Indeed, he was now traveling into Josselyn's old domain, later noting as much in his article "Chesuncook" (published in *The Atlantic* in 1858 and appearing in *The Maine Woods* in 1864). In an essay culled from his journal entries during the trip, Thoreau related how at one point he and his companion had in Old Town visited a patriarchal Indian, "Governor Neptune." Thoreau was particularly taken by the old man's reflection that contemporary moose were not what they once had been; our traveler, interested in further substantiation, noted that

> there may be some truth in what he said about the moose growing larger formerly; for the quaint John Josselyn, a physician who "spent many years in this very district of Maine in the seventeenth century, that the tips of their horns "are sometimes found to be two fathoms asunder"—and he takes care to tell us that a fathom is six feet—"and [they are] in height, from the toe of the forefoot to the pitch of the shoulder, twelve foot, both which hath been taken by some of my sceptique readers to be monstrous lies."

---

19. Josselyn, *An Account*, 235. Even in some of Josselyn's extraordinary observations, admissible due to the state of scientific inquiry in the seventeenth century, there resides a certain charm: for example, his description of the "Troculus" (which we know as a chimney swift) "whose feathers are sharp [and] which they stick into the sides of the Chymney (to rest themselves, their Legs being exceeding short)." So far we might admire his ornithological assessment of what occurs in a swift's chosen "Chymney," but we are soon asked to believe that "they commonly have four or five young ones, and when they go away . . . they never fail to throw down one of their young Birds into the Room by way of Gratitude" (*New Englands Rarities*, 7).

All belief in the chimney swift's magnanimity aside, our astonishment should be tempered if we recall that even in the nineteenth century as careful an observer as Thoreau could for years believe the folktale of the American bittern's making its unnatural noise by pumping water through its bill or by pounding stakes into the soft mud of its favorite marshland. So much so that he once inspected the ground from where this heron had flown, expecting to find either puddles or holes! (*Journal*, 4:123–24).

Thus far Josselyn merely reinforced the truth of Governor Neptune's reminiscence, but Thoreau quotes more from this description of the moose to be found in *An Account:* he adds, "There are certain *transcendentia* in every creature, which are the indelible character of God, and which discover God."

Unfortunately, yet in a manner that illuminates the differing philosophic obsessions of the seventeenth and nineteenth centuries, Thoreau not only misquoted Josselyn (for the line originally read that there are certain *transcendentia* "which are indelible *characters* [my emphasis] of God"; he *omitted* the concluding clause, that "there's a prudential for you, as John Rhodes the fisherman used to say to his mate, Kitt Lux."[20] The core of the passage is not obscured by this selective editing: the "prudential" remains that both Josselyn and Thoreau marvel at this creation called "Moose" and realize, that if read aright, all nature offered such *transcendentia* significant and characteristic of God, a moose thus having something in common with the Oversoul.

It is this same verbal expression (where the word became one with the thing and the object a sign of the spirit) that Thoreau admired in the Indian vocabulary: more than once on his Maine excursions he inquired of his Indian guides the meaning of the native name for Concord River, "Musketicook," and he was pleased when he learned it had a significance verifiable in fact. It is the "Dead-Water Stream," or as he had proposed in *A Week,* the "Grass-ground River."[21] As with so many other Indian words (e.g. "Ktaadn," which meant "Highest Land") here was a language that was fossil poetry, "a purely wild and primitive American sound, as much as the barking of a Chickaree [a red squirrel]."[22] Feeling the force of Josselyn's seventeenth-century vocabulary (also springing securely from the earth), Thoreau must have read with keen interest his assessment that the Indians' speech "is very significant, using but few words, every word having a diverse signification, which is exprest by their gesture," indicating that man himself was still rooted organically to language and reinforcing Thoreau's observation that our English tongue was corrupt. The aboriginal

---

20. Thoreau, *The Maine Woods* (Boston, 1864), 151–52. Josselyn, *An Account,* 270–71. [Author's note: Unfortunately for my argument here, Thoreau in fact did not misquote Josselyn; the Princeton edition of *The Maine Woods* (Princeton: Princeton University Press, 1972) indicates that the edition I had used when I first prepared this essay was erroneous on this matter; see 148. Hereafter I cite the Princeton edition.]

21. Thoreau, *The Maine Woods,* 142; *A Week,* 5.

22. Thoreau, *The Maine Woods,* 136.

language, on the other hand, still flourished in its purity, so alive that "with remarkably few exceptions, the language of their forefathers [was] still copious enough for them."[23] Thoreau could overlook Josselyn's classic exaggeration that the Indians' "speeches in their Assemblies are very gravely delivered, commonly in perfect Hexameter Verse"; it was more important that the seventeenth-century traveler had noted a people who possessed a language that constantly shimmered with primitive meaning and who had no need to pierce rotten diction, their words still being sound to the core.[24]

One evening Thoreau (his thoughts filled with Indians after a lengthy conversation with his native guide, Joe Polis) noted with satisfaction that he "felt that he stood, or rather lay, as near to the primitive man of America that night, as any of its discoverers ever did."[25] His renewed contact with the creative and evocative Indian tongue had again brought to mind his obsession with the symbolic encounter between the sophisticated (albeit enthralled) observer and primitive America.[26] Linked to his incessant search for wildness (which he saw as the only preservation in an age that already heard the steam whistle shrieking through Concord woods) this need to touch Antaeus-like the source of America's vitality is what brought him again and again to writers like Josselyn, a "physician" so well respected that on his first trip to New England he "sought out Mr. Cotton the Teacher of the Boston Church, to whom [he] delivered from Mr. Quarles the poet, the Translation of the 16, 25, 51, 88, 113, 137 Psalms into English Meeter for his approbation"; yet who could also spend eight years away from England tramping the wilderness of Maine, recording his observations on America with a sophistication so "naive" as to be constantly refreshing: for example, his walk one afternoon when he "chanc't to spye a fruit" he thought "like a pine Apple plated with scales." "It was as big as the crown of a Woman's hat" and he "made bold to step unto it, with an intent to have gathered it." But "no sooner had he toucht it, but hundreds of Wasps" were around him! Dropping the wasps' nest Josselyn escaped with but one

---

23. Josselyn, *New Englands Rarities*, 5. Thoreau, *The Maine Woods*, 137.
24. Josselyn, *New Englands Rarities*, 5.
25. Thoreau, *The Maine Woods*, 137.
26. Witness his description of the Maine settler "McCauslin" in his essay "Ktaadn" in the *Union Magazine* for 1848 (later incorporated in *The Maine Woods*): "a man of dry wit and shrewdness, and a general intelligence which I had not looked for in the backwoods. In fact, the deeper you penetrate into the woods, the more intelligent, and in one sense, less countrified do you find the inhabitants; for always the pioneer has been a traveller, and to some extent a man of the world." It is a man like this who in Thoreau's mind is most alert to the primitive, not only in nature, but within himself (*The Maine Woods*, 22).

sting [on the lip], yet he "was swelled so extremely" that on returning home they hardly knew him "but by his garments."[27] Josselyn represented for Thoreau just such an American Adam discovering and new-naming magical beasts in the Garden. And he possessed the added advantage of being a correspondent of the Royal Society—something undoubtedly impressive to one who reported to the great Alexander Agassiz on the sunfish of Walden Pond!

This trip to Maine was but one of many excursions. Thoreau took others to Cape Cod with Ellery Channing and to Minnesota with Horace Mann, Jr.; earlier he had walked westward to Wachusett and had been a Yankee in Canada. We have mentioned his circular journey from Concord, Massachusetts to Concord, New Hampshire, and return, and there would be such explorations closer to home when he sought to know the depths of Walden. But always the expectation was the same: his love for writers like Josselyn, as well as his own attempts to get at the heart of the heart of the country, were linked to his realization shortly after the Ktaadn trip of 1846 that this land was still exceedingly new, and his (or anyone else's) to explore:

> You have only to travel for a few days into the interior and back parts even of many of the old states, to come to that very America which the Northmen and Cabot, and Gosnold and Smith, and Raleigh visited. If Columbus was the first to discover the islands, Americus Vespucius and Cabot, and the Puritans, and we their descendents, have discovered only the shores of America.[28]

Advancing to the Pacific just by leaps we "have left many a lesser Oregon and California unexplored behind us"; and Thoreau, inspired by the thought that men like Josselyn (through their language as well as the character of their observations) had left stirring records that at least one nineteenth-century explorer found enthralling and evocative of those early days, set out in his public and private conversation to leave an equally intriguing chronicle. One really could not yet know whether someday a report of the four seasons at Walden Pond might not be read with pure and utter astonishment, but Thoreau nevertheless took care to make the record and (at least for himself) discovered, like Josselyn, a "Countrie which produceth springs in abundance replenished with excellent waters, having

---

27. Josselyn, *An Account*, 231.
28. Thoreau, *The Maine Woods*, 81.

all the properties ascribed to the best in the world.[29] A good deal of traveling in Concord had uncovered such a source.

It is my contention that people tracing the sources of Thoreau's singular literary development have overlooked influences very close to home. While Josselyn alone can hardly be called a "major influence" on Thoreau, his reference to Josselyn's works, as well as his familiarity with other American exploration and travel narratives, suggests new contours for a reassessment of this author. Could it not be that Thoreau's true affinity is not to people like Emerson, but to those seventeenth-century men who were, in Urian Oakes's words, "the Lord's *Remembrancers* or *Recorders*"? To men like Daniel Gookin or John Eliot, who recognized that a consciousness of the Indian would be with us always and that natives should be dealt with in a considerate (if overly Christian) manner? Or to Edward Johnson whose martial epic, under the guise of chronicling "the Battels of the Lord" in America, was composed more to rouse people from their spiritual torpor by taking stock of what the Lord had revealed to us in the New World? Is it accidental that the excursion was Thoreau's chosen form, or that he would compose a botanical index for his trips to the Maine woods? In the nineteenth century what would make him list the supplies necessary for people seeking to explore the Allagash and East Branch, or to record the nuances of the Penobscot vocabulary?

Henry David Thoreau was not an antiquarian like John Warner Barber or John Hayward, men from whose works he drew information but who remained mere collectors of curious historical and geographic knowledge, knowledge simply not quickened at their touch. Thoreau was an annalist of another sort, a man who used history to free his spirit and as a standard against which to measure the growth of his contemporaries, as well as himself. The chronological annals of Concord—remarkable providences all—were more than historical collections. They were samples of natural and human history that in Thoreau's mind became images or shadows of divine things, or what Josselyn precociously called *transcendentia*. Thoreau's solitary days rowing on the Concord River or standing up to his neck in a swamp were balanced by his conversations with natural men like the farmers Minott and Hosmer and by his philosophical gardening with the likes of Emerson. His "histories" (like Josselyn's) comprised racy narrative as well as organic language: they touched people and things, and

---

29. Josselyn, *An Account*, 241.

all possessed a transcendent integrity stemming from his relationship to this wonder-full new land he found in so many ways still insufficiently explored.

Walking the lanes of Concord with quiet desperate men all about him, Thoreau reflected wryly on the transit of civilization and his contemporaries' insane propensity to disparage wildness. I would like to think that he even remembered Josselyn's humorous account of one New World animal. Beavers "will be tame," Josselyn reported. Witness the one "that not long since was kept at Boston in the Massachusetts Bay, and would run up and down the streets, returning home without a call."[30] Thoreau's literary enterprise was always directed against such unnatural docility, the American's attempt to rationalize his burgeoning commercial spirit. Josselyn, in the face of the majestic American land, at least had possessed the gift of wonder.

---

30. Ibid., 273.

12 | Thoreau's Maine Woods Indians

More Representative Men

Like most other Thoreauvians, I came to *The Maine Woods* after an immersion in *Walden* and at first found the Concord saunterer's encounter with wilderness as problematic as it was engaging. Bushwacking through a landscape that suggested what his home state of Massachusetts might have been like a century earlier, by going to Maine Thoreau brought himself as near as he ever was to get to the kinds of experiences that had so molded early explorers like John Josselyn.

And as well Thoreau was brought near the original inhabitants of America, changed as they were by prolonged contact and interchange with white settlers. Still, in *The Maine Woods* Native Americans like Joe Aitteon, Governor Neptune, and Joe Polis became iconic of that wildness, in fact and spirit, that Thoreau so assiduously sought, and in the essays that compose this work I saw Thoreau celebrating and memorializing their special association with nature.

When I began writing this essay, I thought that I might submit it to an issue of *Harvard English Studies* on the topic of biography that Daniel Aaron was editing, but the deadline for that project passed before I had the time to think through Thoreau's portraits. It finally struck me that Thoreau could so readily accept these nineteenth-century Native Americans, with all their distance from aboriginal man, because he viewed them, finally, as *representative*, in the sense that Thoreau's neighbor used the term in his popular book on the subject of *Representative Men* (1850). These native inhabitants of what had become the state of Maine stood for certain things—certain virtues, we might say—of which Thoreau's contemporaries needed to be reminded, and so in *The Maine Woods* he sought to capture the essence of their character, even as he revealed, in memorable passages like that in which he described himself terrified by the titanic wilderness of Ktaadn, his own ambiguous relation to the nature they embodied.

At the same time that I was working on this essay, Robert F. Sayre was writing his invaluable *Thoreau and the American Indians* (1977), and I wish that I had had the benefit of his exhaustive research. Finally, though, the questions I asked had more to do with biography and character than with the Native Americans in an anthropological sense, and I would like to think that in following that track I made a contribution to our understanding of this writer. I was pleased when the Modern Language Association awarded "Thoreau's Maine Woods Indians" the Norman Foerster Prize for 1977.

My original note to this essay read: "I would like to thank Professor Daniel Aaron of Harvard University for his scholarly example and affectionate guidance, and A. Eddison Welch of Irasburg, Vermont, for providing my first understanding of what it was Thoreau found in the Maine woods."

When in 1850 Ralph Waldo Emerson brought out his fourth book of essays, his title accurately conveyed the substance of what had become a major preoccupation in Transcendentalist circles, the identification of individuals who might serve as "representative men" for the age. His published lectures on "representative genius" suggested that in the modern age, and especially in democratic America, while divine truth was discernible in all individuals, biographers should cease to look for "completeness" in any one man. Contrary to the opinions of Emerson's Scottish correspondent Thomas Carlyle, there could no longer be heroes or hero worship. Once someone accepted the premise that the Oversoul manifested itself in all beings, he had to approach a biographical subject in a new way. With true democratic vigor Emerson declared that there were no "common men." All men were at last of a size, and "the true art [of biography] is only possible on the conviction that every talent has its apotheosis somewhere."[1]

But in assembling his list Emerson failed to abide by his own egalitarian

---

1. Ralph Waldo Emerson, *Works,* Standard Library Edition (Boston: Houghton Mifflin, 1883), 4:38, 35.

proposition. With such subjects as Plato, Swedenborg, Montaigne, Shakespeare, Napoleon, and Goethe, he essentially had composed a hagiography of European intellectual giants, unconsciously committing the sin against America and its democratic principles he had warned against in his 1836 essay *Nature*.[2]

While Emerson still groped among the dry bones of the European past, his Concord neighbor and one-time disciple was continuing his own study of a type of man not given attention in Emerson's effort, a man both very American and representative of traits not even possessed by the multifaceted Shakespeare, acknowledged by most nineteenth-century Romantics as the genuine embodiment of "genius."[3] If Emerson declared that a representative man "must be related to us" and our lives receive from his "some promise of explanation," it was perfectly consistent with Thoreau's heightened sensitivity to what defined the representative man *in America* that he sought his "explanations" from individuals standing in paradoxically close "relation" to the white Americans of this land.[4] Among Thoreau's few published attempts at extended biography are his sketches of the Penobscot Indian guides whom he met on his exploratory trips to the Maine woods. These sketches, later published in one volume as *The Maine Woods*, offer a revealing insight into this other Concordian's idea of the universal representative genius and understanding of how the new American life could be distinguished from the merely European. If Emerson declared all men richer for appreciating his transcendent pantheon, Thoreau offered his readers yet other models, ones so full of natural and primitive vigor that they seemed to encompass the spirit of their American land.[5]

---

2. In the same essay he also complained that the age was "retrospective" and that people no longer enjoyed "an original relation to the universe" because they had become infatuated with the achievement of Europeans.

3. See, for example, Jones Very's assessment of Shakespeare in Miller, *The Transcendentalists: An Anthology* (Cambridge: Harvard University Press, 1950), 346–56; and Herman Melville's fascination with the man, documented in F. O. Matthiessen, *American Renaissance: Art and Expression in the Age of Emerson and Whitman* (New York: Oxford University Press, 1941), 412–17.

4. Emerson, *Works*, 4:12.

5. It should be noted that in the privacy of his journals Thoreau offered extended observations of such Concord friends and acquaintances as George Minott, the "poetical farmer," and George Melvin, who introduced him to new botanical specimens. Both sketches can be found in abbreviated form in F. B. Sanborn, *The Life of Henry David Thoreau* (Boston: Houghton Mifflin, 1917), 423–33. Quite often the men allotted space in the journals are representatives of the white race who possess, as James Fenimore Cooper might have said, "the gifts" of the Red Man.

In his journal for 13 February 1859, Thoreau asked a question that had troubled him for years. Noting how people always had considered America's "indigenous animals so inexhaustibly interesting," he wondered why the American Indian himself had not been treated with similar concern. "If wild men, so much more like ourselves than they are unlike, have inhabited these shores before us, should not an American wish to know particularly what nature of men they are, how they lived there [and] their relations to nature?"[6]

Since his youth Thoreau had been interested in what he termed this "indigenous man of America." His first statement about the importance of the American Indian had come as early as 1837 when, as a Harvard College senior enrolled in one of Henry Tyrell Channing's composition courses, he offered the theme "The Mark or Standard by which a Nation is to be Judged Barbarous or Civilized." In this brief essay he criticized the materialistic tenor of his age and denounced the modern "scientific" view of nature, which made men regard natural objects with a constricted and microscopic vision. The Indian, in contrast, did not view nature atomistically but displayed "a liberal and enlarged view of things," what Thoreau felicitously called a "mountain" prospect that took into consideration the entire landscape. With his larger perspective the Indian could live, think, and die "as a man," while the white race deceived itself into thinking that deductive scientific method could explain all.[7]

Part of Thoreau's Romantic defense of the primitive might be attributed to his disgust at the traumatic economic depression into which civilized America (and his family) had just fallen: it was in the depression year of 1837 that Thoreau left Harvard for the world. But even as his attitude toward the Native American became more realistic, he retained the sense that the Indian races offered the spectacle of man in a vigorously healthy and cosmically symbiotic relationship with nature and so should stand as "representative" of an attitude critically important to a nation rapidly forgetting its relation to the land that defined its uniqueness. As an early journal entry suggested, "the charm of the Indian" was that he stood "free

---

6. *The Journal of Henry David Thoreau,* ed. Bradford Torrey and Francis H. Allen (Cambridge: Riverside, 1906), 9:437. For a recent study of Thoreau and Indians, see D. M. Murray, "Thoreau's Indians and His Developing Art of Characterization," *ESQ: A Journal of the American Renaissance* 21 (4th quarter, 1975): 222–29, where Murray argues that the Indian writings provide "a useful key to his development as an artist."

7. Thoreau's essay was first printed in Sanborn, *Life of Thoreau,* 180–83; but see also Henry D. Thoreau, *Early Essays and Miscellanies,* ed. Joseph Moldenhauer and Edwin Moser (Princeton: Princeton University Press, 1975), 108–11.

and unrestrained in Nature" and was "her inhabitant and not her guest." White Americans had only the "habits of the house," and in the economic stampede of the century it was apparent that this domicile had degenerated into a sordid "prison." If nature and the national ego were, as Perry Miller suggests, inextricably linked, instead of worrying about the examples of a Montaigne or a Napoleon, the American man had to be sure that he understood how underdeveloped he remained if he was not able to read the lessons of his own land.[8]

In light of certain biographical facts, Thoreau's interest in the Indian becomes even more suggestive. In 1846, at the same time as he was living so freely at Walden Pond (thinking and writing about himself because by his later admission there was no one he "knew" as well), he took his first extended trip to the Maine woods, not only to satisfy what he called his "singular yearning toward all wildness," but to have an opportunity to study firsthand the Indians' ways. He made another trip in 1853; and in 1857, within three years of bragging as lustily (and, he would have readers believe, as confidently) as Chanticleer to awaken his neighbors to a more wholesome life, again he was in Maine. He returned to offer a long study not only of himself but of a Penobscot guide, an alter ego who is as interesting a character as Thoreau presented in his published works. Were these forays into the American forest carried out so that he could decide further what made a life significant? Were his biographical sketches of the Maine guides an indication that Thoreau doubted his own capacity as a "civilized" man, a paleface, to experience fully all that was true and good in nature?[9]

The evidence is persuasive. Long before his death in 1862 he had plans to write a large book on the American Indian, and on his saunterings through New England as well as on his last extended trip (to Minnesota in 1861), he took copious notes on the natural history of the forest tribes. Eleven unpublished notebooks of some 540,000 words remained in manuscript, and biographical folklore has him uttering as his last words "moose"

---

8. *Journal,* 1:253. See Perry Miller, "Nature and the National Ego," in *Errand into the Wilderness* (Cambridge: Harvard University Press, 1956), 204–16.

9. Sanborn, *Life of Thoreau,* 209, tells that Thoreau's first trip to Maine was made in 1838 to visit family cousins in Bangor while he investigated the possibility of a schoolteaching job in that area. *Works of Henry David Thoreau* (Cambridge: Riverside, 1894), 1:67. *The Maine Woods,* ed. Joseph Moldenhauer (Princeton: Princeton University Press, 1972), is the edition used throughout.

and "Indians."[10] One can claim that part of the unique quality of Thoreau's thought stems from his intuitive sense that to know truly what it is like to be at home with one's self in America he cannot give his hours of study only to the European giants described by Emerson. Thoreau could point to men in New England who by the "wary independence and aloofness" of their "dim forest life" had preserved an intercourse with native gods. They were people admitted "from time to time" to that "rare and peculiar society with nature" after which Thoreau (and such kindred spirits as John James Audubon and Daniel Boone) always longed, and they had to be surveyed for their representative gifts.[11] That few of these men could articulate their thoughts as well as Goethe or Plato was not at issue, especially at that time and in Thoreau's America. Their genius, just like their startling language, ran in different channels.

Leaving aside the introspective meditation of *A Week on the Concord and Merrimack Rivers* (1849), in his published works we can best trace Thoreau's search for his own representative man from that significant moment in *Walden* (1854) when he introduces readers to the Canadian woodchopper Alek Therien, "a true Homeric or Paphlogonian man" who sometimes visited Thoreau in his woodland hut. While Joel Porte has convincingly described this relationship as another instance of "the Faustian problem of doubleness" that had been evident in European Romantic literature at least since the time of Goethe, it is not farfetched to suggest that, rather than just viewing Therien as "the animal soul whom Thoreau must come to terms with before he can hope to be a unified soul," Thoreau's encounters with him also heightened Thoreau's sense that, before he could unequivocally declare his Walden Pond experiment a success, the added perspective offered by people whose lives suggested (as Therien's did) that "there might be genius in the lowest grades of life, however permanently humble or illiterate," had to be acquired. While containing "an exuberance of animal spirits," Therien still seemed as "bottomless even as Walden Pond was thought to be."[12] Thoreau's attempt to define and locate the primitive he

10. Albert Keiser, *The Indian in American Literature* (New York: Oxford University Press, 1933), fully documents Thoreau's concern with the Indian in his published works; see 209–24.
11. Thoreau, *Works*, 1:68.
12. Alek is not identified by name in *Walden* but journal entries from the same period verify his identity. See Joel Porte, "Emerson, Thoreau, and the Double Consciousness," *New England Quarterly* 41 (March 1968): 40–50. For the woodchopper passage see Henry D. Thoreau, *Walden*, ed. Wayne Shanley (Princeton: Princeton University Press, 1971), 144–50.

encountered in Therien and considered most visible in the American Indian took its mature form in his descriptions of the various Indian guides in the accounts later published as *The Maine Woods*.

One thing to consider is whether or not his association with Therien encouraged Thoreau's first trip to Maine in August 1846. In *Walden* Therien is described as having left Canada in his teens to work in the United States as a lumberman, and proof of his later familiarity with the North Country is evidenced by the fact that on a second trip to Maine in 1853 Thoreau discovered Therien, with twenty or thirty other lumbermen, at "Ansell Smith's clearing" in the middle of the Chesuncook wilderness. We also know that it was during his Walden Pond outing (shortly after he met Therien) that Thoreau left Concord on one of the three trips to the area in which he was most likely to encounter whatever "primitive" men remained in New England. If Thoreau went to the deep woods because he was convinced that, as he had earlier suggested in *A Week on the Concord and Merrimack Rivers,* his genius "dated from an older era than the agricultural," it was equally significant that (as a detailed reading of *The Maine Woods* discloses) he had become interested not only in the wilderness itself but in how a man conceives of himself in relation to it. If America was defined by vast expanses of virgin land, it was important that an American listen for an instant "to the chant of the Indian muse" and understand why an Indian would not "exchange his savageness for civilization."[13] If the biography of such a "wild" man somehow could be assembled, Thoreau might understand better his own race's paradoxical longing for wilderness. His talks with Therien may have crystallized his intent to explore the woodchopper's institutions and to discover whether or not he, Henry Thoreau, was fronting the essential facts of an American life in the civilized wilderness at Walden Pond. He journeyed to the Maine Woods in the hope that he might uncover a man who, in Emerson's words, would become a "lens" through which he could read his own mind more accurately and who could help him adjust the angle of his vision more clearly on an American axis.[14]

But given the sentimentalized popularity the Indian was then enjoying, Thoreau had difficulty in articulating what it was that most attracted him to the Indian genius. Read episodically, *The Maine Woods* reveals Thoreau as a budding, sometimes fumbling, anthropologist whose consecutive jour-

---

13. *Works,* 1:67, 70.
14. Emerson, *Works,* 4:11.

neys to Maine display a gradually increasing sensitivity to the natives he sought to understand. Despite his long-standing interest in the Indians, only on his last trip did he understand precisely what knowledge it was that he had been so long seeking to discover from them. Prior to his actual encounters with the tribes, he labored under the Romantic burden placed on "savages" at least since the time of Rousseau.[15]

This judgment is borne out by the "Ktaadn" essay. As Thoreau later described it, his first trip north of Boston was anything but a success. Beginning to look for his representative man in the Penobscot River settlement of Oldtown, he was disappointed to find the first Indian he encountered not at all the noble savage he expected. His eyes met only a "short, shabby washerwoman-looking Indian" who landed his canoe and took from it "a bundle of skins in one hand and an empty keg or half-barrel in the other." This view of aboriginal man reduced to Yankee trader called forth a lamentation on the white race's influence on these northern tribes, and in a splenetic vein Thoreau reported that by the nineteenth century some Indians had so adopted the white man's ways that their homes had "a very shabby, forlorn, cheerless look" like those further south, and (to Thoreau an even greater disenchantment) it seemed that with them "politics was all the rage," as it presumably was with the Massachusetts citizens he sought to leave behind (*Maine Woods*, 6–7). After this initial disappointment, Thoreau was understandably eager to locate wilder places populated by wilder men and was pleased that his party quickly secured native Indian guides to lead them toward the Ktaadn wilderness, a place that at that time few white men had explored.

In the youthful spirit of his earlier works, though, the essay "Ktaadn" remains characteristically egotistic: it emerges as the story of Thoreau's encounter with his own spirit in the setting of the primitive forest of which he had always dreamed. The Indians have a place in the narrative; but, as the traveler nears the mountain, Louis Neptune and the other guides retreat to the background as Thoreau steps forward to describe his own emotions when he is exposed to the uninhabited wilderness. Earlier in this essay, as though seeking a parallel to his own life at Walden Pond, he meticulously noted each white man's settlement and had tried to describe the lives of other men influenced by the forest. But soon these pioneers, too, cease to

---

15. Roy Harvey Pearce, *Savagism and Civilization: A Study of the Indian and the American Mind* (Baltimore: Johns Hopkins University Press, 1967), offers a good introduction to the prevalent attitudes toward Native Americans in the nineteenth century.

be mentioned as reference points as he continued his inward exploration. These men only struck him as further proof that, with regard to white settlers, "the deeper you penetrate into the woods, the more intelligent, and in one sense, the less countrified do you find the inhabitants" (*Maine Woods*, 22). Although adventurous, they were not natives of the vast spaces, but rather shrewd Yankees who remained within the pale of the lumber-camps and riverways from which they hauled their income.

In contrast, what he found when he reached the summit of the mountain was a frightening solitude, a land "vast, Titanic, and such as man never inhabits." There our bachelor of nature felt as though the "inhuman" land held him at a disadvantage and "pilfered him of some of the divine faculty." What surprised him most was not an idyllic solitude but the presence of a force so strange and overwhelming that it was "not bound to be kind" to him; after experiencing his fill of this awesome emotion he descended the mountain with the lonely revelation that "only daring and insolent men" would travel to such places. No one he knew could assimilate such wild tonic into his system. Even the "simple races" do not climb mountains, he admitted. "Their tops are sacred and mysterious tracts never visited by them." The prospective anthropologist would find no material atop Ktaadn, and it became apparent that, if Thoreau wished to discover what was representative about the Indians, he should not wander long in such wastelands. On future excursions to Maine he needed to discover some literal or figurative middle ground on which to study the aboriginal hunter race, an environment at least conducive to the fellowship of man. The inhabitants of that space perhaps could mediate between the values of civilization and solitude, just as the Transcendentalist poet spun his verse from the relationship between words and things, object and spirit.[16]

The urge Thoreau felt to unearth such truly representative Americans did not weaken; in September 1853, he made another trip, this time to the Chesuncook Lake region of Maine. At this date, with his youthful expectations of the Indians and their forest environment tempered after his first troubled exploration, Thoreau seemed better able to appreciate the seeming inconsistencies in the natives he met along the way, the combination of civilized and savage gifts that had been so disconcerting in Oldtown. But even though the descriptions of the Indians' habits were more sympathetic

---

16. *Maine Woods*, 64–65. The passages mentioned here are among the most startling and puzzling in all of Thoreau's works. Anyone offering a facile definition of Thoreau as proselytizer for the wilderness should know this section of *The Maine Woods* in which the writer displays himself not at all at home in the true physical wilderness.

in "Chesuncook" than in "Ktaadn," what is most significant in the later relation is Thoreau's outrage at the unfeeling savagery in which the Indian partially lived. Just as the earlier essay described Thoreau's initiation into the frightening loneliness of this continent, here one sees a further deflation of his vision of the Red Man, as Thoreau learned that there were civilized amenities sorely missing along the Allagash and its tributaries.

The chief character of this essay, Joe Aitteon, son of the "Governor," had been engaged by Thoreau's party with an understanding that he would be allowed to hunt meat for the market. The usually noncarnivorous Thoreau was unconcerned by this agreement. He had seen animals killed, and it was more to his delight that at last he had found someone resembling the primitive man he was seeking, "a good looking Indian, twenty-four years old, apparently of unmixed blood, short and stout, with a broad face and reddish complexion . . . answering to the description of his race." So eager was Thoreau to believe in this man's natural vigor that, although he heard Aitteon display his corruption by whistling "O Susanna and other such airs" while paddling their canoe, Thoreau still narrowly watched his motions and "listened attentively to his observations," as though ascertaining precisely what gifts this Red Man offered our race when his tunes more truthfully reflected his native background (*Maine Woods,* 85, 90, 95, 107).

He reported closely on Aitteon's activities, but as the trip progressed Thoreau became most interested in the man in his role as hunter, stalking the game by which he and his fellow tribesmen lived. Thoreau carried no firearms, preferring to go as "reporter or Chaplain to the hunters," but he began to admit to a deep curiosity to see a moose "near at hand" and was not sorry "to learn how the Indian managed to kill one." But when the moment finally came, the man from Concord who felt "a strange thrill of savage delight" when he saw even a woodchuck crossing his path (also recall that he was tempted to seize the animal and devour it raw) was shocked by Aitteon's slaughter of the moose. Thoreau's response reveals how much his savage hyperbole always was for rhetorical effect. Even Mr. Sylvester Graham's unbolted flour must have been preferable to meat thus slaughtered on the hoof! (*Maine Woods,* 99).

His description of the event records an interesting transformation. Initially Thoreau was fascinated by Aitteon's behavior when the moose's blood was shed. No matter what civilized tunes the Indian had whistled, he now offered a thrilling sight as he chased the wounded creature "lightly and gracefully, stealing through the bushes with the least possible noise, in a way which no white man does." But once the huge animal was tracked and found floating dead in the stream, Thoreau's attitude turned to outright revulsion. Watching Aitteon attack the carcass with his pocket knife, Thoreau regarded the scene (with true New England fastidiousness and a bit of humanitarian outrage) as nothing but a "tragical business" that "affected the innocence" and simply "destroyed the pleasure" of his adventure in Maine. Rather than taking savage delight in the kill, he was repulsed to see "the warm and palpitating body pierced with a knife" and "the warm milk stream from the rent udder." His description of this denouement did not reflect admiration for the native's skilled woodcraft: the scene only reminded Thoreau of "what a coarse and imperfect use Indians and hunters" often made of the nature that to him most often offered purely spiritual food (*Maine Woods*, 112, 115, 119).

The pastoral innocence of his own beanfields in mind, he admitted that for weeks afterward whenever he considered the episode he could not at all cherish the memory, but felt "the coarser for this part of his woodland experience." Having felt cosmically estranged on top of Ktaadn when he knew for the first time the terror of the infinite spaces, he realized now that, while this novel (to him) experience of savagery was still commonplace in the land he was crossing, the best life for him, and his race, had to be lived not in such violence and gore but "as tenderly as one would pluck a flower." Was he still naive about the Indian's lifestyle? What raw experience was he seeking on those trips to the heart of the country? (*Maine Woods*, 119–20).

My contention thus far has been that Thoreau, as much as Emerson, was interested in discovering and defining representative men for his age and that the nature and intensity of this search is explicitly visible in his discussion of the American Indians he offered in the essays comprising *The Maine Woods*. It is, of course, important to note that Thoreau wrote other brief "lives." One immediately thinks of the astute essays on Raleigh and Carlyle, and more important, of his impressively outraged eulogy for Captain John Brown, whom he canonized with the names "Christian" and "Transcendentalist." Anyone studying the concept of the representative man in Transcendentalist circles cannot ignore these productions. But my point is what was earlier epitomized when Emerson told the audience assembled in 1862 in the Concord meetinghouse to hear him deliver his funeral oration for Thoreau, that by Thoreau's own admission three men of late had greatly influenced his life: John Brown, Walt Whitman, and "his

Indian guide in Maine, Joe Polis."[17] The question of Thoreau's fascination with Indian life, raised by Emerson as he bid a final goodbye to his neighbor, forces the critic to reconsider what it was that, even after the fright and disgust of the first trips in search of his hypothetical nobleman, made him continue his study of this race until he discovered someone commensurate to the capacity for wonder toward the Red Man he had so long carried with him.

With the critic's gift of hindsight we question at what point Thoreau realized that the genius the Indians possessed *already* had been vouchsafed him as he had recorded his own Concord experiences. Earlier he had acknowledged that it was man's awareness of and willingness to confront reality that made the lives of some men more meaningful than others. "The frontiers," he had noted, "are not east or west, north or south, but wherever a man *fronts* a fact." With intriguing wordplay he added that a man should "build for himself a log house with the bark on where he is, *fronting* IT, and wage there an old French war for seventy years, with the Indians and Rangers, or whatever else may come between him and reality, and save his scalp if he can" (*Works*, 1:323). The essence of Thoreau's long-awaited discovery would be that many of the Indians he encountered, despite their obvious failings and corruptions attributable to their exposure to white society, met this test more squarely than his Concord acquaintances, and that in his profoundly simple life the Indian's own consciousness and all outside it (Emerson's Me and Not-Me) were somehow imaginatively linked. This closeness, this blood-knowledge of the final significance of *things*, was what so impressed him about the Red race. Years had passed since his first youthful mention of it, but by the time he met the Penobscot Indian Joe Polis he was able to recognize and appreciate what in his college years he had called that "mountain" prospect the Indians enjoyed. The reticent yet affectionate admiration he felt for his Maine guide who every day saw facts "flower out" into truths is convincing proof that Joe Polis stands as a central figure in any pantheon of representative men Thoreau implicitly established.

---

17. This statement appears to have been dropped from the published version of the oration but Sanborn, *Life of Thoreau*, 383, reported that "Emerson said in his funeral eulogy on Thoreau (which I heard), 'Three men have of late years strongly impressed Mr. Thoreau,—John Brown (in 1857 and 1859), his Indian guide in Maine, Joe Polis (1857), and a third person, not known to this audience.' He meant Whitman." Polis, however, is mentioned by name in the oration; see the reprint in *Henry David Thoreau: A Profile*, ed. Walter Harding and Milton Metzler (New York: Crowell, 1971), 16.

Joe Polis makes his appearance on the first page of the essay on "The Allagash and East Branch," and from the outset it is apparent that Thoreau's relationship to him was more intimate than that with any other Indians. Anthropologically speaking, he again first sought assurance of his subject's authenticity: he carefully noted how typical a native it was he had found as a companion. Stoutly built, with a broad face, and, "as others said, with perfect Indian features and complexion," Joe deserved the appellation as one of the "best" Indians in Oldtown, part of the "aristocracy" of his tribe (*Maine Woods*, 157–58).

But before he could attempt to plummet this man's depths, Thoreau had to learn patience: the Indian's favors were not bestowed indiscriminately. Emerson's task in describing his subjects had been a much easier one: the men he considered were all dead and their normal "lives" openly published to the world; with a living specimen, Thoreau had to labor to penetrate what he described as that "strange remoteness in which the Indian ever dwells to the White man." But the lessons of his last trip to Maine had been well learned, and as he accustomed himself to the Indian's natural reticence he began to take this "remoteness" in stride. Within a day Thoreau's own reserved manner had so won Joe's confidence that Thoreau was able to suggest to the Indian that he should "like to go to school to learn his language." Joe thought well of the idea, and these two unlikely pupils soon decided that during the course of their voyage each would teach the other *all* that he knew! (*Maine Woods*, 168).

It is important, and perfectly consistent with the pervasive concern with language in the Transcendentalist movement, that Thoreau's attempts to "know" the Indian took most productive form through an inquiry into his vocabulary. In "Chesuncook" Thoreau had already admitted the awe he felt while lying awake listening to the Indians converse in their primitive tongue. Taking strange delight in that experience, he concluded that these "purely wild and aboriginal sounds" that had first issued from the wigwams "before Columbus was born" were supreme proof that the Indian was not "the invention of historians and poets" but a being still existing with such primitive vitality that any man listening acutely to the Indian language was brought back to the origin of his own race's experience in the New World. Newly schooled to the meaning of such words as "Musketicook" (the Indian name for Concord River) and hearing Joe's quaint singing in his own vital language, Thoreau's imagination returned him "to the period of the discovery of America" when Europeans "first encountered the simple faith of the Indian." The words of that moving song, expressing Joe's faith in the one Spirit who created the world, were so full of "sentiments of humility and reverence" that Thoreau knew he was with someone who had felt a spiritual presence as he himself had. Here was no rancorous Christian but a truly religious man: Joe's natural piety, his heightened sense that the world was animated and that his words were so expressive that they became one with the things they named, marked him a man to be treated with utmost respect.[18] Through him Thoreau received further confirmation that what makes a life significant, the marrow of its representativeness, often was defined by how one came to know, and to touch, those simple things that were magically alive with spirit.

I could cite numerous instances of the effect Joe had on Thoreau's perceptions, but this new awareness is best illustrated by an anecdote related shortly after Thoreau's nocturnal reflections on the haunting piety of the Indian's song. Awakening about midnight to rake over the coals of the campfire, Thoreau witnessed a strange sight: "partly in the fire, which had ceased to blaze, I saw a perfectly regular elliptical ring of light ... fully as bright as the fire, but not reddish or scarlet like a coal, but a white and slumbering ht, like the glow-worm's." Mustering the courage to approach this shimmering light, he discovered it to be a piece of decaying moosewood shining with phosphorescent glow, the mysterious "foxfire" celebrated in countless myths of the forest. Thoreau was so excited by this discovery that he woke his companion, Edward Hoar, to display this legendary will-o'-the-wisp and soon triumphantly noted how after this fortunate moment he "felt paid" for the hardships of his journey. He wrote that (in a telling phrase that reveals his profound interest in the various communications of nature) the light could hardly have thrilled him more if it had "taken the form of letters, or of the human face" as it revealed itself against the darkness. With the disturbing memories of the preceding trips still with him, he acknowledged that this spectacle had come at a time in his journey when he was "just in the frame of mind to see something wonderful." Then, shifting to a religious metaphor, he acknowledged that prior to this excursion he little had thought that there would be such "a light shining in the darkness of the wilderness" for him (*Maine Woods*, 179–80).

The episode does not close here: the following morning, still unable to

---

18. *Maine Woods,* 169, 178. "Musketicook" is the Indian name for "Grass-Ground River," an apt description of the meandering Concord. It was such accurate identification of word with thing that Thoreau most admired in the Indian language. See my "Thoreau and John Josselyn," *New England Quarterly* 48 (December 1975): 505–18, for further discussion of this topic.

contain his amazement, Thoreau related his nighttime adventure to Joe Polis. The Indian then revealed more about the native mythology of this bewitching phenomenon, and our traveler, with the native's vital and picturesque language still ringing in his ears, finally understood what made the Indian different from his own race. If Joe were so familiar with the natural history of this mysterious event, "nature must have made a thousand [such] revelations to him," most of which remained inaccessible secrets to white men. Thoreau felt privileged to walk for a moment in this charmed circle and noted how he became perfectly content not to dissect the experience further but to "let science slide" while he rejoiced in the light "as if it had been a fellow creature." Scientific explanations of phenomena seemed inappropriate to such graceful moments; and Thoreau, in a vein reminiscent of Emerson when he traced the uses of nature from "commodity" upward, understood that with the Indians' superior vision there was always something magical to be seen within the fabric of nature.[19]

Joe Polis's sophistication aside—he had represented his tribe in the state legislature at Augusta and once even had traveled to Washington, D.C.—he still had insight infrequently granted to people of Thoreau's acquaintance. "One revelation has been made to the Indian, another to the white man," Thoreau humbly admitted. After all his years as a naturalist he knew he had "much to learn of the Indian," a type of knowledge qualitatively different from anything white missionaries, religious or scientific, could present to him. With the Penobscot Joe Polis as a companion traveling did not become what Emerson had called "a fool's paradise." Polis had taught Thoreau to get the axis of his eyes coincident with the axes of things, and he came to feel for a moment what for the white man would always be the evanescent unity of the Me and Not-Me. In so simple a fact as a piece of wood by a campfire had appeared a divine and supernatural light (*Maine Woods*, 181).

Thoreau's relationship to Joe immediately took on new dimensions. After the Indian had explained the simple event in his mythological way, Thoreau could better verbalize the affinity he felt toward the Indian and further discover how expanded his own Concord horizon had become because of their rapport: the woods were no longer "tenantless, but choke-full of

---

19. *Maine Woods*, 180–82. Murray, "Thoreau's Indians," 227, notes that in this part of *The Maine Woods* "Joe Polis is continually present, not only as an object of study but as a companion. The journey is an exploration into grim and shaggy nature, but it is also an exploration into the nature of the guide, whose knowledge is symbolized by the mysterious phosphorescence."

honest spirits as good as myself anyday." His friendship with the primitive man on this more solid footing, Thoreau now detected "a little fun" in the Indian's eyes, something that yielded to Thoreau's "sympathetic smile." He added, with the pun probably intended, that he even found Joe to be "thoroughly good-humored" (*Maine Woods*, 181, 253).

Revelation followed revelation as the Indian taught Thoreau to distinguish the values their differing cultures held. "The Anglo-American can indeed cut down and grub up all this waving forest, and make a stump speech, and vote for Buchanan on its ruins," but for all his pretension to superiority the white man could not "converse with the spirit of the trees he fells" nor read the poetry and mythology that "retire as he advances." Moreover, Joe Polis represented the man who, although he was enough interested in the civilized world to call on Daniel Webster after hearing him deliver his renowned Bunker Hill oration, derived more pleasure and wisdom from less sophisticated recreations like an affectionate conversation with native wildlife. The day Thoreau heard Joe call to the muskrats in "a curious, squeaking, wiry sound" he knew that at last he had gotten "into the wilderness," a place not so much defined by land and space as by a receptivity to the promptings of the natural spirit. With the spread of white settlements, civilization and its discontents were becoming known to the Indian, but his ability to read the poetry and mythology of his environment gave him the stability to lead a life as meaningful as it had been among his ancestors. The Indian's representativeness finally was defined by his being a man who knew in the deepest sense the *anima* of the land he inhabited.[20]

With precious understatement, Thoreau reminded the reader that Joe Polis was "a wild man, indeed, to be talking to a musquash!" and to the prosaic mind Joe might seem far removed from the giants with whom Emerson had concerned himself in his book on great men. This man had founded no religions, written no great books, conquered no continents but was merely a Penobscot Indian, one so domesticated that by his own admission he was a practicing Christian who agonized, as any good Protestant would, over excessive work on the Sabbath. What marked him apart was that in his youth he had been fortunate enough to acquire a natural wisdom "from a wise old Indian with whom he associated" and thus could still see and speak the native wonder his race had always

---

20. *Maine Woods*, 229, 252–53, 206. Thoreau happily reported that, after his visit with Webster, Polis admitted to not liking him. The Indian declared that all the senator said was "not worth the talk about a musquash [muskrat]."

perceived. Now he had transferred some of this wisdom to a traveler from Concord, Massachusetts, who was profoundly moved by the new simple ideas presented to him (*Maine Woods*, 206, 182, 235).

With all this in mind it is significant that in Thoreau's narrative Joe Polis, like Aitteon, kills a moose, but that Thoreau displays no adverse reaction to the incident. He was learning that, contrary to the veiled innocence preached by his friend Emerson, violence and evil were present in the world. But they were to be discerned and then transcended through one's understanding that the uses of nature are, indeed, various, and that in this particular case the animal had been slaughtered by a man who knew in the most poetic, as well as the most practical, sense what it meant to perpetrate the deed. Because of his new tolerance our traveler can be forgiven for indulging in a bit of wry humor when Polis became ill with the colic and "lay groaning under his canoe on the bank, looking woe-begone." "It was only a common case of colic," Thoreau remarked, but it seemed that the Indian, "like the Irish," made "a greater ado about his sickness than a Yankee does."[21] Such inconsequential failings could be overlooked in one of those representative men who in their characters and actions answered questions that ordinary men did not even have the skill to ask.

Thoreau was a man who, as his personal philosophy matured, became increasingly concerned with role models, men who could be termed representative of the gifts necessary to comprehend the complexity that had come to define America. The chaos of the Age of Jackson required that new roles be established—and Thoreau came to view the American Indian as providing an important example of what virtues Americans needed to retain significance in their lives. Unlike others who saw in the Red Man an uncivilized threat to organized society, Thoreau sympathetically probed the aboriginal mind of his continent and ascertained what it was in the Indian spirit that white men sorely lacked in the decadence of their nineteenth-century prosperity, a theme he had addressed differently in *Walden*.

Earlier in life Thoreau had noted in his journal that what he admired most about seventeenth-century exploration writers, the first men who had walked on the virgin continent and encountered the Indian mind, was that their generation, unencumbered by the weight of civilized baggage, "stood nearer to the facts, than this, and hence their books had more life to them." In later years he came to believe that his own inspiring contact with the

---

21. *Maine Woods*, 265–67, 290. Emerson, *Works*, 4:12.

Indians had returned him, at least imaginatively, to those same days, "to the period of the discovery of America, to San Salvador, and the Incas," when the secrets of the world were unraveled naturally as travelers stood open-eyed at the New World's wonder (*Journal*, 7:109; *Maine Woods*, 179). By understanding the Red Man Thoreau jarred his memory into the association between the shimmering present and an ever-vital past; and, at least momentarily, the constricted consciousness of a white American had been dissolved as Thoreau glimpsed what T. S. Eliot later called a timeless world still in time. Well before D. H. Lawrence and William Carlos Williams (and certainly in a more profound way than his older contemporary James Fenimore Cooper) Thoreau sensed that these Red Men possessed a gift so distinct from his whiteness that without an adequate understanding of it the fair-skinned race inevitably faced lives of quiet desperation.

On his trips to Maine Thoreau sadly realized that even by the 1850s the corruption of the Christian world had penetrated to the heart of the American wilderness. But he also discovered, and revealed it impressionistically in his essay on the adventures of Henry Thoreau and Joe Polis in the Allagash wilderness, that it did not matter *where* a man was as long as he drenched himself in reality with the same intensity as the Native Americans. "There is really the same difference between our positions wherever we may be camped," he wrote. We must realize that "some are nearer the frontiers on featherbeds in the towns than others on fir twigs in the backwoods" (*Maine Woods*, 200). *The Maine Woods* offers the important lesson that, as with any story of (and by) a representative man, an author is most to be respected because he knows what representative "genius" is. For Thoreau it resided in the breadth of one's imagination.

If the experience of Walden Pond was to remain important in his eyes (and if it is to remain meaningful to us) Thoreau had to learn the lesson that, as his village neighbor often reminded him, the integrity of one's personal vision is all important. Not one of Emerson's representative men had displayed the same genius as the American Indian, Joe Polis. Swedenborg talking to a muskrat, Plato paddling a canoe, Napoleon explaining the eerie foxfire—all are unimaginable. We need a Joe Polis, and a Henry Thoreau, to remind us that truth is spherical and best approached from any tangent drawn from integrity, be it on State Street or in the Maine woods.

13 | Language and Meaning
An American Tradition

Although in *The Wisdom of Words* (1981) I did not treat Hawthorne and Melville so completely as I might have with regard to their interest in the philosophy of language, early on I had been reminded by Charles Feidelson's *Symbolism and American Literature* (1953) that many of these and other American Romantics' concerns about language and subjectivity were revisited by modernist writers. But what Feidelson and critics in his wake did not recognize was the depth of the antebellum writers' intellectual engagement with the issues of language and meaning, the fact, in other words, that they read widely as well as deeply in philosophical and theological literature that they found germane.

After I had completed what I considered a historical survey of the topic, I realized that perhaps I had neglected to emphasize the difference it made if one adhered to one school or another regarding the relation of language to meaning. I tried to remedy that oversight in this essay, in which I also devoted more time to fascinating secondary figures like the Rhode Island manufacturer Rowland Gibson Hazard and Alexander Bryan Johnson, another amateur philosopher, as well as to more significant intellectuals like the Reverend Horace Bushnell, whose renovations of Christian theology mark him as one of the most important nineteenth-century American churchmen. Since publishing this work, I have been pleased to see Michael Kramer, in his *Imagining Language in America* (1992) revisit Bushnell, particularly the ideological dimensions of his discourse; but I continue to believe that we lack an all-inclusive study of language in relation to epistemology for the antebellum period, a work of scholarship that would be equally at home in literature, philosophy, and theology.

Language and Meaning: An American Tradition   253

This is one of the few essays in which I consciously draw parallels to contemporary matters, in this case, to notions of language and meaning proposed by literary theorists. As I consider this fact in retrospect, I may have done so partly in response—though only half-conscious—to one letter from an outside reviewer of the manuscript of *The Wisdom of Words* who indicated that a particular university press should not publish the work because of the text's seeming innocence of all such matters. In this essay, in other words, I had something to prove, and I was pleased that the piece found a home in the premier journal of American literary history, particularly because I was writing, as I always wanted to, literary history and not criticism.

Scholars have been remiss in not bestowing enough attention on nineteenth-century American thinkers whose assessments of the nature of language provide a sharp focus on American Romantic literature and parallel some of the concerns of contemporary literary theorists. Although in our own intellectual history we do not find a unique systematization of such topics as "coherence" or "signification"—a body of texts to rival Nietzsche's, for example—we do have several thinkers whose ideas about language offer important counterpoint not only to the aesthetic achievement of writers in the American Renaissance who grappled with similar philosophical problems but also to the obsessive concern with semantics evident among contemporary theorists. Until we have recognized the relevance of the linguistic speculation of people like A. B. Johnson and Horace Bushnell (who occupy opposite ends of a spectrum of nineteenth-century American assessments of language and meaning) to the artistic enterprise of Thoreau, Melville, and others among their contemporaries, we neglect an important but little-understood current in American thought, one that connects the early nineteenth century's interest in philology to the explorations into semantics by C. S. Peirce, Ferdinand de Saussure, and the literary modernists.

The reason for the lack of sustained interest in American language study is not hard to uncover. Put quite simply, many American theorists initially developed their ideas within an ideological framework that by modern consensus is now not so relevant as that elaborated by Kant or Hegel. Indeed, as I have shown elsewhere, the Americans' interest in the philosophy of language, even among the most important literary artists, revolved around conservative theological poles.[1] Particularly in New England, debates about language were conducted almost solely with reference to their implications for Protestant theology. What early American thinkers had to say about language, then, does not resonate now so sympathetically as the ideas of those Europeans whose philosophical edifices adapt more easily to the latter part of the twentieth century.

On the other hand, it is important to understand that the theological repercussions of Herder's study of the Hebrew Scriptures, and, more important, the allied investigations of such higher critics as Eichhorn, de Wette, and Strauss, forced nineteenth-century Americans, as much as European Romantics, to a profound reconsideration of the relationship between language and meaning, a restructuring so far-reaching that it created what Thomas Kuhn would call a new "paradigm" for the organization of knowledge, one within which writers of the American Renaissance could express the multiplicity that had come to characterize their moral and intellectual universe.[2] In response to the questions posed by European scholars some American thinkers formulated what we might term particularly *centrifugal* notions of language and meaning. In this essay I outline two of the most important of these formulations and also suggest the relationship of these ideas to the literary achievement of two prominent writers in the American Renaissance.

First, consider the ideas of Alexander Bryan Johnson, whose *A Treatise on Language: or, The Relation which Words Bear to Things* appeared during that *annus mirabilis* of American language study, 1836, the year that also saw the publication of Rowland Gibson Hazard's *Language: Its Connexion with the Present Condition and Future Prospects of Man* and Emerson's

---

1. See my *The Wisdom of Words: Language, Theology, and Literature in the New England Renaissance* (Middletown: Wesleyan University Press, 1981); "The Transcendentalists and Language: The Unitarian Exegetical Background," in *Studies in the American Renaissance, 1979*, ed. Joel Myerson (Boston: Twayne, 1979), 1–16; and "Elizabeth Palmer Peabody and the Philosophy of Language," *ESQ: A Journal of the American Renaissance* 23 (1977), 154–63.

2. See, for example, Hans W. Frei, *The Eclipse of Biblical Narrative: A Study in Eighteenth- and Nineteenth-Century Hermeneutics* (New Haven: Yale University Press, 1974) and Jerry Wayne Brown, *The Rise of Biblical Criticism in America: The New England Scholars* (Middletown: Wesleyan University Press, 1969). Charles Feidelson, in *Symbolism and American Literature* (Chicago: University of Chicago Press, 1953), brilliantly analyzed the notion of ambiguity through which many writers of the American Renaissance expressed themselves, but he neglected the immediate background to the nineteenth century's concern with language and meaning.

Nature, with its important fourth section on language.³ Johnson was one of those amateur philosophers whom nineteenth-century America commonly produced, a businessman from Utica, New York, whose favorite avocation—semantic theory—assured his intellectual resurrection decades later when the originality of his thought finally was discerned. But while for the past thirty years Johnson's radical empiricism has been appreciated by specialists in American philosophy, literary theorists have not noticed how his assessment of the inherent shortcomings of language anticipates the contemporary notion of a self-reflexive linguistic web that has displaced man's special relationship to both word and thing.⁴ Nor have they been aware of how some of Johnson's contemporaries, most notably Thoreau, drew artistic strength from a similar attitude concerning the relationship between words and things.

Johnson contended that too often his contemporaries chose to interpret nature by language rather than vice versa, and he elaborately maintained that words themselves cannot do justice to the infinite variety of the natural world as it affects the senses. Moreover, he was surprised at how easily philosophers, who should know better, were taken in by "sophistries of language" that "cannot enable us to penetrate beyond the range of our senses" and so denied the possibility of empirical verification. Further, he cogently argued that when the sensible signification of a word is removed, the word itself becomes a meaningless husk. By making language "the expositor of nature" instead of "nature the expositor of language," Johnson concluded, men foolishly choose the "paucity" of arbitrarily imposed verbal signs over the richness of the physically verifiable world.⁵

When he republished Johnson's work in 1947 David Rynin succinctly pointed out how Johnson's empirical criticism of language, his notion that "propositions are neither significant nor insignificant, but as they refer to our sensible experience," anticipated the logical positivism of later thinkers,

---

3. Johnson's work reached its final form in 1836; for a description of the evolution of his ideas about language, see David Rynin's introduction to the first modern reprinting of his work: Alexander Bryan Johnson, *A Treatise on Language, edited with a Critical Essay on his Philosophy of Language* (Berkeley and Los Angeles: University of California Press, 1947), 1–23. On Hazard and his work see Harold Durfee, "Language and Religion: Horace Bushnell and Rowland Gibson Hazard," *American Quarterly* 5 (1953): 57–70; and my "Elizabeth Peabody," 156–57.

4. Rynin almost single-handedly resurrected interest in Johnson's importance as a philosopher, but at around the same time others were beginning to discover his ideas. See Charles L. Todd and Russell T. Blackwood, eds., *Language and Value* (New York: Greenwood, 1969), which has an important selection of essays about Johnson's life, work, and influence.

5. Johnson, *A Treatise on Language* (1947 ed.; repr. New York: Dover, 1968), 161.

in particular of Wittgenstein, who in his *Tractatus Logico-Philosophicus* similarly was to declare that "to understand a proposition means to know what is the case if it is true." Long before Pragmatism was codified, Johnson believed that if a statement could not be verified empirically it was not so much false as insignificant.[6]

But, as central as this distinction is to modern positivism, we also must understand how Johnson's description of the inadequacy of language to circumscribe the physical universe ran parallel to the aesthetic and moral lines of force generated by writers who rejected the Emersonian (or, if you will, the Coleridgean) notion of a spiritual link between word and thing. Alarmed by the increasing dependence on the generalized forms provided by words and their concomitant loss of meaning, Johnson urged men who would know "what the universe truly is" to dismiss mere "names" and to "contemplate the universe externally with [their] senses, and internally with [their] consciousness." The information thus obtained, he continued, is the universe; but "the moment this information is clothed in language, either articulately or in thought," man begins to wander "from the substance of the universe to the shadow,—from the realities of creation to the artificial and conventional forms by which men communicate with each other." He gradually discovers, in other words, that he is nothing less than a captive within a linguistic structure (what Saussure would term *langue*), an imprisonment against which Johnson aimed all the logic of his writing (*Treatise on Language*, 161).

Put another way, he was attacking the increasing sovereignty of language, its disturbing independence from the physical world it was made to serve, as well as its establishment as a self-perpetuating organism. For Johnson there always remained a profound distance (rather than, as Emerson argued, a close correspondence) between signifier and signified; and his intense concern with this problem in semantics documents another example of that cultural shift which Michel Foucault has elaborated in *The Order of Things:* from a time when language was thought to have been "given to men by God himself" and so was an "absolutely certain and transparent sign for things" to one in which the authority that had guaranteed the transcendental meaning of language was removed, destroying the "trans-

---

6. See Rynin, in Johnson, *Treatise on Language,* 20–21; and Ludwig Wittgenstein, *Tractatus Logico-Philosophicus* (London: Paul, Trench, and Trubner, 1922), props. 4.024, 3.25, and 4.0031. Also note Max Black, "Johnson's Language Theories in Modern Perspective," in Todd and Blackwood, eds., *Language and Value,* 49–66; and the "Symposium," ibid., 80–89.

parency" that earlier had distinguished all words.[7] Johnson's understanding that language progressively "usurped" the "dignity which truly belongs to creation" was informed by such a disturbing recognition. If "names are at present so identified and confounded with the external existences that we cannot discover the subordination which language bears to the realities of nature," he argued, man will continue to impute to nature "limitations, classifications, ambiguities, imperfections, and properties" that "truly belong to language alone" (*Treatise on Language*, 53).

Still controlled by a predominantly Protestant culture, however, Johnson was unwilling fully to accept the epistemological consequences of his arguments, a failure of nerve most evident in his inability to deal objectively with the words of Scripture. After thoroughly disposing of arguments from natural theology "proving" the existence of God and astutely noting that such words as "God," "heaven," and "hell" were principally "significant of scriptural declarations, and of various words, sentences, and treatises" (that is, they possess only a *verbal* meaning *within a text*), he hedged his statement by allowing that such words still might be "significant of certain individual feelings" that "constitute a vivifying and essential part of their signification to persons who happily possess such feelings in association with such words." Unable to conceive of a universe without a supreme Origin, a transcendental signified, Johnson maintained that while God never could be apprehended directly, nor understand just through the mediation of sound symbols, the word "God" was verified by the internal feelings aroused when the syllable was uttered (*Treatise on Language*, 165).

Such a proof of the existence of (or, at least, of the possibility of meaning for) "God" is, of course, consistent with Johnson's empiricism. But what happened to "God" if *no one* had internal associations with the word, or if the associations were conflicting? "Men must look to revelation alone," Johnson declared, "not for a Saviour only, but for every part of the Godhead, every attribute of Deity." While adding, however, that the God whom such "infidels" as the natural theologians worshipped was but "a creature of language, and apart therefrom possesses no existence," Johnson failed to realize that if all personal testimonies to the truth of revelation

---

7. Michel Foucault, *The Order of Things: An Archaeology of the Human Sciences* (New York: Pantheon, 1970), 36. Foucault continues: "Languages became separated and incompatible with one another only in so far as they had previously lost this original resemblance to the things that had been the prime reason for the existence of language. All the languages known to us are now spoken only against the background of this lost similitude, and in the space that it left vacant."

disappeared and the term "God" came to possess *only* verbal signification, the "death" of God (the displacement of the "origin" or "Archsignifier" that provided meaning) became conceivable.[8] As language is removed from nature, so too is man removed from the ultimate source of linguistic meaning. Caught in a descending spiral as his insufficient understanding of language continues to distance him from raw experience, man relies more and more on verbal forms, even to describe his most powerful religious emotions.

Johnson did not welcome this bleak universe in which signifiers floated freely through space without permanent anchorage, and all his efforts went toward preventing any further loss of meaning in language: hence his stress on the empirical verification of the words men used. But his *Treatise* suggests that the verbal train already had left the station with Johnson fruitlessly shouting after it to return for him and his empirical baggage. Once the belief in a divine origin for language was undercut by a description of the vast network of linguistic families, that is, once language was explained philologically (by Herder, Wilhelm von Humboldt, and others) as originating within certain culturally determined boundaries, no plea for empirical verification could negate the shocking implication that words had a sovereignty, indeed, a tyranny, of their own.

Interestingly, a writer who had begun his literary apprenticeship under Emerson, one of the most insistent defenders of a correspondential notion of language, provocatively explored the imaginative consequences of the problematic relationship of language to the empirical facts it represented. While Thoreau was as aware as Emerson that words were signs of natural facts, and tried as seriously to discern their special relationship to Spirit, he placed the greatest emphasis on the first part of the Emersonian equation: on the relationship of language to nature, which also was Johnson's main concern. But, by the time he published *Walden* in 1854, Thoreau, unlike Johnson, had discovered that language, even with its cultural and semantic limitations, *itself* offered the unique key to nature's well-kept secrets. In essence, he came to believe that only through using words as precisely as possible could an artist approach the very nature of the things he wished to describe. The experiential reference points of language provided a magical power that enabled men to evoke the empirical truth each word contained.

---

8. *Treatise on Language,* 209. On the persistence of religious overtones in Johnson's empirical philosophy see "Alexander Bryan Johnson: Reform and Religion," in Todd and Blackwood, eds., *Language and Value,* 167–82.

There is not space here to trace the development of Thoreau's lifelong interest in matters of language. Suffice it to say that such an understanding entails an acknowledgment not only of his interest in Emerson's thought and the Swedenborgian propositions that underlie it, but also of his fascination with such etymologists as Richard Trench and Walter Whiter, his adoption of Charles Kraitsir's "glossology" into segments of *Walden*, and his appreciation of both the "strong and healthy, but reckless hit-or-miss style" of the early American explorers and the "purely wild and primitive American sound" of the Penobscot Indian vocabulary.[9] The result of such a varied study of language provided Thoreau with a unique conception of how words were related to the facts of nature, an understanding parallel to Johnson's radically empirical view, but also granted him the confidence to derive a profound aesthetic from words that to most people (including Johnson) already seemed threadbare, but that Thoreau restored by deciphering their etymology.

Thoreau's profession, he once declared, was "to be always on the alert to find God in nature, to know his lurking places, to attend all the oratorios, the operas, in nature"; for such works of God as he discerned proved to him, as they had to Johnson, that nature could support more than "one order of understandings." But, just as important, his reading in philology suggested that "the volatile truth of our words should continually betray the inadequacy of the residual statement." With this in mind Thoreau hunted tirelessly for the original meaning of the words men used, seeking the most primitive (and thus the most poetic and evocative) expression they served. "I desire," he once boasted, "to speak somewhere without bounds, like a man in a waking moment, to men in their waking moments." He was convinced, he added, that he could not "exaggerate enough to lay the foundation of a true expression." Such exaggeration implied a challenge to the conventional bounds set by his contemporaries for their words, a task that involved the verbal archaeology he had come to love as he struggled to fit words to the natural thoughts they once described. Like Johnson,

---

9. On Thoreau's wide-ranging interest in language see especially Michael West, "Scatology and Eschatology: The Heroic Dimensions of Thoreau's Wordplay," *PMLA* 89 (1974): 1043–64, and "*Walden*'s Dirty Language: Thoreau and Walter Whiter's Geocentric Etymological Theories," *Harvard Library Bulletin* 22 (1975): 117–28; Gordon V. Boudreau, "Thoreau and Richard C. Trench: Conjectures on the Pickerel Passage in *Walden*," *ESQ: A Journal of the American Renaissance* 20 (1974): 117–24, and my "Thoreau's Maine Woods Indians: More Representative Men," *American Literature* 49 (1977): 366–84, and "Henry Thoreau and the Wisdom of Words," *New England Quarterly* 52 (1979): 38–54.

Thoreau knew that men overestimated the powers of language, but he realized as well that, used properly (that is, with a knowledge of the richness of their primal relationship to nature), words still were poetry. It is, he maintained, a "ridiculous demand which England and America make, that you shall speak so they can understand you," for in such a capitulation lay the dead language Johnson so feared was coming to predominate among his contemporaries.[10] If as an artist Thoreau was to be held prisoner within language's structural web, his kicking and shoving of the cultural detritus that crowded his words more than allowed room for crowing like Chanticleer.

Keeping in mind a passage like that describing the railroad-cut in *Walden*'s "Spring" chapter—a hermeneutical and philological exercise as prodigious as any carried out by his more exegetically inclined countrymen—we understand that to Thoreau the "copious and standard" language of nature reflected not only that words were dependent on natural facts for their meaning, but also that these empirical facts *themselves* represented the ultimate reality.[11] To him the spiritual elements of man's existence (which Johnson felt so obligated to defend in their Protestant version) did not so much lie in the fact of man's transcendence to another sphere as in the permanence of the physical world in which he, as well as his language, were rooted. Whatever correspondence there was between words and things did not so much raise man to a higher level of truth as serve to alert him to the wonder of his sensuous existence. To Thoreau, both words and things delighted the man open to their symbiotic, if often neglected, original relationship.

As though it were a proof-text of Johnson's *Treatise,* then, *Walden* recounts Thoreau's immersion in the oldest fount of inspiration, the original language of nature; and the lesson-plans he read there demanded that his verbal posturing be as "extravagant" as it was. Because of his contemporaries' "remoteness" from nature, Thoreau declared, the "very language of [their] parlors" lost "all its nerve and degenerate[d] into *palaver* wholly."

10. Henry David Thoreau, *The Writings of Henry David Thoreau,* Walden ed., 20 vols. (Boston: Houghton Mifflin, 1906), 8:472; *Walden,* ed. W. Lyndon Shanley, in *The Works of Henry D. Thoreau* (Princeton: Princeton University Press, 1971), 324–25.

11. For a detailed explication of the railroad-cut passage and its relationship to Thoreau's philosophy of language, see my "Thoreau and the Wisdom of Words," 47–52. Also relevant is Joel Porte, *Emerson and Thoreau: Transcendentalists in Conflict* (Middletown: Wesleyan University Press, 1966), 131–90. For a dissenting view, Brian Harding, "Swedenborgian Spirit and Thoreauvian Sense: Another Look at Correspondence," *American Studies* 8 (1974): 65–79.

But if people regained the natural man's insight into nature they would understand why "metaphors and tropes are necessarily so far-fetched." Thus, Thoreau noted elsewhere, "it is salutary to deal with the surface of things," if by "surface" man understands the brimming world of nature and its impact upon the senses. By writing *Walden* Thoreau had learned (as he so beautifully expressed it) that "we are able to comprehend at all what is sublime and noble only by the perpetual instilling and drenching of the reality that surrounds us," a more eloquent formulation of Johnson's notion that to know what the universe truly is, man must dismiss mere names and contemplate natural facts sensually as well as imaginatively.[12]

As Emerson had suggested, somehow words were related to truths; but in Thoreau's writing what words were a *symbol* of—the natural cipher itself—assumed primary importance. Like Johnson's study of the relation that words bear to things, Thoreau's own study of language returned him to the things of this world, not to a shadow universe of transcendental forms that could be contemplated only through language, rather than being experienced continually in nature. It is true, then, as Joel Porte has noted, that in Thoreau the Transcendentalists were harboring a Lockean in their midst, but one who, unlike A. B. Johnson, tried valiantly to derive some meaning from the words used by his nineteenth-century contemporaries.[13] Johnson's assessment of words simply did not account for the original poetry they represented. It did not explain, either, how accurately language represented the limits of man's imagination.

Although Thoreau and Johnson were confident that recourse to the variety of nature offered the possibility for a restoration of meaning to man's language, other thinkers, whom we might consider at the opposite end of the spectrum from the empiricists just discussed, responded differently to the nineteenth-century crisis in language and meaning. Here we should recall Edward Said's provocative reminder that to have an informed view of nineteenth-century literary theory we must understand contemporary attitudes toward scriptural interpretation; attempts like Johnson's to retain the transcendent truths of the Bible within a logically derived system were indicative of a culture's trying encounter with the implications of the Higher Criticism.[14] If language no longer linked man magically to the worlds of

12. Thoreau, *Walden*, 97, 244–45; *Writings*, 9:312.
13. See Porte, *Emerson and Thoreau*, 131–90.
14. Edward Said, *Beginnings: Intention and Method* (New York: Basic Books, 1975), 210–23. There still has been very little exploration of the impact of scriptural studies on

matter and spirit, and thus had no absolute signification, what was the value of theological (or, for that matter, of *any*) discourse? Horace Bushnell, a Congregationalist minister from Hartford, Connecticut, a man steeped in such philosophers as Johnson, Wilhelm von Humboldt, and others who had an interest in language, directly addressed the problem of a universe whose center of meaning seemed indeterminate and whose inhabitants spoke a hopelessly imprecise language. And, interestingly, by using what Johnson had taught him about the inherent ambiguity of language, Bushnell came to espouse a concept of signification diametrically opposed to his. Between the poles of these two men's thoughts the writers of the American Renaissance (and, in particular, Melville) established their aesthetic responses to the critical problems in semantics that troubled so many of their contemporaries.

Bushnell's modernity never has been in doubt, but most critics have been too quick to follow Charles Feidelson's assessment and praise his contribution to the American symbolist tradition without considering why his attempts to "speak of language as regards its significancy" took the turns they did; as in Johnson's *Treatise,* the most revealing portions of Bushnell's "Preliminary Dissertation on the Nature of Language, as Related to Thought and Spirit" (1849) are those that display an acceptance of the idea of a linguistic structure that finally exists independently of those individuals who speak in and through it, and so controls the possibilities of their discourse.[15] But in developing this idea Bushnell stood Johnson on his head, declaring the intrinsic ambiguity of speech the very characteristic that *made possible* man's description and comprehension of his experience. He concluded that Johnson, as well as most New Englanders with whom he

---

American literary theory in the nineteenth century. My *The Wisdom of Words,* esp. chaps. 3 and 5, addresses the question, as does Robert D. Richardson, Jr., *Myth and Literature in the American Renaissance* (Bloomington: Indiana University Press, 1978), from a different perspective. Also see Lawrence Buell, *Literary Transcendentalism: Style and Vision in the American Renaissance* (Ithaca: Cornell University Press, 1973), chaps. 1, 2, and 4.

15. H. Shelton Smith, ed., *Horace Bushnell* (New York: Oxford University Press, 1965), 70; throughout this essay I use the selection from "A Preliminary Dissertation" found in this volume. Bushnell's treatise is found in its entirety in *God in Christ: Three Lectures Delivered at New Haven, Cambridge, and Andover, with a Preliminary Dissertation on Language* (Hartford, Conn.: Brown and Parsons, 1849). Besides Feidelson's treatment of Bushnell in *Symbolism and American Literature* (esp. 151–57), see Durfee, "Language and Religion"; Frederick Kirschenmann, "Horace Bushnell: Cells or Crustacea?" in *Reinterpretation in American Church History,* ed. Jerald Brauer (Chicago: University of Chicago Press, 1968), 67–90; and Donald A. Crosby, *Horace Bushnell's Theory of Language* (The Hague: Mouton, 1975).

was acquainted, had not fully understood the potentiality of language for providing ways to convey the ineffable. As Bushnell understood it, language could be used to establish an "esthetic" theology that depended "not on logical deductions and systematic solutions, but principally on the more cultivated and nicer apprehension of symbol." Despite the importance of Feidelson's preliminary investigation of the ramifications of such statements for Bushnell's literary-minded contemporaries (a discussion now thirty years old), we still have not fully understood the connections between Bushnell's "esthetic" rehabilitation of Congregationalism and the frighteningly ambiguous world of a writer like Melville.[16]

Bushnell's belief that "every human language has, in its words and forms, indelible marks of the personal character and habit of the man by whom it was originally produced," an observation influenced by Herder's notion that the particular genius of a people is visible in their language, formed part of his larger understanding that language, especially in its symbolic dimensions, is best comprehended as an extensive organic structure that continually generates new forms, developing "poetically, mystically, allegorically, dialectically, fluxing through definitions, symbols, changes of subject and object, yet remaining still the same" in regard to the truth to which it referred. If one regarded language in this manner, Bushnell thought, the acrimonious bickering among New England Protestants, a development encouraged by the theologians' erroneous assumption that words were not just "signs or images," but "absolute measures and equivalents of truth," would cease.[17] More important, it also suggested the possibilities for a rhetoric of ambiguity within *any* discourse, particularly within the literary text. Far from embodying divine messages, then, words had to be regarded as linguistic tools to be manipulated within the larger structures of human culture.

Bushnell also stressed that man's attempts to establish the approximate meaning of such mysterious terms as "Trinity" or "Incarnation" always set words in opposition to each other. Because of the inherent imprecision of speech, Bushnell declared, "it follows that language will ever be trying to mend its own deficiencies, by multiplying its forms of representation." To

---

16. Smith, *Bushnell*, 102. Here and in chapter 2 of *The Wisdom of Words* I seek to go beyond Feidelson's groundbreaking discussion in *Symbolism and American Literature*, 162–212.

17. Smith, *Bushnell*, 110, 92, 88. On Herder and language see Robert T. Clark, *Herder: His Life and Thought* (Berkeley and Los Angeles: University of California Press, 1955), 295–97.

describe anything, but in particular *abstract* concepts or feelings, it is necessary "to present the subject on opposite sides or on many sides." Thus, he concluded, "as form battles form, and one form neutralizes another, all the insufficiencies of words are filled out, the contrarieties liquidated, and the mind settles into a full and just apprehension of the pure spiritual truth" (Smith, *Bushnell*, 93).

Certainly this bellicose image of how meaning is established derives, at least partially, from Hegel's conception of speech as a dialectical process of signification and negation, but more probably Bushnell borrowed the thought from Humboldt, who held that "all understanding" is "always the same as a misunderstanding" and "all agreement of feelings and thought is at the same time a growing apart."[18] Moreover, Bushnell's allied proposition that "we never come so near to a truly well-rounded view of any truth as when it is offered paradoxically; that is, under contradictions; that is, under two or more dictions, which taken as dictions, are contrary one to the other," suggests, as Humboldt himself had noted, that "man lives with his objects mainly, in fact exclusively . . . as language turns them over to him."[19] Man knows his world only through the contrarieties in his language, and hence what Bushnell called the "fluxing nature and significance of words," or what Johnson had considered their dangerous imprecision, provided man with countless tangents to the sphericity of truth. We miss much if we do not understand how Bushnell's theory epitomizes America's entry into a world which demanded that its narrators, as James Guetti has noted, "approach a problematic experience by surrounding it with disparate allusions and suggestions, never emphasizing a single perspective as

---

18. See *Humanist without Portfolio: An Anthology of the Writings of Wilhelm von Humboldt*, ed. Marianne Cowan (Detroit: Wayne State University Press, 1963), 235. Also relevant here is Gerald Bruns, *Modern Poetry and the Idea of Language: A Critical and Historical Study* (New Haven: Yale University Press, 1974), 63–67, 242–43.

19. Smith, *Bushnell*, 103; *Humanist without Portfolio*, 294. Bushnell's familiarity with Humboldt's writings on language opens for exploration a whole new area in American critical theory. For example, note the similarity between Bushnell's conception of language and Humboldt's in a passage like this, from the latter: "The mutual interdependence of thought and word illuminates clearly the truth that languages are not really means for representing already known truths but are rather instruments for discovering previously unrecognized ones. The differences between languages are not those of sounds and signs but those of differing world views" (246). Or this: "all language is so rich and fruitful in its eternal youthfulness, its eternal mobility, that the true sense, the sum total of all the connotations of such a word taken as a totality could never be defined or completed, never could be designated in all its grandeur" (247).

definitive."[20] Bushnell's declaration that significance is only established by the indirection and opposition of words resounds as significantly in the troubling romances of Melville as in the enigmatic verse of Emily Dickinson, and in ways that Feidelson never had anticipated.

Even more remarkable for how it anticipates the modernist aesthetic is Bushnell's clarification of what it means to offer truth "paradoxically"; his metaphor for how men use words to order their world was explicitly that of *game-playing*. Unlike so many of his contemporaries, Bushnell was willing to accept as many Protestant creeds as came his way; he perceived his fellow theologians as engaged only in "a kind of battle-dooring of words, blow answering to blow, while the reality of the play, viz., *exercise*, is the same, whichever side of the room is taken, and whether the stroke is given by the right hand or the left" (Smith, *Bushnell*, 100). This notion is strikingly similar to Jacques Derrida's conception of a world governed by structural "free-play," in which "everything became a system where the central signified, the original or transcendental signified, is never absolutely present outside a system of differences."[21] The "pieces" Bushnell wishes man to move in his attempt to force an endgame, to "know" God, are the words available to man within his "langue." They lie waiting to be set into motion, at which time their opposites, their contra-dictions, are also activated. "No good writer," declares Bushnell, "who is occupied in simply expressing truth, is ever afraid of inconsistencies or self-contradictions in his language." Indeed, the multiplication of the verbal figures in any text, the proliferation of the words and the "traces" of meaning that always are present "near" them, are what most distinctively mark the most astute participants in man's strenuous verbal "exercise" (Smith, *Bushnell*, 94).

The stumbling block to these parallels I am trying to establish, though, consists in Bushnell's open acceptance of a "logos in the outward world, answering to the logos or internal reason of the parties," "a vast analogy in things which prepares them, as forms, to be signs or figures of thought"

20. James Guetti, *The Limits of Metaphor: A Study of Melville, Conrad, and Faulkner* (Ithaca: Cornell University Press, 1967), 2. Guetti also notes that "Language can only illuminate itself; it is a deceit, a mask which continually and inevitably recreates itself in a permanent circularity, never reaching away from itself toward the reality, whatever that might be" (28).
21. Jacques Derrida, "Structure, Sign and Play in the Discourse of the Human Sciences," in *The Languages of Criticism and the Sciences of Man: The Structuralist Controversy*, ed. Richard Macksey and Eugenio Donato (Baltimore: Johns Hopkins University Press, 1970), 248–50, 264.

(Smith, *Bushnell*, 76). Like Coleridge, who believed that poetry destroys "the old antithesis of *Words* and *Things*" by "elevating" each word into a thing as it released its compressed, God-given energy, Bushnell believed in a final order to the universe. But his willingness to admit that the distance between man and God was so great that man's understanding of Him, of the center of meaning, could only be achieved through the mediation of the always-insufficient linguistic sign, is what (again) suggests Bushnell's relevance to twentieth-century literary theorists. Like Johnson, he believed that "an immediate, experimental knowledge of God" was the central proof of His existence; but, good heir to Jonathan Edwards that he was, he also acknowledged that man's conception of God, even if supported experientially by the kind of "internal" testimony sanctioned by Coleridge, Schleiermacher, and even Johnson, always remained imperfect, and so had to be comprehended within the verbal forms available to men.[22] Thus, even as Bushnell announced that poetic language had to be incorporated into any discussions of Christian theology, he admitted that "words of thought or spirit are not only inexact in their significance, never measuring the truth or giving its precise equivalent, but always affirm something which is false." They "impute form," he continued, "to that which really is out of form." As much as the various ciphers of language allowed an approach to God, they *never* permitted His circumscription (Smith, *Bushnell*, 92). Words finally were as tied to earth as the humans who set them in motion within the larger structure of their language.

As Derrida suggests, then, the "center" of meaning "also closes off the free-play it opens up and makes possible," for this center is "the point at which the substitution of contents, elements, or terms is no longer possible."[23] What Derrida and other contemporary philosophers are interested in, of course, is that moment (which he calls a "rupture") when man began to think that "the center could not be thought in the form of a being-present, that the center had no natural locus, that it was not a fixed locus, but a function, a sort of non-locus in which an infinite number of sign-

---

22. For Coleridge's influence on Bushnell see Mary Bushnell Cheney, *Life and Letters of Horace Bushnell* (New York: Harpers, 1880), 208–9. Peter C. Carafiol, "James Marsh's American *Aids to Reflection*: Influence through Ambiguity," *New England Quarterly* 49 (1976): 27–45, suggests Coleridge's influence on another important American theologian. The early nineteenth-century Americans' interest in Schleiermacher is largely unexplored; but note, for example, Moses Stuart's translation of his essay on the Trinity *(On the Discrepancies between the Sabellian and Athanasian Methods of Representing the Trinity of the Godhead* [1835]) and George Ripley's long article on him in the *Christian Examiner* 20 (1836): 1–46.

23. Derrida, "Structure, Sign and Play," 248, 259–60.

substitutions came into play" (249). But is it that far from Derrida's notion to Bushnell's understanding that in trying to close the gap between language and meaning we "come to our limits"? "On the one hand there is form," Bushnell explained; "on the other hand is the formless." The former "represents, and is somehow fellow to, the other; how we cannot discover." Moreover, "the more we ponder this mystery, the closer we bring it to our understanding, the more perfectly inscrutable will it appear" (Smith, *Bushnell*, 89).

If in Bushnell's world the center of meaning, the ultimate locus of signification, had not disappeared, its very diffusion had made it similar to that "function" Derrida describes, where an "infinite number of sign substitutions" come into play around its very inscrutability. It is true that Bushnell's theology helped later Protestants to formulate a "Christian comprehensiveness" in regard to doctrine, but one wonders whether his followers understood how amorphous, if not finally vacant, their universe had become, once signification was determined by an elaborate set of substitutions so different from the empirical assurances on which Thoreau established his aesthetic.

Among Bushnell's contemporaries Herman Melville most thoroughly investigated the "rupture" between language and meaning. Witness, for example, the haunting universe of *The Confidence-Man*. Written amid the turmoil following the critical failure of *Pierre* (1852), this turgid book directly attacks the problem of meaning in a world in which language has become nothing but verbal manipulation toward selfish ends. Set in the geographical center of America—on a Mississippi steamboat mockingly called the *Fidèle*—on April Fool's Day, *The Confidence-Man* revolves around an elaborate charade that has at its heart the proposition that, given the crisis in rhetoric and meaning the nineteenth century was witnessing, men no longer could believe in anything other men said or did. Confidence—or, to consider the term's religious significance, as Melville clearly intended, *faith*—had become inexpedient, if not impossible, in a society in which language was reduced to verbal chicanery, attached neither to thing nor spirit, but only to the egotistical whims of those who used it to forward their own designs.[24]

24. The best essays to treat Melville's linguistic and epistemological concerns in *The Confidence-Man* are Cecilia Tichi, "Melville's Craft and the Theme of Language Debased in *The Confidence-Man*," ELH 39 (1972): 639–58, and Henry Sussman, "The Deconstructor as Politician: Melville's *Confidence-Man*," *Glyph IV*, Johns Hopkins Textual Studies (Baltimore: Johns Hopkins University Press, 1978), 32–56.

Moreover, it is a revealing indication of Melville's sensitivity to one of his culture's most disturbing problems that not the least of the confidence man's ploys concerned the meaning of Scripture itself, in which one is asked to place the final confidence. At the conclusion of his tale, after having dispensed with such Transcendentalists as Emerson and Thoreau through his introduction of Mark Winsome and his disciple Egbert (Winsome is described as an idealist whose language is peppered with inconsistencies and whose philosophical propositions are comprehensible only to himself), Melville raises the question, as Bushnell himself might have, of how a phrase like "An enemy speaketh sweetly with his lips" can be found in Scripture if admirers of the Bible purport that, above all else, the good book counsels faith and trust among men. The old man with the Bible excuses the phrase by claiming it only a part of the Apocrypha and so of "uncertain credit," but the confidence man, alias the cosmopolitan, pronounces the deeper truth. "Fact is, when all is bound up together [as the two Testaments and the Apocrypha are]," he declares, "it's sometimes confusing."[25]

Melville further explored this problem of pluralistic interpretation—of discerning meaning in a decentered universe—in *Moby-Dick,* his most ambitious examination of the different philosophical and theological "grammars" one needs to read the "text" of an object, in this case a white whale. As this novel unfolds, the crew of the *Pequod* are forced to construct their own "etymologies" of the whale in order to understand its meaning and the reason for Ahab's violent hatred of it.

The famous chapter dealing with "The Whiteness of the Whale" offers the starkest challenge to conventional interpretations of objective reality and best reflects the similarity of Melville's understanding of semantics to Bushnell's. As though foreshadowing the famous question Melville later would ask about the Indian Hater in *The Confidence-Man,* in this chapter he allows Ishmael candidly to inquire how something can be both good and bad *at the same time;* that is, how whiteness could represent something beautiful and yet terrifying, "not so much a color as the visible absence of color, and at the same time the concrete of all colors." The answer lies in the reader's grasp of how Ishmael's survival depends on an understanding of the "comprehensive" vision counseled by thinkers like Bushnell. The whale, like the great truths of the Christian religion, cannot be understood in one way or the other, but only as a symbol of the final unapproachability

---

25. Herman Melville, *The Confidence-Man,* ed. Herschel Parker (New York: Norton, 1971), 167–71, 209.

of any objective fact. What identifies reality is the sum of each man's understanding, and the error of men like Ahab is that they take one truth to themselves and attempt to call it their own to the exclusion of all others, a fault endemic to many nineteenth-century American theologians and philosophers.[26]

Similarly, the mysterious hold the doubloon nailed to the masthead by Ahab exercises over his crew also is linked to the problem of pluralistic interpretation. Like the doctrine of the Trinity or the meaning of the Eucharist, the coin can be "read" differently by different individuals. But the most accurate transcription of its meaning is made by Pip, who here represents a sensibility we recognize as peculiarly deracinated. Symbolically drowned in the immensity of wisdom he gained after his plunge to the depths of the ocean, Pip responds to the confusion of symbols in what most observers would call a cryptic manner. "I look, you look, he looks; we look, ye look, they look," he declares. Pip has, indeed, been studying Murray's *Grammar,* as one of the crew declares. In addition, though, his sinking to the ocean's depths (where "strange shapes of the unwarped primal world glided to and fro") had provided him with the knowledge that any individual object exists only as the *sum* of the different "grammars" men bring to its interpretation. All objectivity vanishes in acts of personal interpretation, and the doubloon's message, like the mystery of the whale, is finally accessible only through a multiplicity of readings.[27]

Such examples of Melville's interest in language and interpretation could easily be multiplied, particularly by considering his *Pierre; or, The Ambiguities.* But these few suggestions should make my point apparent: although there is no proof that Melville knew Bushnell's work, he became the novelist of Bushnell's imaginative universe, a realm where meaning was,

---

26. T. Walter Herbert, Jr., *Moby-Dick and Calvinism: A World Dismantled* (New Brunswick: Rutgers University Press, 1977) is helpful in sifting through Melville's religious ideas in this novel. Also see Paul Brodtkorb, Jr., *Ishmael's White World: A Phenomenological Reading of Moby-Dick* (New Haven: Yale University Press, 1965); and Guetti, on Melville, particularly 15ff. where he notes that in the "Cetology" chapter of *Moby-Dick* we see epitomized a central narrative technique in the novel, "the exploitation of special and artificial kinds of language that serve to draw our attention to the limitations of such language and thus communicate in both a positive and a negative way." Rodolphe Gasché, "The Scene of Writing: A Deferred Outset," *Glyph 1,* Johns Hopkins Textual Studies (Baltimore: Johns Hopkins University Press, 1977), 150–71, is also relevant here.

27. Here, of course, Melville sounds much like Bushnell, whose advocacy of "Christian comprehensiveness" allowed him to support such pluralistic interpretations of meaning. See Smith, *Bushnell,* 88–93, 100–103. Feidelson's chapter on Melville is still relevant here; see *Symbolism and American Literature,* 162–212.

indeed, established by frequent dictions and contra-dictions, the acknowledgment of which allowed the only possible understanding of the ideas and objects named by language. In Melville's novels and stories, language is not viewed as a magical mirror that reflects the relationship of words and things without distortion. Rather, words become in themselves nothing but verbal signs that provide "meaning" as they are endlessly multiplied around that which they once had encapsulated. The discovery of "meaning" in language had become so private an affair—almost an individual meditative exercise—that one could convey a knowledge of reality only through a rhetoric of ambiguity, a mode of expression suitable to a world that had no final center of linguistic or semantic authority.

Such a profound shift in the way men regarded "truth" had prevented Melville from investigating theological or moral problems through the unambiguously sentimental modes he might have used twenty-five years earlier; the world he inhabited, with all its confusion over how one establishes meaning in language, could no longer be described through the stock formulas of a Washington Irving or a James Fenimore Cooper. Indeed, I do not think it far-fetched to suggest that both Melville's and Hawthorne's preoccupation with the "romance" as a prose style originated in the epistemological confusion to which their age was reduced. Their desire to create in their novels a "neutral territory . . . where the Actual and Imaginary may meet, and each imbue itself with the nature of the other" stemmed from their inability to tell the stories of their age in any other ways but those that teach "through a far more subtle process than the ostensible one." In a world in which Moby-Dick is either God or the Devil, stylistic clarity was not so important as a rhetoric with which the author could perform such mental, and linguistic, gymnastics.[28]

If, as Ishmael declares, "man's insanity is heaven's sense," the words our finest literary artists invoke to convey their "sanity" often may seem contradictory. That is, I suppose, part of the lesson taught us by that group of critics loosely called the "deconstructionists." What is of more immediate interest here, though, is how within a few decades in early nineteen-

---

28. See the prefaces to Hawthorne's novels in Norman Holmes Pearson, ed., *The Complete Novels and Selected Tales of Nathaniel Hawthorne* (New York: Modern Library, 1937). Joel Porte, *The Romance in America: Studies in Cooper, Poe, Hawthorne, Melville, and James* (Middletown: Wesleyan University Press, 1969) offers a good introduction to this genre of American prose; see esp. 95–151. He does not, however, stress problems of language and meaning in the way I suggest here.

century America there was formulated a set of responses to the central problem in contemporary semantic theory—how meaning is established when no "absolute signified" can be located—that reveal a significant contribution to our own critical debates. It is not so great a distance from the radical empiricism of A. B. Johnson, who found the word always inferior to the thing it named, to the philological explorations of Thoreau, who determined that far back in a word's history its richness was indeed comparable to what it expressed, as it is from either of these two thinkers to the aesthetic universe of Bushnell and Melville, in which any expression of truth depended on an acknowledgment of the inherent imprecision of the language men use.

Put another way, Johnson and Thoreau wished to tell the truth "straight," as firmly and accurately as words allowed them to, while Bushnell and Melville, like Emily Dickinson, told it "slant," through indirections and contradictions that challenge readers poetically rather than empirically. I intend no value judgment here, but I do suggest that critics eager to trace a particularly American aesthetic take care to distinguish what in reality are two very different ways of seeing, and speaking, the world. There were, of course, numerous other figures—Hawthorne, Emerson, and Whitman in the literary sphere, and James Marsh, Rowland Gibson Hazard, and Josiah W. Gibbs in the philosophical—who contributed to this important American dialogue over language and meaning.[29] But before we explore their formulations more thoroughly we must understand that such explorations must occur within the boundaries established by such figures as Johnson and Bushnell, Thoreau, and Melville. By 1855 the American Renaissance had provided numerous examples of brilliant and forceful verbal expression, but all these works were based on the knowledge that once God was absent, or at least distant, from an author's invocation of language, God's creatures had to establish their own systems of meaning to replace His. Theirs was no small achievement, and the variety of their responses to this problem in semantics should make us even more appreciative of the focus they provide for our own dialogues about language and meaning.

29. In *The Wisdom of Words*, I treat the importance of these thinkers as they influenced the development of a rhetoric of ambiguity in American prose. Also see Peter C. Carafiol, "James Marsh: Transcendental Puritan," *ESQ: A Journal of the American Renaissance* 21 (1975): 127–36; Durfee, on Hazard; David Porter, *Emerson and Literary Change* (Cambridge: Harvard University Press, 1978); and Catharine Albanese, *Corresponding Motion: Transcendental Religion and the New America* (Philadelphia: Temple University Press, 1977), all of whom touch on the subject of language in the various authors they study.

Index

Aarslef, Hans, 159, 176
An Account of Two Voyages to New England (Josselyn), 222–23, 223 n. 3, 228–29
"The Act of Thought in Virginia" (Simpson), 29
The Adventurous Muse (Spengemann), 25–26
Advertisements for the Unexperienced Planters of New England (Smith), 223
Aesthetic Papers, 181
Aitteon, Joe, 243–44
Alcott, Bronson
   Concord Days, 1
   Conversations with Children on the Gospels, 187
   on language, 159, 171–72, 178
   Temple School, 171–72, 173, 186–89
   view of Christ, 172, 187
"The Allagash and East Branch" (Thoreau), 246
Allyn, Joseph, 194
almanacs, 47, 123, 126–33
Alvord Carriage Company, 194, 200, 201
American Antiquarian Society, 9, 44, 114
The American Jeremiad (Bercovitch), 19, 21–22
American Literary Scholarship, 44
American Romantic literature
   continuities seen with colonial period, 34
   and study of language, 253–54
American Studies, 13
American Thought and Religious Typology (Brumm), 20
An American Triptych: Anne Bradstreet, Emily Dickinson, Adrienne Rich (Martin), 42

Ames, Nathaniel, 47
Andover Theological Seminary, 164
Andros, Sir Edmund, 68
Ashborn guitar factory, 192–93, 195–96
   accessories, 207–11
   accounting journals, 192–93, 192 n. 5, 216–19
   banjos, 206, 206 n. 27, 219 n. 43
   banking, 217
   buildings, 199
   capos, 207, 210–11
   contract work, 200–201
   designs, 204–6, 205 n. 25, 207
   distributors, 197, 204, 215–17, 218, 220
   dividends, 218
   employees, 198, 202, 211–14
   establishment, 198–99
   guitar string manufacture, 199, 199 n. 18, 209–10
   instrument cases, 210
   labor costs, 199 n. 18, 212–13, 214–15
   materials, 201–4, 217
   prices, 195 n. 11, 207
   production levels, 199 n. 18, 204
   production methods, 205–6, 211–12
   purchased parts, 211 n. 34
   success, 196–98
   suppliers, 199, 201–3
   tools, 199–200, 201
   tuning mechanisms, 207–8
   water power, 198
   woods used, 202–4, 205 n. 25, 206
Ashborn, James
   arrival in Torrington, 194–95

design of capos, 210–11
family, 195
patents, 207–8, 211
travel to New York, 217–18
Aspirations and Anxieties: New England Workers and the Mechanized Factory System, 1815–1850 (Zonderman), 141
Astrology and the Popular Press (Capp), 47
Audubon, John James, 224

Badger, William, 212 n. 35
Balfour, Walter, 150
banjos, 206, 206 n. 27, 219 n. 43
Barber, John Warner, 194, 225, 225 n. 8, 232
barter, in Howe's printing business, 134, 137–38
Bercovitch, Sacvan, 13, 19–22, 24, 26 n. 32, 40, 41, 49, 50, 51, 64
Beverley, Robert, 51–52
Bible
  analogies in Puritan literature, 20
  conflicts over readings of, 159–60, 162–69
  Higher Criticism, 157–58, 163, 163 n. 14
  language theorists on, 257–58, 261–62
  Melville on, 268
  Transcendentalists' views of, 171–72
Billings, William, 117–19, 119 n. 13
Bishop, J., 136
Blanchard, Amos, 141–42
Blodget, Joseph, 125
Bolton, Nathaniel, 125
bookbinding, 135
book, history of. *See* history of the book
Booter, Andrew, 213
Bosco, Ronald A., 45
Boston, politics, 66–67, 70
The Bostonians (James), 174
Bouwsma, William J., 6
Bowdoin, William, 143
Bradford, William, 42–43
Bradstreet, Anne, 41–42
Bradstreet, Simon, 103
Breck, Robert, 110
Breen, T. H., 51
Breitwieser, Mitchell, 40–41
Brenton, Jahleel, 67
Bridenbaugh, Carl, 32
Bridenbaugh, Jessica, 32
British North American literature. *See* colonial American literature

Brown, John, 244
Brumm, Ursula, 20
Buckminster, Joseph Stevens, 163, 163 n. 14, 164
Bullough, Vern L., 47
Burke, Peter, 44
Bushman, Richard, 104
Bushnell, Horace, 252
  God in Christ, 181, 182–83
  influence on Melville, 269–70
  on language, 173, 181, 182–83, 184–85, 262–67, 264 n. 19, 271
  "Preliminary Dissertation on the Nature of Language, as Related to Thought and Spirit," 262
Butts, Francis, 21
"By Dens of Lions: Notes on Stylization in Early Puritan Captivity Narratives" (Minter), 46
Byrd, William, II, 30–31

Calef, Robert, 65, 78
Canada, Phips' campaigns in, 69, 69 n. 8, 74
Capp, B. S., 47
Carey, Mathew, 115, 119
Caribbean literature, 32–33
Carlyle, Thomas, 235
Channing, William Ellery, 164, 165, 166, 179, 231
Charles II, king of England, 67
Chauncy, Charles, 97
Chauncy, Isaac, 101
"Chesuncook" (Thoreau), 228, 243, 246
Chickering, Jonas, 200 n. 19
Clarke, Dorus, 142 n. 2
Clark, Edward W., 46
Clark, Lyman, 198
clergy. *See also* Puritanism
  autonomy, 63
  criticism of, 129
  Hampshire Association, 63, 90, 92, 99, 101
  missionary work in factory villages, 142, 142 n. 2, 156
  William Williams on, 104–6
Coe, Israel, 194
Colacurcio, Michael, 25–26
Coleridge, Samuel Taylor, 266
Collins, Nathaniel, 90
Colman, Benjamin, 31, 88, 98, 101, 103, 106, 109

colonial American literature, study of, 14
  British influence, 18, 25, 30–31
  Caribbean, 32–33
  continuities school, 16–17, 18, 21, 22–24, 34, 38, 39–40, 41–43, 49–51
  criticism of continuities school, 24–26
  focus on American uniqueness, 17, 18, 33, 49
  focus on New England, 17, 27, 33, 50
  heroes in, 75 n. 21
  historians and, 53–54
  influence of study of nineteenth-century literature, 24, 25
  monographs, 33–34
  natural history writing, 222, 223–24
  new directions in, 51–53
  popular, 44–49, 52, 53
  Puritan influence, 18, 20, 24
  regions outside New England, 27, 28, 29–30, 31–33, 52
  Southern, 27–30
  studies of genres, 43–44
  travel narratives, 222, 223–24
Colonial British America (Greene and Pole), 16, 18
The Coming of Industrial Order: Town and Factory Life in Rural Massachusetts, 1810–1860 (Prude), 141
communion
  Emerson's views, 169–70
  Stoddard's views, 39, 62, 78, 83, 87–88, 102, 103
  theological debate on, 39
Concord Days (Alcott), 1
The Confidence-Man (Melville), 267–68
Connecticut
  Torrington, 193
  Wolcottville, 192–93, 194, 197
Connecticut River Valley
  church in, 62–63, 63 n. 19, 96–97
  church leaders, 92
  theological debates, 35–36, 55, 90–91, 110
Conversations with Children on the Gospels (Alcott), 187
Cooke, Elisha, 66, 66 n. 4
Cooke, Parsons
  attacks on other denominations, 148–52, 155
  career, 142, 155
  education, 146
  Farewell Sermon, 154
  ministry in Ware Factory Village, 145, 146, 147–48, 152–54, 155–56
  A Remonstrance Against Established Religion in Massachusetts, 148
  resignation, 154
  temperance sermon, 152–54
  theological views, 146–47
  Unitarianism, an Exclusive System, 148
Cook, Winthrop, 202, 203
Cooper, James Fenimore, 54
"Cotton Mather" (Bercovitch), 20–21
Cotton Mather and Benjamin Franklin: The Price of Representative Personality (Breitwieser), 40–41
Crawford, Michael J., 96
Cressy, David, 44
Cumberland, Richard, 32–33
Curtiss, Willys, 199
Cutler, Alonzo, 136

Daly, Robert, 37, 42
Damon, Asa, 136
Danforth, Samuel, 52, 97
The Danger of Not Reforming Known Evils (Williams), 98, 102–3
Davidson, Cathy N., 48
Davison, Phineas, 125, 135
Davis, Richard Beale, 27–28, 29
Davis, Thomas M., 36, 55
Davis, Virginia L., 36
Dayton, Arvid, 203, 203 n. 23
Decalves, Alonso, 124
Delbanco, Andrew, 13, 22, 64
Derrida, Jacques, 265, 266–67
devotional literature, 47
Dexter, Thomas, 143
The Dial, 181
Dickinson, Emily, 38, 41
Directions for Such as are Concerned to Obtain a True Repentance and Conversion to God (Williams), 99, 107, 108–9
Discourse Concerning the Danger of Apostasy (Mather), 83
A Discourse concerning the Subject of Baptisme (Mather), 82
A Discourse of Matters Pertaining to Religion (Parker), 171
Discoverers, Explorers, Settlers (Franklin), 43
Ditson, Oliver, 197 n. 14

"Divinity School Address" (Emerson), 163, 170–71
The Doctrine of Instituted Churches (Stoddard), 63, 86–88, 101
Dorchester (Mass.), 57, 57 n. 5
Downs, Clark, 202
Dublin, Thomas, 141
Dunn, Samuel, 123, 125
Durfee, Harold, 181
The Duty and Interest of a People . . . (Williams), 99, 107, 108
Dwight, Timothy, 120

Early American Literature, 15
The Eclipse of Biblical Narrative: A Study in Eighteenth- and Nineteenth-Century Hermeneutics (Frei), 157
economy. See also factory villages
  barter in, 134, 137–38
  of New England, 137–38, 141–42
  rural, 115–17, 121–22, 137, 138–39
education
  Alcott on, 186
  Puritan, 47
  Temple School, 171–72, 186–89
  Transcendentalists' view of, 188–89
Edwards, Jonathan
  character, 80
  conflict with Williams family, 109–13
  A Faithful Narrative, 109–10
  funeral sermon for Williams, 96, 96 n. 1, 111–12
  ministry at Northampton, 99
  ordination, 92
  revivals, 95, 107–8
  scholarship on, 96
  on Stoddard, 79, 92–93
  theology, 104, 106, 161
Edward Taylor (Grabo), 35
"Edward Taylor and the Momentum of Metaphor" (Griffith), 37
Eichhorn, T. G., 163
Eliot, John, 232
Elliott, Emory, 18, 24, 45, 48
Emerson, Ralph Waldo
  "Divinity School Address, 163, 170–71
  on language, 158, 159, 169–71, 173, 184, 255, 258
  "The Lord's Supper," 169–70
  Nature, 158, 170, 184, 236, 236 n. 2, 255
  "The Poet," 171
  Representative Men, 234, 235–36
  on Thoreau, 244–45
  view of Christ, 170–71
Enfield (Mass.), 122–23, 139
  controversies in church, 90–91
  culture, 129
  economy, 138
  Howe's printing work for, 136
Essay Concerning Human Understanding (Locke), 161–62, 177
Essay for the Recording of Illustrious Providences (Mather), 46
An Essay to Prove the Interest of the Children of Believers in the Covenant (Williams), 99
An Examination of the Power of the Fraternity (Stoddard), 90–92
The Example of Edward Taylor (Keller), 38

factories. See also Ashborn guitar factory
  financing, 195 n. 11
  labor specialization, 200, 200 n. 19
  standardization in, 205
  textile, 143, 193, 196
  in Torrington, 193–94
  transition from craft production, 216, 219, 219 n. 44
  wage levels, 212–13, 212 n. 35
factory villages. See also Ware Factory Village; Wolcottville (Conn.)
  missionary work in, 142, 142 n. 2, 156
  social impact of, 141–42, 151–52
  studies of, 141
  Universalism in, 150
A Faithful Narrative (Edwards), 109–10
Feidelson, Charles, 24, 252, 262, 263, 265
feminist literary criticism, 42
Field, C. E., 136
Figures or Types of the Old Testament (Mather), 20
The First Principles of New England, 82
Firth, Hall & Pond, 216
Firth, John, 203 n. 22, 215–16
Firth, Pond & Company, 215–16
  distribution of Ashborn guitars, 197, 204, 215, 216–17, 218, 220
  income, 215
  relationship with Ashborn factory, 209, 211, 211 n. 34

Index 277

Folsom, James K., 46
Foster, Asabel, 136
Foster, Stephen, 81
Foucault, Michel, 256
Franklin, Benjamin, 31
Franklin, Wayne, 43
Free-Mason's Almanac for 1826, 127
Frei, Hans, 157
Fremont, John, 224
French Canada, Phips' campaigns in, 69, 69 n. 8, 74
From Colony to Province (Miller), 79
Frothingham, Octavius Brooks, 175–76
Furet, François, 44

Gaustad, Edwin, 96
Geertz, Clifford, 21
Geib, Susan, 134
Gilmore, William J., 114, 116
Glossology: Being a Treatise on the Nature of Language and the Language of Nature (Kraitsir), 186
God, proofs of existence, 257–58
God in Christ (Bushnell), 181
God's Altar (Daly), 37
Goen, C. C., 95, 108, 109–10
Goodnow, Russell, 199
Gookin, Daniel, 225, 232
The Gospel Order Revived (Colman, Woodbridge and Bradstreet), 103
Grabo, Norman S., 35
Grainger, James, 33
Gramsci, Antonio, 21
Gray, Moses, 135
Great Awakening, 95–96, 99–100
The Great Salvation Revealed and Offered in the Gospel (Williams), 98, 98 n. 5, 105–7
Greenblatt, Stephen Jay, 40
Greene, Jack P., 16, 18, 25, 27, 50
Green, Gardner, 144
Greenwich (Mass.), 139
  culture, 128
  differences among inhabitants, 122–23
  economy, 121–22
  Howe's printing business, 116–17, 120, 123, 134–39
  location, 120–22
Griesbach, Johann Jakob, 163
Griffin, Edward Dorr, 145, 146, 147, 156
Griffith, Clark, 37

Griffith, John, 42
Gross, Robert, 128
Grusin, Richard, 157
Guetti, James, 264–65
A Guide to Christ (Stoddard), 103
guitars. *See also* Ashborn guitar factory
  manufacturers, 197 n. 14, 205 n. 26, 219–20
  popularity, 195
  prices, 195 n. 11

Half-Way Covenant, 58, 60–61, 82–83, 84 n. 11
Hall & Son. *See* William Hall & Son
Hall, Chester, 135
Hall, David D., 13, 44
Hall, James, 216
Hall, William, 203 n. 22, 215–16
Hambrick-Stowe, Charles E., 47
Hamilton, Alexander, 30
Hampshire Association, 63, 90, 92, 99, 101
Harlan, David, 64
Hartford (Conn.), 57
Hart, Timothy, 213, 214
Harvard College, 97
Harvard University, 13
  Divinity School, 149, 163–64
Hatfield (Mass.), 98
Hawthorne, Nathaniel, 10–11
Haynes, Lemuel, 124
Hayward, John, 225, 225 n. 8, 232
Hazard, Rowland Gibson, 177, 179–81, 185, 254
Hegel, G. W. F., 264
Heimert, Alan, 22
Herder, J. G., 163 n. 14, 263
  The Study of Hebrew Poetry, 176–78, 254
Higginson, Francis, 223
Higher Criticism, 157–58, 163, 163 n. 14
History and Present State of Virginia (Beverley), 51–52
history of the book, 44, 53, 114–15
  in rural America, 115–17, 122
History of the Tuesday Club (Hamilton), 30
history, study of
  intellectual, 4
  separated from literature, 14–15
  with study of literature, 13–14, 15–16, 53–54
Hoar, Edward, 247

278 Index

Holcomb & Lyon, 201
Holley, F. N., 196
Hollinger, David, 4–5, 6–7
Holmes, Israel, 194
Hopkins, Asa, 216
Howard, Alan B., 37, 42
Howe, Daniel Walker, 22
Howe, Elias, 197 n. 14
Howe, John
  account books, 134–38
  almanacs, 123, 126–33
  barter by, 134, 137–38
  bookbinding, 135
  book published by, 133
  customers, 134–38
  father, 117–20
  humor on women, 131–33
  humorous stories, 128–29, 128 n. 43, 131–33
  job printing, 123, 135–37
  Printer's Book, 134, 136–37
  printing business, 116–17, 120, 123, 127–28, 138–39
  publication of local writers, 123, 124–25
  social criticism, 129–30
  types of printing work, 123–26, 133–34
Howe, Solomon, 117–20, 119 n. 13
  music, 118–20, 123, 124
  poetry, 125–26
Hubbard, William, 81
Huke, John, 212–13, 214
Humboldt, Wilhelm von, 264, 264 n. 19
Hungerford, Austin N. *See also* Ashborn guitar factory
  accounting journals, 192–93, 192 n. 5, 216–19
  career, 196
  travel to New York, 218
Hungerford, John, 194, 196, 201, 203

Imagining Language in America (Kramer), 252
"The Indian Captivity Narrative as Ritual" (VanDerBeets), 46
Indian captivity narratives, 46, 98
Indians
  languages, 229–30, 246
  Thoreau's interest in, 228, 234–35, 236–39, 240–44, 245–51
industrialization. *See* factories; factory villages
The Inexcusableness of Neglecting the Worship of God (Stoddard), 102

intellectual history, 4
Intellectual Life in Jefferson's Virginia (Davis), 28
Intellectual Life in the Colonial South, 1585–1763 (Davis), 27–28
Inwood, Alexander, 213, 214
" 'I spake as a child': Authority, Metaphor, and *The New-England Primer*" (Watters), 47

James II, king of England, 67–68
James, Henry, 174
J. Atkins & Company, 199
J. Firth & Hall, 203, 203 n. 22
Johnson, Alexander Bryan, 254–58, 261, 271
  influence, 262–63
  A Treatise on Language: or, The Relation which Words Bear to Things, 254
Johnson, Edward, 225, 232
Johnson, Thomas H., 34
Joslin, William, 135
Josselyn, Henry, 222 n. 1
Josselyn, John
  An Account of Two Voyages to New England, 222–23, 223 n. 3, 228–29
  descriptions of animals and birds, 228–29, 228 n. 19
  influence on Thoreau, 225–28, 230–33
  on New Englanders, 226 n. 14
  New Englands Rarities Discovered, 222, 223 n. 3, 226
  place in American literature, 223–24
  Thoreau on, 222
  travels in America, 223 n. 3, 230–31
  vocabulary, 226, 229
  writing based on observation, 227–28
"A Journey from *Patapsco* to *Annapolis*, April 4, 1730" (Lewis), 30
Judd, Martin, 213, 214

Kant, Immanuel, 159, 163, 168, 169
Keach, Benjamin, 20
Keller, Karl, 38
Kelley, Dennis, 213
Knight, Janice, 13
Kolodny, Annette, 43
Kouwenhoven, John A., 38
Kraitsir, Charles
  career, 181–82
  Glossology: Being a Treatise on the Nature of Language and the Language of Nature, 186

influence on Thoreau, 158, 259
on language, 179, 182, 183–86
The Significance of the Alphabet, 182
Kramer, Michael, 252
"Ktaadn" (Thoreau), 230 n. 26, 241–42
Kuhn, Thomas, 254

Lamb, Charles, 212, 213, 214
Lambert, Frank, 95
Lammon, Cecilia, 137
Langdon, Edward, 201
Language: Its Connexion with the Present Condition and Future Prospects of Man (Hazard), 179, 254
language
　Alcott on, 159, 171–72, 178
　ambiguity of, 167, 262
　of Bible, 257–58, 261–62
　Bushnell on, 173, 181, 182–83, 184–85, 262–67, 264 n. 19, 271
　development of, 177–78
　Emerson on, 158, 159, 169–71, 173, 184, 255, 258
　empirical view, 161–63
　etymology, 185–86, 259
　evolution of theories, 256–57
　Hazard on, 179–81
　importance to writers, 157–58, 253–54, 271
　of Indians, 229–30, 246
　Johnson on, 254–58, 261, 271
　Kraitsir on, 179, 182, 183–86
　Melville on, 267–70, 271
　Peabody on, 173, 176–79, 181, 182, 185–86
　physical aspects, 183–85
　relationship to nature, 178, 182, 184, 255, 258–61
　sounds of, 183–85
　teaching of, 171–72, 184, 186–89
　Thoreau on, 158, 159, 173, 258–61, 271
　Transcendentalists' views of, 157, 159, 161, 169–70, 173, 176, 178, 189
　twentieth-century theorists, 265, 266–67, 270–71
　Unitarian view of, 157–58, 159, 160, 161–63, 166–67, 166 n. 20, 177
　universality of, 178, 183–85
　words as symbols, 261, 263–66, 268–69
The Language of Canaan (Lowance), 20, 23
The Language of Puritan Feeling (Leverenz), 48

Larkin, Benjamin, 119
Lawrence, D. H., 23, 41
Lawson, John, 224
The Lay of the Land (Kolodny), 43
Learned, Moses, 116
Lemay, J. A. Leo, 28, 29–30
The Letters of Elizabeth Palmer Peabody, American Renaissance Woman (Ronda), 174–75
Leverenz, David, 48
Levin, David, 42–43
Lewalski, Barbara Kiefer, 39
Lewis, Richard, 30
Life of Phips (Mather), 64–65
　contemporary criticism, 65
　credibility, 71 n. 14
　objectives of, 65–66, 70–72, 78
　publication, 65 n. 1
　treatment of career, 73–78
Literacy and the Social Order (Cressy), 44
literary criticism
　of Edward Taylor, 37–39
　feminist, 42
　structuralism, 265
　twentieth-century, 43, 253, 255–56, 265, 266
literature, study of. *See also* colonial American literature
　American Romantic, 34, 253–54
　with history study, 13–14, 15–16, 53–54
　lack of interest in language, 253–54
　separated from history, 14–15
Literature and Society in Early Virginia, 1608–1840 (Davis), 27
Livre et Société dans la France du XVIII siècle (Furet), 44
Locke, John, 160–63, 168, 188
　Essay Concerning Human Understanding, 161–62, 177
Loomis, Elisha, 213
"The Lord's Supper" (Emerson), 169–70
Lott, Eric, 190–91
Love & Theft: Blackface Minstrelsy and the American Working Class (Lott), 190–91
Lowance, Mason I., Jr., 20, 23, 24
Lucas, Paul, 100–102
Lynn (Mass.), 155

Magnalia Christi Americana (Mather), 20–21, 26, 64, 66

Magoon, Isaac, 135
Maine, Thoreau's trips to, 228–30, 234, 238, 238 n. 9, 240, 246–51
The Maine Woods (Thoreau), 228, 230 n. 26, 234–35, 236, 240–44, 247–48, 251
Mann, Horace, Jr., 231
manufacturing. *See* factories
manufacturing villages. *See* factory villages
Manville, Burris, 212, 213, 214
Martin, Christian F., 197 n. 14, 198, 205 n. 26
Martin, Wendy, 42
Martz, Louis L., 35
Maryland, literature, 28, 29–30
Massachusetts. *See also* Connecticut River Valley; *and specific towns*
  charter, 68, 69
  politics, 66–67, 70
  Swift River Valley, 121–22, 124, 137, 139
Massachusetts Agricultural Almanac for 1821, 127, 130
Masson, Margaret W., 45
Mather, Cotton
  accused of witchcraft, 70
  Life of Phips, 64–66, 70–78
  Magnalia Christi Americana, 20–21, 26, 64, 66
  Phips as church member, 69, 74
  pirate narrative, 45
  scholarship on, 40–41
  theological debates, 39, 88
Mather, Eleazer
  death, 56
  influence, 55–56, 57, 63
  ministry, 56
  move to Northampton, 57, 58
  A Serious Exhortation to the Present and Rising Generation, 57, 59–61
  sermons, 57, 59–61
  views on church membership, 58, 59
Mather, Increase, 56
  criticism of Stoddard, 83–84, 85, 88, 101
  Discourse Concerning the Danger of Apostasy, 83
  A Discourse concerning the Subject of Baptisme, 82
  Essay for the Recording of Illustrious Providences, 46
  negotiations with English, 66 n. 4, 68, 69
  opponents, 66 n. 4
  Phips and, 68, 69
  preface to *The First Principles of New England*, 82
  theological debates, 39, 58, 82
Mather, Richard, 57 n. 5
The Mathers (Middlekauff), 40
Mather, Samuel, 20
Matthiessen, F. O., 13
Maul, George, 197 n. 14
Melville, Herman
  The Confidence-Man, 267–68
  on language, 267–70, 271
  Moby-Dick, 268–69
Men of Letters in Colonial Maryland (Lemay), 28
Merriam, Ebenezer, 116, 119
Merriam, George, 116
Middlekauff, Robert, 40, 41
Miller, Perry, 13, 14, 19, 21, 77, 79, 96, 100, 157, 161, 238
Minds, James, 136
Minter, David L., 46
Moby-Dick (Melville), 268–69
Moore, John Weeks, 219, 220
More Wonders of the Invisible World (Calef), 65
Morison, Samuel Eliot, 13
Morris, Emery, 202, 207, 212
Morse, Cyrus, 137
Murdock, Kenneth B., 13
Murrin, John, 52
music
  popular, 190–91
  publishing, 118–19
  of Solomon Howe, 118–20, 123, 124
musical instruments, 192. *See also* guitars
  banjos, 206, 206 n. 27, 219 n. 43
  distribution, 197 n. 14
  manufacturers, 200, 200 n. 19, 215–16
  prices, 195 n. 11

Native Americans. *See* Indians
"Natural History of Massachusetts" (Thoreau), 226 n. 12
natural history writing, English, 222, 223–24
Nature (Emerson), 158, 170, 184, 236, 236 n. 2, 255
nature
  early travel writers on, 222, 223–24
  idealistic view of, 168
  Josselyn on, 227–29, 228 n. 19

Index   281

language's relationship to, 178, 182, 184, 255, 258–61
Thoreau on, 172–73, 240, 242
Naugatuck Railroad, 196–97, 197 n. 13
Naugatuck River, 193–94, 198, 214
Neptune, Louis, 228, 241
Newcomb, Anson, 137
Newcomb, Barzillai, 134
New England
  economy, 115–17, 121–22, 137–38, 141–42
  English nature writers on, 222, 223–24, 226 n. 14
  industrialization, 200, 200 n. 19, 216, 219, 219 n. 44
  labor in, 198, 202, 211–14
  literary scholars' focus on, 17, 27, 33, 50
  railroads, 197, 197 n. 13
  theological debates in nineteenth century, 158–60, 161, 162–63
  Transcendentalists in, 175–76
The New England Puritan, 155
New-Englands Errand in the Wilderness (Danforth), 52
New Englands Plantation (Higginson), 223
New Englands Rarities Discovered (Josselyn), 222, 223 n. 3, 226
A New Voyage to Carolina (Lawson), 224
New York City
  manufacturing, 200, 200 n. 19
  music business, 197 n. 14, 212 n. 35, 215–16
North American Review, 185
Northampton (Mass.)
  church membership controversies, 58–59, 60–61, 83
  clergy authority debates, 62–63
  Eleazer Mather's ministry, 56, 59–61
  settlement of, 57–58
  Stoddard's ministry, 62–63, 83, 84–85
Norton, Andrews, 158, 163–64, 166–67, 166 n. 20
  A Statement of Reasons for Not Believing the Doctrines of the Trinitarians, 166, 166 n. 20

Oakes, Urian, 232
Observations on the Growth of the Mind (Reed), 160
Oegger, Guillaume, 158

Of Plymouth Plantation (Bradford), 42–43
"The Old Manse" (Hawthorne), 10–11
Old Sturbridge Village, 8, 140
Olney, Anthony, 143
Oracles of Empire: Poetry, Politics, and Commerce in British America, 1690–1750 (Shields), 13
The Order of Things (Foucault), 256
Orthodoxies in Massachusetts: Rereading American Puritanism (Knight), 13

Palmer, Ralph, 199
Panormo, Louis, 205
Parker, Isaac, 148, 149–50, 150 n. 22
Parker, Theodore
  A Discourse of Matters Pertaining to Religion, 171
  on language, 159, 165, 173
Parkman, John, 137
Parrott, F. W., 201
Patterson, O. A., 136
Peabody, Elizabeth Palmer
  career, 174–75
  and Channing, 179
  and Kraitsir, 182, 185
  on language, 173, 176–79, 181, 182, 185–86
  letters, 174–75
  publishing activities, 179, 179 n. 8, 181, 182
  The Record of a School, Exemplifying the Principles and Methods of Moral Culture, 186
  review of Bushnell, 181, 182–83, 184–85
  review of Herder, 176–78
  scholarship on, 174
  teaching, 182, 186–89
  in Transcendentalist movement, 175, 176
Pedlar in Divinity: George Whitefield and the Transatlantic Revivals (Lambert), 95
Pennsylvania, literature, 32
Perkins, David, 10
Perry, William, 124
Phelps, Anson G., 194
philology, 159, 176, 258
Phips, Sir William
  association with Mathers, 68–69, 71–72
  career, 67–69, 73–75
  character, 73–76
  crimes charged with, 67
  critics, 70, 76–77

death, 67, 78
expeditions, 67–68, 74
as governor, 66–67, 69–70
Life of Phips, 64–66, 70–78
military campaigns, 69, 69 n. 8, 74–75
patriotism, 76
Phoenix Bank, 217
Pietas in Patriam: The Life of His Excellence Sir William Phips, Knt. See *Life of Phips*
A Plea for God (Williams), 98
"The Poet" (Emerson), 171
poetry
  of Anne Bradstreet, 41–42
  broadside verse, 130, 131–33
  of Taylor, 35, 37, 38
  topical verse, 52, 125
Pole, J. R., 16, 18, 25, 27, 50
Polis, Joe, 245–50, 248 n. 19, 249 n. 20, 251
Pond, Sylvanus, 216
Pope, Robert G., 14
Popular Culture in Early Modern Europe (Burke), 44
popular literature
  almanacs, 47, 123, 126–33
  in colonial America, 44–49
  devotional, 47
  Indian captivity narratives, 46
  published by Howe, 124–25
  readers of, 53
  of revivals, 48
  ribald humor, 131–33
  sermons, 45, 48
  sex manuals, 47
  topical verse, 52, 125
  on witchcraft, 46–47
Porte, Joel, 239–40, 261
Power and the Pulpit in Puritan New England (Elliott), 48
pragmatism
  of Johnson, 256
  of Stoddard, 79–80
  of Transcendentalists, 175–76
"Preliminary Dissertation on the Nature of Language, as Related to Thought and Spirit" (Bushnell), 262
The Presence of Christ (Stoddard), 90
printers
  John Howe, 116–17, 120, 123–39
  music publishing, 119
  in rural areas, 116–17

Prophetic Waters (Seelye), 25–26, 43–44
Protestant Poetics and the Seventeenth-Century Religious Lyric (Lewalski), 39
Prude, Jonathan, 141
publishers. *See also* printers
  Elizabeth Palmer Peabody, 179, 179 n. 8, 181, 182
  music, 118–19
  rural, 115–17, 133, 138–39
  urban, 115
Puritan Influences in American Literature (Elliott), 24
Puritanism. *See also* clergy
  change in, 81–84, 93
  debates on church membership requirements, 35–36, 57, 58–59, 60–61
  education, 47
  Half-Way Covenant, 58, 60–61, 82–83, 84 n. 11
  influence on literature, 18, 20, 24
  literature, 20–22, 35, 46–48, 49–50
  meditative verse, 35
  Reforming Synod of 1679, 84
  revivals, 48, 95–97, 99–100
  scholarship on, 64
  sermons, 45, 48, 52
  Stoddard's view of, 78 n. 23, 80–81, 86–88, 89–92, 100–102
  Synod of 1662, 58, 82
  theological debates, 35–37, 55, 82–84, 87, 90–92
  view of society, 73
The Puritan Ordeal (Delbanco), 13
The Puritan Origins of the American Self (Bercovitch), 19, 20, 21, 64
Puritans among the Indians (Vaughan and Clark), 46
Putnam, Mary Lowell, 185
Pynchon, William, 58

Quabbin (Mass.) *See* Greenwich (Mass.)
Quabbin (Underwood), 122, 128
Quebec, Phips' military campaigns, 69, 69 n. 8, 74

Rabinowitz, Richard, 140
railroads, 197, 197 n. 13
Reading Becomes a Necessity of Life: Material and Cultural Life in Rural New England, 1780–1835 (Gilmore), 114
Rebels and Gentlemen: Philadelphia in the Age

of *Franklin* (Bridenbaugh and Bridenbaugh), 32
The Record of a School, Exemplifying the Principles and Methods of Moral Culture (Peabody), 186
The Redeemed Captive Returning to Zion (Williams), 98
Reed, Augustus, 147
Reed, Sampson, 160–61, 187
  influence on Emerson, 158
  Observations on the Growth of the Mind, 160
Reforming Synod of 1679, 84
Regeneration through Violence (Slotkin), 23–24, 44, 46
A Remonstrance Against Established Religion in Massachusetts (Cooke), 148
Renaissance Self-Fashioning (Greenblatt), 40
Representative Men (Emerson), 234, 235–36
Revere, Paul, 118
revivals
  Great Awakening, 95–96, 99–100
  led by Stoddard, 78, 98 n. 5
  popular literature of, 48
  scholarship on, 95–97
  in Ware Factory Village, 147
  Williams' role in, 107–8
rhetoric
  in American literature, 21–22
  jeremiads, 21–22
Richards, James, 134
Richardson, Robert D., Jr., 41
Riley, Edward, 215
Rinders, Cornelius, 212, 214
Robinson, Joseph, 137
Ronda, Bruce A., 174
Rosenmeier, Jesper, 42
Rowe, Karen E., 38–39
Royce, Harvey, 136
Royce, Joseph G., 133
rural economy. *See also* factory villages
  barter in, 134, 137–38
  books in, 122
  publishing in, 115–17, 122, 138–39
  use of cash, 137
Russell, John, 84, 84 n. 11
Rutman, Darrett B., 14
Rynin, David, 255

Sabin, Darius, 135
The Safety of Appearing at the Day of Judgment in the Righteousness of Christ (Stoddard), 84–86, 101–2
Said, Edward, 261
Saint and Singer (Rowe), 38–39
Saybrook Platform, 63 n. 19, 101
Sayre, Robert F., 235
Schafer, Thomas, 92, 104
Scheick, William J., 13, 37
Schmidt, Louis, 197 n. 14
Schuldiner, Michael, 37
Seasons of Grace: Colonial New England's Revival Tradition in Its British Context (Crawford), 96
Seelye, John, 25–26, 43–44
A Serious Exhortation to the Present and Rising Generation (Mather), 57
Sewall, Samuel, 107, 224
Shakespeare, William, 236
Shaw, Chaney, 135
Shepard, Odell, 186
Sherman, George, 213, 214
Shields, David, 13
The Significance of the Alphabet (Kraitsir), 182
Silverman, Kenneth, 40, 41
Simpson, Lewis P., 29
Sloan, James, 137
Slotkin, Richard, 23–24, 44, 46
Small Books and Pleasant Histories (Spufford), 44
Smith & Hawley, 202
Smith, Benjamin F., 198, 198 n. 16, 213–14
Smith, Chester, 213, 214
Smith, John, 51, 223
So Dreadfull a Judgment: Puritan Responses to King Philip's War, 1676–1677 (Slotkin and Folsom), 46
Southern colonies, literature of, 27–30
Spengemann, William C., 24–26, 32
Spooner, Alden, 116
Springfield (Mass.), 57–58, 110
Spufford, Margaret, 44
The Spy (Cooper), 54
Stanford, Ann, 41
Stanford, Donald E., 35
A Statement of Reasons for Not Believing the Doctrines of the Trinitarians (Norton), 166, 166 n. 20
Sterling, James, 30
Stiles, Ezra, 97
Stoddard, Solomon

on the church, 78 n. 23, 80–81, 86–88, 89–92, 100–102
on church membership, 35–36, 62, 83
on communion, 39, 62, 78, 83, 87–88, 102, 103
conflicts with Mathers, 56–57, 83–84, 85–86, 88–89
daughter, 98
The Doctrine of Instituted Churches, 63, 86–88, 101
evangelism, 84–85, 103, 104, 112
An Examination of the Power of the Fraternity, 90–92
funeral, 99
A Guide to Christ, 103
The Inexcusableness of Neglecting the Worship of God, 102
influence, 55, 80, 92–94, 100, 101, 103 n. 14
intellectual development, 100–102
ministry in Northampton, 62–63, 83, 84–85
on New England's history, 80–81, 87, 88–89, 93–94
pragmatism, 79–80
The Presence of Christ, 90
revivals, 78, 98 n. 5
The Safety of Appearing at the Day of Judgment in the Righteousness of Christ, 84–86, 101–2
scholarship on, 100
Stowell, Marion Barber, 47
structuralism, 265
Stuart, Moses, 158, 163, 164–66, 170
The Study of Hebrew Poetry (Herder), 176–78, 254
The Study of Language in England, 1780–1860 (Aarslef), 176
The Sugar-Cane: A Poem in Four Books (Grainger), 33
Swedenborg, Emanuel, 161
Swift River Valley, 121–22, 139. *See also* Greenwich (Mass.)
  economy, 137
  local writers, 124
Symbolism and American Literature (Feidelson), 24, 252
Synod of 1662, 58, 82

Tappan, John, 144–45
Taylor, Edward
  poetry, 35, 37, 38
  role in theological debates, 35–36, 39, 55, 84, 101
  scholarship on, 34–39, 47
  Upon the Types of the Old Testament, 39
Temple School, 171–72, 186–89
Tennent, Gilbert, 105
Terry, Ezekiel, 116, 125
Therien, Alek, 239–40
Thomas, Isaiah, 115
Thompson, James, 135, 136
Thoreau and the American Indians (Sayre), 235
Thoreau, Henry David, 140
  "The Allagash and East Branch," 246
  "Chesuncook," 228, 243, 246
  on Christianity, 172–73
  Emerson on, 244–45
  foxfire experience, 247–48
  on history, 11
  on hunting, 243–44, 250
  influence of early travel writers, 222, 224–26, 230–33, 250
  influence of Josselyn, 225–28, 230–33
  influences, 244–45
  interest in Indian languages, 229–30, 246
  interest in Indians, 228, 234–35, 236–39, 240–44, 245–51
  on Josselyn, 222, 228–29
  journals, 236 n. 5
  "Ktaadn," 230 n. 26, 241–42
  on language, 158, 159, 173, 258–61, 271
  The Maine Woods, 228, 230 n. 26, 234–35, 236, 240–44, 247–48, 251
  "Natural History of Massachusetts," 226 n. 12
  on nature, 172–73, 240, 242
  relationship with Joe Polis, 245–50, 248 n. 19
  on representative men, 239–40, 242, 249, 251
  travels, 231
  travel writing, 232–33
  trips to Maine, 228–30, 234, 238, 238 n. 9, 240, 246–51
  Walden, 158, 239–40, 258, 259, 260–61
  A Week on the Concord and Merrimack Rivers, 172–73, 221, 225, 226, 229
  on wilderness, 240, 242
  writing based on observation, 227–28

Thornton, Isaac, 211–12, 213, 214
Thwing, Thomas, 145, 156
Tinkham, Samuel, 137
tools, in guitar factory, 199–200, 201
topical verse, 52, 125
Torrington (Conn.), 193. *See also* Wolcottville (Conn.)
Tractatus Logico-Philosophicus (Wittgenstein), 256
Transcendental Hermeneutics: Institutional Authority and the Higher Criticism of the Bible (Grusin), 157
Transcendentalism in New England, 175–76
The Transcendentalists: An Anthology (Miller), 157
Transcendentalists
  on Christianity, 171
  on education, 188–89
  Elizabeth Palmer Peabody as, 175, 176
  on language, 157, 159, 161, 169–70, 173, 176, 178, 189
  pragmatism, 175–76
Transforming Women's Work: New England Lives in the Industrial Revolution (Dublin), 141
A Treatise on Language: or, The Relation which Words Bear to Things (Johnson), 254
Trinitarians
  conflict with Unitarians, 163–66
  philosophy of language, 159–60, 164–66
Tropologia (Keach), 20
True Travels (Smith), 51
Turell, Jane, 31
Turner, Victor, 21
typology, 19–23, 91
Typology and Early American Literature, 19–23
"The Typology of the Female as a Model for the Regenerate: Puritan Preaching, 1690–1730" (Masson), 45

Ulrich, Laurel Thatcher, 45
Underwood, Francis H., 122–23, 128, 129, 138
Union Manufacturing Company, 196
Unitarianism
  attacked by Cooke, 148–50
  conflict with Trinitarians, 159, 163–64
  philosophy of language, 157–58, 159, 160, 161–63, 166–67, 166 n. 20, 177
  popularity in factory villages, 142
  theology, 165–66, 168–69
  in Ware Factory Village, 144, 153
  in Ware Manufacturing Company, 144–45
Unitarianism, an Exclusive System (Cooke), 148
Universalism
  attacked by Cooke, 148, 150–52
  popularity in factory villages, 142, 150
  in Ware Factory Village, 144
Upon the Types of the Old Testament (Taylor), 39

VanDerBeet, Richard, 46
Vaughan, Alden T., 46
"Vertuous Women Found: New England Ministerial Literature, 1668–1735" (Ulrich), 45
violence, in American literature, 23

Wadhams Manufacturing Company, 201
Walden (Thoreau), 158, 239–40, 258, 259, 260–61
Warden, Gilbert, 137
Ware (Mass.)
  differences with Ware Factory Village, 143, 147–48
  history, 140–41, 142–43
Ware Factory Village
  churches in, 143–45, 146, 153
  establishment, 143
  Howe's printing for businesses in, 136, 137
  ministers, 142 n. 2, 144, 145, 146, 155–56
  revivals, 147
  social disruption caused by, 143
  temperance controversy, 152–54
  water power, 142
Ware, Henry, 149, 163–64
Ware Manufacturing Company, 143, 144–45
Warham, John, 57, 63
Watters, David H., 47
Webster, Daniel, 249, 249 n. 20
A Week on the Concord and Merrimack Rivers (Thoreau), 172–73, 221, 225, 226, 229
Welton, Ebenezer, 203–4
Wendell, Barrett, 71–72
Wenska, Walter P., 43
The West Indian: A Comedy (Cumberland), 32–33
White, Elizabeth Wade, 41
White, Noah, 124, 134, 135

Whiter, Walter, 158
Whitman, Walt, 244
Wilder, S. V. S., 144–45, 144 n. 9, 147
Willard, Samuel, 64–65, 66, 67, 70
William III, king of England, 67, 69
William Hall & Son, 215–16
  distribution of Ashborn guitars, 197, 204, 215, 216–17, 218, 220
  piano manufacture, 200
  relationship with Ashborn factory, 200, 203, 209, 210, 211, 211 n. 34
  wages, 212 n. 35
Williams, Daniel E., 45
Williams, Israel, 110, 111–12
Williams, John, 92, 97–98, 101, 102
  The Redeemed Captive Returning to Zion, 98
Williams, Raymond, 21, 22
Williams, Roger, 19
Williams, Stephen, 104–5
Williams, William
  anticipation of Millennium, 107, 113
  on church membership, 95
  as clergyman, 98–99
  contemporary views of, 97
  on conversion, 108–9
  The Danger of Not Reforming Known Evils, 98, 102–3
  death, 99, 113
  Directions for Such as are Concerned to Obtain a True Repentance and Conversion to God, 99, 107, 108–9
  The Duty and Interest of a People . . ., 99, 107, 108
  education, 97
  Edwards and, 109–10, 113
  An Essay to Prove the Interest of the Children of Believers in the Covenant, 99
  evangelism, 112
  funeral, 96, 96 n. 1, 111–12
  The Great Salvation Revealed and Offered in the Gospel, 98, 98 n. 5, 105–7
  in Hampshire Association, 99, 101
  influence, 103, 113
  marriage, 98
  A Plea for God, 98
  role in theological debates, 55, 92, 104
  on role of ministers, 104–6
  scholarship on, 95, 112
  sermons, 98–99, 102–3
  sons, 110–13
Williams, William Carlos, 23
Wilson, John B., 176
Wing, Warren P., 135–36
Wise, John, 98
witchcraft
  hysteria, 57, 69–70
  popular literature on, 46–47
Wittgenstein, Ludwig, 256
Wolcottville (Conn.)
  Ashborn guitar factory, 192–93
  establishment, 194
  railroad, 197
Wolcottville Brass Company, 194, 201, 203
women, ribald humor on, 131–33
Woodbridge, John, 146
Woodbridge, Jonathan Edwards, 142 n. 2
Woodbridge, Timothy, 101, 103
Wood, Gordon, 6
Woodrow, Thomas, 213
Woods, Leonard, 146
Worlds of Wonder, Days of Judgment: Popular Religious Belief in Early New England (Hall), 13
Wright, Andrew, 119, 123
Wyman, Amos H., 137

Yale, Cyrus, 156
Young, Ernest, 213

Zonderman, David A., 141

About the Author

Philip F. Gura is Professor of English and Adjunct Professor of American Studies and Religious Studies at the University of North Carolina at Chapel Hill. He is the author of *The Wisdom of Words: Language, Theology, and Literature in the American Renaissance* (Wesleyan, 1981) and *A Glimpse of Sion's Glory: Puritan Radicalism in New England, 1620–1660* (Wesleyan, 1984) and editor, with Joel Myerson, of *Critical Essays on American Transcendentalism* (G. K. Hall, 1982).

www.ingramcontent.com/pod-product-compliance
Lightning Source LLC
Chambersburg PA
CBHW031546300426
44111CB00006BA/197